ETHICAL CHOICE

ETHICAL CHOICE

A CASE STUDY APPROACH

Robert N. Beck
John B. Orr

The Free Press
A Division of Macmillan Publishing Co., Inc.
New York

Collier Macmillan Publishers
London

COPYRIGHT © 1970 BY The Free Press

A DIVISION OF MACMILLAN PUBLISHING CO., INC.

The Free Press

A DIVISION OF MACMILLAN PUBLISHING CO., INC.

866 Third Avenue, New York, N.Y. 10022

Collier Macmillan Canada, Ltd.

Library of Congress Catalog Card Number: 70–122282

Printed in the United States of America

PRINTING NUMBER

9   10

To Our Students

PREFACE

Broadly divided into topics central both to individual and to social ethics, this volume is designed as an introductory text in ethics. Planned for use either as a text or as a supplementary source, it seeks to develop a problem-oriented, case-study approach to ethical reasoning. Materials have been selected that are the product of a philosopher or theologian who is attempting to address a concrete moral or social problem in the light of his articulated theory of values. Through such materials, the editors hope to show the role of value theory in shaping styles of problem analysis, to offer opportunities for students to view the interrelationships of value theory and 'factual' materials in moral reasoning, and to provide well constructed examples of ethical argument. Three concluding essays by the editors discuss and seek to amplify these and related matters.

The case study approach seems particularly germane to ethical studies. In using it for this anthology, the editors have had three educational goals in mind: to suggest the continuing importance of practical philosophy or the need to develop theories of commitment; to encourage students to be involved in the analysis of important moral issues with special reference to the concept of analytical sensitivities developed in the study of philosophy; and to view systematically the relation between theories of commitment and the justification of positions on particular issues. Thus, it is hoped that this anthology will show the anchorage of ethical theory in primary human concerns as well as illuminate the pluralism of ethical traditions within Western society. In brief, the anthology aims at providing a fund of illustrative material that can help students relate course content to matters of obvious personal and social importance, and at enlivening the study of ethics by offering examples of moral reasoning tied directly to major traditions in value theory.

The following are the organizational principles used by the editors. A number of widely adopted textbooks in ethics have been examined to determine the theorists and traditions most often cited. Case studies have been selected on the basis of their potential usefulness in supplementing those citations—although a few materials have been included solely because of their peculiar importance or interest. A limited number of topical headings in individual and social ethics have been chosen, and selections are organized under them. The selections represent diverse theoretical traditions, the intent being to allow students to note contrasting styles of problem analysis which, in turn, are shaped to some extent by contrasting ethical theories. In a syllabus at the end of the book, the editors have regrouped the selections according to theoretical traditions. By following the regrouping, instructors so inclined can adopt the materials in the anthology to the 'traditions' approach in the study of ethics as well as to a 'problems' approach.

Brief introductions to the various sections are provided. In general, the selections speak for themselves. But within the short compass of a headnote, the editors indicate points of comparison and contrast, thus dramatizing issues, and identify problems of theoretical concern. Where relevant, some attention is given to the phenomenology of the decision-making process, and suggestions are made about the interrelations of conclusions on issues and value choices.

Work on the anthology was a joint effort of the editors, although a division of labour was required. Robert N. Beck is primarily responsible for Part I, the introduction "Moral Experience," and the editorial essay, "Commitment and Practical Philosophy." John B. Orr worked especially on Part II and contributed the essays, "The Logic of Moral Argument" and "A Postscript Concerning Case Study Ethics."

We wish to thank the many people whose effort and counsel have been useful to us, as well as publishers and authors for their permission to use materials. A special remark of appreciation, however, must go to our students. Their interests and concerns have helped us to learn—if only a little—the arts of introduction and dialogue.

R. N. B.
J. B. O.

CONTENTS

PREFACE   vii

INTRODUCTION: MORAL EXPERIENCE   xiii

PART I

Studies in Individual Ethics

SECTION ONE: TRUTH

Truth and Character: *Plato*   5
How Princes Should Keep Faith: *Niccolo Machiavelli*   16
Altruistic Lying: *Immanuel Kant*   19
Truth and Freedom: *John Stuart Mill*   24
On Truth and Falsity: *Friedrich Nietzsche*   30
Truthfulness and Uprightness: *Nicolai Hartmann*   39
What is Meant by 'Telling the Truth'?: *Dietrich Bonhoeffer*   43

SECTION TWO: SUICIDE

On Suicide: *Seneca*   53
Suicide: *St. Augustine*   59
Whether It Is Lawful to Kill Oneself? *St. Thomas Aquinas*   67
On Suicide: *David Hume*   69
On Suicide: *Arthur Schopenhauer*   77
Is Life Worth Living?: *William James*   82
Suicide and Meaning: *Albert Camus*   88

SECTION THREE: SEXUAL INTEGRITY

Humanae Vitae: *Paul VI*	98
The Aesthetic Validity of Marriage: *Sören Kierkegaard*	105
Sex and Birth Control: *Walter Lippmann*	117
Love and Situation Ethics: *Joseph Fletcher*	128
Sex and Values: *Peter A. Bertocci*	133
Sexual Perversion: *Thomas Nagel*	137

SECTION FOUR: ALIENATION

The Unhappy Consciousness: *G. W. F. Hegel*	153
Alienated Labor: *Karl Marx*	160
The Metropolis and Mental Life: *Georg Simmel*	171
Self-Alienation: *Frederick A. Weiss*	184
The Present Situation: *Karl Jaspers*	199
World Alienation: *Hannah Arendt*	206

PART II

Studies in Social Ethics

SECTION FIVE: PROPERTY AND WELFARE

On Property: *John Locke*	220
What is Property?: *Pierre-Joseph Proudhon*	228
The Distribution of Welfare: *John Stuart Mill*	240
Apollinian and Faustian Money: *Oswald Spengler*	252
The Transformation of Welfare: *Charles Frankel*	259
Guaranteed Income and Expanded Freedom: *Erich Fromm*	269

SECTION SIX: VIOLENCE

On Revolution: *Aristotle*	278
On the State of Men Without Civil Society: *Thomas Hobbes*	286
Reflections on Violence: *Georges Sorel*	292
The State and Violence: *Leo Tolstoy*	300
Illusions about Violence: *Reinhold Niebuhr*	306
Ethics and Revolution: *Herbert Marcuse*	311

SECTION SEVEN: PUNISHMENT

Capital Punishment: *Marchise de Beccaria*   320
The Rationale of Punishment: *Jeremy Bentham*   326
Some Remarks on Punishment: *F. H. Bradley*   341
A Defense of Capital Punishment: *John J. Ford*   345
Justice and Criminality: *John Dewey*   355
Punishment and Responsibility: *Moritz Schlick*   359

SECTION EIGHT: WAR

Concerning the Just War: *St. Augustine*   368
The Right of the State Over the Individual in War:
    T. H. Green   373
The Moral Equivalent of War: *William James*   382
An Appeal to the Intellectuals of Europe: *Bertrand Russell*   390
The War Has Taken Place: *Maurice Merleau-Ponty*   398
War As Crucifixion: *H. Richard Niebuhr*   404

PART III

Editorial Essays

Commitment and Practical Philosophy: *Robert N. Beck*   413
The Logic of Moral Argument: *John B. Orr*   418
A Postscript Concerning Case Study Ethics: *John B. Orr*   426

BIBLIOGRAPHICAL ESSAY   430
SYSTEMATIC OUTLINE OF SELECTIONS   434
INDEX   437

MORAL
EXPERIENCE

All of us constantly face certain kinds of situations which it is usual to call moral or ethical. Not always, to be sure, are we certain of ourselves as we recognize or classify them in this way; nor are we likely, apart from philosophy, to reflect on them as a kind or class of situation at all. So diverse in nature and context are they that we may fail initially to see them as having anything in common. Still, ethical problems are related, and if we give heed, less to the situations than to the questions they raise, we will see that in these very questions is found the relatedness that links diverse situations as ethical ones. And ethical reflection, we may say, is directed toward certain kinds of questions about human situations and problems, no matter how diverse they may seem.

What is it, then, that constitutes a problem or question as ethical? 'Ethics' is derived from the Greek word *ethos*, which means character and, in the plural, manners. The synonym 'morals' derives from the Latin *moralis*, which Cicero used to render the Greek *ethikos*, and also means character and manners or customs.[1] Such etymologies suggest that the ethical refers to one's own relationship (character) to his and other's conduct (manners and customs). In reference to philosophical

---

[1] We shall use 'ethics' and 'morals' as synonyms here, although a few philosophers have suggested distinctions between the two concepts.

usage, this is partly right, yet partly misleading. Ethical experience and reflection are about human conduct; but what is omitted is the problem of evaluation, of judging by reference to the right and the good.

To see a bit more directly what ethical questions and concerns are about, we may turn to an illustration.[2] In November, 1915, a Chicago surgeon named J. H. Haiselden refused to operate on a baby boy four days old. Though contrary to accepted medical ethics, he did this, he said, "in the interest of the human race and more particularly of American manhood." The baby was extremely defective and would probably remain so throughout life. Dr. Haiselden believed the infant to be dying, although its life could have been prolonged if an operation had been performed. The doctor's position was that, given the consent of the parents (which consent was given), "nature should be allowed to take her course." When no other doctor or nurse intervened, the result was that the child was allowed to die.

Needless to say, the moral reaction to Dr. Haiselden's decision was immediate and widespread. The Chicago Anti-Cruelty League and the Illinois Humane Society held meetings, and threats of court action were made. Surprisingly, however, these two societies announced themselves in agreement with Dr. Haiselden. The result was that he was exonerated by a coroner's jury, which settled the legal question. But many voices expressing moral judgments were nevertheless heard as well. Miss Jane Addams of Hull House condemned the act absolutely. Only the One who gave life can take it away, she said; and she asked, what right does this doctor have to take a human life? Everything is born into the world with an inherent right to live. "The letting of that baby die when its life could have been saved is a crime against the race instead of the benefaction claimed." A specialist in children's diseases wrote that when an animal is disabled it is shot, so when a child takes all the pleasure out of life for its parents, and is helpless, it should not be allowed to give unhappiness to the living. Still another opinion was expressed by one writer who said that he believed that a child with congenital malformation to such a degree that the mental development necessary to a self-reliant individual is prevented should be permitted to die. "The only good or value for the child is in this capacity of development." Finally, still others suggested that all children born with congenital abnormalities are a detriment to society. Therefore, they said, it is humane to cut off their future sufferings and those of society.

[2] This case is reported and discussed by W. M. Urban in his *Fundamentals of Ethics* (New York: Henry Holt and Company, 1930), pp. 41–49.

Few people will deny either that Dr. Haiselden faced a moral situation, or that the various spokesmen mentioned in the illustration made moral judgments on his action. Let us look closely at the illustration to see just what made it a moral one. First of all, we note that Dr. Haiselden was called upon to *act* in the light of a choice or decision. He was not reacting mechanically or simply responding to a stimulus like the knee-jerk reflex: he was choosing to act in such a way that some (then non-existent) end would be achieved. Thus, ethical situations, we may say, involve human action rather than mere behavior and response; or—as an older terminology had it—they are voluntary rather than involuntary.

Within the domain of the voluntary, we find four factors or data whose presence defines situations as ethical more fully. The first of these is the experience of choice. This datum is very difficult to treat briefly, for discussions of it often turn quickly to one of the most vexing and difficult of all philosophic problems, that of free will. But clearly, Dr. Haiselden had a choice to make. Indeed, whether he believed in determinism or not, or whether we do or not, he still faced a situation in which he believed (1) that there were alternatives, (2) that he was called upon to choose because the outcome of the situation depended to some degree upon his choice, and (3) that he was in a situation in which he could have acted otherwise. Apart from some such experience, one would hesitate to call Dr. Haiselden's situation a moral one at all. And it is just for this reason also that critics—Jane Addams and the others—made their moral judgments: if Haiselden's actions were simply a development and outcome like the growth of a flower, one might grade them as appropriate or not; but one would hardly censor them and call them blameworthy or commendable. If we adopt the word 'choice' for this datum, we can say that the possibility of choice is a necessary condition of the moral experience.[3]

The second observation to make about the experiences suggested in the illustration is that the issue of choice and the outcome of action are related to the question of value. Values, or what was believed to be valuable, were at stake; goods and evils were set in opposition to each other. Such a concern with values is another identifying mark of ethical experience.

[3] The influence and importance of freedomism and determinism for ethics have been exaggerated: these are theories about choice, not alternative theories or acceptance or denial of choice. This is not to say, however, that the problem of free will is not one of the most significant and—for many students—interesting problems in philosophy.

A value (or good) is whatever is approved, esteemed, or desired. Enjoyment is often taken as a rough synonym of value. Disvalue is evil or that which is disapproved or suffered. Now people differ in what they take to be of value: Miss Addams said life itself, others said happiness, or utility, or individual development. Such differences of opinion about what is valuable suggest a distinction between what might be called a true value and a false or only apparent value. A true value, if such can be found, would be one which has been judged so by an adequate criterion of value.

Third, we find in our illustration the datum of obligation, of what ought to be, and therewith the concept of right as against wrong. Of course, the participants in the debate differed about what ought to have been done, and they therefore differed about what they considered right and wrong in the situation. Still, it is because of a sense of obligation, a belief that some choices are right, others wrong, that we can speak of Haiselden's action as moral at all.

Philosophers have interpreted the nature, meaning, and role of this datum of obligation differently, though almost all of them have believed it to be a central factor for morality. Sometimes, as with Immanuel Kant, the experience of obligation is seen to be the very core of the moral experience, so that obedience in action to the necessities of duty constitutes the moral experience, and defines duty and rightness as well.[4] For other philosophers, value experience is more basic, so that for them what ought to be is determined by what is recognized as valuable.

The fourth and final datum we find in our illustration is the rule—the moral law or principle—to which the debaters appealed in their judgments of the possible goodness or rightness of Dr. Haiselden's action. Not always are moral laws as explicit as they are in the illustration, but at least possible reference to a principle is taken by many philosophers as another necessary condition for the moral experience. Miss Addams, we remember, appealed to the principle of an inherent right to live; Haiselden himself spoke of the development of American manhood; and the others appealed to happiness, usefulness, and self-realization. It is such rules or principles that define and identify what people believe are true values and valid, binding obligations.

---

[4] Students may sense here an ambiguity in the terms 'moral' and 'ethical.' Sometimes they mean simply 'pertaining to morality', and are thus descriptive; at other times they mean 'the right' and are thus evaluative or normative. The context of the use of these terms will usually help to determine which meaning is intended.

Thus, we find the data of choice, value, obligation, and principle essential to the moral experience. They constitute that experience, though of course they also pose the problems that concern us as we reflect on the human situations involving them. We ask about values: are there any which we (and perhaps all men) should acknowledge? In what ways are they binding on us? Are there distinctively moral values, and how might they be related to other values? We wonder about obligation: what is our duty? What basis or justification does it have? And we ask about principle: is there a moral law which is definitive for human beings in their choices and decisions? As we become more reflective on these and similar questions about the data of morality, we become at the same time more philosophical about them.

Philosophical ethics is a disciplined inquiry into these problems. As philosophers have developed the field, they have worked on three general levels. The first of these is largely *descriptive* and seeks to identify the moral experience in a descriptive way. We have been on this level in discussing the case of Dr. Haiselden. Much of the work here is now done by social scientists, though before the rise of such disciplines as psychology and sociology, moral philosophers had to do this kind of inquiry themselves. Some contemporary philosophers, in an activity called phenomenology, however, also attempt descriptive accounts of morality. A second level of inquiry is *normative ethics* (normative means what ought to be). Here philosophers try to work out acceptable judgments regarding what ought to be in choice and value. "We ought to keep our promises" and "justice is a virtue" are examples of normative judgments that many philosophers find acceptable. Finally, there is a third level of philosophical inquiry usually called *critical* or *meta-ethics*. On this level, philosophers seek to work out a theory of the meaning and justification of our judgments of obligation and value. Meta-ethics does not propound any moral principle or goal (except possibly by implication), but rather consists entirely of philosophical analysis. What is the meaning of 'good'? and, Can ethical judgments be justified or warranted? are typical problems for meta-ethics.

A survey of the data of ethics and a summary of levels of ethical inquiry cover a rather extensive amount of material for an introduction to ethics. Yet there is one more topic which should be mentioned before we can turn to the case studies below. That topic is the general types of ethical theory. Fortunately, though there are a number of variations on them, ethical theories fall into only two main classes. Consider once again the Haiselden case. A number of spokesmen (including the doctor himself) sought to state and justify their normal judgments in terms of the consequences that they believed would follow from a certain choice. Theories thus appealing to consequences are called *teleological* (from *telos*-end). According to them, an act is right or obligatory if a certain value is brought into being by it. To be sure, theorists differ about this value: it may be taken to be pleasure, or happiness, or self-realization,[5] or survival. These differences give rise to a variety of teleological systems. The second general type of theory, called *deontological* (from *deontos*-necessity, obligation), holds that there is an inherent rightness—apart from all consequences—in at least certain actions and that therefore we are obliged by that rightness apart from consequences altogether. Miss Addam's view that life is an absolute good is an example of such a deontological judgment. Students will find that the positions taken by philosophers on the issues in the selections below will reflect their adherence to one or the other of these two types of theory.

Much of our discussion thus far falls within that part of ethics dealing with individual conduct. But the philosopher's interest in ethics is not limited to the individual alone. There is also the field of social behavior, including institutions, programs, and 'social actions' such as punishment and war. These too are the object of reflective philosophical concern, for problems of choice, value, and obligation arise with regard to them as well. Is war good or right as a means of national policy? Does the welfare state support or hinder the development of moral values? Is punishment a justifiable social institution? And if so, why? Though obviously asked in a different context from those posed in individual ethics, such questions also come directly under the purview of the moral philosopher.

The materials below include case studies in both individual and social ethics. Although specific in nature, the topics are discussed by philosophers and writers who approach them with well defined and articulate theories of value and obligation. The positions they take on specific issues are therefore to some degree justified or grounded in principle, and they provide us opportunities to follow cases of philosophical reasoning involving both specific problems and philosophical systems. (It does not follow, of course, that all these writers are right:

---

[5] Some philosophers believe self-realization ethics to be a third major alternative rather than classify it as we have done. Important as this possibility is, we shall not discuss it further here, although it is included in the "Systematic Outline of Selections" at the end of the book.

they could not be, for they differ among themselves!) The consequence of such study, it is hoped,[6] will be to help the individual toward formulating a fruitful ethical hypothesis—even though we must remember with Spinoza that all good things are as difficult as they are rare.

[6] Fuller discussion of the case studies approach in ethics is found in the editorial essay below, "A Postscript Concerning Case Study Ethics."

Part I

Studies in Individual Ethics

TRUTH

Frequently met in the concrete moral situations of individuals, the problem of truth-telling—of speaking 'the truth, the whole truth, and nothing but the truth'—is deceptively simple. To say what is, to speak with words which conform to thoughts, to act in the light of what one believes to be the case: such injunctions seem easy and imperative. Furthermore, much of the Western moral and religious tradition places a high value on truthfulness—although, somewhat strangely, the Decalogue does not contain a commandment against lying and deceitfulness. Despite all this, however, moral complications arise when we reflect on the imperative to be always truthful or wonder about the principle (if any) that might justify truthfulness. Should one tell a dying person the nature of his illness or a potential murderer the escape route of his intended victim? Should a child, in his innocence, be told the 'whole truth' about sex, regardless of the possible psychological consequences to him? Such a list of questions can be extended almost without end.

Moral philosophers usually begin their discussions of the problem of truth by distinguishing (as does Hartmann in the selection below) between truth as a logical value and as a moral value. The logical value is applicable to those judgments or statements which assert what is the case. In this use, truth is of course a very important value, and it is a special object of study for logicians and epistemologists. ('Epistemology' means theory of knowledge.) But such a meaning is not a moral one, for it is not related to obligation or duty, and it therefore does not command or lay requirements on anyone. Truth in the moral sense is or involves an act of will such that one's word and action agree with one's thoughts, and one's thoughts are directed or guided by one's understanding of what is the case. Truthfulness is thus always a personal value (as are all moral values), whereas logical truth is impersonal.

Analysis of questions similar to those mentioned above raises a number of critical problems. Commitment to truth in speech and action implies duty and value. Is truthfulness a value? Is it possibly among the highest values, or is it subordinate to some other value or principle? There is also the issue of whether truth is something properly prized as valuable in itself (an *intrinsic* value) or as a means to some other end (an *instrumental* value). A somewhat different, though related, question arises in reference to a possible duty to be truthful: what is such a duty, if any, and what ground or justification might be found to substantiate it? Still another set of issues surrounds the question of being truthful in contrast to speaking truthfully. Existentialist writers have reemphasized this question, stressing that men living truthfully will be open to the being which they are and to the being around them. Some existentialists have also pushed on toward an even more radical question, namely, of whether men can in fact live with the truth.

The selections which follow explore a variety of issues arising from considerations such as have been indicated briefly here. Plato believes that truth and reality are important in the development of the best of human beings. Machiavelli, writing during the political stirrings of the early Renaissance, argues that truth should be subordinated (at least by rulers) to other values—in his case, to power and political stability. The most rigorous interpretation of truth as a duty is given by Kant, who argues that we owe truthfulness in all our statements to all men as an absolute duty. We therefore are never justified in lying to anyone, even out of the most altruistic of motives. John Stuart Mill holds that the pursuit of truth is a value which entails another value, namely, political freedom. Nietzsche raises the problem of being truthful and discusses a series of suggestive consequences of that problem. Hartmann finds truthfulness justified as a moral value because it is a demand of love. Finally, Bonhoeffer believes that 'telling the truth' depends on the situation in which one speaks and acts and that therefore one is obliged, not by true statements, but by the imperative to make concrete situations truthful.

PLATO (428–348 B.C.)

Truth and Character

[*Socrates*:] Thus, Glaucon, I said, after pursuing a lengthened inquiry we have, not without difficulty, discovered who are true philosophers and who are not.

[*Glaucon*:] Yes, he replied; probably it was not easy to abridge the inquiry.

Apparently not, I said. However that may be, I think, for my part, that the result would have been brought out still more clearly, if we had to speak of this only, without discussing the many points that still await our notice, if we wish to ascertain wherein the superiority of a righteous over an unrighteous life consists.

Then what are we to do next?

We have only to take the step next in order. Since those who are able to apprehend the eternal and immutable, are philosophers, while those who are incapable of this and who wander in the region of change and multiformity, are not philosophers, which of the two, tell me, ought to be governors of a state?

What must I reply, if I am to do justice to the question?

Ask yourself which of the two are to be thought capable of guarding the laws and customs of states, and let these be appointed guardians.

You are right.

Can there be any question as to whether a blind man, or one with quick sight, is the right person to guard and keep any thing?

There can be no question about it.

Then do you think that there is a particle of difference between the condition of blind persons, and the state of those who are absolutely destitute of the knowledge of things as they really are, and who possess in their soul no distinct exemplar, and cannot, like painters, fix their eyes on perfect truth as a perpetual standard of reference, to be contemplated with the minutest care, before they proceed to deal with earthly canons about things beautiful and just and good, laying them down where they are required, and where they already exist watching over their preservation?

The selection is from *The Republic of Plato*, trans. J. L. Davies and D. J. Vaughan (London: Macmillan and Co., 1895).

No, indeed, there is not much difference.

Shall we then appoint such persons to the office of guardians, in preference to those who not only have gained a knowledge of each thing in its reality, but in practical skill are not inferior to the former, and come behind them in no other department of excellence?

Why, if these latter are not wanting in the other qualifications, it would be perfectly absurd to choose any others. For just the point in which they are superior may be said to be the most important of all.

Then shall we proceed to explain how the same persons will be enabled to possess both qualifications?

By all means.

If so, we must begin by gaining a thorough insight into their proper character, as we said at the outset of this discussion. And I think, if we agree tolerably on that point, we shall also agree that the two qualifications may be united in the same persons, and that such characters, and no others, are the proper governors of states.

How so?

With regard to the philosophic nature, let us take for granted that its possessors are ever enamoured of all learning, that will reveal to them somewhat of that real and permanent existence, which is exempt from the vicissitudes of generation and decay.

Let it be granted.

Again, I said, let us also assume that they are enamoured of the whole of that real existence, and willingly resign no part of it, be it small or great, honoured or slighted; as we shewed on a previous occasion, in speaking of the ambitious and the amorous.

You are right.

Now then proceed to consider, whether we ought not to find a third feature in the character of those who are to realize our description.

What feature do you mean?

I mean truthfulness, that is, a determination never to admit falsehood in any shape, if it can be helped, but to abhor it, and love the truth.

Yes, it is probable we shall find it.

Nay, my friend, it is not only probable, but absolutely inevitable, that one who is by nature prone to any passion, should be well pleased with everything that is bound by the closest ties to the beloved object.

True, he said.

And can you find any thing allied to wisdom more closely than truth?

Certainly not.

And is it possible for the same nature to love wisdom, and at the same time love falsehood?

Unquestionably it is not.

Consequently, the genuine lover of knowledge must, from his youth up, strive intensely after all truth.

Yes, he must thoroughly.

Well, but we cannot doubt that when a person's desires set strongly in one direction, they run with corresponding feebleness in every other channel, like a stream whose waters have been diverted into another bed.

Undoubtedly they do.

So that when the current has set towards science, and all its branches, a man's desires will, I fancy, hover around pleasures that are purely mental, abandoning those in which the body is instrumental, — provided that the man's love of wisdom is real, not artificial.

It cannot be otherwise.

Again, such a person will be temperate and thoroughly un covetous: for he is the last person in the world to value those objects, which make men anxious for money at any cost.

True.

Once more, there is another point which you ought to take into consideration, when you are endeavouring to distinguish a philosophic from an unphilosophic character.

What is that?

You must take care not to overlook any taint of meanness. For surely little-mindedness thwarts above everything the soul that is destined ever to aspire to grasp truth, both divine and human, in its integrity and universality.

That is most true.

And do you think that a spirit full of lofty thoughts, and privileged to contemplate all time, and all existence, can possibly attach any great importance to this life?

No, it is impossible.

Then such a person will not regard death as a formidable thing, will he?

Certainly not.

So that a mean and cowardly character can have no part, as it seems, in true philosophy.

I think it cannot.

What then? Can the man whose mind is well-regulated, and free from covetousness, meanness, pretentiousness, and cowardice, be by any possibility hard to deal with or unjust?

No; it is impossible.

Therefore, when you are noticing the indications of a philosophical or unphilosophical temper, you must also observe in early youth whether the mind is just and gentle, or unsociable and fierce.

Quite so. . . .

Very well, I proceeded; this will make one demonstration for us. The following must make a second, if it shall be approved.

What is it?

Since the soul of each individual has been divided into three parts corresponding to the three classes in the state, our position will admit, I think, of a second demonstration.

What is it?

It is the following. As there are three parts, so there appear to me to be three pleasures, one appropriate to each part; and similarly three appetites, and governing principles.

Explain yourself.

According to us, one part was the organ whereby a man learns, and another that whereby he shews spirit. The third was so multiform that we were unable to address it by a single appropriate name; so we named it after that which is its most important and strongest characteristic. We called it appetitive, on account of the violence of the appetites of hunger, thirst, and sex, and all their accompaniments; and we called it peculiarly money-loving, because money is the chief agent in the gratification of such appetites.

Yes, we were right.

Then if we were to assert that the pleasure and the affection of this third part have gain for their object, would not this be the best summary of the facts upon which we should be likely to settle by force of argument, as a means of conveying a clear idea to our minds, whenever we spoke of this part of the soul? and shall we not be right in calling it money-loving and gain-loving?

I confess I think so, he replied.

Again, do we not maintain that the spirited part is wholly bent on winning power and victory and celebrity?

Certainly we do.

Then would the title of strife-loving and honour-loving be appropriate to it?

Yes, most appropriate.

Well, but with regard to the part by which we learn, it is obvious to every one that its entire and constant aim is to know how the truth stands, and that this of all the elements of our nature feels the least concern about wealth and reputation.

Yes, quite the least.

Then shall we not do well to call it knowledge-loving and wisdom-loving?

Of course we shall.

Does not this last reign in the souls of some persons, while in the souls of other people one or other of the two former, according to circumstances, is dominant?

You are right.

And for these reasons may we assert that men may be primarily classed under the three heads of lovers of wisdom, of strife, and of gain?

Yes, certainly.

And that there are three kinds of pleasures, respectively underlying the three classes?

Exactly so.

Now are you aware, I continued, that if you choose to ask three such men each in his turn, which of these lives is pleasantest, each will extol his own beyond the others? Thus the money-making man will tell you, that compared with the pleasures of gain, the pleasures of being honoured or of acquiring knowledge are worthless, except in so far as they can produce money.

True.

But what of the honour-loving man? Does he not look upon the pleasure derived from money as a vulgar one, while, on the other hand, he regards the pleasure derived from learning as a mere vapour and absurdity, unless honour be the fruit of it?

That is precisely the case.

And[1] must we not suppose that the lover of wisdom regards all the other pleasures as, by comparison, very far inferior to the pleasure of knowing how the truth stands, and of being constantly occupied with this pursuit of knowledge; and that he calls those other pleasures strictly necessary, because, if they were not necessary, he would feel no desire for them?

---

[1] The passage is undoubtedly corrupt. In default of a better emendation we have adopted the proposal of Stallbaum, who reads μὴ οἰώμεθα instead of ποιώμεθα, and οὔσας, πάνυ πόῤῥω, instead of οὐ πάνυ πόῤῥω *Trs.*

We may be certain that it is so, he replied.

Then whenever a dispute is raised as to the pleasures of each kind and the life itself of each class, not in reference to degrees of beauty and deformity, of morality and immorality, but in reference merely to their position in the scale of pleasure, and freedom from pain,—how can we know which of the three men speaks most truly?

I am not quite prepared to answer.

Well; look at the question in this light. What must be the instrument employed in passing a judgment, in order that such a judgment may be correct? Must it not be experience, wisdom, and reasoning? or can one find a better organ of judging than these?

Of course we cannot.

Then observe. Of the three men, which is the best acquainted by experience with all the pleasures which we have mentioned? Does the lover of gain study the nature of real truth to such an extent as to be, in your opinion, acquainted with the pleasure of knowledge better than the lover of wisdom is acquainted with the pleasure of gain?

There is a great difference, he replied. The lover of wisdom is compelled to taste the pleasures of gain from his childhood: whereas the lover of gain is not compelled to study the nature of the things that really exist, and thus to taste the sweetness of this pleasure, and become acquainted with it: rather I should say, it is not easy for him to do this, even if he has the inclination.

Hence, I proceeded, the lover of wisdom is far superior to the lover of gain in practical acquaintance with both the pleasures.

He is indeed.

But what of the lover of honour? Is he acquainted with the pleasure of wisdom as thoroughly as the lover of wisdom is acquainted with the pleasure of honour?

Nay, said he; honour waits upon them all, if each works out the object of his pursuit. For the rich man is honoured by many people, as well as the courageous and the wise; so that all are acquainted with the nature of the pleasure to be derived from the fact of being honoured. But the nature of the pleasure to be found in the contemplation of truth, none can have tasted, except the lover of wisdom.

Then, as far as practical acquaintance goes, the lover of wisdom is the best judge of the three.

Quite so.

Also we know that he alone can lay claim to wisdom as well as experience.

Undoubtedly.

Once more; the organ by which judgment is passed is an organ belonging, not to the lover of gain or of honour, but to the lover of wisdom.

What is that organ?

We stated, I believe, that judgment must be passed by means of reasoning. Did we not?

We did.

And reasoning is, in an especial degree, the organ of the lover of wisdom.

Certainly.

Consequently, if wealth and gain were the best instruments for deciding questions as they arise, the praise and the censure of the lover of gain would necessarily be most true.

Quite so.

And if honour, victory, and courage, were the best instruments for the purpose, the sentence of the lover of honour and of strife would be most true, would it not?

Obviously it would.

But since experience, wisdom, and reasoning, are the best instruments,—what then?

Why of course, he replied, the praise of the lover of wisdom and of reasoning is the truest.

Then, if the pleasures are three in number, will the pleasure of this part of the soul, by which we learn, be pleasantest? and will the life of that man amongst us, in whom this part is dominant, be also most pleasant?

Unquestionably it will; at any rate, the man of wisdom is fully authorized to praise his own life.

And what life, I asked, does the judge pronounce second, and what pleasure second?

Obviously, the pleasure of the warlike and honour-loving man. For it approaches the first more nearly than the pleasure of the money-making man does.

Then the pleasure of the lover of gain is to be placed last, as it appears.

Undoubtedly, he replied.

Thus will the unjust man be twice in succession foiled, and twice conquered by the just. And now for the third and last time, address yourself, like a combatant in the great games, to Olympian Zeus, the Preserver, and observe that in the pleasure of all but the wise man there is something positively unreal and ungenuine, and slight as the rude outline of a picture, as I think I have been told by some learned man. And let me say, that a fall in this bout will be the heaviest and most decisive of all.

Quite so: but explain yourself.

I shall find what we want, I replied, if you will respond while I prosecute the inquiry.

Put your questions by all means.

Tell me then, I proceeded, do we not assert that pain is the opposite of pleasure?

Assuredly we do.

And also that there is such a thing as a simultaneous absence both of pleasure and of pain?

Certainly there is.

In other words, you admit that there is a point midway between the two at which the mind reposes from both. Is not that your meaning?

It is.

Have you forgotten the language which people hold when they are ill?

Give me a specimen of it.

They tell us that nothing is pleasanter than health, but that, before they were ill, they had not found out its supreme pleasantness.

I remember.

Do you not also hear persons who are in excessive pain say, that nothing is so pleasant as relief from pain?

I do.

And I think you find that, on many other similar occasions, persons, when they are uneasy, extol as supremely pleasant, not positive joy, but the absence of, and repose from, uneasiness.

True, he replied; and perhaps the reason is, that at such times this relief does become positively pleasant and delightful.

In the same way we might expect, that when a person's joy has ceased, the repose from pleasure will be painful.

Perhaps not.

Thus the repose, which we described just now as midway between pleasure and pain, must be now one, now the other.

So it would seem.

Can that, which is neither pleasure nor pain, become both?

I think so.

Again, pleasure and pain, when present in the mind are both of them emotions, are they not?

They are.

But was not the simultaneous absence of pleasure and of pain shewn just now to indicate a state of undoubted repose, midway between the two?

It was.

Then how can it be right to regard the absence of pain as pleasant, or the absence of pleasure as painful?

It cannot be right.

Hence, the repose felt at the times we speak of is not really, but only appears to be, pleasant by the side of what is painful, and painful by the side of what is pleasant; and these representations will in no instance stand the test of comparison with veritable pleasure, because they are only a species of enchantment.

I confess that the argument points to that conclusion.

In the next place turn your eyes to pleasures which do not grow out of pains, to prevent your imagining, as perhaps at the present moment you might do, that it is a law of nature that pleasure should be a cessation of pain, and pain a cessation of pleasure.

Pray where am I to look, and what pleasures do you mean?

Among many others, I replied, you may, if you will, take as the best example for your consideration the pleasures of smell; which, without the existence of any previous uneasiness, spring up suddenly in extraordinary intensity, and when they are over, leave no pain behind.

That is quite true.

Then do not let us be persuaded that genuine pleasure consists in the release from pain, or that genuine pain consists in the release from pleasure.

No.

But it is certain that, speaking roughly, most of the so-called pleasures which reach the mind through the body, and the keenest of them, belong to this species; that is to say, they are a kind of release from pain.

They are.

Does not the same remark apply to those pleasures and pains of anticipation which precede them?

It does.

Now, are you aware what the character of these pleasures is, and what they most resemble?

What?

Do you believe that there is in the nature of things a real Above, and Below, and an Intermediate?

Yes, I do.

And do you imagine that a person, carried from below to that intermediate position, could help fancying that he is being carried above? And when he is stationary in that situation, and looks to the place from whence he has been carried, do you imagine that he can help supposing his position to be above, if he has not seen the real Above?

For my own part, he replied, I assure you I cannot imagine how such a person is to think differently.

Well, supposing him to be carried to his old place, would he think that he is being carried below, and would he be right in so thinking?

Of course he would.

And will not all this happen to him, because he is not acquainted with the real Above, and Between, and Below?

Obviously it will.

Then can you wonder, that persons unacquainted with truth, besides holding a multitude of other unsound opinions, stand to pleasure and pain and their intermediate, in such a position, that though when they are carried to what is painful, they form a correct opinion of their condition, and are really in pain; yet, when they are carried from pain to the middle point between pain and pleasure, they obstinately imagine that they have arrived at fulness of pleasure,— which they have never experienced, and consequently are deceived by contrasting pain with the absence of pain, like persons who, not knowing white, contrast gray with black, and take it for white?

No, indeed, I cannot wonder at it; nay, I should wonder much more if it were not so.

Well, consider the question in another light. Are not hunger and thirst, and similar sensations, a kind of emptiness of the bodily constitution?

Undoubtedly.

Similarly, are not ignorance and folly an emptiness of the mental constitution?

Yes, certainly.

Will not the man who eats, and the man who gets understanding be filled?

Of course.

And will fulness, induced by a real substance, be more true or less true than that induced by a less real substance.

Obviously, the more real the substance, the more true is the fulness.

Then do you think that pure being enters more largely into the constitution of the class of substances like bread and meat and drink, and food generally, than into the constitution of that species of things which includes true opinion and science and understanding, and in a word, all virtue? In forming your judgment look at the matter thus. Do you believe that real existence is essentially the attribute of that which is closely connected with the unchanging and immortal and with truth, and which is itself unchanging and immortal, and appears in substances like itself; or, is it rather the attribute of that which is closely connected with the changeful and mortal, and which is itself changeful and mortal, and appears in things of kindred mould?

It is the attribute of the former in a very superior degree, he replied.

And does science enter at all less largely, than real existence, into the substance of the unchanging?

Certainly not.

Well, does truth enter less largely?

No.

That is to say, if truth enters less largely, real existence enters less largely also?

Necessarily so.

Speaking universally, does not the cultivation of the body in all its branches contain truth and real existence in a less degree than the cultivation of the soul in all its branches?

Yes, in a much less degree.

And do you not regard the body itself as less true and real than the soul?

I do.

And is not that, which is filled with substances more real, and which is itself more real, really more filled than that which is filled with things less real, and which is itself less real?

Undoubtedly it is.

Hence, as it is pleasant to a subject to be filled with the things that are naturally appropriate to it, that subject which is really more filled, and filled with real substances, will in a more real and true sense be productive of true pleasure; whereas that subject which partakes of things less real, will be less really and less securely filled, and will participate in a less true and less trustworthy pleasure.

The conclusion is absolutely inevitable, he replied.

Those, therefore, who are unacquainted with wisdom and virtue, and who spend their time in perpetual banqueting and similar indulgences, are carried down, as it appears, and back again only as far as the midway point on the upward road; and between these limits they roam their life long, without ever overstepping them so as to look up towards, or be carried to, the true Above: and they have never been really filled with what is real, or tasted sure and unmingled pleasure; but, like cattle, they are always looking downwards, and hanging their heads to the ground, and poking them into their dining-tables, while they graze and get fat and propagate their species; and, to satiate their greedy desire for these enjoyments, they kick and butt with hoofs and horns of iron, till they kill one another under the influence of ravenous appetites; because they fill with things unreal the unreal and incontinent part of their nature.

Certainly, Socrates, said Glaucon, you describe like an oracle the life of the majority of persons.

And does it not follow that they consort with pleasures mingled with pain which are mere phantoms and rude outlines of the true pleasure, and which are so coloured by simple juxtaposition to pain, that they appear in each case to be extravagantly great, and beget a frantic passion for themselves in the breasts of the foolish people, and are made subjects of contention, like that phantom of Helen, for which, according to Stesichorus, the combatants at Troy fought, in ignorance of the true Helen?

Such a state of things, he replied, follows as a matter of course.

NICCOLO MACHIAVELLI (1469-1527)

How Princes Should Keep Faith

Every one understands how praiseworthy it is in a Prince to keep faith, and to live uprightly and not craftily. Nevertheless, we see from what has taken place in our own days that Princes who have set little store by their word, but have known how to overreach men by their cunning, have accomplished great things, and in the end got the better of those who trusted to honest dealing.

Be it known, then, that there are two ways of contending, one in

The selection is from Niccolo Machiavelli, *The Prince,* trans. Ninian Hill Thomson (Oxford: The Clarendon Press, 1897).

accordance with the laws, the other by force; the first of which is proper to men, the second to beasts. But since the first method is often ineffectual, it becomes necessary to resort to the second. A Prince should, therefore, understand how to use well both the man and the beast. And this lesson has been covertly taught by the ancient writers, who relate how Achilles and many others of these old Princes were given over to be brought up and trained by Chiron the Centaur; since the only meaning of their having for instructor one who was half man and half beast is, that it is necessary for a Prince to know how to use both natures, and that the one without the other has no stability.

But since a Prince should know how to use the beast's nature wisely, he ought of beasts to choose both the lion and the fox; for the lion cannot guard himself from the toils, nor the fox from wolves. He must therefore be a fox to discern toils, and a lion to drive off wolves.

To rely wholly on the lion is unwise; and for this reason a prudent Prince neither can nor ought to keep his word when to keep it is hurtful to him and the causes which led him to pledge it are removed. If all men were good, this would not be good advice, but since they are dishonest and do not keep faith with you, you, in return, need not keep faith with them; and no Prince was ever at a loss for plausible reasons to cloak a breach of faith. Of this numberless recent instances could be given, and it might be shown how many solemn treaties and engagements have been rendered inoperative and idle through want of faith in Princes, and that he who has best known to play the fox has had the best success.

It is necessary, indeed, to put a good colour on this nature, and to be skilful in simulating and dissembling. But men are so simple, and governed so absolutely by their present needs, that he who wishes to deceive will never fail in finding willing dupes. One recent example I will not omit. Pope Alexander VI had no care or thought but how to deceive, and always found material to work on. No man ever had a more effective manner of asseverating, or made promises with more solemn protestations, or observed them less. And yet, because he understood this side of human nature, his frauds always succeeded.

It is not essential, then, that a Prince should have all the good qualities which I have enumerated above, but it is most essential that he should seem to have them; I will even venture to affirm that if he has and invariably practises them all, they are hurtful, whereas the appearance of having them is useful. Thus, it is well to seem merciful, faithful, humane, religious, and upright, and also to be so; but the mind should remain so balanced that were it needful not to be so, you should be able and know how to change to the contrary.

And you are to understand that a Prince, and most of all a new Prince, cannot observe all those rules of conduct in respect whereof men are accounted good, being often forced, in order to preserve his Princedom, to act in opposition to good faith, charity, humanity, and religion. He must therefore keep his mind ready to shift as the winds and tides of Fortune turn, and, as I have already said, he ought not to quit good courses if he can help it, but should know how to follow evil courses if he must.

A Prince should therefore be very careful that nothing ever escapes his lips which is not replete with the five qualities above named, so that to see and hear him, one would think him the embodiment of mercy, good faith, integrity, humanity, and religion. And there is no virtue which it is more necessary for him to seem to possess than this last; because men in general judge rather by the eye than by the hand, for every one can see but few can touch. Every one sees what you seem, but few know what you are, and these few dare not oppose themselves to the opinion of the many who have the majesty of the State to back them up.

Moreover, in the actions of all men, and most of all of Princes, where there is no tribunal to which we can appeal, we look to results. Wherefore if a Prince succeeds in establishing and maintaining his authority, the means will always be judged honourable and be approved by every one. For the vulgar are always taken by appearances and by results, and the world is made up of the vulgar, the few only finding room when the many have no longer ground to stand on.

A certain Prince of our own days, whose name it is as well not to mention,[1] is always preaching peace and good faith, although the mortal enemy of both; and both, had he practised them as he preaches them, would, oftener than once, have lost him his kingdom and authority.

---

[1] A later reference by Machiavelli suggests that he had Ferdinand and Isabella of Spain in mind here. *Eds.*

IMMANUEL KANT (1724–1804)

Altruistic Lying

In the work, "*France in the Year 1797*," Sixth Part, No. 1, "*Concerning Political Reactions*," by Benjamin Constant, the following passage occurs on page 123:

> The moral principle, that it is a duty to tell the truth, would, if taken unconditionally and separately, make all society an impossibility. Of this we have a proof in the very immediate consequences which a German philosopher has drawn from this principle; he going so far as to maintain, that a lie—told to a murderer, who asks us whether a friend of ours, whom he is persecuting, has not hidden himself in our house—would be a crime.[1]

On page 124, the French philosopher refutes this principle in the following manner:

> It is a duty to tell the truth. The conception of duty is inseparable from that of right or law. A duty is that which corresponds in one being to the rights of another. Where there are no rights there are no duties. Hence it is a duty to tell the truth, but a duty only towards him who has a right to the truth. But no man has a right to a truth which harms others.

The $\pi\rho\hat{\omega}\tau o\nu\ \psi\epsilon\hat{\upsilon}\delta o\varsigma$, or first error, lies here in the proposition "*that it is a duty to tell the truth, which we owe only to him who has a right to the truth.*"

It is to be remarked, first, that the expression "to have a right to a truth" is a phrase without any sense. One ought rather to say that man has a right to his own veracity, i.e., to the subjective truth in his person. For that I have a right objectively to a truth means: I depend—altogether as in the mine and thine—upon my *will* whether a given proposition is to be true or false; which would establish a strange logic.

---

[1] I hereby acknowledge that I really said this in some sentence, which I cannot, however, now recall to mind.—I. KANT.

The selection is from Immanuel Kant, "Concerning A Pretended Right To Lie From Motives of Humanity," trans. A. E. Kroeger, *Journal of Speculative Philosophy*, Vol. 7, 1873.

Now the first question is, whether a man has the authority, or the right, to be untruthful in cases where he cannot escape answering by either Yes or No. The second question is, whether he is not even obliged to be untruthful in that statement, which an unjust compulsion forces him to make, for the purpose of preventing a threatened crime to be committed upon either him or another.

Truthfulness in statements which we cannot avoid making is the formal duty which each one owes to all men,[2] no matter how great a disadvantage may result therefrom to him or to another; and although I inflict no wrong upon the person who unjustly compels a statement from me, by falsifying it, I yet by such a falsification—which may, therefore, be also called a lie, though not in a legal sense—commit a general wrong. Namely, in this: I do all in my power to bring about a state of things wherein no statement whatever any longer finds belief, hence wherein all rights based upon agreements crumble away and lose their power, which is a wrong committed upon mankind in general.

Hence the lie, defined simply as a wilful untrue statement made to another man, needs not the additional definition that it must inflict harm upon another, as the lawyers define it: *mendacium est falsiloquium in prejudicium alteris.* For it always hurts another; and if not another man, at least mankind in general by making the source of all right useless.

This good-humored lie may, however, become punishable, by accident (*casus*), under civil law, since that which escapes punishment merely by accident can also be adjudged a wrong by external laws. For instance: if you by telling a lie have prevented some one, who intended to commit murder, from the deed, then *you* are legally responsible for all the consequences that may arise from your lie; whereas, if you keep strictly to the truth, public justice can prefer no charge against you, let the unforseen results be what they may. It is quite possible, that, after you have honestly replied to the murderer, upon his asking whether his intended victim is in your house, by saying Yes, the person may have escaped from your house unobserved and thus avoided the murderer, in which case the deed would be prevented; whereas, if you had told a lie and said that the person was not in your house, whilst he has really escaped—although unknown to you—and

[2] I do not like here to carry the principle so far as to say: *untruthfulness* is a violation of the duty one owes to himself. For this duty belongs to morality; but here we speak only of a legal duty. Morality considers in every wrong only the turpitude which the liar draws upon himself.

the murderer had met and killed him, you could justly be charged with the death of the victim. For if you had stated the truth to the best of your knowledge, the murderer, in looking up his victim in your house, might have been caught by the arrival of some of your neighbors, and the deed might thus have been prevented. Hence whosoever *lies*—no matter with what good intention—is legally amenable to and must suffer the consequences of his lie before a civil tribunal, however unforseen these consequences may have been. For truthfulness is a duty which must be considered as the basis of all duties that are based upon agreements, the law of which agreements would become utterly uncertain and useless if the least exception were admitted.

Hence it is a holy—unconditionally commanding, and by no conveniences to be limited—Imperative of reason to be *truthful*—that is, honest—in all our statements. Quite just and at the same time correct is M. Constant's remark concerning the decrial of such strict principles, of which it is said that they lose themselves in impracticable ideas, and should, therefore, be discarded. He says:

> Whenever a principle, that has been proved to be true, seems to be inapplicable, it is because we do not know the *middle principle*, which contains the means of application.

He cites the doctrine of Equality, as forming the first link of the social chain, thus:

> No man can be bound by other laws than those which he has assisted to frame. Nevertheless, although in a very limited society this principle can be immediately applied, and needs no middle or mediating principle in order to become universal, still in a very numerous society must be added a new and mediating principle, namely, that the individual men can assist in the framing of laws either in their own person *or by representatives.* Whosoever should try to apply the first principle to a numerous society without adding the other mediating one, would inevitably bring about the ruin of that society. Yet this circumstance would prove only the ignorance or inability of the legislator, but would prove nothing against the principle itself.

M. Constant concludes thus: "A principle that has been recognized as true must, therefore, never be abandoned, no matter what apparent danger it seems to incur."

And yet the good man had just before repudiated the unconditional principle of truthfulness on account of the danger it seemed to threaten society, and only because he could discover no middle principle which might seem calculated to prevent this danger, and because really there is no such middle principle to be inserted here.

Adopting M. Constant's terminology, the "French philosopher" mistook the act whereby some one harms (*nocet*) another in telling a truth which he cannot avoid stating, with an act whereby he wrongs (*laedit*) another. It was simply an accident (*casus*) that the truthfulness of the statement harmed the refugee of the house, and it was in no manner a free *deed*, in legal meaning. For a pretended right to demand of another that he should lie for my benefit, would involve results opposed to all justice. But every man has not only a right but the strictest duty to be truthful in his statements, and this duty he cannot avoid whether it harms him or others. Hence he himself does not inflict harm upon whomsoever may suffer from that truthfulness; the harm is *caused* by accident. For he who acts is not free to choose; truthfulness being his unconditional duty, if he is bound to speak at all.

Hence the "German philosopher" cannot admit this proposition: "To tell the truth is a duty only towards him who has a right to the truth"; firstly, because its formula is not clear, since truth is not a possession to which we may deny the right to one and admit it to the other; but, secondly and chiefly, because the duty of truthfulness—of which alone we speak here—makes no distinction between persons to whom we may owe this duty and those toward whom we may repudiate it, but is an *unconditioned* duty which is valid in all circumstances.

Now, in order to proceed from a *Metaphysic of Rights*—which abstracts from all conditions of experience—to a *Fundamental Principle of Policy*—which applies the conceptions of that *metaphysic* to cases of experience—and thus to arrive at the solution of the problem of such a *policy* which shall be conformable to the *Metaphysic of Rights*, the philosopher must furnish:

1. *An Axiom*—that is, an apodictically certain proposition—which results immediately from the definition of External right. In other words, a harmony of the freedom of each individual with the freedom of every one according to a general law.

2. *A Postulate*—of the external public law, as the united will of all according to the principle of *Equality*, without which there would be no freedom of any single individual.

3. *A Problem*—what must, therefore, be done in order to

establish harmony, according to the principles of freedom and equality, in ever so large a society; that is, by means of a representative system.

This result or means would then become the fundamental principle of policy or politics, and the establishment and regulation whereof, obtained from an empirical knowledge of men, would have in view only the mechanism of the administration of law, and how that might be best effected. Right must never be made to conform to policy, but policy must always be made to conform to right.

M. Constant says: "A principle recognized as true"—and I add, an *à priori* recognized and hence apodictic principle—"must never be abandoned, no matter how apparently it incurs danger."

But here we ought to interpret the word "danger" as relating not to any—accidental—*harm*, but, generally, to *doing wrong*. The latter would occur if I were to make the duty of truthfulness, which is altogether unconditioned and which in statements is the supreme legal condition, a conditioned and subordinate duty. But furthermore, although by telling a certain lie I may really not do any one any wrong, yet I violate thereby the principle of right *generally* in regard to all absolutely necessary statements—I do a wrong *formaliter*, though not *materialiter*—which is much worse than to do an injustice to somebody, since such an injustice does not always presuppose an intention in principle on the part of the subject.

Whoever does not listen, with indignation at the expressed suspicion that he might be a liar, to an inquiry whether in his now-to-be-made statement he intends to be truthful or not, but rather asks for permission to consider whether there might not be possible exceptions to his truthfulness, is already a liar *in potentia;* since he shows that he does not recognize truthfulness as a duty in itself, but keeps in mind exceptions to a rule which in its nature admits of no exceptions, since in admitting them it would directly contradict itself.

All legal-practical principles must contain strict truth, and the here so-called middle principle can contain only a closer determination of their application or occurring cases according to rules of policy, but never exceptions, since exceptions annihilate that universality on account whereof alone they are called *principles*.

JOHN STUART MILL (1806-1873)

Truth and Freedom

. . . We can never be sure that the opinion we are endeavouring to stifle is a false opinion; and if we were sure, stifling it would be an evil still.

First: the opinion which it is attempted to suppress by authority may possibly be true. Those who desire to suppress it, of course deny its truth; but they are not infallible. They have no authority to decide the question for all mankind, and exclude every other person from the means of judging. To refuse a hearing to an opinion, because they are sure that it is false, is to assume that *their* certainty is the same thing as *absolute* certainty. All silencing of discussion is an assumption of infallibility. Its condemnation may be allowed to rest on this common argument, not the worse for being common.

Unfortunately for the good sense of mankind, the fact of their fallibility is far from carrying the weight in their practical judgement, which is always allowed to it in theory; for while every one well knows himself to be fallible, few think it necessary to take any precautions against their own fallibility, or admit the supposition that any opinion, of which they feel very certain, may be one of the examples of the error to which they acknowledge themselves to be liable. Absolute princes, or others who are accustomed to unlimited deference, usually feel this complete confidence in their own opinions on nearly all subjects. People more happily situated, who sometimes hear their opinions disputed, and are not wholly unused to be set right when they are wrong, place the same unbounded reliance only on such of their opinions as are shared by all who surround them, or to whom they habitually defer: for in proportion to a man's want of confidence in his own solitary judgement, does he usually repose, with implicit trust, on the infallibility of 'the world' in general. And the world, to each individual, means the part of it with which he comes in contact; his party, his sect, his church, his class of society: the man may be called by comparison, almost liberal and large-minded to whom it means anything so comprehensive as his own country or his own age. Nor is his faith in this collective authority at all shaken by his being aware that other ages, countries, sects, churches, classes, and parties have thought, and even

The selection is from John Stuart Mill, *On Liberty* (London : Oxford University Press, 1859).

now think, the exact reverse. He devolves upon his own world the responsibility of being in the right against the dissentient worlds of other people; and it never troubles him that mere accident has decided which of these numerous worlds is the object of his reliance, and that the same causes which make him a Churchman in London, would have made him a Buddhist or a Confucian in Pekin. Yet it is as evident in itself, as any amount of argument can make it, that ages are no more infallible than individuals; every age having held many opinions which subsequent ages have deemed not only false but absurd; and it is as certain that many opinions, now general, will be rejected by future ages, as it is that many, once general, are rejected by the present.

The objection likely to be made to this argument would probably take some such form as the following. There is no greater assumption of infallibility in forbidding the propagation of error, than in any other thing which is done by public authority on its own judgement and responsibility. Judgement is given to men that they may use it. Because it may be used erroneously, are men to be told that they ought not to use it at all? To prohibit what they think pernicious, is not claiming exemption from error, but fulfilling the duty incumbent on them, although fallible, of acting on their conscientious conviction. If we were never to act on our opinions, because those opinions may be wrong, we should leave all our interests uncared for, and all our duties unperformed. An objection which applies to all conduct can be no valid objection to any conduct in particular. It is the duty of governments, and of individuals, to form the truest opinions they can; to form them carefully, and never impose them upon others unless they are quite sure of being right. But when they are sure (such reasoners may say), it is not conscientiousness but cowardice to shrink from acting on their opinions, and allow doctrines which they honestly think dangerous to the welfare of mankind, either in this life or in another, to be scattered abroad without restraint, because other people, in less enlightened times, have persecuted opinions now believed to be true. Let us take care, it may be said, not to make the same mistake: but governments and nations have made mistakes in other things, which are not denied to be fit subjects for the exercise of authority: they have laid on bad taxes, made unjust wars. Ought we therefore to lay on no taxes, and, under whatever provocation, make no wars? Man, and governments, must act to the best of their ability. There is no such thing as absolute certainty, but there is assurance sufficient for the purposes of human life. We may, and must, assume our opinion to be true for the guidance of our own conduct: and it is assuming no more when we forbid bad men to pervert society by the propagation of opinions which we regard as false and pernicious.

I answer, that it is assuming very much more. There is the greatest difference between presuming an opinion to be true, because, with every opportunity for contesting it, it has not been refuted, and assuming its truth for the purpose of not permitting its refutation. Complete liberty of contradicting and disproving our opinion is the very condition which justifies us in assuming its truth for purposes of action; and on no other terms can a being with human faculties have any rational assurance of being right.

When we consider either the history of opinion, or the ordinary conduct of human life, to what is it to be ascribed that the one and the other are no worse than they are? Not certainly to the inherent force of the human understanding; for, on any matter not self-evident, there are ninety-nine persons totally incapable of judging of it, for one who is capable; and the capacity of the hundredth person is only comparative; for the majority of the eminent men of every past generation held many opinions now known to be erroneous, and did or approved numerous things which no one will now justify. Why is it, then, that there is on the whole a preponderance among mankind of rational opinions and rational conduct? If there really is this preponderance—which there must be unless human affairs are, and have always been, in an almost desperate state—it is owing to a quality of the human mind, the source of everything respectable in man either as an intellectual or as a moral being, namely, that his errors are corrigible. He is capable of rectifying his mistakes, by discussion and experience. Not by experience alone. There must be discussion, to show how experience is to be interpreted. Wrong opinions and practices gradually yield to fact and argument: but facts and arguments, to produce any effect on the mind, must be brought before it. Very few facts are able to tell their own story, without comments to bring out their meaning. The whole strength and value, then, of human judgement, depending on the one property, that it can be set right when it is wrong, reliance can be placed on it only when the means of setting it right are kept constantly at hand. In the case of any person whose judgement is really deserving of confidence, how has it become so? Because he has kept his mind open to criticism of his opinions and conduct. Because it has been his practice to listen to all that could be said against him; to profit by as much of it as was just, and expound to himself, and upon occasion to others, the fallacy of what was fallacious. Because he has felt, that the only way in which a human being can make some approach to knowing the whole of a subject, is by hearing what can be said about it by persons of every variety of opinion, and studying all modes in which it can be looked at by every character of mind. No wise man ever acquired his wisdom in any mode but this; nor is it in the nature of human intellect to become wise in any other manner. The steady habit of correcting and completing his own opinion by collating it with those of others, so far from causing doubt and hesitation in carrying it into practice, is the only stable foundation for a just reliance on it: for, being cognisant of all that can, at least obviously, be said against him, and having taken up his position against all gainsayers—knowing that he has sought for objections and difficulties, instead of avoiding them, and has shut out no light which can be thrown upon the subject from any quarter—he has a right to think his judgement better than that of any person, or any multitude, who have not gone through a similar process.

It is not too much to require that what the wisest of mankind, those who are best entitled to trust their own judgement, find necessary to warrant their relying on it, should be submitted to by that miscellaneous collection of a few wise and many foolish individuals, called the public. The most intolerant of churches, the Roman Catholic Church, even at the canonization of a saint, admits, and listens patiently to, a 'devil's advocate'. The holiest of men, it appears, cannot be admitted to posthumous honours, until all that the devil could say against him is known and weighed. If even the Newtonian philosophy were not permitted to be questioned, mankind could not feel as complete assurance of its truth as they now do. The beliefs which we have most warrant for, have no safeguard to rest on, but a standing invitation to the whole world to prove them unfounded. If the challenge is not accepted, or is accepted and the attempt fails, we are far enough from certainty still; but we have done the best that the existing state of human reason admits of; we have neglected nothing that could give the truth a chance of reaching us: if the lists are kept open, we may hope that if there be a better truth, it will be found when the human mind is capable of receiving it; and in the meantime we may rely on having attained such approach to truth, as is possible in our own day. This is the amount of certainty attainable by a fallible being, and this the sole way of attaining it. . . .

But what! (it may be asked) Is the absence of unanimity an indispensable condition of true knowledge? Is it necessary that some part of mankind should persist in error, to enable any to realize the truth? Does a belief cease to be real and vital as soon as it is generally received—and is a proposition never thoroughly understood and felt unless some doubt of it remains? As soon as mankind have unanimously accepted a truth, does the truth perish within them? The highest aim and best result of improved intelligence, it has hitherto been thought, is to unite mankind more and more in the acknowledgement of all important truths: and does the intelligence only last as long as it has not achieved its object? Do the fruits of conquest perish by the very completeness of the victory?

I affirm no such thing. As mankind improve, the number of doctrines which are no longer disputed or doubted will be constantly on the increase: and the well-being of mankind may almost be measured by the number and gravity of the truths which have reached the point of being uncontested. The cessation, on one question after another, of serious controversy, is one of the necessary incidents of the consolidation of opinion; a consolidation as salutary in the case of true opinions, as it is dangerous and noxious when the opinions are erroneous. But though this gradual narrowing of the bounds of diversity of opinion is necessary in both senses of the term, being at once inevitable and indispensable, we are not therefore obliged to conclude that all its consequences must be beneficial. The loss of so important an aid to the intelligent and living apprehension of a truth, as is afforded by the necessity of explaining it to, or defending it against, opponents, though not sufficient to outweigh, is no trifling drawback from, the benefit of its universal recognition. Where this advantage can no longer be had, I confess I should like to see the teachers of mankind endeavouring to provide a substitute for it; some contrivance for making the difficulties of the question as present to the learner's consciousness, as if they were pressed upon him by a dissentient champion, eager for his conversion.

But instead of seeking contrivances for this purpose, they have lost those they formerly had. The Socratic dialectics, so magnificently exemplified in the dialogues of Plato, were a contrivance of this description. They were essentially a negative discussion of the great questions of philosophy and life, directed with consummate skill to the purpose of convincing any one who had merely adopted the commonplaces of received opinion, that he did not understand the subject—that he as yet attached no definite meaning to the doctrines he professed; in order that, becoming aware of his ignorance, he might be put in the way to attain a stable belief, resting on a clear apprehension both of the meaning of doctrines and of their evidence. The school disputations of the middle ages had a somewhat similar object. They were intended to make sure that the pupil understood his own opinion, and (by necessary correlation) the opinion opposed to it, and could enforce the grounds of the one and confute those of the other. These last mentioned contests had indeed the incurable defect, that the premises appealed to were taken from authority, not from reason; and, as a discipline to the mind, they were in every respect inferior to the powerful dialectics which formed the intellects of the *Socratici viri*: but the modern mind owes far more to both than it is generally willing to admit, and the present modes of education contain nothing which in the smallest degree supplies the place either of the one or of the other. A person who derived all his instruction from teachers or books, even if he escape the besetting temptation of contenting himself with cram, is under no compulsion to hear both sides; accordingly it is far from a frequent accomplishment, even among thinkers, to know both sides; and the weakest part of what everybody says in defence of his opinion, is what he intends as a reply to antagonists. It is the fashion of the present time to disparage negative logic—that which points out weaknesses in theory or errors in practice, without establishing positive truths. Such negative criticism would indeed be poor enough as an ultimate result; but as a means to attaining any positive knowledge or conviction worthy the name, it cannot be valued too highly; and until people are again systematically trained to it, there will be few great thinkers, and a low general average of intellect, in any but the mathematical and physical departments of speculation. On any other subject no one's opinions deserve the name of knowledge, except so far as he has either had forced upon him by others, or gone through of himself, the same mental process which would have been required of him in carrying on an active controversy with opponents. That, therefore, which when absent, it is so indispensable, but so difficult, to create, how worse than absurd it is to forgo, when spontaneously offering itself! If there are any persons who contest a received opinion, or who will do so if law or opinion will let them, let us thank them for it, open our minds to listen to them, and rejoice that there is some one to do for us what we otherwise ought, if we have any regard for either the certainty or the vitality of our convictions, to do with much greater labour for ourselves.

FRIEDRICH NIETZSCHE (1844–1900)

On Truth and Falsity

In some remote corner of the universe, effused into innumerable solar-systems, there was once a star upon which clever animals invented cognition. It was the haughtiest, most mendacious moment in the history of this world, but yet only a moment. After Nature had taken breath awhile the star congealed and the clever animals had to die.—Someone might write a fable after this style, and yet he would not have illustrated sufficiently, how wretched, shadow-like, transitory, purposeless and fanciful the human intellect appears in Nature. There were eternities during which this intellect did not exist, and when it has once more passed away there will be nothing to show that it has existed. For this intellect is not concerned with any further mission transcending the sphere of human life. No, it is purely human and none but its owner and procreator regards it so pathetically as to suppose that the world revolves around it. If, however, we and the gnat could understand each other we should learn that even the gnat swims through the air with the same pathos, and feels within itself the flying centre of the world. Nothing in Nature is so bad or so insignificant that it will not, at the smallest puff of that force cognition, immediately swell up like a balloon, and just as a mere porter wants to have his admirer, so the very proudest man, the philosopher, imagines he sees from all sides the eyes of the universe telescopically directed upon his actions and thoughts.

It is remarkable that this is accomplished by the intellect, which after all has been given to the most unfortunate, the most delicate, the most transient beings only as an expedient, in order to detain them for a moment in existence, from which without that extra-gift they would have every cause to flee as swiftly as Lessing's son.[1] That

---

[1] The German poet, Lessing, had been married for just a little over one year to Eva König. A son was born and died the same day, and the mother's life was despaired of. In a letter to his friend Eschenburg the poet wrote: "... and I lost him so unwillingly, this son! For he had so much understanding! so much understanding! Do not suppose that the few hours of fatherhood have made

---

The selection is from Nietzsche's essay, "On Truth and Falsity in their Ultramoral Sense," in Oscar Levy (ed.), *The Complete Works of Friedrich Nietzsche* (London: T. N. Foulis, 1911), Vol. 2, pp. 173–187

haughtiness connected with cognition and sensation, spreading blinding fogs before the eyes and over the senses of men, deceives itself therefore as to the value of existence owing to the fact that it bears within itself the most flattering evaluation of cognition. Its most general effect is deception; but even its most particular effects have something of deception in their nature.

The intellect, as a means for the preservation of the individual, develops its chief power in dissimulation; for it is by dissimulation that the feebler, and less robust individuals preserve themselves, since it has been denied them to fight the battle of existence with horns or the sharp teeth of beasts of prey. In man this art of dissimulation reaches its acme of perfection: in him deception, flattery, falsehood and fraud, slander, display, pretentiousness, disguise, cloaking convention, and acting to others and to himself in short, the continual fluttering to and fro around the *one* flame—Vanity: all these things are so much the rule, and the law, that few things are more incomprehensible than the way in which an honest and pure impulse to truth could have arisen among men. They are deeply immersed in illusions and dream-fancies; their eyes glance only over the surface of things and see "forms"; their sensation nowhere leads to truth, but contents itself with receiving stimuli and, so to say, with playing hide-and-seek on the back of things. In addition to that, at night man allows his dreams to lie to him a whole life-time long, without his moral sense ever trying to prevent them; whereas men are said to exist who by the exercise of a strong will have overcome the habit of snoring. What indeed *does* man know about himself? Oh! that he could but once see himself complete, placed as it were in an illuminated glass-case! Does not nature keep secret from him most things, even about his body, *e.g.*, the convolutions of the intestines, the quick flow of the blood-currents, the intricate vibrations of the fibres, so as to banish and lock him up in proud, delusive knowledge? Nature threw away the key; and woe to the fateful curiosity which might be able for a moment to look out and down through a crevice in the chamber of consciousness, and discover that man, indifferent to his own ignorance, is resting on the pitiless, the greedy, the insatiable, the

---

me an ape of a father! I know what I say. Was it not understanding, that they had to drag him into the world with a pair of forceps? that he so soon suspected the evil of this world? Was it not understanding, that he seized the first opportunity to get away from it?..."

Eva König died a week later.—*Tr.*

murderous, and, as it were, hanging in dreams on the back of a tiger. Whence, in the wide world, with this state of affairs, arises the impulse to truth?

As far as the individual tries to preserve himself against other individuals, in the natural state of things he uses the intellect in most cases only for dissimulation; since, however, man both from necessity and boredom wants to exist socially and gregariously, he must needs make peace and at least endeavour to cause the greatest *bellum omnium contra omnes* to disappear from his world. This first conclusion of peace brings with it a something which looks like the first step towards the attainment of that enigmatical bent for truth. For that which henceforth is to be "truth" is now fixed; that is to say, a uniformly valid and binding designation of things is invented and the legislature of language also gives the first laws of truth: since here, for the first time, originates the contrast between truth and falsity. The liar uses the valid designations, the words, in order to make the unreal appear as real; *e.g.*, he says, "I am rich," whereas the right designation for his state would be "poor." He abuses the fixed conventions by convenient substitution or even inversion of terms. If he does this in a selfish and moreover harmful fashion, society will no longer trust him but will even exclude him. In this way men avoid not so much being defrauded, but being injured by fraud. At bottom, at this juncture too, they hate not deception, but the evil, hostile consequences of certain species of deception. And it is in a similarly limited sense only that man desires truth: he covets the agreeable, life-preserving consequences of truth; he is indifferent towards pure, ineffective knowledge; he is even inimical towards truths which possibly might prove harmful or destroying. And, moreover, what after all are those conventions of language? Are they possibly products of knowledge, of the love of truth; do the designations and the things coincide? Is language the adequate expression of all realities?

Only by means of forgetfulness can man ever arrive at imagining that he possesses "truth" in that degree just indicated. If he does not mean to content himself with truth in the shape of tautology, that is, with empty husks, he will always obtain illusions instead of truth. What is a word? The expression of a nerve-stimulus in sounds. But to infer a cause outside us from the nerve-stimulus is already the result of a wrong and unjustifiable application of the proposition of causality. How should we dare, if truth with the genesis of language, if the point of view of certainty with the designations had alone been decisive; how indeed should we dare to say: the stone is hard; as if "hard" was known to us otherwise; and not merely as an entirely subjective stimulus! We divide things according to genders; we designate the tree as masculine,[2] the plant as feminine;[3] what arbitrary metaphors! How far flown beyond the canon of certainty! We speak of a "serpent";[4] the designation fits nothing but the sinuosity, and could therefore also appertain to the worm. What arbitrary demarcations! what one-sided preferences given sometimes to this, sometimes to that quality of a thing! The different languages placed side by side show that with words truth or adequate expression matters little: for otherwise there would not be so many languages. The "Thing-in-itself" (it is just this which would be the pure ineffective truth) is also quite incomprehensible to the creator of language and not worth making any great endeavour to obtain. He designates only the relations of things to men and for their expression he calls to his help the most daring metaphors. A nerve-stimulus, first transformed into a percept! First metaphor! The percept again copied into a sound! Second metaphor! And each time he leaps completely out of one sphere right into the midst of an entirely different one. One can imagine a man who is quite deaf and has never had a sensation of tone and of music; just as this man will possibly marvel at Chladni's sound figures in the sand, will discover their cause in the vibrations of the string, and will then proclaim that now he knows what man calls "tone"; even so does it happen to us all with language. When we talk about trees, colours, snow and flowers, we believe we know something about the things themselves, and yet we only possess metaphors of the things, and these metaphors do not in the least correspond to the original essentials. Just as the sound shows itself as a sand-figure, in the same way the enigmatical x of the Thing-in-itself is seen first as nerve-stimulus, then as percept, and finally as sound. At any rate the genesis of language did not therefore proceed on logical lines, and the whole material in which and with which the man of truth, the investigator, the philosopher works and builds, originates, if not from Nephelococcygia, cloud-land, at any rate not from the essence of things.

Let us especially think about the formation of ideas. Every word becomes at once an idea not by having, as one might presume, to serve as a reminder for the original experience happening but

---

[2] In German *the tree—der Baum—*is masculine.—*Tr.*
[3] In German *the plant—die Pflanze—*is feminine.—*Tr.*
[4] *Cf.* the German *die Schlange* and *schlingen*, the English *serpent* from the Latin *serpere.*—*Tr.*

once and absolutely individualised, to which experience such word owes its origin, no, but by having simultaneously to fit innumerable, more or less similar (which really means never equal, therefore altogether unequal) cases. Every idea originates through equating the unequal. As certainly as no one leaf is exactly similar to any other, so certain is it that the idea "leaf" has been formed through an arbitrary omission of these individual differences, through a forgetting of the differentiating qualities, and this idea now awakens the notion that in nature there is, besides the leaves, a something called *the* "leaf," perhaps a primal form according to which all leaves were woven, drawn, accurately measured, coloured, crinkled, painted, but by unskilled hands, so that no copy had turned out correct and trustworthy as a true copy of the primal form. We call a man "honest"; we ask why has he acted so honestly to-day? Our customary answer runs, "On account of his honesty." *The* Honesty! That means again: the "leaf" is the cause of the leaves. We really and truly do not know anything at all about an essential quality which might be called *the* honesty, but we do know about numerous individualised, and therefore unequal actions, which we equate by omission of the unequal, and now designate as honest actions; finally out of them we formulate a *qualitas occulta* with the name "Honesty." The disregarding of the individual and real furnishes us with the idea, as it likewise also gives us the form; whereas nature knows of no forms and ideas, and therefore knows no species but only an *x*, to us inaccessible and indefinable. For our antithesis of individual and species is anthropomorphic too and does not come from the essence of things, although on the other hand we do not dare to say that it does not correspond to it; for that would be a dogmatic assertion and as such just as undemonstrable as its contrary.

What therefore is truth? A mobile army of metaphors, metonymies, anthropomorphisms: in short a sum of human relations which become poetically and rhetorically intensified, metamorphosed, adorned, and after long usage seem to a nation fixed, canonic and binding; truths are illusions of which one has forgotten that they *are* illusions; worn-out metaphors which have become powerless to affect the senses; coins which have their obverse effaced and now are no longer of account as coins but merely as metal.

Still we do not yet know whence the impulse to truth comes, for up to now we have heard only about the obligation which society imposes in order to exist: to be truthful, that is, to use the usual metaphors, therefore expressed morally: we have heard only about the obligation to lie according to a fixed convention, to lie gregariously in a style binding for all. Now man of course forgets that matters are going thus with him; he therefore lies in that fashion pointed out unconsciously and according to habits of centuries' standing—and by *this very unconsciousness,* by this very forgetting, he arrives at a sense for truth. Through this feeling of being obliged to designate one thing as "red," another as "cold," a third one as "dumb," awakes a moral emotion relating to truth. Out of the antithesis "liar" whom nobody trusts, whom all exclude, man demonstrates to himself the venerableness, reliability, usefulness of truth. Now as a *"rational"* being he submits his actions to the sway of abstractions; he no longer suffers himself to be carried away by sudden impressions, by sensations, he first generalises all these impressions into paler, cooler ideas, in order to attach to them the ship of his life and actions. Everything which makes man stand out in bold relief against the animal depends on this faculty of volatilising the concrete metaphors into a schema, and therefore resolving a perception into an idea. For within the range of those schemata a something becomes possible that never could succeed under the first perceptual impressions: to build up a pyramidal order with castes and grades, to create a new world of laws, privileges, sub-orders, delimitations, which now stands opposite the other perceptual world of first impressions and assumes the appearance of being the more fixed, general, known, human of the two and therefore the regulating and imperative one. Whereas every metaphor of perception is individual and without its equal and therefore knows how to escape all attempts to classify it, the great edifice of ideas shows the rigid regularity of a Roman Columbarium and in logic breathes forth the sternness and coolness which we find in mathematics. He who has been breathed upon by this coolness will scarcely believe, that the idea too, bony and hexahedral, and permutable as a die, remains however only as the *residuum of a metaphor,* and that the illusion of the artistic metamorphosis of a nerve-stimulus into percepts is, if not the mother, then the grandmother of every idea. Now in this game of dice, "Truth" means to use every die as it is designated, to count its points carefully, to form exact classifications, and never to violate the order of castes and the sequences of rank. Just as the Romans and Etruscans for their benefit cut up the sky by means of strong mathematical lines and banned a god as it were into a *templum,* into a space limited in this fashion, so every nation has above its head such a sky of ideas divided up mathematically, and it understands the demand for truth to mean that every conceptual god is to be looked for only in *his* own sphere. One may here well admire man, who succeeded in piling up an infinitely complex dome of ideas on a movable foundation and as it were on running water, as a powerful genius of architecture. Of course in order to obtain hold on such a foundation it must be as an edifice piled up out of cobwebs, so fragile, as to be carried away by the waves: so firm, as not to be blown asunder by every wind. In this way man as an architectural genius rises high above the bee; she builds with wax, which she brings together out of nature; he with the much more delicate material of ideas, which he must first manufacture within himself. He is very much to be admired here—but not on account of his impulse for truth, his bent for pure cognition of things. If somebody hides a thing behind a bush, seeks it again and finds it in the self-same place, then there is not much to boast of, respecting this seeking and finding; thus, however, matters stand with the seeking and finding of "truth" within the realm of reason. If I make the definition of the mammal and then declare after inspecting a camel, "Behold a mammal," then no doubt a truth is brought to light thereby, but it is of very limited value, I mean it is anthropomorphic through and through, and does not contain one single point which is "true-in-itself," real and universally valid, apart from man. The seeker after such truths seeks at the bottom only the metamorphosis of the world in man, he strives for an understanding of the world as a human-like thing and by his battling gains at best the feeling of an assimilation. Similarly, as the astrologer contemplated the stars in the service of man and in connection with their happiness and unhappiness, such a seeker contemplates the whole world as related to man, as the infinitely protracted echo of an original sound: man; as the multiplied copy of the one arch-type: man. His procedure is to apply man as the measure of all things, whereby he starts from the error of believing that he has these things immediately before him as pure objects. He therefore forgets that the original metaphors of perception *are* metaphors, and takes them for the things themselves.

Only by forgetting that primitive world of metaphors, only by the congelation and coagulation of an original mass of similes and percepts pouring forth as a fiery liquid out of the primal faculty of human fancy, only by the invincible faith, that *this* sun, *this* window, *this* table is a truth in itself: in short only by the fact that man forgets himself as subject, and what is more as an *artistically creating* subject: only by all this does he live with some repose, safety and consequence. If he were able to get out of the prison walls of this faith, even for an instant only, his "self-consciousness" would be destroyed at once.

Already it costs him some trouble to admit to himself that the insect and the bird perceive a world different from his own, and that the question, which of the two world-perceptions is more accurate, is quite a senseless one, since to decide this question it would be necessary to apply the standard of *right perception*, i.e., to apply a standard which *does not* exist. On the whole it seems to me that the "right perception"—which would mean the adequate expression of an object in the subject—is a nonentity full of contradictions: for between two utterly different spheres, as between subject and object, there is no causality, no accuracy, no expression, but at the utmost an *aesthetical* relation, I mean a suggestive metamorphosis, a stammering translation into quite a distinct foreign language, for which purpose however there is needed at any rate an intermediate sphere, an intermediate force, freely composing and freely inventing. The word "phenomenon" contains many seductions, and on that account I avoid it as much as possible, for it is not true that the essence of things appears in the empiric world. A painter who had no hands and wanted to express the picture distinctly present to his mind by the agency of song, would still reveal much more with this permutation of spheres, than the empiric world reveals about the essence of things. The very relation of a nerve-stimulus to the produced percept is in itself no necessary one; but if the same percept has been reproduced millions of times and has been the inheritance of many successive generations of man, and in the end appears each time to all mankind as the result of the same cause, then it attains finally for man the same importance as if it were *the* unique, necessary percept and as if that relation between the original nerve-stimulus and the percept produced were a close relation of causality: just as a dream eternally repeated, would be perceived and judged as though real. But the congelation and coagulation of a metaphor does not at all guarantee the necessity and exclusive justification of that metaphor.

Surely every human being who is at home with such contemplations has felt a deep distrust against any idealism of that kind, as often as he has distinctly convinced himself of the eternal rigidity, omnipresence, and infallibility of nature's laws: he has arrived at the conclusion that as far as we can penetrate the heights of the telescopic and the depths of the microscopic world, everything is quite secure, complete, infinite, determined, and continuous. Science will have to dig in these shafts eternally and successfully and all things found are sure to have to harmonise and not to contradict one another. How little does this resemble a product of fancy, for if it were one it would necessarily betray somewhere its nature of appearance and unreality. Against this it may be objected in the first place that if each of us had for himself a different sensibility, if we ourselves were only able to perceive sometimes as a bird, sometimes as a worm, sometimes as a plant, or if one of us saw the same stimulus as red, another as blue, if a third person even perceived it as a tone, then nobody would talk of such an orderliness of nature, but would conceive of her only as an extremely subjective structure. Secondly, what is, for us in general, a law of nature? It is not known in itself but only in its effects, that is to say in its relations to other laws of nature, which again are known to us only as sums of relations. Therefore all these relations refer only one to another and are absolutely incomprehensible to us in their essence; only that which we add: time, space, *i.e.*, relations of sequence and numbers, are really known to us in them. Everything wonderful however, that we marvel at in the laws of nature, everything that demands an explanation and might seduce us into distrusting idealism, lies really and solely in the mathematical rigour and inviolability of the conceptions of time and space. These however we produce within ourselves and throw them forth with that necessity with which the spider spins; since we are compelled to conceive all things under these forms only, then it is no longer wonderful that in all things we actually conceive none but these forms: for they all must bear within themselves the laws of number, and this very idea of number is the most marvellous in all things. All obedience to law which impresses us so forcibly in the orbits of stars and in chemical processes coincides at the bottom with those qualities which we ourselves attach to those things, so that it is we who thereby make the impression upon ourselves. Whence it clearly follows that that artistic formation of metaphors, with which every sensation in us begins, already presupposes those forms, and is therefore only consummated within them; only out of the persistency of these primal forms the possibility explains itself, how afterwards out of the metaphors themselves a structure of ideas could again be compiled. For the latter is an imitation of the relations of time, space and number in the realm of metaphors.

NICOLAI HARTMANN (1882–1950)

Truthfulness and Uprightness

Truth and truthfulness are not the same. Both are of value, but only the latter is a moral value. Truth is the objective agreement of thought, or conviction, with the existing situation. The agreement is not in the least dependent upon the free will of man. Hence it has no moral value.

Truthfulness, on the other hand, is agreement of one's word with one's thought, or conviction. It is in the power of man to establish this agreement; he bears the responsibility of doing so. Truthfulness is a moral value. One's word, the object of which is to be a witness to one's real opinion, conviction and attitude, ought to achieve this end solely. For as this is its object, everyone assumes involuntarily that one's word is truthful—unless there exists some special ground for distrust. The thing said is taken as really meant. Nothing is presupposed, but that the sense peculiar to the words will be fulfilled. Herein consists the natural and good trust of anyone who is not morally corrupted, the faith he puts in the words he hears. The lie is the misuse of this good trust. It is not simply a violation of the sense of the words, but at the same time a deception of another person, based upon his trustfulness.

Inasmuch as words are not the only form of expressing one's actual attitude of mind, there is together with truthfulness of word also truthfulness of act, of allowing oneself to appear to be such or such, indeed of conduct in general. One can tell a lie by means of a deed, by one's bearing, one's pose. Straightforwardness, or uprightness, is related to pretence not otherwise than truthfulness to a lie. Still, mere silence can be a lie. One who pretends and conceals is a liar in the wider sense of the word.

A lie injures the deceived person in his life; it leads him astray. Sincere expression is a good for the other person, since he can depend upon it; and under these circumstances it is a high and inestimable good. One might accordingly think that the dispositional value of truthfulness is only a special instance of neighbourly love. A lie is, in

The selection is from *Ethics,* 3 vols., trans. Stanton Coit (New York: The Macmillan Company; London: Geo. Allen and Unwin, Ltd., 1932), Vol. 2, pp. 281-285. Distributed by Humanities Press, New York. Used by permission of Geo. Allen and Unwin, Ltd.

fact, loveless. This connection may exist; and a trace of it must always be at hand. But it is not the distinguishing mark of truthfulness as such. There is something here besides. The unloving man, for instance, is merely less worthy from the moral point of view, but he is not reprehensible, not despicable. But the untruthful man is indeed so. He heaps upon himself an odium of an entirely different kind. He is "branded" as a liar, as one in whom we can have no confidence, as an untrustworthy person. Trustworthiness is a quite distinctive moral value; it inheres as a constituent element in what gives a man "integrity." The liar is precisely the man who cannot be regarded as an "integer," his worth as a witness is damaged.

In truthfulness and uprightness there is an element of purity. A lie is a kind of stain—which one cannot say of a failure to love; it is a degradation of one's own personality, something to be ashamed of. In it there is always a certain breach of trust. And there is also in it an element of cowardice. For in truthfulness there inheres "the courage of truth." All this distinguishes it from neighbourly love. A truthful man may in some other respects be immoral; likewise one who loves may be untruthful. For there are lies which do not at all injure the person who is deceived; indeed, there are some which one commits out of genuine love. And conversely, there is a truthfulness which is highly unloving.

But, despite everything, the essential connection between truth and truthfulness is by no means broken. Objective truth is still the value which is intended and striven for by the truthful person. It is the goods-value upon which truthfulness is based. The situation which the truth-speaker aims to bring about is that the other person shall experience the truth. Upon this reference to objective truth—in which the general connection between the intended value and the value of the intention reappears—depends the high situational value of truthfulness in private as well as in public life. There is also a public truthfulness, just as there is a fraudulent and falsified public opinion. Freedom of speech, of conviction, of instruction, of confession, is a fundamental moral requirement of a healthy communal life. In the ethos of nations the struggle for such freedom is a special chapter on truthfulness; likewise the official lie, the deliberate misleading of the masses to attain particular ends, even down to the practice of official calumniation and instigation to hatred, constitute another special chapter. Truthfulness as a community-value is a permanent ideal of the moral life, which in history forever meets with new obstacles.

VALUATIONAL CONFLICTS BETWEEN TRUTHFULNESS AND THE SO-CALLED "NECESSARY LIE"

Truthfulness as a value, with its specific moral claim, admits of no exception at all. What is called the necessary lie is always an anti-value—at least from the point of view of truthfulness as a value. No end can justify deliberate deception as a means—certainly not in the sense of causing it to cease to be a moral wrong.

Still we are confronted here with a very serious moral problem, which is by no means solved by the simple rejection of each and every lie. There are situations which place before a man the unescapable alternative either of sinning against truthfulness or against some other equally high, or even some higher, value. A physician violates his professional duty, if he tells a patient who is dangerously ill the critical state of his health; the imprisoned soldier who, when questioned by the enemy, allows the truth about his country's tactics to be extorted from him, is guilty of high treason; a friend, who does not try to conceal information given to him in strictest personal confidence, is guilty of breach of confidence. In all such cases the mere virtue of silence is not adequate. Where suspicions are aroused, mere silence may be extremely eloquent. If the physician, the prisoner, the possessor of confidential information will do their duty of warding off a calamity that threatens, they must resort to a lie. But if they do so, they make themselves guilty on the side of truthfulness.

It is a portentous error to believe that such questions may be solved theoretically. Every attempt of the kind leads either to a one-sided and inflexible rigorism concerning one value at the expense of the rest, or to a fruitless casuistry devoid of all significance—not to mention the danger of opportunism. Both rigorism and casuistry are offences against the intention of genuine moral feeling. The examples cited are so chosen that truthfulness always seems to be inferior to the other value which is placed in opposition to it. It is the morally mature and seriously minded person who is here inclined to decide in favour of the other value and to take upon himself the responsibility for the lie. But such situations do not permit of being universalized. They are extreme cases in which the conflict of conscience is heavy enough and in which a different solution is required according to the peculiar ethos of the man. For it is inherent in the essence of such moral conflicts that in them value stands against value and that it is not possible to escape from them without being guilty. Here it is not the values as such in their pure ideality which are in conflict; between the claim of truthfulness as such and the duty of the soldier or friend there exists no antinomy at all. The conflict arises from the structure of the situation. This makes it impossible to satisfy both at the same time. But if from this one should think to make out a universal justification of the necessary lie, one would err, as much as if one were to attempt a universal justification for violating one's duty to one's country or the duty of keeping one's promise.

Nevertheless a man who is in such a situation cannot avoid making a decision. Every attempt to remain neutral only makes the difficulty worse, in that he thereby violates both values; the attempt not to commit oneself is at bottom moral cowardice, a lack of the sense of responsibility and of the willingness to assume it; and often enough it is also due to moral immaturity, if not to the fear of others. What a man ought to do, when he is confronted with a serious conflict that is fraught with responsibility, is this: to decide according to his best conscience; that is, according to his own living sense of the relative height of the respective values, and to take upon himself the consequences, external as well as inward, ultimately the guilt involved in the violation of the one value. He ought to carry the guilt and in so doing become stronger, so that he can carry it with pride.

Real moral life is not such that one can stand guiltless in it. And that each person must step by step in life settle conflicts, insoluble theoretically, by his own free sense of values and his own creative energy, should be regarded as a feature of the highest spiritual significance in complete humanity and genuine freedom. Yet one must not make of this a comfortable theory, as the vulgar mind makes of the permissible lie, imagining that one brings upon oneself no guilt in offending against clearly discerned values. It is only unavoidable guilt which can preserve a man from moral decay.

DIETRICH BONHOEFFER (1906–1945)

What is Meant by 'Telling the Truth'?

From the moment in our lives at which we learn to speak we are taught that what we say must be true. What does this mean? What is meant by 'telling the truth'? What does it demand of us?

It is clear that in the first place it is our parents who regulate our relation to themselves by this demand for truthfulness; consequently, in the sense in which our parents intend it, this demand applies strictly only within the family circle. It is also to be noted that the relation which is expressed in this demand cannot simply be reversed. The truthfulness of a child towards his parents is essentially different from that of the parents towards their child. The life of the small child lies open before the parents, and what the child says should reveal to them everything that is hidden and secret, but in the converse relationship this cannot possibly be the case. Consequently, in the matter of truthfulness, the parents' claim on the child is different from the child's claim on the parents.

From this it emerges already that 'telling the truth' means something different according to the particular situation in which one stands. Account must be taken of one's relationships at each particular time. The question must be asked whether and in what way a man is entitled to demand truthful speech of others. Speech between parents and children is, in the nature of the case, different from speech between man and wife, between friends, between teacher and pupil, government and subject, friend and foe, and in each case the truth which this speech conveys is also different.

It will at once be objected that one does not owe truthful speech to this or that individual man, but solely to God. This objection is correct so long as it is not forgotten that God is not a general principle, but the living God who has set me in a living life and who demands service of me within this living life. If one speaks of God one must not simply disregard the actual given world in which one lives; for if one does that one is not speaking of the God who entered into the world in Jesus Christ, but rather of some metaphysical idol. And it is precisely this which is determined by the way in which, in my

The selection is from *Ethics* (tr. Neville Horton Smith) (New York: The Macmillan Company; London: SCM Press, Ltd., 1961), pp. 326–334. Used by permission of the publishers.

actual concrete life with all its manifold relationships, I give effect to the truthfulness which I owe to God. The truthfulness which we owe to God must assume a concrete form in the world. Our speech must be truthful, not in principle but concretely. A truthfulness which is not concrete is not truthful before God.

'Telling the truth,' therefore, is not solely a matter of moral character; it is also a matter of correct appreciation of real situations and of serious reflection upon them. The more complex the actual situations of a man's life, the more responsible and the more difficult will be his task of 'telling the truth.' The child stands in only one vital relationship, his relationship to his parents, and he, therefore, still has nothing to consider and weigh up. The next environment in which he is placed, his school, already brings with it the first difficulty. From the educational point of view it is, therefore, of the very greatest importance that parents, in some way which we cannot discuss here, should make their children understand the differences between these various circles in which they are to live and the differences in their responsibilities.

Telling the truth is, therefore, something which must be learnt. This will sound very shocking to anyone who thinks that it must all depend on moral character and that if this is blameless the rest is child's play. But the simple fact is that the ethical cannot be detached from reality, and consequently continual progress in learning to appreciate reality is a necessary ingredient in ethical action. In the question with which we are now concerned, action consists of speaking. The real is to be expressed in words. That is what constitutes truthful speech. And this inevitably raises the question of the 'how?' of these words. It is a question of knowing the right word on each occasion. Finding this word is a matter of long, earnest and ever more advanced effort on the basis of experience and knowledge of the real. If one is to say how a thing really is, *i.e.*, if one is to speak truthfully, one's gaze and one's thought must be directed towards the way in which the real exists in God and through God and for God.

To restrict this problem of truthful speech to certain particular cases of conflict is superficial. Every word I utter is subject to the requirement that it shall be true. Quite apart from the veracity of its contents, the relation between myself and another man which is expressed in it is in itself either true or untrue. I can speak flatteringly or presumptuously or hypocritically without uttering a material untruth; yet my words are nevertheless untrue, because I am disrupting and destroying the reality of the relationship between man and wife, superior and subordinate, etc. An individual utterance is always part of a total reality which seeks expression in this utterance. If my utterance is to be truthful it must in each case be different according to whom I am addressing, who is questioning me, and what I am speaking about. The truthful word is not in itself constant; it is as much alive as life itself. If it is detached from life and from its reference to the concrete other man, if 'the truth is told' without taking into account to whom it is addressed, then this truth has only the appearance of truth, but it lacks its essential character.

It is only the cynic who claims 'to speak the truth' at all times and in all places to all men in the same way, but who, in fact, displays nothing but a lifeless image of the truth. He dons the halo of the fanatical devotee of truth who can make no allowance for human weaknesses; but, in fact, he is destroying the living truth between men. He wounds shame, desecrates mystery, breaks confidence, betrays the community in which he lives, and laughs arrogantly at the devastation he has wrought and at the human weakness which 'cannot bear the truth'. He says truth is destructive and demands its victims, and he feels like a god above these feeble creatures and does not know that he is serving Satan.

There is a truth which is of Satan. Its essence is that under the semblance of truth it denies everything that is real. It lives upon hatred of the real and of the world which is created and loved by God. It pretends to be executing the judgement of God upon the fall of the real. God's truth judges created things out of love, and Satan's truth judges them out of envy and hatred. God's truth has become flesh in the world and is alive in the real, but Satan's truth is the death of all reality.

The concept of living truth is dangerous, and it gives rise to the suspicion that the truth can and may be adapted to each particular situation in a way which completely destroys the idea of truth and narrows the gap between truth and falsehood, so that the two become indistinguishable. Moreover, what we are saying about the necessity for discerning the real may be mistakenly understood as meaning that it is by adopting a calculating or schoolmasterly attitude towards the other man that I shall decide what proportion of the truth I am prepared to tell him. It is important that this danger should be kept in view. Yet the only possible way of countering it is by means of attentive discernment of the particular contents and limits which the real itself imposes on one's utterance in order to make it a truthful one. The dangers which are involved in the concept of living truth must never impel one to abandon this concept in favour of the formal and cynical concept of truth. We must try to make this clear. Every utterance or word lives and has its home in a particular environment. The word in the family is different from the word in business or in public. The word which has come to life in the warmth of a personal relationship is frozen to death in the cold air of public existence. The word of command, which has its habitat in public service, would sever the bonds of mutual confidence if it were spoken in the family. Each word must have its own place and keep to it. It is a consequence of the wide diffusion of the public word through the newspapers and the wireless that the essential character and the limits of the various different words are no longer clearly felt and that, for example, the special quality of the personal word is almost entirely destroyed. Genuine words are replaced by idle chatter. Words no longer possess any weight. There is too much talk. And when the limits of the various words are obliterated, when words become rootless and homeless, then the word loses truth, and then indeed there must almost inevitably be lying. When the various orders of life no longer respect one another, words become untrue. For example, a teacher asks a child in front of the class whether it is true that his father often comes home drunk. It is true, but the child denies it. The teacher's question has placed him in a situation for which he is not yet prepared. He feels only that what is taking place is an unjustified interference in the order of the family and that he must oppose it. What goes on in the family is not for the ears of the class in school. The family has its own secret and must preserve it. The teacher has failed to respect the reality of this institution. The child ought now to find a way of answering which would comply with both the rule of the family and the rule of the school. But he is not yet able to do this. He lacks experience, knowledge, and the ability to express himself in the right way. As a simple no to the teacher's question the child's answer is certainly untrue; yet at the same time it nevertheless gives expression to the truth that the family is an institution *sui generis* and that the teacher had no right to interfere in it. The child's answer can indeed be called a lie; yet this lie contains more truth, that is to say, it is more in accordance with reality than would have been the case if the child had betrayed his father's weakness in front of the class. According to the measure of his knowledge, the child acted correctly. The blame for the lie falls back entirely upon the teacher. An experienced man in the same position as the child would have been able to correct his questioner's error while at the same time avoiding a formal untruth in his answer, and he would thus have found the 'right word'. The lies of children, and of inexperienced people in general, are often to be ascribed to the fact that these people are faced with situations which they do not fully understand. Consequently, since the term lie is quite properly understood as meaning something which is quite simply and utterly wrong, it is perhaps unwise to generalize and extend the use of this term so that it can be applied to every statement which is formally untrue. Indeed here already it becomes apparent how very difficult it is to say what actually constitutes a lie.

The usual definition of the lie as a conscious discrepancy between thought and speech is completely inadequate. This would include, for example, even the most harmless April-fool joke. The concept of the 'jocular lie', which is maintained in Catholic moral theology, takes away from the lie its characteristic features of seriousness and malice (and, conversely, takes away from the joke its characteristic features of harmless playfulness and freedom); no more unfortunate concept could have been thought of. Joking has nothing whatever to do with lying, and the two must not be reduced to a common denominator. If it is now asserted that a lie is a deliberate deception of another man to his detriment, then this would also include, for example, the necessary deception of the enemy in war or in similar situations.[1] If this sort of conduct is called lying, the lie thereby acquires a moral sanction and justification which conflicts in every possible way with the accepted meaning of the term. The first conclusion to be drawn from this is that the lie cannot be defined in formal terms as a discrepancy between thought and speech. This discrepancy is not even a necessary ingredient of the lie. There is a way of speaking which is in this respect entirely correct and unexceptionable, but which is, nevertheless, a lie. This is exemplified when a notorious liar for once tells 'the truth' in order to mislead, and when an apparently correct statement contains some deliberate ambiguity or deliberately omits the essential part of the truth. Even a deliberate silence may constitute a lie, although this is not by any means necessarily the case.

From these considerations it becomes evident that the essential character of the lie is to be found at a far deeper level than in the discrepancy between thought and speech. One might say that the man who stands behind the word makes his word a lie or a truth. But even

[1] Kant, of course, declared that he was too proud ever to utter a falsehood; indeed he unintentionally carried this principle *ad absurdum* by saying that he would feel himself obliged to give truthful information even to a criminal looking for a friend of his who had concealed himself in his house.

this is not enough; for the lie is something objective and must be defined accordingly. Jesus calls Satan 'the father of the lie' (John 8.44). The lie is primarily the denial of God as He has evidenced Himself to the world. 'Who is a liar but he that denieth that Jesus is the Christ?' (I John 2.22). The lie is a contradiction of the word of God, which God has spoken in Christ, and upon which creation is founded. Consequently the lie is the denial, the negation and the conscious and deliberate destruction of the reality which is created by God and which consists in God, no matter whether this purpose is achieved by speech or by silence. The assigned purpose of our words, in unity with the word of God, is to express the real, as it exists in God; and the assigned purpose of our silence is to signify the limit which is imposed upon our words by the real as it exists in God.

In our endeavours to express the real we do not encounter this as a consistent whole, but in a condition of disruption and inner contradiction which has need of reconciliation and healing. We find ourselves simultaneously embedded in various different orders of the real, and our words, which strive toward the reconciliation and healing of the real, are nevertheless repeatedly drawn in into the prevalent disunion and conflict. They can indeed fulfil their assigned purpose of expressing the real, as it is in God, only by taking up into themselves both the inner contradiction and the inner consistency of the real. If the words of men are to be true they must deny neither the Fall nor God's word of creation and reconciliation, the word in which all disunion is overcome. For the cynic the truthfulness of his words will consist in his giving expression on each separate occasion to the particular reality as he thinks he perceives it, without reference to the totality of the real; and precisely through this he completely destroys the real. Even if his words have the superficial appearance of correctness, they are untrue. 'That which is far off, and exceeding deep; who can find it out?' (Eccl. 7.24).

How can I speak the truth?

1. By perceiving who causes me to speak and what entitles me to speak.

2. By perceiving the place at which I stand.

3. By relating to this context the object about which I am making some assertion.

It is tacitly assumed in these rules that all speech is subject to certain conditions; speech does not accompany the natural course of life in a continual stream, but it has its place, its time and its task, and consequently also its limits.

1. Who or what entitles or causes me to speak? Anyone who speaks without a right and a cause to do so is an idle chatterer. Every utterance is involved in a relation both with the other man with a thing, and in every utterance, therefore, this twofold reference must be apparent. An utterance without reference is empty. It contains no truth. In this there is an essential difference between thought and speech. Thought does not in itself necessarily refer to the other man, but only to a thing. The claim that one is entitled to say what one thinks is in itself completely unfounded. Speech must be justified and occasioned by the other man. For example, I may in my thoughts consider another man to be stupid, ugly, incapable or lacking in character, or I may think him wise and reliable. But it is quite a different question whether I have the right to express this opinion, what occasion I have for expressing it, and to whom I express it. There can be no doubt that a right to speak is conferred upon me by an office which is committed to me. Parents can blame or praise their child, but the child is not entitled to do either of these things with regard to his parents. There is a similar relation between teacher and pupil, although the rights of the teacher with regard to the children are more restricted than those of the father. Thus in criticizing or praising his pupil the teacher will have to confine himself to single particular faults or achievements, while, for example, general judgements of character are the business not of the teacher but of the parents. The right to speak always lies within the confines of the particular office which I discharge. If I overstep these limits my speech becomes importunate, presumptuous, and, whether it be blame or praise, offensive. There are people who feel themselves called upon to 'tell the truth', as they put it, to everyone who crosses their path.[2]

[2] *Editor's note.* Unfinished. A letter of December, 1943, contains the following passage on this problem. "I have been thinking again about the problem of talking about one's own fear (in air raids), a problem I wrote to you about quite recently. I believe that under the guise of 'honesty' something is here presented as being 'natural' which is really fundamentally a symptom of sin; it is really exactly like talking in public about sexual matters. The point is precisely that 'truthfulness' does not mean the disclosure of everything that exists. God Himself made clothes for man (Gen. 3.21); and this means that *in statu corruptionis* many things in man are to remain concealed, and that if it is too late to eradicate evil, it is at least to be kept hidden. Exposure is cynical; and even if the cynic appears to himself to be specially honest, or if he sets himself up to be a fanatical devotee of truth, he nevertheless fails to achieve the truth which is of decisive importance, namely, the truth that since the Fall there has been a need also for concealment and

secrecy. For me the greatness of Stifter[3] lies in the fact that he refrains from intruding upon the inner life of man; he respects its secret and looks at men, so to speak, only quite discreetly, always from without and not at all from within. Any sort of curiosity is quite foreign to him. It made a great impression on me once when Frau ____ told me with genuine horror of a film in which the life of a plant was shown in quick motion. She and her husband had found this intolerable as an unauthorized intrusion in the mystery of life. That is Stifter's point of view, too. But is there not a connexion between all this and the so-called 'hypocrisy' of the British, which is contrasted with the 'honesty' or 'frankness' of the Germans? I think we Germans have never properly understood the meaning of 'concealment,' that is to say, ultimately the *status corruptionis* of the world. Kant in his *Anthropology* makes the very sound remark that anyone who fails to grasp the significance of the false appearances in the world, and who opposes them, is a traitor to humanity. Nietzsche says that "every profound mind has need of a mask." In my view 'telling the truth' means saying how something is in reality *i.e.*, respect for secrecy, confidence and concealment. 'Betrayal', for example, is not truth; nor are frivolity, cynicism etc. What is concealed must be disclosed only at confession, *i.e.*, before God."

[3] Adalbert Stifter (1805–1868), Austrian writer of the realist school. *Eds.*

SUICIDE

Unlike truthfulness, suicide involves an option which is not seriously faced by many people. Still, the problem of suicide is undoubtedly reflected upon by most individuals at some time in their lives, either when they themselves are in periods of anxiety or depression or when news of a suicide comes to them. The special qualities of the act of suicide are finality and ultimacy; for the suicide commits an act which is final because it cannot be undone, and which is ultimate (as far as earthly life is concerned, at least) because it destroys the basis—human consciousness—for any and all meaning and value. Reflection on these qualities may take one far into the field of normative ethics, and, if one is philosophical, into meta-ethical questions as well.

Our concern with suicide here requires some initial clarification, for not all taking (or giving) of one's life is normally considered suicide. Even ethical theories which teach principles of self-directed action and development can include reference to giving one's life for others or sacrificing one's life when such is the highest value of which one is capable. Thus, a war hero who falls on a grenade to save his company or the donor of a kidney who subsequently dies is not usually considered a suicide. Rather (though this is very much a matter requiring philosophical clarification) suicide is an individual-centered, life-taking act whose motive is ceasing the struggle for values and resigning the search for meaning.

Mention of motives suggests a number of issues that are raised by a study of suicide. Chief among them are the worth of life itself, the justification of that worth, and the control over individual life that one ought to have. In these issues is found again the basic concern of ethics with values, principles, and obligations. The problem of the worth of life involves decisions about values. Is life itself a value? Is it an intrinsic value or is it solely instrumental? In the letter comprising the selection from his writings, Seneca suggests that not life but the quality or value of life is the important matter. He therefore believes that reason, as man's capacity for determining quality, can at certain times advise us to die. Augustine and Aquinas reflect Christian doctrine in their teaching that suicide is always a disvalue or an evil. In direct opposition to Stoic teaching, Augustine finds no authority for suicide, nor, he believes, does suicide ever indicate any greatness of spirit. Aquinas expands on Augustine's statements and relates suicide to the natural law tradition of ethics. He too finds that life, as a God-given gift, is to be prized as a value and that its willful cessation is always an evil.

These references to Augustine and Aquinas also touch on a second issue, that of moral principle. Life for them has the value it does because of the ultimate belief that all being (and therefore all good) derives from God. A very different principle is found in the writing of David Hume, one of the great representatives of social utilitarianism. Finding no valid religious, legal, or moral argument against suicide, he concludes that suicide may be consistent with, even useful for, the good of society as well as of self. Schopenhauer, though not considered a utilitarian, uses roughly the same sort of principle as Hume in considering the value of suicide, yet he draws a rather different conclusion. After reviewing a number of opinions on suicide, he finds that anxiety may indeed compel one to break off with life. But suicide remains a very clumsy act, for it abolishes the consciousness which should be aware of the cessation of the anxieties it is to accomplish.

Like the second, the third major problem raised by the question of suicide is implicit in the illustrations used above. This is the problem of moral obligation, of whether suicide is ever 'right'. Seneca, himself a suicide, teaches that under certain circumstances reason can advise or oblige us to die. Augustine and Aquinas find an opposite obligation, namely, always to support and protect life. Hume believes that the principle of usefulness to self or society may sometimes make it right to commit suicide, but Schopenhauer finds suicide clumsy, if not exactly morally wrong. Somewhat more subtle analyses of the problem of obligation, however, are given in the last two selections by William James and Albert Camus. James finds that the worth of living (as against dying) and the consequent obligation to live are not so much 'givens' as accomplishments: by believing and living with these convictions, we can produce or bring about the value and the obligation. This reference to produced consequences is at the very heart of James's pragmatism. Finally, Camus, reflecting existentialist themes, observes that suicide is not a form of revolt as some would have it, but it is rather an ultimate acceptance of the 'absurd' (the threat of meaninglessness) and death. Yet, he says, revolt is what gives life its meaning—indeed, revolt in the presence of the absurd gives life all the purpose and value it has.

SENECA (4 B.C.–65 A.D.)

On Suicide

After a long space of time I have seen your beloved Pompeii.[1] I was thus brought again face to face with the days of my youth. And it seemed to me that I could still do, nay, had only done a short time ago, all the things which I did there when a young man. We have sailed past life, Lucilius, as if we were on a voyage, and just as when at sea, to quote from our poet Vergil,

Lands and towns are left astern,[2]

even so, on this journey where times flies with the greatest speed, we put below the horizon first our boyhood and then our youth, and then the space which lies between young manhood and middle age and borders on both, and next, the best years of old age itself. Last of all, we begin to sight the general bourne of the race of man. Fools that we

[1] Probably the birthplace of Lucilius.
[2] *Aeneid*, iii. 72.

Reprinted by permission of the publishers and The Loeb Classical Library from R. M. Gumere, trans., Seneca, *Epistulae Morales*, Vol. II. Cambridge, Mass., Harvard University Press.

are, we believe this bourne to be a dangerous reef; but it is the harbour, where we must some day put in, which we may never refuse to enter; and if a man has reached this harbour in his early years, he has no more right to complain than a sailor who has made a quick voyage. For some sailors, as you know, are tricked and held back by sluggish winds, and grow weary and sick of the slow-moving calm; while others are carried quickly home by steady gales.

You may consider that the same thing happens to us; life has carried some men with the greatest rapidity to the harbour, the harbour they were bound to reach even if they tarried on the way, while others it has fretted and harassed. To such a life, as you are aware, one should not always cling. For mere living is not a good, but living well. Accordingly, the wise man will live as long as he ought, not as long as he can.[3] He will mark in what place, with whom, and how he is to conduct his existence, and what he is about to do. He always reflects concerning the quality, and not the quantity, of his life. As soon as there are many events in his life that give him trouble and disturb his peace of mind, he sets himself free. And this privilege is his, not only when the crisis is upon him, but as soon as Fortune seems to be playing him false; then he looks about carefully and sees whether he ought, or ought not, to end his life on that account. He holds that it makes no difference to him whether his taking-off be natural or self-inflicted, whether it comes later or earlier. He does not regard it with fear, as if it were a great loss; for no man can lose very much when but a driblet remains. It is not a question of dying earlier or later, but of dying well or ill. And dying well means escape from the danger of living ill.

That is why I regard the words of the well-known Rhodian[4] as most unmanly. This person was thrown into a cage by his tyrant, and fed there like some wild animal. And when a certain man advised him to end his life by fasting, he replied: "A man may hope for anything while he has life." This may be true; but life is not to be purchased at any price. No matter how great or how well-assured certain rewards

---

[3] Although Socrates says (*Phaedo,* 61 f.) that the philosopher must, according to Philolaus, not take his own life against the will of God, the Stoics interpreted the problem in different ways. Some held that a noble purpose justified suicide; others that any reason was good enough. *Cf. Ep.* lxxvii. 5 ff.

[4] Telesphorus of Rhodes, threatened by the tyrant Lysimachus. On the proverb see Cicero, *Ad Att.* ix. 10. 3, and Terence, *Heauton.* 981 *modo liceat vivere, est spes.*

may be, I shall not strive to attain them at the price of a shameful confession of weakness. Shall I reflect that Fortune has all power over one who lives, rather than reflect that she has no power over one who knows how to die? There are times, nevertheless, when a man, even though certain death impends and he knows that torture is in store for him, will refrain from lending a hand to his own punishment; to himself, however, he would lend a hand.[5] It is folly to die through fear of dying. The executioner is upon you; wait for him. Why anticipate him? Why assume the management of a cruel task that belongs to another? Do you grudge your executioner his privilege, or do you merely relieve him of his task? Socrates might have ended his life by fasting; he might have died by starvation rather than by poison. But instead of this he spent thirty days in prison awaiting death, not with the idea "everything may happen," or "so long an interval has room for many a hope" but in order that he might show himself submissive to the laws[6] and make the last moments of Socrates an edification to his friends. What would have been more foolish than, scorning death, at the same time to be afraid of poison?[7]

Scribonia, a woman of the stern old type, was an aunt of Drusus Libo.[8] This young man was as stupid as he was well born, with higher ambitions than anyone could have been expected to entertain in that epoch, or a man like himself in any epoch at all. When Libo had been carried away ill from the senate-house in his litter, though certainly with a very scanty train of followers—for all his kinsfolk undutifully deserted him, when he was no longer a criminal but a corpse,—he began to consider whether he should commit suicide, or await death. Scribonia said to him: "What pleasure do you find in doing another man's work?" But he did not follow her advice; he laid violent hands upon himself. And he was right, after all; for when a man is doomed to die in two or three days at his enemy's pleasure, he is really "doing another man's work" if he continues to live.

No general statement can be made, therefore, with regard to

---

[5] *I.e.*, if he must choose between helping along his punishment by suicide, or helping himself by staying alive under torture and practising the virtues thus brought into play, he will choose the latter,—*sibi commodare*.

[6] See the imaginary dialogue in Plato's *Crito* (50 ff.) between Socrates and the Laws—a passage which develops this thought.

[7] And to commit suicide in order to escape poisoning.

[8] For a more complete account of this tragedy see Tacitus, *Annals*, ii. 27 ff. Libo was duped by Firmius Catus (16 A.D.) into seeking imperial power, was detected, and finally forced by Tiberius to commit suicide.

the question whether, when a power beyond our control threatens us with death, we should anticipate death, or await it. For there are many arguments to pull us in either direction. If one death is accompanied by torture, and the other is simple and easy, why not snatch the latter? Just as I shall select my ship when I am about to go on a voyage, or my house when I propose to take a residence, so I shall choose my death when I am about to depart from life. Moreover, just as a long-drawn-out life does not necessarily mean a better one, so a long-drawn-out death necessarily means a worse one. There is no occasion when the soul should be humoured more than at the moment of death. Let the soul depart as it feels itself impelled to go;[9] whether it seeks the sword, or the halter, or some draught that attacks the veins, let it proceed and burst the bonds of its slavery. Every man ought to make his life acceptable to others besides himself, but his death to himself alone. The best form of death is the one we like. Men are foolish who reflect thus: "One person will say that my conduct was not brave enough; another, that I was too headstrong; a third, that a particular kind of death would have betokened more spirit." What you should really reflect is: "I have under consideration a purpose with which the talk of men has no concern!" Your sole aim should be to escape from Fortune as speedily as possible; otherwise, there will be no lack of persons who will think ill of what you have done.

You can find men who have gone so far as to profess wisdom and yet maintain that one should not offer violence to one's own life, and hold it accursed for a man to be the means of his own destruction; we should wait, say they, for the end decreed by nature. But one who says this does not see that he is shutting off the path to freedom. The best thing which eternal law ever ordained was that it allowed to us one entrance into life, but many exits. Must I await the cruelty either of disease or of man, when I can depart through the midst of torture, and shake off my troubles? This is the one reason why we cannot complain of life: it keeps no one against his will. Humanity is well situated, because no man is unhappy except by his own fault. Live, if you so desire; if not, you may return to the place whence you came.

---

[9] When the "natural advantages" (τὰ κατὰ φύσιν) of living are outweighed by the corresponding disadvantages, the honourable man may, according to the general Stoic view, take his departure. Socrates and Cato were right in so doing, according to Seneca; but he condemns (*Ep.* xxiv. 25) those contemporaries who had recourse to suicide as a mere whim of fashion.

You have often been cupped in order to relieve headaches.[10] You have had veins cut for the purpose of reducing your weight. If you would pierce your heart, a gaping wound is not necessary; a lancet will open the way to that great freedom, and tranquillity can be purchased at the cost of a pin-prick.

What, then, is it which makes us lazy and sluggish? None of us reflects that some day he must depart from this house of life; just so old tenants are kept from moving by fondness for a particular place and by custom, even in spite of ill-treatment. Would you be free from the restraint of your body? Live in it as if you were about to leave it. Keep thinking of the fact that some day you will be deprived of this tenure; then you will be more brave against the necessity of departing. But how will a man take thought of his own end, if he craves all things without end? And yet there is nothing so essential for us to consider. For our training in other things is perhaps superfluous. Our souls have been made ready to meet poverty; but our riches have held out. We have armed ourselves to scorn pain; but we have had the good fortune to possess sound and healthy bodies, and so have never been forced to put this virtue to the test. We have taught ourselves to endure bravely the loss of those we love; but Fortune has preserved to us all whom we loved. It is in this one matter only that the day will come which will require us to test our training.

You need not think that none but great men have had the strength to burst the bonds of human servitude; you need not believe that this cannot be done except by a Cato,—Cato, who with his hand dragged forth the spirit which he had not succeeded in freeing by the sword. Nay, men of the meanest lot in life have by a mighty impulse escaped to safety, and when they were not allowed to die at their own convenience, or to suit themselves in their choice of the instruments of death, they have snatched up whatever was lying ready to hand, and by sheer strength have turned objects which were by nature harmless into weapons of their own. For example, there was lately in a training-school for wild-beast gladiators a German, who was making ready for the morning exhibition; he withdrew in order to relieve himself,—the only thing which he was allowed to do in secret and without the presence of a guard. While so engaged, he seized the stick of wood, tipped with a sponge, which was devoted to the vilest uses, and stuffed it, just as it

[10] By means of the *cucurbita*, or cupping-glass. *Cf.* Juvenal, xiv. 58 *caput ventosa cucurbita quaerat.* It was often used as a remedy for insanity or delirium.

was, down his throat; thus he blocked up his windpipe, and choked the breath from his body. That was truly to insult death! Yes, indeed; it was not a very elegant or becoming way to die; but what is more foolish than to be over-nice about dying? What a brave fellow! He surely deserved to be allowed to choose his fate! How bravely he would have wielded a sword! With what courage he would have hurled himself into the depths of the sea, or down a precipice! Cut off from resources on every hand, he yet found a way to furnish himself with death, and with a weapon for death. Hence you can understand that nothing but the will need postpone death. Let each man judge the deed of this most zealous fellow as he likes, provided we agree on this point,—that the foulest death is preferable to the cleanest slavery.

Inasmuch as I began with an illustration taken from humble life, I shall keep on with that sort. For men will make greater demands upon themselves, if they see that death can be despised even by the most despised class of men. The Catos, the Scipios, and the others whose names we are wont to hear with admiration, we regard as beyond the sphere of imitation; but I shall now prove to you that the virtue of which I speak is found as frequently in the gladiators' training-school as among the leaders in a civil war. Lately a gladiator, who had been sent forth to the morning exhibition, was being conveyed in a cart along with the other prisoners,[11] nodding as if he were heavy with sleep, he let his head fall over so far that it was caught in the spokes; then he kept his body in position long enough to break his neck by the revolution of the wheel. So he made his escape by means of the very wagon which was carrying him to his punishment.

When a man desires to burst forth and take his departure, nothing stands in his way. It is an open space in which Nature guards us. When our plight is such as to permit it, we may look about us for an easy exit. If you have many opportunities ready to hand, by means of which you may liberate yourself, you may make a selection and think over the best way of gaining freedom; but if a chance is hard to find, instead of the best, snatch the next best, even though it be something unheard of, something new. If you do not lack the courage, you will not lack the cleverness, to die. See how even the lowest class of slave, when suffering goads him on, is aroused and discovers a way to deceive even the most watchful guards! He is truly great who not only has given himself the order to die, but has also found the means.

---

[11] *Custodia* in the sense of "prisoner" (abstract for concrete) is a post-Augustan usage. See *Ep.* v. 7, and Summers' note.

I have promised you, however, some more illustrations drawn from the same games. During the second event in a sham sea-fight one of the barbarians sank deep into his own throat a spear which had been given him for use against his foe. "Why, oh why," he said, "have I not long ago escaped from all this torture and all this mockery? Why should I be armed and yet wait for death to come?" This exhibition was all the more striking because of the lesson men learn from it that dying is more honourable than killing.

What, then? If such a spirit is possessed by abandoned and dangerous men, shall it not be possessed also by those who have trained themselves to meet such contingencies by long meditation, and by reason, the mistress of all things? It is reason which teaches us that fate has various ways of approach, but the same end, and that it makes no difference at what point the inevitable event begins. Reason, too, advises us to die, if we may, according to our taste; if this cannot be, she advises us to die according to our ability, and to seize upon whatever means shall offer itself for doing violence to ourselves. It is criminal to "live by robbery";[12] but, on the other hand, it is most noble to "die by robbery." Farewell.

ST. AUGUSTINE (354–430)

Suicide

THAT THERE IS NO AUTHORITY WHICH ALLOWS CHRISTIANS TO BE THEIR OWN DEATHS IN WHAT CAUSE SOEVER

For it is not for nothing that we never find it commanded in the holy canonical scriptures, or but allowed, that either for attaining of immortality, or avoiding of calamity, we should be our own

[12] *I.e.*, by robbing oneself of life; but the antithesis to Vergil's phrase (*Aen.* ix. 613) is artificial.

From *The City of God* by St. Augustine, translated by John Healy. Revised and newly edited by R. V. G. Tasker. Everyman's Library. Reprinted by permission of E. P. Dutton & Co., Inc., and J. M. Dent and Sons, Ltd.

destructions: we are forbidden it in the law: 'Thou shalt not kill':[1] especially because it adds not 'thy neighbour'; as it doth in the prohibition of false witness, 'Thou shalt not bear false witness against thy neighbour': yet let no man think that he is free of this latter crime, if he bear false witness against himself: because he that loves his neighbour, begins his love from himself: seeing it is written: 'Thou shalt love thy neighbour as thyself.'[2] Now, if he be no less guiltless of false witness that testifieth falsely against himself, than he that doth so against his neighbour (since in that commandment where false witness is forbidden, it is forbidden to be practised against one's neighbour, whence misunderstanding conceits may suppose that it is not forbidden to bear false witness against oneself), how much plainer is it to be understood, that a man may not kill himself, seeing that unto the commandment 'Thou shalt not kill' nothing being added excludes all exception both of others, and of him to whom the command is given. And therefore some would extend the extent of this precept even unto beasts and cattle, and would have it unlawful to kill any of them. But why not unto herbs also, and all things that grow and are nourished by the earth? for though these kinds cannot be said to have sense or feeling, yet they are said to be living: and therefore they may die; and consequently by violent usage be killed. Wherefore the apostle speaking of these kind of seeds saith thus: 'Fool, that which thou sowest is not quickened except first it die.'[3] And the psalmist saith: 'He destroyed their vines with hail,'[4] but what? Shall we therefore think it sin to cut up a twig, because the commandment says: 'Thou shalt not kill,' and so involve ourselves in the foul error of the Manichees? Wherefore setting aside these dotages, when we read this precept: 'Thou shalt not kill'; if we hold it not to be meant of fruits or trees, because they are not sensitive; nor of unreasonable creatures, either going, flying, swimming, or creeping, because they have no society with us in reason, which God the Creator hath not made common both to them and us; and therefore by His just ordinance, their deaths and lives are both most serviceable and useful unto us; then it follows necessarily, that 'Thou shalt not kill,' is meant only of men: 'Thou shalt not kill,' namely, 'neither thyself, nor another.' For he that kills himself, kills no other but a man.

[1] Exod. xx. 13, 16.
[2] Matt. xxii. 39.
[3] 1 Cor. xv. 36.
[4] Ps lxxviii. 47.

THAT VOLUNTARY DEATH CAN NEVER BE ANY SIGN OF MAGNANIMITY OR GREATNESS OF SPIRIT

Whosoever have committed this homicide upon themselves, may perhaps be commended of some for their greatness of spirit, but never for their soundness of judgment. But indeed if you look a little deeper into the matter, it cannot be rightly termed magnanimity, when a man being unable to endure either casual miseries or other oppressions, to avoid them, destroyeth himself. For that mind discovereth itself to be of the greatest infirmity, that can neither endure hard bondage in its body, nor the fond opinion of the vulgar: and worthily is that spirit entitled great, that can rather endure calamities than avoid them: and in respect of its own purity and enlightened conscience, can set at naught the trivial censures of mortal men, which are most commonly enclouded in a mist of ignorance and error. If we shall think it a part of magnanimity to put a man's self to death, then is Cleombrotus most worthy of this magnanimous title, who having read Plato's book of the immortality of the soul, cast himself headlong from the top of a wall, and so leaving this life, went unto another which he believed was better. For neither calamity, nor guiltiness, either true or false, urged him to avoid it by destroying himself, but his great spirit alone was sufficient to make him catch at his death, and break all the pleasing fetters of this life. Which deed notwithstanding, that it was rather great than good, Plato himself, whom he read, might have assured him; who (be sure) would have done it, or taught it himself, if he had not discerned by the same instinct whereby he discerned the soul's eternity, that this was in no case to be practised, but rather utterly prohibited.

OF CATO, WHO KILLED HIMSELF, BEING NOT ABLE TO ENDURE CAESAR'S VICTORY

But many have killed themselves for fear to fall into the hands of their foes. We dispute not here *de facto*, whether it hath been done or no, but *de jure*, whether it were to be done or no. For sound reason is before example to be sure, to which also all examples do consent, being such as by their excellence in goodness are worthily imitable. Neither patriarch, prophet, nor apostle ever did this: yet our Lord Jesus Christ, when He admonished His disciples[5] in persecution to flee from city to city, might have willed them in such cases to make a quick dispatch of themselves, and so to avoid their persecutors, had He held

[5] Matt. x. 23.

it fit. But if He never gave any such admonition, or command, that any to whom He promised a mansion of eternity at their deaths, should pass unto their deaths on this fashion (let the heathen that know not God produce all they can); it is plainly unlawful for any one that serveth the only true God to follow this course. But, indeed, besides Lucretia (of whom, I think, we have sufficiently argued before),[6] it is hard for them to find one other example, worth prescribing as a fit authority for others to follow, besides that Cato only that killed himself at Utica: not that he alone was his own deathsman, but because he was accounted as a learned and honest man, which may beget a belief that to do as he did were to do well. What should I say of his act more than his friends (and some of them learned men) have said who showed far more judgment in dissuading the deed, and censuring it as the effect of a spirit rather dejected than magnanimous? And of this did Cato himself leave a testimony in his own famous son. For if it were base to live under Caesar's victory, why did he advise his son to this, willing him to entertain a full hope of Caesar's clemency? Yea, why did he not urge him to go willingly to his end with him? If it were laudable in Torquatus to kill his son that had fought and foiled his enemy (though herein he had broken the dictator's command), why did conquered Cato spare his overthrown son, that spared not himself? Was it more vile to be a conqueror against law, than to endure a conqueror against honour? What shall we say then, but that even in the same measure that he loved his son, whom he both hoped and wished that Caesar would spare, in the same did he envy Caesar's glory, which Caesar should have got in sparing of him also, or else (to mollify this matter somewhat) he was ashamed to receive such courtesy at Caesar's hands.

THAT THE CHRISTIANS EXCEL REGULUS IN THAT VIRTUE, WHEREIN HE EXCELLED MOST

But those whom we oppose will not have their Cato excelled by our Job, that holy man, who chose rather to endure such horrible torments in his flesh, than by adventuring upon death to avoid all those vexations: and other saints of high credit and undoubted faith in our scriptures, all of whom made choice rather to endure the tyranny of their enemies, than be their own butchers. But now we will prove out of their own records that Regulus was Cato's better in this glory. For Cato never overcame Caesar, unto whom he scorned to be subject,

[6] I. xix

and chose to murder himself rather than be servant unto him. But Regulus overcame the Africans, and in his generalship, returned with diverse noble victories unto the Romans, never with any notable loss of his citizens, but always of his foes: and yet being afterwards conquered by them, he resolved rather to endure slavery under them, than by death to free himself from them. And therein he both preserved his patience under the Carthaginians, and his constancy unto the Romans, neither depriving the enemy of his conquered body, nor his countrymen of his unconquered mind: neither was it the love of this life that kept him from death. This he gave good proof of, when, without dread, he returned back unto his foes, to whom he had given worse cause of offence in the senate house with his tongue than ever he had done before in the battle with his force: and therefore, this so great a conqueror and contemner of this life, who had rather that his foes should take it from him by any torments, than that he should give death to himself, howsoever, must needs hold, that it was a foul guilt for a man to be his own murderer. Rome, amongst all her worthies and virtuous spirits, cannot show one better than he was; for he, for all his great victories, continued most poor: nor could mishap crush him: for with a fixed, resolved, and an undaunted courage, returned he unto his deadliest enemies. Now, if those magnanimous and heroical defenders of their earthly fatherland, and those true and sound servants of their indeed false gods (who had power to cut down their conquered foes by law of arms), seeing themselves afterwards to be conquered of their foes, nevertheless would not be their own butchers, but although they feared not death at all, yet would rather endure to be slaves to their foes' superiority, than to be their own executioners: how much more then should the Christians, that adore the true God, and aim wholly at the eternal dwellings, restrain themselves from this foul wickedness, whensoever it pleaseth God to expose them for a time to taste of temporal extremities, either for their trial, or for correction sake, seeing that He never forsaketh them in their humiliation, for whom He, being most high, humbled Himself so low: especially seeing that they are persons whom no laws of arms or military power can allow to destroy the conquered enemies!

THAT SIN IS NOT TO BE AVOIDED BY SIN

What a pernicious error then is here crept into the world, that a man should kill himself, because either his enemy has injured him, or means to injure him, whereas he may not kill his enemy, whether he have offended him, or be about to offend him! This is rather to be feared indeed, that the body, being subject unto the enemy's lust, with touch of some enticing delight do not allure the will to consent to this impurity: and therefore (say they) it is not because of another's guilt, but for fear of one's own, that such men ought to kill themselves before sin be committed upon them. Nay, the mind that is more truly subject unto God and His wisdom than unto carnal concupiscence will never be brought to yield unto the lust of its own flesh be it never so provoked by the lust of another's: but if it be a damnable crime, and a detestable wickedness to kill oneself at all (as the Truth in plain terms saith it is), what man will be so fond as to say: Let us sin now, lest we sin hereafter; let us commit murder now, lest we fall into adultery hereafter? If wickedness be so predominant in such a one, as he or she will not choose rather to suffer in innocence than to escape by guilt, is it not better to adventure on the uncertainty of the future adultery, than the certainty of the present murder? is it not better to commit such a sin as repentance may purge, than such a one as leaves no place at all for repentance? This I speak for such as for avoiding of guilt (not in others but in themselves) and fearing to consent to the lust in themselves which another's lust inciteth, do imagine that they ought rather to endure the violence of death: but far be it from a Christian soul that trusteth in his God, that hopeth in Him and resteth on Him; far be it (I say) from such, to yield unto the delights of the flesh in any consent unto uncleanness. But if that concupiscential disobedience, which dwelleth as yet in our dying flesh, do stir itself by its own licence against the law of our will; how can it be but faultless in the body of him or her that never consenteth, when it stirs without guilt in the body that sleepeth!

OF SOME UNLAWFUL ACTS DONE BY THE SAINTS, AND BY WHAT OCCASION THEY WERE DONE

But there were some holy women (say they) in these times of persecution, who, flying from the spoilers of their chastities, threw themselves headlong into a swift river which drowned them, and so they died, and yet their martyrdoms are continually honoured with religious memorials in the Catholic Church. Well, of these I dare not judge rashly in anything. Whether the Church have any sufficient testimonies that the divine will advised it to honour these persons' memories, I cannot tell; it may be that it hath. For what if they did not this through mortal fear, but through heavenly instinct? not in error, but in obedience, as we must not believe but that Samson did? And if God command, and this command be clearly and doubtlessly discerned to be His, who dare call this obedience into question? Who dare calumniate the duty of holy love? But every one that shall resolve to sacrifice his son unto God shall not be cleared of guilt in such a resolution, because Abraham was praised for it. For the soldier, that in his order and obeisance to his governor (under whom he fighteth lawfully) killeth a man, the city never makes him guilty of homicide: nay, it makes him guilty of falsehood and contempt if he do not labour in all that he can to do it. But if he had killed the man of his own voluntary pleasure, then had he been guilty of shedding human blood, and so he is punished for the doing of that unbidden, for the not doing of which being bid he should also have been punished. If this be thus at the general's command, then why not at the Creator's? He, therefore, that heareth it said, 'Thou shalt not kill thyself,' must kill himself if He command him, whom we may in no way gainsay: only he is to mark whether this divine command be not involved in any uncertainty. By the ear we do make conjecture of the conscience, but our judgment cannot penetrate into the secrets of hearts: 'No man knows the things of a man, but the spirit of a man which is in him.'[7] This we say, this we affirm, this we universally approve, that no man ought to procure his own death for fear of temporal miseries; because in doing this he falleth into eternal: neither may he do it to avoid the sins of others, for in this he maketh himself guilty of a deadly guilt, whom others' wickedness could not make guilty: nor for his own sins past, for which he had more need to wish for life, that he might repent himself of them: nor for any desire of a better life to be hoped for after death; because such as are guilty of the loss of their own life, never enjoy any better life after their death.

WHETHER WE OUGHT TO FLEE FROM SIN WITH VOLUNTARY DEATH

There is one reason of this proposition as yet to handle, which seems to prove it commodious for a man to suffer a voluntary death: namely lest either alluring pleasures or tormenting pains should enforce him to sin afterwards. Which reason if we will give scope unto, it will run out so far, that one would think that men should be exhorted to this voluntary butchery, even then, when by the fount of regeneration[8] they are purified from all their sins. For then is the time to beware of

[7] 1 Cor. ii. 11.
[8] Titus iii. 5.

all sins to come, when all that is past is pardoned. And if voluntary death do this, why is it not fittest then? Why doth he that is newly baptized forbear his own throat? Why doth he thrust his freed head again into all these imminent dangers of this life, seeing he may so easily avoid them all by his death; and it is written: 'He that loveth danger shall fall therein'?[9] Why then doth he love those innumerable dangers? or if he do not love them, why undertakes he them? Is any man so fondly perverse and so great a contemner of truth, that if he think one should kill himself to eschew the violence of one oppressor lest it draw him into sin, will nevertheless avouch that one should live still, and endure this whole world at all times, full of all temptations, both such as may be expected from one oppressor, and thousands besides without which no man doth nor can live? What is the reason then, why we do spend so much time in our exhortations, endeavouring to animate those whom we have baptized, either unto virginity, or chaste widowhood, or honest and honourable marriage; seeing we have both far shorter and far better ways to abandon all contagion and danger of sin; namely in persuading every one immediately after that remission of his sins which he hath newly obtained in baptism, to betake him at once to a speedy death, and so send him forthwith away unto God, both fresh and fair? If any man think that this is fit to be persuaded, I say not he dotes, but I say he is plain mad. With what face can he say unto a man: Kill thyself, lest unto thy small sins thou add a greater by living in slavery unto a barbarous unchaste master? How can he (but with guilty shame) say unto a man: Kill thyself now that thy sins are forgiven thee, lest thou fall into the like again or worse, by living in this world, so fraught with manifold temptation, so alluring with unclean delights, so furious with bloody sacrileges, so hateful with errors and terrors? It is a shame and a sin to say the one, and therefore is it so likewise to do the other. For if there were any reason of just force to authorize this fact, it must needs be that which is fore-alleged. But it is not that; therefore there is none. Loathe not your lives then, you faithful of Christ, though the foe hath made havoc of your chastities. You have a great and true consolation, if your conscience bear you faithful witness that you never consented unto their sins who were suffered to commit such outrages upon you.

---

[9] Ecclus. iii. 26.

Whether It Is Lawful to Kill Oneself?

We proceed thus to the Fifth Article:

Objection 1. It would seem lawful for a man to kill himself. For murder is a sin in so far as it is contrary to justice. But no man can do an injustice to himself, as is proved in *Ethic.*v.11.[1] Therefore no man sins by killing himself.

Obj. 2. Further, It is lawful, for one who exercises public authority, to kill evildoers. Now he who exercises public authority is sometimes an evildoer. Therefore he may lawfully kill himself.

Obj. 3. Further, It is lawful for a man to suffer spontaneously a lesser danger that he may avoid a greater: Thus it is lawful for a man to cut off a decayed limb even from himself, that he may save his whole body. Now sometimes a man, by killing himself, avoids a greater evil, for an example an unhappy life, or the shame of sin. Therefore a man may kill himself.

Obj. 4. Further, Samson killed himself, as related in Judges xvi, and yet he is numbered among the saints (Heb.xi). Therefore it is lawful for a man to kill himself.

Obj. 5. Further, It is related (2 Mach.xiv.42) that a certain Razias killed himself, *choosing to die nobly rather than to fall into the hands of the wicked, and to suffer abuses unbecoming his noble birth.* Now nothing that is done nobly and bravely is unlawful. Therefore suicide is not unlawful.

On the contrary, Augustine says (*De Civ. Dei i.*20): *Hence it follows that the words "Thou shalt not kill" refer to the killing of a man; not another man; therefore, not even thyself. For he who kills himself, kills nothing else than a man.*

I answer that, It is altogether unlawful to kill oneself, for three reasons. First, because everything naturally loves itself, the result being that everything naturally keeps itself in being, and resists corruption so far as it can. Wherefore suicide is contrary to the inclination of

---

[1] The reference is to Aristotle's *Nicomachean Ethics. Eds.*

The selection is from Vol. 2 of Thomas Aquinas, *Summa Theologica* (New York: Benziger Brothers, Inc.; London: Burns & Oaks, Ltd., 1925), Part 2, Question 64, A5. Used by permission of the publishers.

nature, and to charity whereby every man should love himself. Hence suicide is always a mortal sin, as being contrary to the natural law and to charity.

Secondly, because every part, as such, belongs to the whole. Now every man is part of the community, and so, as such, he belongs to the community. Hence by killing himself he injures the community, as the Philosopher declares (*Ethic*.v.ii).

Thirdly, because life is God's gift to man, and is subject to His power, Who kills and makes to live. Hence whoever takes his own life, sins against God, even as he who kills another's slave, sins against that slave's master, and as he who usurps himself judgment of a matter not entrusted to him. For it belongs to God alone to pronounce sentence of death and life, according to Deut.xxxii.39, *I will kill and I will make to live.*

Reply Obj. 1. Murder is a sin, not only because it is contrary to justice, but also because it is opposed to charity which a man should have towards himself: in this respect suicide is a sin in relation to oneself. In relation to the community and to God, it is sinful, by reason also of its opposition to justice.

Reply Obj. 2. One who exercises public authority may lawfully put to death an evildoer, since he can pass judgment on him. But no man is judge of himself. Wherefore it is not lawful for one who exercises public authority to put himself to death for any sin whatever: although he may lawfully commit himself to the judgment of others.

Reply Obj. 3. Man is made master of himself through his free-will: wherefore he can lawfully dispose of himself as to those matters which pertain to this life which is ruled by man's free-will. But the passage from this life to another and happier one is subject not to man's free-will but to the power of God. Hence it is not lawful for man to take his own life that he may pass to a happier life, nor that he may escape any unhappiness whatsoever of the present life, because the ultimate and most fearsome evil of this life is death, as the Philosopher states (*Ethic*.iii.6). Therefore to bring death upon oneself in order to escape the other afflictions of this life, is to adopt a greater evil in order to avoid a lesser. In like manner it is unlawful to take one's own life on account of one's having committed a sin, both because by so doing one does oneself a very great injury, by depriving oneself of the time needful for repentance, and because it is not lawful to slay an evildoer except by the sentence of the public authority. Again it is unlawful for a woman to kill herself lest she be violated, because she ought not to commit on herself the very great sin of suicide, to avoid the lesser sin of another. For she commits no sin in being violated by force, provided she does not consent, since *without consent of the mind there is no stain on the body*, as the Blessed Lucy declared. Now it is evident that fornication and adultery are less grievous sins than taking a man's, especially one's own, life: since the latter is most grievous, because one injures oneself, to whom one owes the greatest love. Moreover it is most dangerous since no time is left wherein to expiate it by repentance. Again it is not lawful for anyone to take his own life for fear he should consent to sin, because *evil must not be done that good may come* (Rom.iii.8) or that evil may be avoided, especially if the evil be of small account and an uncertain event, for it is uncertain whether one will at some future time consent to a sin, since God is able to deliver man from sin under any temptation whatever.

Reply Obj. 4. As Augustine says (*De Civ. Dei* i.21), *not even Samson is to be excused that he crushed himself together with his enemies under the ruins of the house, except the Holy Ghost, Who had wrought many wonders through him, had secretly commanded him to do this.* He assigns the same reason in the case of certain holy women, who at the time of persecution took their own lives, and who are commemorated by the Church.

Reply Obj. 5. It belongs to fortitude that a man does not shrink from being slain by another, for the sake of the good of virtue, and that he may avoid sin. But that a man take his own life in order to avoid penal evils has indeed an appearance of fortitude (for which reason some, among whom was Razias, have killed themselves, thinking to act from fortitude), yet it is not true fortitude, but rather a weakness of soul unable to bear penal evils, as the Philosopher (*Ethic.*iii.7) and Augustine (*De Civ. Dei* i.22,23) declare.

DAVID HUME (1711–1776)

On Suicide

One considerable advantage that arises from philosophy, consists in the sovereign antidote which it affords to superstition and false religion. All other remedies against that pestilent distemper are vain, or at least uncertain. Plain good sense, and the practice of the world,

The selection is from the fourth volume of *The Philosophical Works of David Hume* (Boston: Little, Brown and Company, 1854).

which alone serve most purposes of life, are here found ineffectual: history, as well as daily experience, furnish instances of men endowed with the strongest capacity for business and affairs, who have all their lives crouched under slavery to the grossest superstition. Even gaiety and sweetness of temper, which infuse a balm into every other wound, afford no remedy to so virulent a poison, as we may particularly observe of the fair sex, who, though commonly possessed of these rich presents of nature, feel many of their joys blasted by this importunate intruder. But when sound philosophy has once gained possession of the mind, superstition is effectually excluded; and one may fairly affirm, that her triumph over this enemy is more complete than over most of the vices and imperfections incident to human nature. Love or anger, ambition or avarice, have their root in the temper and affections, which the soundest reason is scarce ever able fully to correct; but superstition being founded on false opinion, must immediately vanish when true philosophy has inspired juster sentiments of superior powers. The contest is here more equal between the distemper and the medicine; and nothing can hinder the latter from proving effectual, but its being false and sophisticated.

It will here be superfluous to magnify the merits of Philosophy by displaying the pernicious tendency of that vice of which it cures the human mind. The superstitious man, says Tully,[1] is miserable in every scene, in every incident in life; even sleep itself, which banishes all other cares of unhappy mortals, affords to him matter of new terror, while he examines his dreams, and finds in those visions of the night prognostications of future calamities. I may add, that though death alone can put a full period to his misery, he dares not fly to this refuge, but still prolongs a miserable existence, from a vain fear lest he offend his Maker, by using the power with which that beneficent Being has endowed him. The presents of GOD and nature are ravished from us by this cruel enemy; and notwithstanding that one step would remove us from the regions of pain and sorrow, her menaces still chain us down to a hated being, which she herself chiefly contributes to render miserable.

It is observed by such as have been reduced by the calamities of life to the necessity of employing this fatal remedy, that if the unseasonable care of their friends deprive them of that species of death which they proposed to themselves, they seldom venture upon any other, or can summon up so much resolution a second time, as to execute their

[1] De Divin. lib. ii.

purpose. So great is our horror of death, that when it presents itself under any form besides that to which a man has endeavored to reconcile his imagination, it acquires new terrors, and overcomes his feeble courage: but when the menaces of superstition are joined to this natural timidity, no wonder it quite deprives men of all power over their lives, since even many pleasures and enjoyments, to which we are carried by a strong propensity, are torn from us by this inhuman tyrant. Let us here endeavor to restore men to their native liberty, by examining all the common arguments against suicide, and showing that that action may be free from every imputation of guilt or blame, according to the sentiments of all the ancient philosophers.

If suicide be criminal, it must be a transgression of our duty either to God, our neighbor, or ourselves. To prove that suicide is no transgression of our duty to God, the following considerations may perhaps suffice. In order to govern the material world, the almighty Creator has established general and immutable laws, by which all bodies, from the greatest planet to the smallest particle of matter, are maintained in their proper sphere and function. To govern the animal world, he has endowed all living creatures with bodily and mental powers; with senses, passions, appetites, memory, and judgment, by which they are impelled or regulated in that course of life to which they are destined. These two distinct principles of the material and animal world continually encroach upon each other, and mutually retard or forward each other's operation. The powers of men and of all other animals are restrained and directed by the nature and qualities of the surrounding bodies; and the modifications and actions of these bodies are incessantly altered by the operation of all animals. Man is stopped by rivers in his passage over the surface of the earth; and rivers, when properly directed, lend their force to the motion of machines, which serve to the use of man. But though the provinces of the material and animal powers are not kept entirely separate, there results from thence no discord or disorder in the creation; on the contrary, from the mixture, union, and contrast of all the various powers of inanimate bodies and living creatures, arises that sympathy, harmony, and proportion, which affords the surest argument of Supreme Wisdom. The providence of the Deity appears not immediately in any operation, but governs every thing by those general and immutable laws which have been established from the beginning of time. All events, in one sense, may be pronounced the action of the Almighty; they all proceed from those powers with which he has endowed his creatures. A house which falls by its own weight, is not brought to ruin by his providence, more than one destroyed by the hands of men; nor are the human faculties less his workmanship than the laws of motion and gravitation. When the passions play, when the judgment dictates, when the limbs obey; this is all the operation of God; and upon these animate principles, as well as upon the inanimate, has he established the government of the universe. Every event is alike important in the eyes of that infinite Being, who takes in at one glance the most distant regions of space, and remotest periods of time. There is no event, however important to us, which he has exempted from the general laws that govern the universe, or which he has peculiarly reserved for his own immediate action and operation. The revolution of states and empires depends upon the smallest caprice or passion of single men; and the lives of men are shortened or extended by the smallest accident of air or diet, sunshine or tempest. Nature still continues her progress and operation; and if general laws be every broke by particular volitions of the Deity, it is after a manner which entirely escapes human observation. As, on the one hand, the elements and other inanimate parts of the creation carry on their action without regard to the particular interest and situation of men; so men are intrusted to their own judgment and discretion in the various shocks of matter, and may employ every faculty with which they are endowed, in order to provide for their ease, happiness, or preservation. What is the meaning then of that principle, that a man, who, tired of life, and hunted by pain and misery, bravely overcomes all the natural terrors of death, and makes his escape from this cruel scene; that such a man, I say, has incurred the indignation of his Creator, by encroaching on the office of divine providence, and disturbing the order of the universe? Shall we assert, that the Almighty has reserved to himself, in any peculiar manner, the disposal of the lives of men, and has not submitted that event, in common with others, to the general laws by which the universe is governed? This is plainly false: the lives of men depend upon the same laws as the lives of all other animals; and these are subjected to the general laws of matter and motion. The fall of a tower, or the infusion of a poison, will destroy a man equally with the meanest creature; an inundation sweeps away every thing without distinction that comes within the reach of its fury. Since therefore the lives of men are for ever dependent on the general laws of matter and motion, is a man's disposing of his life criminal, because in every case it is criminal to encroach upon these laws, or disturb their operation? But this seems absurd: all animals are intrusted to their own prudence and skill for their conduct in the world; and have full authority, as far as their power extends, to alter all the operations of nature. Without the exercise of this authority, they could not subsist a moment; every action, every motion of a man, innovates on the order of some parts of matter, and diverts from their ordinary course the general laws of motion. Putting together therefore these conclusions, we find that human life depends upon the general laws of the matter and motion, and that it is no encroachment on the office of Providence to disturb or alter these general laws: has not every one of consequence the free disposal of his own life? And may he not lawfully employ that power with which nature has endowed him? In order to destroy the evidence of this conclusion, we must show a reason why this particular case is excepted. Is it because human life is of such great importance, that it is a presumption for human prudence to dispose of it? But the life of a man is of no greater importance to the universe than that of an oyster: and were it of ever so great importance, the order of human nature has actually submitted it to human prudence, and reduced us to a necessity, in every incident, of determining concerning it.

Were the disposal of human life so much reserved as the peculiar province of the Almighty, that it were an encroachment on his right for men to dispose of their own lives, it would be equally criminal to act for the preservation of life as for its destruction. If I turn aside a stone which is falling upon my head, I disturb the course of nature; and I invade the peculiar province of the Almighty, by lengthening out my life beyond the period, which, by the general laws of matter and motion, he had assigned it.

A hair, a fly, an insect, is able to destroy this mighty being whose life is of such importance. Is it an absurdity to suppose that human prudence may lawfully dispose of what depends on such insignificant causes? It would be no crime in me to divert the Nile or Danube from its course, were I able to effect such purposes. Where then is the crime of turning a few ounces of blood from their natural channel? Do you imagine that I repine at Providence, or curse my creation, because I go out of life, and put a period to a being which, were it to continue, would render me miserable? Far be such sentiments from me. I am only convinced of a matter of fact which you yourself acknowledge possible, that human life may be unhappy; and that my existence, if further prolonged, would become ineligible: but I thank Providence, both for the good which I have already enjoyed, and for the power with which I am endowed of escaping the ills that threaten me.[2] To

---

[2] Agamus Deo gratias, quod nemo in vita teneri potest. Seneca, Epist xii.

you it belongs to repine at Providence, who foolishly imagine that you have no such power; and who must still prolong a hated life, though loaded with pain and sickness, with shame and poverty. Do not you teach, that when any ill befalls me, though by the malice of my enemies, I ought to be resigned to Providence; and that the actions of men are the operations of the Almighty, as much as the actions of inanimate beings? When I fall upon my own sword, therefore, I receive my death equally from the hands of the Deity as if it had proceeded from a lion, a precipice, or a fever. The submission which you require to Providence, in every calamity that befalls me, excludes not human skill and industry, if possibly by their means I can avoid or escape the calamity. And why may I not employ one remedy as well as another? If my life be not my own, it were criminal for me to put it in danger, as well as to dispose of it; nor could one man deserve the appellation of *hero*, whom glory or friendship transports into the greatest dangers; and another merit the reproach of *wretch* or *miscreant*, who puts a period to his life from the same or like motives. There is no being which possesses any power or faculty, that it receives not from its Creator; nor is there any one, which by ever so irregular an action, can encroach upon the plan of his providence or disorder the universe. Its operations are his works equally with that chain of events which it invades; and whichever principle prevails, we may for that very reason conclude it to be most favored by him. Be it animate or inanimate; rational or irrational; it is all the same case: its power is still derived from the Supreme Creator, and is alike comprehended in the order of his providence. When the horror of pain prevails over the love of life; when a voluntary action anticipates the effects of blind causes; it is only in consequence of those powers and principles which he has implanted in his creatures. Divine Providence is still inviolate, and placed far beyond the reach of human injuries.[3] It is impious, says the old Roman superstition, to divert rivers from their course, or invade the prerogatives of nature. It is impious, says the French superstition, to inoculate for the smallpox, or usurp the business of Providence, by voluntarily producing distempers and maladies. It is impious, says the modern European superstition, to put a period to our own life, and thereby rebel against our Creator: and why not impious, say I, to build houses, cultivate the ground, or sail upon the ocean? In all these actions we employ our powers of mind and body to produce some innovation in the course of nature; and in none of them do we any more. They are all of them therefore

[3] Tacit. Ann. lib. i.

equally innocent, or equally criminal. *But you are placed by Providence, like a sentinel, in a particular station; and when you desert it without being recalled, you are equally guilty of rebellion against your Almighty Sovereign, and have incurred his displeasure*—I ask, Why do you conclude that Providence has placed me in this station? For my part, I find that I owe my birth to a long chain of causes, of which many depended upon voluntary actions of men. *But Providence guided all these causes, and nothing happens in the universe without its consent and coöperation.* If so, then neither does my death, however voluntary, happen without its consent; and whenever pain or sorrow so far overcome my patience, as to make me tired of life, I may conclude that I am recalled from my station in the clearest and most express terms. It is Providence surely that has placed me at this present moment in this chamber: but may I not leave it when I think proper, without being liable to the imputation of having deserted my post or station? When I shall be dead, the principles of which I am composed will still perform their part in the universe, and will be equally useful in the grand fabric, as when they composed this individual creature. The difference to the whole will be no greater than betwixt my being in a chamber and in the open air. The one change is of more importance to me than the other; but not more so to the universe.

It is a kind of blasphemy to imagine that any created being can disturb the order of the world, or invade the business of Providence. It supposes, that that being possesses powers and faculties which it received not from its Creator, and which are not subordinate to his government and authority. A man may disturb society, no doubt, and thereby incur the displeasure of the Almighty: but the government of the world is placed far beyond his reach and violence. And how does it appear that the Almighty is displeased with those actions that disturb society? By the principles which he has implanted in human nature, and which inspire us with a sentiment of remorse if we ourselves have been guilty of such actions, and with that of blame and disapprobation, if we ever observe them in others. Let us now examine, according to the method proposed, whether Suicide be of this kind of actions, and be a breach of our duty to our *neighbor* and to *society*.

A man who retires from life does no harm to society: he only ceases to do good; which, if it is an injury, is of the lowest kind. All our obligations to do good to society seem to imply something reciprocal. I receive the benefits of society, and therefore ought to promote its interests; but when I withdraw myself altogether from society, can I be bound any longer? But allowing that our obligations to do good were perpetual, they have certainly some bounds; I am not obliged to do a small good to society at the expense of a great harm to myself: why then should I prolong a miserable existence, because of some frivolous advantage which the public may perhaps receive from me? If upon account of age and infirmities, I may lawfully resign any office, and employ my time altogether in fencing against these calamities, and alleviating as much as possible the miseries of my future life; why may I not cut short these miseries at once by an action which is no more prejudicial to society? But suppose that it is no longer in my power to promote the interest of society; suppose that I am a burden to it; suppose that my life hinders some person from being much more useful to society: in such cases, my resignation of life must not only be innocent, but laudable. And most people who lie under any temptation to abandon existence, are in some such situation; those who have health, or power, or authority, have commonly better reason to be in humor with the world.

A man is engaged in a conspiracy for the public interest; is seized upon suspicion; is threatened with the rack; and knows from his own weakness that the secret will be extorted from him: could such a one consult the public interest better than by putting a quick period to a miserable life? This was the case of the famous and brave Strozi of Florence. Again, suppose a malefactor is justly condemned to a shameful death; can any reason be imagined why he may not anticipate his punishment, and save himself all the anguish of thinking on its dreadful approaches? He invades the business of Providence no more than the magistrate did who ordered his execution; and his voluntary death is equally advantageous to society, by ridding it of a pernicious member.

That Suicide may often be consistent with interest and with our duty to ourselves, no one can question, who allows that age, sickness, or misfortune, may render life a burden, and make it worse even than annihilation. I believe that no man ever threw away life while it was worth keeping. For such is our natural horror of death, that small motives will never be able to reconcile us to it; and though perhaps the situation of a man's health or fortune did not seem to require this remedy, we may at least be assured, that any one who, without apparent reason, has had recourse to it, was cursed with such an incurable depravity or gloominess of temper as must poison all enjoyment, and render him equally miserable as if he had been loaded with the most grievous misfortunes. If Suicide be supposed a crime, it is only cowardice can impel us to it. If it be no crime, both prudence and

courage should engage us to rid ourselves at once of existence when
it becomes a burden. It is the only way that we can then be useful to
society, by setting an example, which, if imitated, would preserve to
every one his chance for happiness in life, and would effectually free
him from all danger or misery.[4]

ARTHUR SCHOPENHAUER (1788–1860)

On Suicide

As far as I see it is only the monotheistic, that is, the Jewish
religions, whose votaries regard suicide as a crime. This is the more
surprising as neither in the Old, nor in the New Testament is there to
be found any prohibition, or even any decided disapproval of it. Teachers
of religion, therefore, have to base their condemnation of suicide on
philosophical grounds of their own, with which, however, it goes so

[4] It would be easy to prove that suicide is as lawful under the Christian
dispensation as it was to the Heathens. There is not a single text of Scripture
which prohibits it. That great and infallible rule of faith and practice which
must control all philosophy and human reasoning, has left us in this particular
to our natural liberty. Resignation to Providence is indeed recommended in
Scripture; but that implies only submission to ills that are unavoidable, not to
such as may be remedied by prudence or courage. *Thou shalt not kill*, is evidently meant to exclude only the killing of others, over whose life we have no
authority. That this precept, like most of the Scripture precepts, must be
modified by reason and common sense, is plain from the practice of magistrates, who punish criminals capitally, notwithstanding the letter of the law.
But were this commandment ever so express against suicide, it would now
have no authority, for all the law of *Moses* is abolished, except so far as it is
established by the law of nature. And we have already endeavored to prove
that suicide is not prohibited by that law. In all cases Christians and Heathens
are precisely upon the same footing; *Cato* and *Brutus*, *Arrea* and *Portia*
acted heroically; those who now imitate their example ought to receive the
same praises from posterity. The power of committing suicide is regarded
by *Pliny* as an advantage which men possess even above the Deity himself.
"Deus non sibi potest mortem consciscere si velit, quod homini dedit optimum
in tantis vitæ pœnis."—Lib. II. cap. 7.

The selection is from Arthur Schopenhauer, *Selected Essays,* ed. Ernest Belfort Bax
(London: George Bell and Sons, 1909), pp. 257–262.

badly, that they seek to supply what in their arguments lacks strength, by the vigour of their expressions of disgust, that is, by abuse. We have to hear, accordingly, that suicide is the greatest cowardice, that it is only possible in madness, and similar twaddle, or even the entirely senseless phrase that suicide is "wrong," whereas obviously no one has a greater right over anything in the world than over his own person and life. Suicide, as already remarked, is even accounted a crime, and with it is allied, especially in brutal, bigoted England, a shameful burial, and the invalidation of the testament, for which reason the jury almost always bring in a verdict of insanity. Let us before anything else allow moral feeling to decide in the matter and compare the impression which the report that an acquaintance had committed a crime, such as a murder, a cruelty, a fraud, a theft, makes upon us, with that of the report of his voluntary death. While the first calls forth energetic indignation, the greatest disgust, a demand for punishment or for vengeance, the latter will excite only sorrow and sympathy, mingled more often with an admiration of his courage than with the moral disapproval which accompanies a bad action. Who has not had acquaintances, friends, or relations, who have willingly departed from the world? And are we to think with horror of each of these as of a criminal? *Nego ac pernego.* I am rather of the opinion that the clergy should, once for all, be challenged to give an account, with what right they, without being able to show any biblical authority, or any valid philosophical arguments, stigmatize in the pulpit and in their writings an action committed by many men honoured and beloved by us, as a *crime*, and refuse those who voluntarily leave the world an honourable burial—it should, however, be clearly understood that reasons are required, and that no mere empty phrases or abusive epithets will be accepted in place of them. The fact that criminal jurisprudence condemns suicide is no ecclesiastically valid reason, besides being extremely ridiculous. For what punishment can frighten him who seeks death? If we punish the attempt at suicide, it is the clumsiness whereby it failed that we punish.

The ancients, moreover, were a long way from regarding the matter in this light. Pliny ("Histor. Nat.," lib. 28, c. 1; vol. iv., p. 351 Ed. Bip.), says: *Vitam quidem non adeo expetendam censemus, ut quoque modo trahenda sit. Quisquis es talis, aeque morier, etiam cum obscoenus vixeris, aut nefandus. Quapropter hoc primum quisque in remediis animi sui habeat: ex omnibus bonis, quae homini tribuit natura, nullum melius esse tempestiva morte: idque in ea optimum, quod illam sibi quisque praestare poterit.*" He also says (lib. 2, c. 7; vol. i., p. 125):

"*Ne Deum quidem posse omnia. Namque nec sibi potest mortem consciscere; si velit, quod homini dedit optimum in tantis vitae poenis,* etc.[1] In Massillia, and in the island of Chios, indeed, the hemlock was publicly handed to him who could give sufficient reasons for leaving life ("Val. Max.," l. ii. c. 6, § 7 et 8)[2] And how many heroes and wise men of antiquity have not ended their lives by a voluntary death! Aristotle indeed says ("Eth. Nicom.," v. 15) that suicide is a wrong against the state, although not against one's own person. Stobaeus, however, in his exposition of the Ethics of the Peripatetics, quotes the proposition (Ecl. eth. II., c. 7, p. 286): Φευλτύν δὲ τὸν βίον γίγνεσθαι τοῖς μὲν ἀγαθοῖς ἐν ταῖς ἄγαν ἀτυχίαις τοῖς δὲ κακοῖς καὶ ἐν ταῖς ἄγαν εὐτυχίαις. (*Vitam autem relinquendem esse bonis in nimiis quidem miseriis, pravis vero in nimium quoque secundis.*) And in a similar way, p. 312: Διὸ καὶ γαμήσειν, καὶ παιδοποιήσεσθαι, καὶ πολιτεύσεοθαι etc., καὶ καθόλου τὴν ἀρετὴν ἀσκοῦντα καὶ μένειν ἐν τῷ βίῳ, καὶ πάλιν, εἰ δέοι, πύτε δι' ἀνάγκας ἀπαλλαγήσεσθαι, ταφῆς προνοήσαντα, etc. (*Ideoque et uxorem ducturum, et liberos procreaturum, et ad civitatem accessurum,* etc. *Atque omnino virtutem colendo tum vitam servaturum, tum iterum, cogente necessitate, relictarum,* etc.).[3]

We find suicide celebrated by the Stoics as a noble and heroic deed, as might be confirmed by hundreds of extracts, the strongest being from Seneca. Again, with the Hindoo, as is well known, suicide often occurs as a religious action, especially as widow burning, also as immolation beneath the wheels of the Car of Juggernaut, as self-sacrifice to the crocodiles of the Ganges, or of the holy pond of the

[1] "We don't think that life is so much to be sought (desirable) that it must be drawn out by any possible means. Whoever you are, you will die equally, even though you may have lived a foul or abominable life. Therefore each person should have this in first place among the means of relieving his mind: namely, of all the good things which nature has provided for man, none is better than a timely death. The best thing of all in death is that each man is able to fulfill it for himself." He also says . . . , "Not even God can do everything. He can't commit suicide; if he should wish to, which he has granted to man as the greatest compensation of life, etc." *Eds.*
[2] On the Island of Chios it was also the custom that the aged should voluntarily put themselves to death. See "Valerius Maximus," lib. ii. c. 6; Heraclides Ponticus, "Fragmenta de Rebus Publicis," ix.; Ælian, "Var. Hist.," iii. 37; Strabo, lib. x. cap. 5, § 6, ed. Kramer.
[3] "That life may be abandoned by good men in excessive miseries, by evil men in very great prosperity." And in a similar way, p. 312: "Therefore he will marry, he will beget children, he will serve the state, etc. And in all respects pursuing virtue he will remain in life, then again if it be necessary, he will free himself, providing for death for himself in advance." *Eds.*

temple, and otherwise. In the same way, at the theatre, that mirror of life, where we see for example in the celebrated Chinese piece "L'Orphelin de la Chine" (trad. p. St. Julien, 1834,) almost all the noble characters end by suicide without its being anywhere indicated, or its occurring to the onlooker, that they have committed a crime. On our own stage, indeed, it is not otherwise, *e.g.*, Palmira in Mahomet, Mortimer in Maria Stuart, Othello, the Countess Terzky. Is Hamlet's monologue the meditation of a crime? It says certainly that if we were sure to be absolutely destroyed by death it would, considering the structure of the world, be unconditionally to choose. "But there lies [*sic* tr.] the rub." The reasons, however, against suicide which have been put forward by the clergy of the monotheistic, that is, Jewish religion, and the philosophers who accommodate themselves to them, are feeble sophisms easy of refutation. (See my "Treatise on the Foundation of Morals," § 5.) Hume has furnished the most thorough-going refutation of them in his "Essay on Suicide," which first appeared after his death, and was immediately suppressed by the shameful bigotry and scandalous priestly tyranny of England, for which reason only a few very copies were sold, secretly and at a high price, so that for the preservation of this and of another treatise of the great man, we have to thank the Basel reprint: "Essays on Suicide and the Immortality of the Soul, by the late David Hume. Basel, 1799. Sold by James Decker, pp. 124, 8vo." But that a purely philosophical treatise coming from one of the first thinkers and writers of England, refuting the current reasons against suicide, had in its native land to be smuggled through like a forbidden thing, until it found refuge abroad, redounds to the greatest shame of the English nation. It shows at the same time the kind of good conscience the Church has on this question. I have pointed out the only valid moral reason against suicide in my chief work, vol. i. § 69. It lies in that suicide is opposed to the attainment of the highest moral goal, since it substitutes for the real emancipation from this world of sorrow, a merely apparent one. But from this mistake to a crime, such as the Christian clergy seek to stamp it, is a very long way.

Christianity bears in its innermost essence the truth that suffering (the Cross) is the true purpose of life; hence it rejects, as opposed to this, suicide, which antiquity, from a lower standpoint, approved and even honoured. The foregoing reason against suicide is, however, an ascetic one, and as such only applies to a much higher ethical standpoint than that which European moral philosophers have ever occupied. But if we descend from this very high standpoint there is no longer any valid moral reason for condemning suicide. The extraordinarily energetic zeal of the clergy of the monotheistic religions against it, which is supported neither by the Bible nor by valid reasons, must rest, it would seem, therefore, on a concealed basis. Might it not be that the voluntary surrender of life is a poor compliment for him who said πάντα καλὰ λίαν ["all things are exceedingly good"]? Once more, then, it would be the obligatory optimism of these religions which arraigns suicide in order not to be arraigned by it.

We shall find on the whole that as soon as the terrors of life counterbalance the terrors of death man makes an end of his life. The resistance to these terrors is nevertheless considerable; they stand as it were as warders before the gate of exit. There is no one living perhaps who would not have made an end of his life if this end were something purely negative, a sudden cessation of existence. But there is something positive in it—the destruction of the body. This frightens men back simply because the body is the phenomenon of the Will-to-Live.

Meanwhile the struggle with these warders is not so hard as a rule as it may seem to us from afar, and indeed in consequence of the antagonism between intellectual and corporeal sufferings. When, for instance, we suffer corporeal pain severely and continuously, we are indifferent to all other trouble; our recovery alone seriously concerns us. Just in the same way severe mental sorrows make us unsusceptible to corporeal—we despise them. Even if they acquire the preponderance, this is a welcome diversion to us, a pause in our mental suffering. It is this which makes suicide easier, inasmuch as the corporeal pain associated with it loses all importance in the eyes of one tortured by excessive mental suffering. The above is especially noticeable with those who are driven to suicide through a purely morbid but none the less intense melancholy. It does not cost such persons any self-conquest, they do not require to form any resolution, but as soon as the keepers provided for them leave them for two minutes they quickly make an end of their life. When in disturbed, horrible dreams, anxiety has reached its highest pitch, it brings us of itself to awakening, and therewith all these horrors of a night vanish. The same thing happens in the dream of life, where also the highest degree of anxiety compels us to break it off.

Suicide may also be regarded as an experiment, a question which we put to nature, and to which we wish to compel the answer, to wit, what change the existence and the knowledge of man experiences through death. But it is a clumsy one, for it abolishes the identity of the consciousness which should receive the answer.

WILLIAM JAMES (1842-1910)

Is Life Worth Living?

With many men the question of life's worth is answered by a temperamental optimism that makes them incapable of believing that anything seriously evil can exist. Our dear old Walt Whitman's works are the standing text-book of this kind of optimism: the mere joy of living is so immense in Walt Whitman's veins that it abolishes the possibility of any other kind of feeling. . . .

If moods like this could be made permanent and constitutions like these universal, there would never be any occasion for such discourses as the present one. No philosopher would seek to prove articulately that life is worth living, for the fact that it absolutely is so would vouch for itself, and the problem disappear in the vanishing of the question rather than in the coming of anything like a reply. But we are not magicians to make the optimistic temperament universal; and alongside of the deliverances of temperamental optimism concerning life, those of temperamental pessimism always exist and oppose to them a standing refutation. . . .

To come immediately to the heart of my theme, then, what I propose is to imagine ourselves reasoning with a fellow-mortal who is on such terms with life that the only comfort left him is to brood on the assurance "you may end it when you will." What reasons can we plead that may render such a brother (or sister) willing to take up the burden again? Ordinary Christians, reasoning with would-be suicides, have little to offer them beyond the usual negative "thou shalt not." God alone is master of life and death, they say, and it is a blasphemous act to anticipate his absolving hand. But can we find nothing richer or more positive than this, no reflections to urge whereby the suicide may actually see, and in all sad seriousness feel, that in spite of adverse appearances even for him life is worth living still? . . .

And now, in turning to what religion may have to say to the question, I come to what is the soul of my discourse. Religion has meant many things in human history, but when from now onward I use the word I mean to use it in the supernaturalist sense, as signifying that the so-called order of nature that constitutes this world's

The selection is from William James, "Is Life Worth Living?", *International Journal of Ethics*, VI (1895–1896).

experience is only one portion of the total Universe, and that there stretches beyond this visible world an unseen world of which we now know nothing positive, but in its relation to which the true significance of our present mundane life consists. A man's religious faith (whatever more special items of doctrine it may involve) means for me essentially his faith in the existence of an unseen order of some kind in which the riddles of the natural order may be found explained. In the more developed religions this world has always been regarded as the mere scaffolding or vestibule of a truer, more eternal world, and affirmed to be a sphere of education, trial, or redemption. One must in some fashion die to this world before one can enter into life eternal. The notion that this physical world of wind and water, where the sun rises and the moon sets, is absolutely and ultimately the divinely aimed at and established thing, is one that we find only in very early religions, such as that of the most primitive Jews. It is this natural religion (primitive still in spite of the fact that poets and men of science whose good-will exceeds their perspicacity keep publishing it in new editions tuned to our contemporary ears) that has suffered definitive bankruptcy in the opinion of a circle of persons, amongst whom I must count myself, and who are growing more numerous every day. For such persons the physical order of Nature, taken simply as Science knows it, cannot be held to reveal any one harmonious spiritual intent. It is mere *weather*, as Chauncey Wright called it, doing and undoing without end.

Now I wish to make you feel, if I can, that we have a *right* to believe that the physical order is only a partial order; we have a right to supplement it by an unseen spiritual order which we assume on trust, if only thereby life may seem to us better worth living again. But as such a trust will seem to some of you sadly mystical and execrably unscientific, I must first say a word or two to weaken the veto which you may consider that Science opposes to our act.

There is included in human nature an ingrained naturalism and materialism of mind which can only admit facts that are actually tangible. Of this sort of mind the entity called "Science" is the idol. Fondness for the word "scientist" is one of the notes by which you may know its votaries; and its short way of killing any opinion that it disbelieves in is to call it "unscientific." It must be granted that there is no slight excuse for this. Science has made such glorious leaps in the last three hundred years, and extended our knowledge of Nature so enormously both in general and in detail; men of science, moreover, have as a class displayed such admirable virtues, that it is no wonder if the worshippers of Science lose their head. In this very University, accordingly, I have heard more than one teacher say that all the fundamental conceptions of truth have already been found by Science, and that the future has only the details of the picture to fill in. But the slightest reflection on the real conditions will suffice to show how barbaric such notions are. They show such a lack of scientific imagination, that it is hard to see how one who is actively advancing any part of Science can make a mistake so crude. Think how many absolutely new scientific conceptions have arisen in our own generation, how many new problems have been formulated that were never thought of before, and then cast an eye upon the brevity of Science's career. . . . Is it credible that such a mushroom knowledge, such a growth overnight as this, *can* represent more than the minutest glimpse of what the Universe will really prove to be when adequately understood? No! our Science is a drop, our ignorance a sea. Whatever else be certain, this at least is certain: that the world of our present natural knowledge *is* enveloped in a larger world of *some* sort of whose residual properties we at present can frame no positive idea. . . .

Now, when I speak of trusting our religious demands, just what do I mean by "trusting"? Is the word to carry with it license to define in detail an invisible world and to anathematize and excommunicate those whose trust is different? Certainly not! Our faculties of belief were not primarily given us to make orthodoxies and heresies withal; they were given us to live by. And to trust our religious demands means first of all to live in the light of them, and to act as if the invisible world which they suggest were real. It is a fact of human nature that men can live and die by the help of a sort of faith that goes without a single dogma or definition. The bare assurance that this natural order is not ultimate but a mere sign or vision, the external staging of a man-stories universe, in which spiritual forces have the last word and are eternal; this bare assurance is to such men enough to make life seem worth living in spite of every contrary presumption suggested by its circumstances on the natural plane. Destroy this inner assurance, vague as it is, however, and all the light and radiance of existence is extinguished for these persons at a stroke. Often enough the wild-eyed look at life,—the suicidal mood—will then set in.

And now the application comes directly home to you and me. Probably to almost every one of us here the most adverse life would seem well worth living if we only could be *certain* that our bravery and patience with it were terminating and eventuating and bearing fruit somewhere in an unseen spiritual world. But granting we are not certain, does it then follow that a bare trust in such a world is a fool's paradise and lubberland, or rather that it is a living attitude in which we are free to indulge? Well, we are free to trust at our own risks anything that is not impossible and that can bring analogies to bear in its behalf. That the world of physics is probably not absolute, all the converging multitude of arguments that make in favor of idealism tend to prove. And that our whole physical life may lie soaking in a spiritual atmosphere, a dimension of Being that we at present have no organ for apprehending, is vividly suggested to us by the analogy of the life of our domestic animals. Our dogs, for example, are *in* our human life but not *of* it. They witness hourly the outward body of events whose inner meaning cannot, by any possible operation, be revealed to their intelligence, events in which they themselves often play the cardinal part. My terrier bites a teasing boy, for example, and the father demands damages. The dog may be present at every step of the negotiations, and see the money paid without an inkling of what it all means, without a suspicion that it has anything to do with *him*. And he never *can* know in his natural dog's life. . . .

Now turn from this to the life of man. In the dog's life we see the world invisible to him because we live in both worlds. In human life, although we only *see* our world, and his within it, yet encompassing these worlds a still wider world may be there unseen by us; and to believe in that world *may* be the most essential function that our lives in this world have to perform. But "*may*be! *may*be!" one hears the positivist contemptuously exclaim; "what use can a scientific life have for maybes?" But the "scientific" life itself has much to do with maybes, and human life at large has everything to do with them. So far as man stands for anything, and is productive or originative at all, his entire vital function may be said to be to deal with maybes. Not a victory is gained, not a deed of faithfulness or courage is done, except upon a maybe; not a service, not a sally of generosity, not a scientific exploration or experiment or text-book, that *may* not be a mistake. It is only by risking our persons from one hour to another that we live at all. And often enough our faith beforehand in an uncertified result *is the only thing that makes the result come true*. Suppose, for instance, that you are climbing a mountain and have worked yourself into a position from which the only escape is by a terrible leap. Have faith that you *can* successfully make it, and your feet are nerved to its accomplishment. But mistrust yourself, and think of all the sweet things you have heard the scientists say of *maybes*, and you will hesitate so long that, at last, all unstrung and trembling, and launching yourself in a moment of despair, you roll in the abyss. In such a case (and it belongs to an enormous class), the part of wisdom as well as of courage is to *believe what is in the line of your needs,* for only by the belief is the need fulfilled. Refuse to believe, and you shall indeed be right, for you shall irretrievably perish. But believe, and again you shall be right, for you shall save yourself. You *make* one or the other of two possible universes true by your trust or mistrust, both universes having been only *maybes,* in this particular, before you contributed your act. . . .

Now, it appears to me that the question whether life is worth living is subject to conditions logically much like these. It does, indeed, depend on you the liver. If you surrender to the nightmare view and crown the evil edifice by your own suicide, you have indeed made a picture totally black. Pessimism, completed by your act, is true beyond a doubt, so far as your world goes. Your mistrust of life has removed whatever worth your own enduring existence might have given to it; and now, throughout the whole sphere of possible influence of that existence, the mistrust has proved itself to have had divining power. But suppose, on the other hand, that instead of giving way to the nightmare view you cling to it that this world is not the *ultimatum.* Suppose you find yourself a very well-spring, as Wordsworth says, of

> *Zeal, and the virtue to exist by faith*
> *As soldiers live by courage; as, by strength*
> *Of heart, the sailor fights with roaring seas.*

Suppose, however thickly evils crowd upon you, that your unconquerable subjectivity proves to be their match, and that you find a more wonderful joy than any passive pleasure can bring in trusting ever in the larger whole. Have you not now *made* life worth living on *these* terms? What sort of a thing would life really be, with *your* qualities ready for a tussle with it, if it only brought fair weather and gave these higher faculties of yours no scope? Please remember that optimism and pessimism are definitions of the world, and that our own reactions on the world, small as they are in bulk, are parts of it, and necessarily help to determine the definition. They may be the decisive elements in determining the definition. A large mass can have its unstable equilibrium overturned by the addition of a feather's weight. A long phrase may have its sense reversed by the addition of the three letters *n, o, t.* This life *is* worth living, we can say, since it is what we make it, from the moral point of view, and we are bound to make it from that point of view, so far as we have anything to do with it, a success.

Now, in this description of faiths that verify themselves I have assumed that our faith in an invisible order is what inspires those efforts and that patience of ours is what makes this visible order good for moral men. Our faith in the seen world's goodness (goodness now meaning fitness for successful moral and religious life) has verified itself by leaning on our faith in the unseen world. But will our faith in the unseen world similarly verify itself? Who knows?

Once more it is a case of *maybe.* And once more *maybes* are the essence of the situation. I confess that I do not see why the very existence of an invisible world *may* not in part depend on the personal response which any one of us may make to the religious appeal. God himself, in short, *may* draw vital strength and increase of very being from our fidelity. For my own part, I do not know what the sweat and blood and tragedy of this life mean, if they mean anything short of this. If this life be not a real fight, in which something is eternally gained for the Universe by success, it is no better than a game of private theatricals from which one may withdraw at will. But it *feels* like a real fight; as if there were something really wild in the Universe which we, with all our idealities and faithfulnesses, are needed to redeem. And first of all to redeem our own hearts from atheisms and fears. For such a half-wild, half-saved universe our nature is adapted. The deepest thing in our nature is this *Binnenleben* (as a German doctor lately has called it), this dumb region of the heart in which we dwell alone with our willingnesses and unwillingnesses, our faiths and fears. As through the cracks and crannies of subterranean caverns the earth's bosom exudes its waters, which then form the fountain-heads of springs, so in these crepuscular depths of personality the sources of all our outer deeds and decisions take their rise. Here is our deepest organ of communication with the nature of things; and compared with these concrete movements of our soul all abstract statements and scientific arguments, the veto, for example, which the strict positivist pronounces upon our faith, sound to us like mere chatterings of the teeth. For here possibilities, not finished facts, are the realities that we encounter; and to quote my friend William Salter, of the Philadelphia Ethical Society, "as the essence of courage is to stake one's life on a possibility, so the essence of faith is to believe that the possibility exists."

These, then, are my last words to you: Be not afraid of life.

Believe that life *is* worth living, and your belief will help create the fact. The "scientific proof" that you are right may not be clear before the day of judgment (or some stage of Being which that expression may serve to symbolize) is reached. But the faithful fighters of this hour, or the beings that then and there will represent them, may then turn to the faint-hearted, who here decline to go on, with words like those with which Henry IV greeted the tardy Crillon after a great victory had been gained: "Hang yourself, Crillon! we fought at Arques, and you were not there."

ALBERT CAMUS (1914–1960)

Suicide and Meaning

Now I can broach the notion of suicide. It has already been felt what solution might be given. At this point the problem is reversed. It was previously a question of finding out whether or not life had to have a meaning to be lived. It now becomes clear, on the contrary, that it will be lived all the better if it has no meaning. Living an experience, a particular fate, is accepting it fully. Now, no one will live this fate, knowing it to be absurd, unless he does everything to keep before him that absurd brought to light by consciousness. Negating one of the terms of the opposition on which he lives amounts to escaping it. To abolish conscious revolt is to elude the problem. The theme of permanent revolution is thus carried into individual experience. Living is keeping the absurd alive. Keeping it alive is, above all, contemplating it. Unlike Eurydice, the absurd dies only when we turn away from it. One of the only coherent philosophical positions is thus revolt. It is a constant confrontation between man and his own obscurity. It is an insistence upon an impossible transparency. It challenges the world anew every second. Just as danger provided man the unique opportunity of seizing awareness, so metaphysical revolt extends awareness to the whole of experience. It is that constant presence of man in his own eyes. It is not aspiration, for

From THE MYTH OF SISYPHUS, by Albert Camus, trans. by Justin O'Brien. ©
*Copyright 1955 by Alfred A. Knopf, Inc. Hamish Hamilton, London, Ltd. Reprinted
by permission of the publisher.*

it is devoid of hope. That revolt is the certainty of a crushing fate, without the resignation that ought to accompany it.

This is where it is seen to what a degree absurd experience is remote from suicide. It may be thought that suicide follows revolt—but wrongly. For it does not represent the logical outcome of revolt. It is just the contrary by the consent it presupposes. Suicide, like the leap, is acceptance at its extreme. Everything is over and man returns to his essential history. His future, his unique and dreadful future—he sees and rushes toward it. In its way, suicide settles the absurd. It engulfs the absurd in the same death. But I know that in order to keep alive, the absurd cannot be settled. It escapes suicide to the extent that it is simultaneously awareness and rejection of death. It is, at the extreme limit of the condemned man's last thought, that shoelace that despite everything he sees a few yards away, on the very brink of his dizzying fall. The contrary of suicide, in fact, is the man condemned to death.

That revolt gives life its value. Spread out over the whole length of a life, it restores its majesty to that life. To a man devoid of blinders, there is no finer sight than that of the intelligence at grips with a reality that transcends it. The sight of human pride is unequaled. No disparagement is of any use. That discipline that the mind imposes on itself, that will conjured up out of nothing, that face-to-face struggle have something exceptional about them. To impoverish that reality whose inhumanity constitutes man's majesty is tantamount to impoverishing him himself. I understand then why the doctrines that explain everything to me also debilitate me at the same time. They relieve me of the weight of my own life, and yet I must carry it alone. At this juncture, I cannot conceive that a skeptical metaphysics can be joined to an ethics of renunciation.

Consciousness and revolt, these rejections are the contrary of renunciation. Everything that is indomitable and passionate in a human heart quickens them, on the contrary, with its own life. It is essential to die unreconciled and not of one's own free will. Suicide is a repudiation. The absurd man can only drain everything to the bitter end, and deplete himself. The absurd is his extreme tension, which he maintains constantly by solitary effort, for he knows that in that consciousness and in that day-to-day revolt he gives proof of his only truth, which is defiance. This is a first consequence.

If I remain in that prearranged position which consists in drawing all the conclusions (and nothing else) involved in a newly discovered notion, I am faced with a second paradox. In order to remain faithful to that method, I have nothing to do with the problem of metaphysical liberty. Knowing whether or not man is free doesn't interest me. I can experience only my own freedom. As to it, I can have no general notions, but merely a few clear insights. The problem of "freedom as such" has no meaning. For it is linked in quite a different way with the problem of God. Knowing whether or not man is free involves knowing whether he can have a master. The absurdity peculiar to this problem comes from the fact that the very notion that makes the problem of freedom possible also takes away all its meaning. For in the presence of God there is less a problem of freedom than a problem of evil. You know the alternative: either we are not free and God the all-powerful is responsible for evil. Or we are free and responsible but God is not all-powerful. All the scholastic subtleties have neither added anything to nor subtracted anything from the acuteness of this paradox.

This is why I cannot get lost in the glorification or the mere definition of a notion which eludes me and loses its meaning as soon as it goes beyond the frame of reference of my individual experience. I cannot understand what kind of freedom would be given me by a higher being. I have lost the sense of hierarchy. The only conception of freedom I can have is that of the prisoner or the individual in the midst of the State. The only one I know is freedom of thought and action. Now if the absurd cancels all my chances of eternal freedom, it restores and magnifies, on the other hand, my freedom of action. That privation of hope and future means an increase in man's availability.

Before encountering the absurd, the everyday man lives with aims, a concern for the future or for justification (with regard to whom or what is not the question). He weighs his chances, he counts on "someday," his retirement or the labor of his sons. He still thinks that something in his life can be directed. In truth, he acts as if he were free, even if all the facts make a point of contradicting that liberty. But after the absurd, everything is upset. That idea that "I am," my way of acting as if everything has a meaning (even if, on occasion, I said that nothing has)—all that is given the lie in vertiginous fashion by the absurdity of a possible death. Thinking of the future, establishing aims for oneself, having preferences—all this presupposes a belief in freedom, even if one occasionally ascertains that one doesn't feel it. But at that moment I am well aware that that higher liberty, that freedom to *be*, which alone can serve as basis for a truth, does not exist. Death is there as the only reality. After death the chips are down. I am not even free, either, to perpetuate myself, but a slave, and, above all, a slave without hope of an eternal revolution, without recourse to contempt. And who without revolution and without contempt can remain a slave? What freedom can exist in the fullest sense without assurance of eternity?

But at the same time the absurd man realizes that hitherto he was bound to that postulate of freedom on the illusion of which he was living. In a certain sense, that hampered him. To the extent to which he imagined a purpose to his life, he adapted himself to the demands of a purpose to be achieved and became the slave of his liberty. Thus I could not act otherwise than as the father (or the engineer or the leader of a nation, or the postoffice sub-clerk) that I am preparing to be. I think I can choose to be that rather than something else. I think so unconsciously, to be sure. But at the same time I strengthen my postulate with the beliefs of those around me, with the presumptions of my human environment (others are so sure of being free, and that cheerful mood is so contagious!). However far one may remain from any presumption, moral or social, one is partly influenced by them and even, for the best among them (there are good and bad presumptions), one adapts one's life to them. Thus the absurd man realizes that he was not really free. To speak clearly, to the extent to which I hope, to which I worry about a truth that might be individual to me, about a way of being or creating, to the extent to which I arrange my life and prove thereby that I accept its having a meaning, I create for myself barriers between which I confine my life. I do like so many bureaucrats of the mind and heart who only fill me with disgust and whose only vice, I now see clearly, is to take man's freedom seriously.

The absurd enlightens me on this point: there is no future. Henceforth this is the reason for my inner freedom. I shall use two comparisons here. Mystics, to begin with, find freedom in giving themselves. By losing themselves in their god, by accepting his rules, they become secretly free. In spontaneously accepted slavery they recover a deeper independence. But what does that freedom mean? It may be said, above all, that they *feel* free with regard to themselves, and not so much free as liberated. Likewise, completely turned toward death (taken here as the most obvious absurdity), the absurd man feels released from everything outside that passionate attention crystallizing in him. He enjoys a freedom with regard to common rules. It can be seen at this point that the initial themes of existential philosophy keep their entire value. The return to consciousness, the escape from every-day sleep represent the first steps of absurd freedom. But it is existen-tial *preaching* that is alluded to, and with it that spiritual leap which basically escapes consciousness. In the same way (this is my second comparison) the slaves of antiquity did not belong to themselves. But they knew that freedom which consists in not feeling respon-sible.[1] Death, too, has patrician hands, which, while crushing, also liberate.

Losing oneself in that bottomless certainty, feeling henceforth sufficiently remote from one's own life to increase it and take a broad view of it—this involves the principle of a liberation. Such new in-dependence has a definite time limit, like any freedom of action. It does not write a check on eternity. But it takes the place of the illusions of *freedom*, which all stopped with death. The divine availability of the condemned man before whom the prison doors open in a certain early dawn, that unbelievable disinterestedness with regard to every-thing except for the pure flame of life—it is clear that death and the absurd are here the principles of the only reasonable freedom: that which a human heart can experience and live. This is a second conse-quence. The absurd man thus catches sight of a burning and frigid, transparent and limited universe in which nothing is possible but everything is given, and beyond which all is collapse and nothingness. He can then decide to accept such a universe and draw from it his strength, his refusal to hope, and the unyielding evidence of a life without consolation.

But what does life mean in such a universe? Nothing else for the moment but indifference to the future and a desire to use up everything that is given. Belief in the meaning of life always implies a scale of values, a choice, our preferences. Belief in the absurd, according to our definitions, teaches the contrary. But this is worth examining.

Knowing whether or not one can live *without appeal* is all that interests me. I do not want to get out of my depth. This aspect of life being given me, can I adapt myself to it? Now, faced with this particular concern, belief in the absurd is tantamount to substituting the quantity of experiences for the quality. If I convince myself that this life has no other aspect than that of the absurd, if I feel that its

---

[1] I am concerned here with a factual comparison, not with an apology of humility. The absurd man is the contrary of the reconciled man.

whole equilibrium depends on that perpetual opposition between my conscious revolt and the darkness in which it struggles, if I admit that my freedom has no meaning except in relation to its limited fate, then I must say that what counts is not the best living but the most living. It is not up to me to wonder if this is vulgar or revolting, elegant or deplorable. Once and for all, value judgments are discarded here in favor of factual judgments. I have merely to draw the conclusions from what I can see and to risk nothing that is hypothetical. Supposing that living in this way were not honorable, then true propriety would command me to be dishonorable.

The most living; in the broadest sense, that rule means nothing. It calls for definition. It seems to begin with the fact that the notion of quantity has not been sufficiently explored. For it can account for a large share of human experience. A man's rule of conduct and his scale of values have no meaning except through the quantity and variety of experiences he has been in a position to accumulate. Now, the conditions of modern life impose on the majority of men the same quantity of experiences and consequently the same profound experience. To be sure, there must also be taken into consideration the individual's spontaneous contribution, the "given" element in him. But I cannot judge of that, and let me repeat that my rule here is to get along with the immediate evidence. I see, then, that the individual character of a common code of ethics lies not so much in the ideal importance of its basic principles as in the form of an experience that it is possible to measure. To stretch a point somewhat, the Greeks had the code of their leisure just as we have the code of our eight-hour day. But already many men among the most tragic cause us to foresee that a longer experience changes this table of values. They make us imagine that adventurer of the everyday who through mere quantity of experiences would break all records (I am purposely using this sports expression) and would thus win his own code of ethics.[2] Yet let's avoid romanticism and just ask ourselves what such an attitude may mean to a man with his mind made up to take up his bet and to observe strictly what he takes to be the rules of the game.

Breaking all records is first and foremost being faced with the

---

[2] Quantity sometimes constitutes quality. If I can believe the latest restatements of scientific theory, all matter is constituted by centers of energy. Their greater or lesser quantity makes its specificity more or less remarkable. A billion ions and one ion differ not only in quantity but also in quality. It is easy to find an analogy in human experience.

world as often as possible. How can that be done without contradictions and without playing on words? For on the one hand the absurd teaches that all experiences are unimportant, and on the other it urges toward the greatest quantity of experiences. How, then, can one fail to do as so many of those men I was speaking of earlier—choose the form of life that brings us the most possible of that human matter, thereby introducing a scale of values that on the other hand one claims to reject?

But again it is the absurd and its contradictory life that teaches us. For the mistake is thinking that that quantity of experiences depends on the circumstances of our life when it depends solely on us. Here we have to be over-simple. To two men living the same number of years, the world always provides the same sum of experiences. It is up to us to be conscious of them. Being aware of one's life, one's revolt, one's freedom, and to the maximum, is living, and to the maximum. Where lucidity dominates, the scale of values becomes useless. Let's be even more simple. Let us say that the sole obstacle, the sole deficiency to be made good, is constituted by premature death. Thus it is that no depth, no emotion, no passion, and no sacrifice could render equal in the eyes of the absurd man (even if he wished it so) a conscious life of forty years and a lucidity spread over sixty years.[3] Madness and death are his irreparables. Man does not choose. The absurd and the extra life it involves *therefore do not depend on man's will,* but on its contrary, which is death.[4] Weighing words carefully, it is altogether a question of luck. One just has to be able to consent to this. There will never be any substitute for twenty years of life and experience.

By what is an odd inconsistency in such an alert race, the Greeks claimed that those who died young were beloved of the gods. And that is true only if you are willing to believe that entering the ridiculous world of the gods is forever losing the purest of joys, which is feeling, and feeling on this earth. The present and the succession of presents before a constantly conscious soul is the ideal of the absurd man. But

---

[3] Same reflection on a notion as different as the idea of eternal nothingness. It neither adds anything to nor subtracts anything from reality. In psychological experience of nothingness, it is by the consideration of what will happen in two thousand years that our own nothingness truly takes on meaning. In one of its aspects, eternal nothingness is made up precisely of the sum of lives to come which will not be ours.

[4] The will is only the agent here: it tends to maintain consciousness. It provides a discipline of life, and that is appreciable.

the word "ideal" rings false in this connection. It is not even his vocation, but merely the third consequence of his reasoning. Having started from an anguished awareness of the inhuman, the meditation on the absurd returns at the end of its itinerary to the very heart of the passionate flames of human revolt.[5]

[5] What matters is coherence. We start out here from acceptance of the world. But Oriental thought teaches that one can indulge in the same effort of logic by choosing against the world. That is just as legitimate and gives this essay its perspectives and its limits. But when the negation of the world is pursued just as rigorously, one often achieves (in certain Vedantic schools) similar results regarding, for instance, the indifference of works. In a book of great importance, *Le Choix*, Jean Grenier establishes in this way a veritable "philosophy of indifference."

SEXUAL INTEGRITY

With the problem of sexual integrity, we return to an issue that is close to and affects every human being. Whatever else man is and whatever ideals are believed important for him, he is a sexual being, and his sexuality influences his total conduct. But sexuality is primarily a 'given', and the moral problem arises in connection with the values, principles, and obligations that are believed relevant to that given.

Sex is not only an object of concern for the moralist. Biologists study sex as a part of the physiology of the human organism; psychologists examine manifestations—and often perversions—of sex in human behavior; and sociologists investigate the role of sex (and related institutions such as the family) in man's social relations. Important as they are, however, such scientific studies do not touch the essential problem for the moralist which is, not how does one *describe* sexuality, but rather how *ought* one to relate to or control his sexuality. That is, the moral question is a normative one, and descriptive, scientific studies, no matter how accurate or exhaustive, do not answer that question.

In addition to sharpening the problem of normative judgments (the question is not really raised here: any moral situation does that), sexuality also brings into focus the issue of the interpenetration of values. Simply as given, sex is a biological act, like digestion or circulation. It can also be experienced simply as a biological act. But for most human beings, sex is more than biological, for the question of quality or value also enters and superimposes itself. That is, sex in itself, however important a means and a drive, points toward and perhaps really depends on other values. Much of the Western moral tradition has stressed the coalescence of sex with the value of love, and one can possibly also add, with character and truth values. But while this problem of the relation of sex to other values (which is also a problem of instrumental and intrinsic values) is central to much ethical discussion, a consequence has often resulted—at least in popular thought—that many have judged harmful. This is an extreme suppression or repression of sex, often for the sake of some other supposed value. This consequence has frequently led to distortions, many thinkers believe, not only in attitudes toward sex, but in the experience of other values as well. These latter observations are part of what has been called the sexual revolution of the twentieth century. Whether some of the current opinions about sex constitute a revolution or whether greater ethical insight is being achieved as the pill and a mobile society change the context of sexual behavior in the twentieth century are debatable matters. But discussion of sex seems intensified in our day, and this is reflected in the relatively recent date of most of the selections.

The selections begin with Pope Paul's encyclical, *Humanae Vitae,* which argues that sex has a twofold meaning, union and procreation. Such a meaning implies that the proper role and expression of sex are found only within the bonds of family life. And since children are the supreme gift of marriage, artificial birth control methods are illicit. Throughout the encyclical, Paul's argument reflects the tradition of natural law ethics and Catholic Christianity. The second selection is taken from volume two of Kierkegaard's *Either/Or.* In volume one, Kierkegaard describes the life of sensuous immediacy, pleasure, or the "esthetic," as he calls it. Absent from this life, however, is any notion of duty and therewith, Kierkegaard believes, of love. In volume two he sketches for his readers a "higher" level of life, the ethical (and ultimately, the religious). Sexuality as immediate is limited and doomed to existential disappointment or boredom. Love, though based upon and retaining the sensuous, is distinguished from sexuality by "the impress of eternity" and by duty. Hence, Kierkegaard concludes, love accepts—even demands—marriage and is ultimately experienced only through Christianity.

The remaining selections reflect somewhat more directly contemporary discussions of sex, love, and marriage. Lippmann notes the inadequacy of older rules but nevertheless suggests that if the convention of marriage correctly interprets human experience, then it will be the conclusion that will emerge from current experimentation and discussion. In his situation ethics, Joseph Fletcher rejects both the legalism of formal rules and mere spontaneous reaction. The moral life is rather a search for values in the differing situations of life, guided by love. Sex has become a moral dilemma primarily as a result of repressive legalism. Rejecting that legalism, Fletcher believes that sex may or may not be experienced with integrity in different situations, depending on the other values realized. Bertocci argues that the connections of sex to other values is critical, though this is often overlooked in discussions of sex. He urges that marriage is normally the context within which this range of values becomes explicit and can be pursued. The final selection by Thomas Nagel is a study of sexual perversion. Sex, he says, involves a natural development of attraction and perception of oneself and another. For the integrity of sexual perversion, a wholistic pattern is required. Sexual perversion can therefore be understood as involving partial or blocked pattern development.

PAUL VI (1897—)

Humanae Vitae

A Total Vision of Man

The problem of birth, like every other problem regarding human life, is to be considered, beyond partial perspectives—whether of the biological or psychological demographic or sociological orders—in the light of an integral vision of man and of his vocation, not only his natural and earthly, but also his supernatural and eternal vocation. And since, in the attempt to justify artificial methods of birth control, many have appealed to the demands both of conjugal love and of "responsible parenthood" it is good to state very precisely the true concept of these two great realities of married life, referring principally

The selection is from Pope Paul's encyclical on birth control, *Humanae Vitae,* published in translation in *The Catholic Free Press,* Worcester, Mass., Vol. 18; No. 31, August 2, 1968, pp. 11, 12.

to what was recently set forth in this regard, and in a highly authoritative form, by the Second Vatican Council in its pastoral constitution Gaudium et Spes.

Conjugal Love

Conjugal love reveals its true nature and nobility when it is considered in its supreme origin, God, who is love, "the Father, from whom every family in heaven and on earth is named."

Marriage is not, then, the effect of chance or the product of evolution of unconscious natural forces; it is the wise institution of the Creator to realize in mankind His design of love. By means of the reciprocal personal gift of self, proper and exclusive to them, husband and wife tend towards the communion of their beings in view of mutual personal perfection, to collaborate with God in the generation and education of new lives.

For baptized persons, moreover, marriage invests the dignity of a sacramental sign of grace, inasmuch as it represents the union of Christ and of the Church.

Its Characteristics

Under this light, there clearly appear the characteristic marks and demands of conjugal love, and it is of supreme importance to have an exact idea of these.

This love is first of all fully human, that is to say, of the senses and of the spirit at the same time. It is not, then, a simple transport of instinct and sentiment, but also, and principally, an act of the free will, intended to endure and to grow by means of the joys and sorrows of daily life, in such a way that husband and wife become one only heart and one only soul, and together attain their human perfection.

Then, this love is total, that is to say, it is a very special form of personal friendship, in which husband and wife generously share everything, without undue reservations or selfish calculations. Whoever truly loves his marriage partner loves not only for what he receives, but for the partner's self, rejoicing that he can enrich his partner with the gift of himself.

Again, this love is faithful and exclusive until death. Thus in fact do bride and groom conceive it to be on the day when they freely and in full awareness assume the duty of the marriage bond. A fidelity, this, which can sometimes be difficult, but is always possible, always noble and meritorious, as no one can deny. The example of so many married persons down through the centuries show, not only that fidelity is according to the nature of marriage, but also that it is a source of profound and lasting happiness and finally, this love is fecund for it is not exhausted by the communion between husband and wife, but is destined to continue, raising up new lives. "Marriage and conjugal love are by their nature ordained toward the begetting and educating of children. Children are really the supreme gift of marriage and contribute very substantially to the welfare of their parents."

Responsible Parenthood

Hence conjugal love requires in husband and wife an awareness of their mission of "responsible parenthood," which today is rightly much insisted upon, and which also must be exactly understood. Consequently it is to be considered under different aspects which are legitimate and connected with one another.

In relation to the biological processes, responsible parenthood means the knowledge and respect of their functions; human intellect discovers in the power of giving life biological laws which are part of the human person.

In relation to the tendencies of instinct or passion, responsible parenthood means that necessary dominion which reason and will must exercise over them.

In relation to physical, economic, psychological and social conditions, responsible parenthood is exercised, either by the deliberate and generous decision to raise a numerous family, or by the decision, made for grave motives and with due respect for the moral law, to avoid for the time being, or even for an indeterminate period, a new birth.

Responsible parenthood also and above all implies a more profound relationship to the objective moral order established by God, of which a right conscience is the faithful interpreter. The responsible exercise of parenthood implies, therefore, that husband and wife recognize fully their own duties towards God, towards themselves, towards the family and towards society, in a correct hierarchy of values.

In the task of transmitting life, therefore, they are not free to proceed completely at will, as if they could determine in a wholly autonomous way the honest path to follow; but they must conform their activity to the creative intention of God, expressed in the very nature of marriage and of its acts, and manifested by the constant teaching of the Church.

Respect for the Nature and Purpose of the Marriage Act

These acts, by which husband and wife are united in chaste intimacy, and by means of which human life is transmitted, are, as the council recalled, "noble and worthy," and they do not cease to be lawful if, for causes independent of the will of husband and wife, they are foreseen to be infecund, since they always remain ordained towards expressing and consolidating their union. In fact, as experience bears witness, not every conjugal act is followed by a new life. God has wisely disposed natural laws and rhythms of fecundity which, of themselves, cause a separation in the succession of births. Nonetheless the Church, calling men back to the observance of the norms of the natural law, as interpreted by their constant doctrine, teaches that each and every marriage act (quilibet matrimonii usus) must remain open to the transmission of life.

Two Inseparable Aspects: Union and Procreation

That teaching, often set forth by the magisterium, is founded upon the inseparable connection, willed by God and unable to be broken by man on his own initiative, between the two meanings of the conjugal act: the unitive meaning and the procreative meaning. Indeed, by its intimate structure, the conjugal act, while most closely uniting husband and wife, capacitates them for the generation of new lives, according to laws inscribed in the very being of man and of woman. By safeguarding both these essential aspects, the unitive and the procreative, the conjugal act preserves in its fullness the sense of true mutual love and its ordination towards man's most high calling to parenthood. We believe that the men of our day are particularly capable of seizing the deeply reasonable and human character of this fundamental principle.

Faithfulness to God's Design

It is in fact justly observed that a conjugal act imposed upon one's partner without regard for his or her condition and lawful desires is not a true act of love, and therefore denies an exigency of right moral order in the relationships between husband and wife. Hence, one who reflects well must also recognize that a reciprocal act of love, which jeopardizes the responsibility to transmit life which God the Creator, according to particular laws, inserted therein, is in contradiction with the design constitutive of marriage, and with the will of the Author of life. To use this divine gift destroying, even if only partially, its meaning and its purpose is to contradict the nature both of man and of woman and of their most intimate relationship, and therefore it is to contradict also the plan of God and His will. On the other hand, to make use of the gift of conjugal love while respecting the laws of the generative process means to acknowledge oneself not to be the arbiter of the sources of human life, but rather the minister of the design established by the Creator. In fact, just as man does not have un-limited dominion over his body in general, so also, with particular reason, he has no such dominion over his generative faculties as such, because of their intrinsic ordination towards raising up life, of which God is the principle. "Human life is sacred," Pope John XXIII recalled: "from its very inception it reveals the creating hand of God."

Illicit Ways of Regulating Birth

In conformity with these landmarks in the human and Christian vision of marriage, we must once again declare that the direct inter-ruption of the generative process already begun, and, above all, directly willed and procured abortion, even if for thereapeutic reasons, are to be absolutely excluded as licit means of regulating birth.

Equally to be excluded, as the teaching authority of the Church has frequently declared, is direct sterilization, whether perpetual or temporary, whether of the man or of the woman. Similarly excluded is every action which, either in anticipation of the conjugal act, or in its accomplishment, or in the development of its natural consequences, proposes, whether as an end or as a means, to render procreation impossible.

To justify conjugal acts made intentionally infecund, one cannot invoke as valid reasons the lesser evil, or the fact that such acts would constitute a whole together with the fecund acts already performed or to follow later, and hence would share in one and the same moral good-ness. In truth, if it is sometimes licit to tolerate a lesser evil in order to avoid a greater evil or to promote a greater good it is not licit even for the gravest reasons, to do evil so that good may follow there-from that is, to make into the object of a positive act of the will something which is intrinsically disordered, and hence unworthy of the human person, even when the intention is to safeguard or promote individual, family or social well-being. Consequently it is an error to think that a conjugal act which is deliberately made infecund and so is intrinsically dishonest could be made honest and right by the ensemble of a fecund conjugal life.

Licitness of Therapeutic Means

The Church, on the contrary, does not at all consider illicit the use of those therapeutic means truly necessary to cure diseases of the organism, even if an impediment to procreation, which may be foreseen, should result therefrom, provided such impediment is not, for whatever motive, directly willed.

Licitness of Recourse to Infecund Periods

To this teaching of the Church on conjugal morals, the objection is made today, as we observed earlier, that it is the prerogative of the human intellect to dominate the energies offered by irrational nature and to orient them towards an end conformable to the good of man. Now, some may ask: in the present case, is it not reasonable in many circumstances to have recourse to artificial birth control if, thereby, we secure the harmony and peace of the family, and better conditions for the education of the children already born? To this question it is necessary to reply with clarity: the Church is the first to praise and recommend the intervention of intelligence in a function which so closely associates the rational creature with his Creator; but she affirms that this must be done with respect for the order established by God.

If, then, there are serious motives to space out births, which derive from the physical or psychological conditions of husband and wife, or from external conditions, the Church teaches that it is then licit to take into account the natural rhythms immanent in the generative functions, for the use of marriage in the infecund periods only, and in this way to regulate birth without offending the moral principles which have been recalled earlier.

The Church is coherent with herself when she considers recourse to the infecund periods to be licit, while at the same time condemning, as being always illicit, the use of means directly contrary to fecundation, even if such use is inspired by reasons which may appear honest and serious. In reality, there are essential differences between the two cases; in the former, the married couple make legitimate use of a natural disposition; in the latter, they impede the development of natural processes. It is true that, in the one and the other case, the married couple are concordant in the positive will of avoiding children for plausible reasons, seeking the certainty that offspring will not arrive; but it is also true that only in the former case are they able to renounce the use of marriage in the fecund periods when, for just motives, procreation is not desirable, while making use of it during infecund periods to manifest their affection and to safeguard their mutual fidelity. By so doing, they give proof of a truly and integrally honest love.

Upright men can even better convince themselves of the solid grounds on which the teaching of the Church in this field is based, if they care to reflect upon the consequences of methods of artificial birth control. Let them consider, first of all, how wide and easy a road would thus be opened up towards conjugal infidelity and the general lowering of morality. Not much experience is needed in order to know human weakness, and to understand that men—especially the young, who are so vulnerable on this point—have need of encouragement to be faithful to the moral law, so that they must not be offered some easy means of eluding its observance. It is also to be feared that the man, growing used to the employment of anti-conceptive practices, may finally lose respect for the woman and, no longer caring for her physical and psychological equilibrium, may come to the point of considering her as a mere instrument of selfish enjoyment, and no longer as his respected and beloved companion.

Let it be considered also that a dangerous weapon would thus be placed in the hands of those public authorities who take no heed of moral exigencies. Who could blame a government for applying to the solution of the problems of the community those means acknowledged to be licit for married couples in the solution of a family problem? Who will stop rulers from favoring, from even imposing upon their peoples, if they were to consider it necessary, the method of contraception which they judge to be most efficacious? In such a way men, wishing to avoid individual, family, or social difficulties encountered in the observance of the divine law, would reach the point of placing at the mercy of the intervention of public authorities the most personal and most reserved sector of conjugal intimacy.

Consequently, if the mission of generating life is not to be exposed to the arbitrary will of men, one must necessarily recognize unsurmountable limits to the possibility of man's domination over his own body and its functions; limits which no man, whether a private individual or one invested with authority, may licitly surpass. And such limits cannot be determined otherwise than by the respect due to the integrity of the human organism and its functions, according to the principles recalled earlier, and also according to the correct understanding of the "principle of totality" illustrated by our predecessor Pope Pius XII.

The Church Guarantor of True Human Values

It can be foreseen that this teaching will perhaps not be easily received by all: Too numerous are those voices—amplified by the modern means of propaganda—which are contrary to the voice of the Church. To tell the truth, the Church is not surprised to be made, like her divine founder, a "sign of contradiction," yet she does not because of this cease to proclaim with humble firmness the entire moral law, both natural and evangelical. Of such laws the Church was not the author, nor consequently can she be their arbiter; she is only their depository and their interpreter, without ever being able to declare to be licit that which is not so by reason of its intimate and unchangeable opposition to the true good of man.

In defending conjugal morals in their integral wholeness, the Church knows that she contributes towards the establishment of a truly human civilization; she engages man not to abdicate from his own responsibility in order to rely on technical means; by that very fact she defends the dignity of man and wife. Faithful to both the teaching and the example of the Saviour, she shows herself to be the sincere and disinterested friend of men, whom she wishes to help, even during their earthly sojourn, "to share as sons in the life of the living God, the Father of all men."

SÖREN KIERKEGAARD (1813–1855)

The Aesthetic Validity of Marriage

Now for the matter in hand. There are two things I must especially regard as my task: to show the aesthetic significance of marriage; and to show how the aesthetic element in it may be held

[This material is from a letter by Judge Williams addressed to his "young friend," that is, "A ," who is the author and editor of the first volume of *Either/Or.* This accounts for the use of the second person pronoun throughout the work. Both the names are, of course, pseudonyms adopted by Kierkegaard. "A" had written of the immediate or pleasure-filled life, and Judge Williams responds to him to discuss love and marriage from an ethical standpoint. *Eds.*]

The selection is from Sören Kierkegaard, *Either/Or,* two vols., trans. Walter Lowrie and L. M. Swenson (Princeton: Princeton University Press, 1946), vol. 2, pp. 8–124, with omissions. Used by permission of the publisher.

fast in spite of the manifold obstacles of actual life. In order, however, that you may abandon yourself with the more security to the edification which this little treatise may possibly procure you, I will let a little polemical prelude precede my discussions, and in it take due account of your sarcastic observations. But with that I hope also that I shall have paid due tribute to the piratical states and can then calmly pursue my calling; for after all I am within my calling when I who am a married man fight in behalf of marriage—*pro aris et focis*.[1] I assure you I take this matter so much to heart that I, who ordinarily do not feel tempted to write books, might actually be tempted to do so, if only I might hope to save a single marriage from the hell into which perhaps it has precipitated itself, or to render a few people more capable of realizing the most beautiful task proposed to men.

As a precautionary measure I will occasionally allude to my wife and my relation to her—not as though I presumed to represent our marriage as the normative example, but partly because the poetical descriptions which are purely fanciful have no very special convincing power, and partly because I count it of importance to show that even in commonplace situations it is possible to preserve the aesthetical. You have known me for many years, you have known my wife for five, you find her quite pretty, or rather attractive, and so do I; and yet I know very well that she is not so pretty by day as in the evening, that a certain sad, almost ailing trait vanishes only in the course of the day, and that it is forgotten when in the evening she can really lay claim to be charming. I know very well that her nose is not the perfection of beauty, that it is too small; but it turns itself saucily to the world, and I know that this little nose has given occasion to so much pleasant banter that, if it were within my jurisdiction, I would never wish for her a more beautiful one. This is a much deeper appreciation of the significance of the accidental in life than that about which you are so enthusiastic. I thank God for all this good and forget the weak points.

This, however, is of minor importance. But there is one thing for which I thank God with my whole soul, namely, that she is the only one I have ever loved, the first one; and there is one thing for which I pray God with my whole heart, that He will give me strength never to want to love any other. This is a family prayer in which she too takes part; for every feeling, every mood, acquires for me a higher significance for the fact that I make her a partaker of it. All feeling, even the highest religious emotions, are able to assume an easy air when people

[1]For altar and hearth, i.e., house and home. *Tr.*

always agree in them. In her presence I am at once priest and congregation. And if sometimes I might be unkind enough not to be mindful of this good and ungrateful enough not to give thanks for it, she will then remind me of it. Look you, my young friend, this is not the coquetry of the first days of love-making; it is not an essay in experimental eroticism, as when in the period of his engagement pretty much every man has proposed to himself and to his fiancée the question whether she has been in love before, or whether he himself has loved anyone before; but this is the downright seriousness of life, and yet it is not cold, uncomely, unerotic, unpoetic. And truly I take it very much to heart that she really loves me and that I really love her—not as though in the course of years our marriage might not attain as much solidity as most others, but the point with me is to renew constantly the first love, and this again in such a way that for me it has just as much religious as aesthetic significance; for to me God has not become so supermundane that He might not concern Himself about the covenant He himself has established betwixt man and woman, and I have not become too spiritual to feel also the significance of the worldly side of life. And all the beauty inherent in the pagan erotic has validity also in Christianity, insofar as it can be combined with marriage. This renewal of our first love is not merely a sad reflection or a poetic recollection of something that has been experienced—that sort of thing produces fatigue, but this is action. Generally, the moment comes soon enough when one has to be content with recollection. One ought as long as possible to keep love's fresh spring open. . . .

Romantic love shows that it is immediate by the fact that it follows a natural necessity. It is based upon beauty; in part upon sensuous beauty, in part upon the beauty which can be conceived through and with and in the sensuous yet not as if it came to evidence through a deliberation, but in such a way that it is constantly on the point of expressing itself, peeking out through the sensuous form. In spite of the fact that this love is essentially based upon the sensuous, it is noble, nevertheless, by reason of the consciousness of eternity which it embodies; for what distinguishes all love from lust is the fact that it bears an impress of eternity. The lovers are sincerely convinced that their relationship is in itself a complete whole which never can be altered. But since this assurance is founded only upon a natural determinant, the eternal is thus based upon the temporal and thereby cancels itself. Since this assurance has undergone no test, has found no higher attestation, it shows itself to be an illusion, and for this reason it is so easy to make it ridiculous. People should not, however, be so ready to do this, and it is truly disgusting to see in modern comedy these experienced, intriguing, dissolute women who know that love is an illusion. I know no creature so abominable as such a woman. No debauchery is so loathsome to me, and nothing is so revolting as to see a lovable young girl in the hands of such a woman. Truly this is more terrible than to imagine her in the hands of a club of seducers. It is sad to see a man who learned to discount every substantial value in life, but to see a woman on this false path is horrible. Romantic love, however, as I have said, presents an analogy to morality by reason of the presumptive eternity which ennobles it and saves it from being mere sensuality. For the sensual is the momentary. The sensual seeks instant satisfaction, and the more refined it is, the better it knows how to make the instant of enjoyment a little eternity. The true eternity in love, as in true morality, delivers it, therefore, first out of the sensual. But in order to produce this true eternity a determination of the will is called for. But of this I shall say more later.

Our age has perceived very clearly the weak points of romantic love, and its ironical polemic against it has sometimes been thoroughly amusing—whether it has remedied its defects, and what it has put in its place, we shall now see. One may say that it has taken two paths, one of which is seen at the first glance to be a false one, that is, an immoral path; the other is more respectable, but to my mind it misses the deeper values of love, for if love is in fact founded upon the sensuous, every one can easily see that this "immediate" faithfulness of theirs is foolishness. What wonder then that women want emancipation —one of the many ugly phenomena of our age for which men are responsible. The eternal element in love becomes an object of derision, the temporal element alone is left, but this temporal again is refined into the sensuous eternity, into the eternal instant of the embrace. What I say here applies not only to a seducer here and there who sneaks about in the world like a beast of prey; no, it is appropriate to a numerous chorus of highly gifted men, and it is not only Byron who declares that love is heaven, marriage is hell.[2] It is very evident that there is in this a reflection, something which romantic love does not have. For romantic love is quite willing to accept marriage too, willing to accept the blessing of the Church as a pretty adjunct to the festivity, without attaching to it any real significance on its own account. By reason of its disposition to reflection the love here in question has

---

[2] "To Eliza"—"Though women are angels, yet wedlock's the devil. "*Tr.*

with a terrible firmness and induration of mind made up a new definition[3] of what unhappy love is, namely, to be loved when one no longer loves—the opposite of loving without requital. And verily, if this tendency were aware what profundity is implied in these few words, it would itself shrink from it. For apart from all the experience, shrewdness and cunning this definition reveals, it contains also a presentiment that conscience exists. So then the moment remains the principal thing, and how often one has heard these shameless words addressed by such a lover to a poor girl who could love only once: "I do not demand so much, I am content with less; far be it from me to require that you shall continue to love me to all eternity, if only you love me at the instant when I wish it." Such lovers know very well that the sensuous is transient, they know also what is the most beautiful instant, and therewith they are content.

Such a tendency is, of course, absolutely immoral; yet on the path of thought it brings us in a way nearer our goal, forasmuch as it lodges a formal protest against marriage. Insofar as the same tendency seeks to assume a more decent appearance it does not confine itself merely to the single instance but extends this to a longer period, yet in such a way that instead of receiving the eternal into its consciousness it receives the temporal, or it entangles itself in this opposition between the temporal and the eternal by supposing a possible alteration in the course of time. It thinks that for a time one can well enough endure living together, but it would keep open a way of escape, so as to be able to choose if a happier choice might offer itself. This reduces marriage to a civil arrangement; one need only report to the proper magistrate that this marriage is ended and another contracted, just as one reports a change of domicile. Whether this is an advantage to the State I leave undecided—for the individual in question it must truly be a strange relationship. Hence, one does not always see it realized, but the age is continually threatening us with it. And verily it would require a high degree of impudence to carry it out—I do not think this word is too strong to apply to it—just as on the part of the female participant in this association it would betray a frivolity bordering on depravity. There is, however, an entirely different disposition of mind which might get this notion into its head, and that is a disposition which I would deal with here more especially, since it is very characteristic of our age. For in fact such a plan may originate

---

[3] *Papirer* III, p. 129, shows that the reference is to *Gabrielle de Belle-isle* by A. Dumas. *Tr.*

either in an *egoistic* or in a *sympathetic melancholy*. People have now been talking long enough about the frivolity of this age; I believe it is now high time to talk a little about its melancholy, and I hope that by this everything will be better clarified. Or is not melancholy the defect of our age? Is it not this which resounds even in its frivolous laughter? Is it not melancholy which has deprived us of courage to command, of courage to obey, of power to act, of the confidence necessary to hope? And now when the good philosophers are doing everything to give intensity to the actual, shall we not become so crammed full of it that we are suffocated? Everything is cut out except the present—what wonder then that for the constant dread of forfeiting this, one forfeits it. Well, it is true enough that we ought not to vanish in an evanescent hope, and that this is not the way to become transfigured in the clouds; but in order truly to enjoy one must have air, and not only in moments of sorrow is it important to have the heavens opened, but also in the time of joy to have a free vista and the folding doors thrown open wide. It is true that enjoyment apparently loses by this a certain degree of the intensity it has by the help of such an alarming limitation; but it is not likely that thereby much will be lost, for this intensity has a good deal in common with the intense enjoyment of the Strasbourg geese which costs them their lives. It might perhaps prove rather difficult to make you perceive this; but on the other hand I surely do not need to explain to you the significance of the intensity one attains in a different way. For in this respect you have great virtuosity—you *cui di dederunt formam, divitias, artemque fruendi. . . .*[4]

We have now seen how romantic love was built upon an illusion, and that the eternity it claims was built upon the temporal, and that although the knight was sincerely convinced of its absolute durability, there nevertheless was no certainty of this, inasmuch as its trials and temptations have hitherto been in a medium which was entirely external. Such being the case, it was able with a pretty piety to accept marriage along with love, although, after all, this acquired no very deep significance. We have seen how this immediate and beautiful but also very naïve love, being embodied in the consciousness of a reflective age, must become the object of its mockery and of its irony; and we have seen too what such an age was capable of substituting for it. Such an age embodied marriage in its consciousness and in part

---

[4] Upon whom the gods bestowed beauty, wealth and the power of enjoyment. Horace's *Letters* I, 4, 6. *Tr.*

declared itself on the side of love in such a way as to exclude marriage, in part on the side of marriage in such a way as to exclude love. Hence, in a recent play a sensible little seamstress, speaking of the love of fine gentlemen, makes the shrewd observation, "You love us but you don't marry us; the fine ladies you don't love, but you marry them."

Herewith this little treatise (as I am compelled to call what I am here writing, although at first I thought only of a big letter) has reached the point from which marriage can be viewed in the right light. That marriage belongs essentially to Christianity, that the pagan nations have not brought it to perfection, in spite of the sensuousness of the Orient and all the beauty of Greece, that not even Judaism has been capable of this, in spite of the truly lyrical elements to be found in it—all this you will be ready to concede without compelling me to argue the matter, and this all the more because it is sufficient to remember that the contrast between the sexes has nowhere been made a subject for such deep reflection that the other sex has received complete justice. But within Christianity also love has had to encounter many fates before we learned to see the deep, the beautiful and the true implications of marriage. Since, however, the immediately preceding age was an age of reflection, as is ours also to a certain degree, it is not so easy a matter to prove this, and since in you I have found so great a virtuoso in bringing the weaker sides into prominence, the task of convincing you of the side which I have undertaken to defend is doubly difficult. I owe you, however, the admission that I am much indebted to you for your polemic. When I think of the multifarious expressions of it which I possess in their dispersion, and imagine them gathered into a unity, your polemic is so talented and inventive that it is a good guide for one who would defend the other side. For your attacks are not so superficial that (if only you or another would think them through) they might not contain the truth, even though neither you nor your adversary observe this in the moment of conflict.

Inasmuch as it appeared to be a defect on the part of romantic love that it was not reflective, it might seem reasonable to let true conjugal love begin with a kind of doubt. This might seem all the more necessary in view of the fact that we approach this subject with the prepossessions of a reflective age. I am by no means prepared to deny that a marriage might be artificially accomplished after such a doubt; but the question remains nevertheless whether the nature of marriage is not substantially altered by this, since it presupposes a divorce between love and marriage. The question is whether it is essential to marriage to annihilate the first love because of doubt as to the possibility of realizing it, in order to make conjugal love possible and actual through this annihilation, so that the marriage of Adam and Eve was really the only one in which immediate love was preserved inviolate, and that again chiefly for the reason which Musaeus[5] wittily suggests, there was no possibility of loving anybody else. The question, remains whether immediate love, the first love, would be secured against this scepticism by being assumed in a higher concentric immediacy, so that conjugal love would be in no need of plowing under the beautiful hopes of first love, but conjugal love itself would be first love, seasoned with an admixture of determinants which would not detract from it but would ennoble it. This is a difficult problem to prove, and yet it is of prodigious importance, lest in the ethical sphere we might have such a cleavage as exists in the intellectual sphere between faith and knowledge. And how beautiful it would be, my dear friend—you will not deny it, for after all your heart is susceptible to love, and your head is only too well acquainted with doubt—how beautiful it would be if the Christian might venture to call his God the God of love, in such a way as to think therewith of that unspeakably blissful feeling, the eternal force in the world—earthly love.

In the foregoing discussion I dealt with romantic and reflective love as discursive points of view, but now we are to see to what extent the higher unity is a return to immediate love, and accordingly to what extent (apart from the more which it contains) it contains also what was comprised in the first. It is now clear enough that reflective love constantly consumes itself, and that it stops arbitrarily now at this point, now at another; it is clear that it points beyond itself to the higher position, but the question is whether this higher experience cannot come at once into touch with the first love. Now this higher experience is the religious, in which the reflective understanding comes to an end; and just as for God nothing is impossible, so too for the religious individual nothing is impossible. In the religious sphere love finds again the infinity which it vainly sought in the sphere of reflection. But in case the religious, higher though it certainly is than everything earthly, does not stand in an eccentric relation to immediate love but in a concentric relation, unity might be brought about without any necessity for the pain which religion indeed can heal but which, nevertheless, always remains a profound pain. One very rarely sees this matter made the subject of serious deliberation, because those who have feeling for romantic love do not bother much about marriage,

[5] *Volksmärchen der Deutschen,* Gotha, 1887–89, III, p. 219. *Tr.*

and because on the other hand so many marriages unfortunately are contracted without the deeper erotic which is assuredly the most beautiful thing in a purely human existence. Christianity holds firmly to marriage. So in case conjugal love is unable to contain all of the first erotic, Christianity does not represent the highest development of the human race, and without doubt it is a secret dread of such an incongruity which is largely responsible for the despair which permeates modern lyric both in verse and in prose.

So you see what a task I have undertaken in endeavoring to show that romantic love can be united with and can persist in marriage, yea, that marriage is the true transfiguration of romantic love. This is not by any means to cast disparagement upon the marriages which have been rescued from reflection and its shipwreck, nor would I be so unsympathetic as to grudge them my admiration; it is not to be denied that much can be done in this way, nor ought it to be forgotten that the whole tendency of the age often makes such marriages a dolorous necessity. As for this "necessity," however, it must be remembered that every generation, and each individual in the generation, begins life anew to a certain extent, and that for each one severally there is a possibility of escaping this maelstrom, and it must be remembered, too, that one generation should learn from the other, and that hence there is a likelihood that after reflection has made such a sorry spectacle of one generation the successive generation will be more fortunate. And however many painful confusions life may still have in store, I fight for two things: for the prodigious task of showing that marriage is the transfiguration of first love, that it is its friend, not its enemy; and for the task (which to others is very trivial but to me is all the more important) of showing that my humble marriage has had such a meaning for me, so that from it I derive strength and courage to fulfill constantly this task. . . .

Let us then cast up the account once for all. You talk so much about the erotic embrace—what is that in comparison with the matrimonial embrace! What richness of modulation in the matrimonial "Mine!" in comparison with the erotic! It reechoes not only in the seductive eternity of the instant, not only in the illusory eternity of fantasy and imagination, but in the eternity of clear consciousness, in the eternity of eternity. What power there is in the matrimonial "Mine!"—for will, resolution and purpose have a deeper tone. What energy and pliability!—for what is so hard as will, and what so soft? What power of movement!—not merely the confusing enthusiasm of obscure impulses; for marriage is made in heaven, and duty permeates the whole body of the universe to its utmost limits and prepares the way and gives assurance that to all eternity no obstacle shall be able to unsettle love! So let Don Juan keep the leafy bower, and the knight the starry dome of heaven, if he can see nothing above it; marriage has its heaven still higher up. Such is marriage; and if it is not thus, it is not the fault of God, nor of Christianity, nor of the wedding ceremony; it is not due to cursing nor to blessing, but it is man's own fault. And is it not a sin and a shame that men write books in such a way as to make people perplexed about life, make them tired of it before they begin, instead of teaching them how to live! And this would be a painful truth, even if they were in the right, but in fact, it is a lie. They teach us to sin, and those who have not the courage for that they make equally unhappy in other ways. Unfortunately, I myself am too much influenced by the aesthetic not to know that the word "husband" grates upon your ears. But I don't care. If the word husband has fallen into discredit and almost become laughable, it is high time for one to seek to restore it to honor. And if you say "Such a sight as this one never sees, although one often enough sees marriages," this does not disquiet me; for the fact that one sees marriages every day entails the consequence that one more rarely sees the greatness in marriage, especially in view of the fact that people do everything to belittle it. For have not you and your sort carried the thing so far that the maiden who gives her hand before the altar is regarded as a more imperfect being than these heroines in your romances with their "first love"?

Now that I have listened patiently to you and your outburst, you perhaps will forgive me for coming forward with my little observations. (Your outburst, by the way, was perhaps wilder than you were aware; but even though you have not thoroughly understood these emotions within you, yet when marriage comes to meet you as a reality, you will see that within you there will be a raging storm, though presumably you will not confide in any one.) A man loves only once in his life—the heart clings to its first love—marriage! Harken and be amazed at the harmonious accord of these three spheres. It is the same thing, except that it is expressed aesthetically, religiously, and ethically. One loves but once. To effect a realization of this, marriage joins in—and in case people who do not love each other take it into their heads to get married, the Church is not responsible. A man loves only once—this refrain is heard from the most various quarters: from the fortunate to whom every new day gives a glad reassurance; and from the unfortunate. Of the latter there are properly only two classes: those who are always aspiring after the ideal; and those who will not stick to it. The last are the real seducers. One meets them rather seldom, because an uncommon aptitude is always requisite for this. I have known one, but he too admitted that a man loves only once; his wild lusts, however, love was unable to tame. "Yes," say these people, "one loves only once, one marries two or three times." Here the two spheres are again united; for aesthetics says, "No," and the Church with ecclesiastical ethics looks with suspicion upon the second marriage. To me this is of the utmost importance; for if it were true that one loves several times, marriage would be a questionable institution; it might seem that the erotic suffered harm from the arbitrary exaction of the religious, which requires as a rule that one should love only once, and disposes of the business of the erotic as cavalierly as though it were to say, "You can marry once, and that's the end of it." . . .

This is one of the points to which we constantly return—you, as it seems, against your will and without being quite clear what it involves, I with full consciousness of its significance: the point, namely, that the illusory or naive eternity of first or romantic love cancels itself out, in one way or another. Just because you try to retain love in this immediate form, try to make yourself believe that true freedom consists in being outside oneself, intoxicated by dreams, therefore you fear the metamorphosis, not regarding it as such but as something altogether heterogeneous which implies the death of first love, and hence your abhorrence of duty. For, of course, if duty has not already subsisted as a germ in first love, it is absolutely disturbing when it makes its appearance. But such is not the case with conjugal love. Already in the ethical and religious factors it has duty in it, and when this appears before it, it is not as a stranger, a shameless intruder, who nevertheless has such authority that one dare not by virtue of the mysteriousness of love show him the door. No, duty comes as an old friend, an intimate, a confidant, whom the lovers mutually recognize in the deepest secret of their love. And when he speaks it is nothing new he has to say, and when he has spoken the individuals humble themselves under it, but at the same time are uplifted just because they are assured that what he enjoins is what they themselves wish, and that his commanding it is merely a more majestic, a more exalted, a divine way of expressing the fact that their wish can be realized. It would not have been enough if he had encouraged them by saying, "It can be done, love can be preserved," but when he says, "It shall be preserved," there is in that an authority which answers to the heart-felt desire of love. Love drives out fear; but yet when love is for a moment fearful for itself, fearful of its own salvation, duty is the nutriment of all others love stands in need of; for it says, "Fear not, you shall conquer," speaking not futuristically, for that only suggests hope, but imperatively, and in this lies an assurance which nothing can shake.

So then you regard duty as the enemy of love; I regard it as its friend. You will, perhaps, be content at hearing this declaration, and with your customary mockery will congratulate me on such an interesting and uncommon friend. I, on the other hand, will by no means be satisfied with this reply but will take the liberty of carrying the war into your own territory. If duty, once it has appeared in consciousness, is an enemy of love, then love must do its best to conquer it; for you, after all, would not think of love as a being so impotent that it cannot vanquish every opposition. On the other hand, you think that when duty makes its appearance it is all over with love, and you think also that duty, early or late, must make its appearance, not merely in conjugal love but also in romantic love; and the truth is that you are afraid of conjugal love because it has in it duty to such a degree that when it makes its appearance you cannot run away from it. In romantic love, on the other hand, you think this is all right, for as soon as the instant arrives when duty is mentioned, love is over, and the arrival of duty is the signal for you, with a very courtly bow, to say farewell. Here you see again what your eulogies of love amount to. If duty is the enemy of love, and if love cannot vanquish this enemy, then love is not the true conquerer. The consequence is that you must leave love in the lurch. When once you have got the desperate idea that duty is the enemy of love, your defeat is certain, and you have done just as much to disparage love and deprive it of its majesty as you have done to show despite of duty, and yet it was only the latter you meant to do. You see, this again is despair, whether you feel the pain of it or seek in despair to forget it. If you cannot reach the point of seeing the aesthetical, the ethical and the religious as three great allies, if you do not know how to conserve the unity of the diverse appearances which everything assumes in these diverse spheres, then life is devoid of meaning, then one must grant that you are justified in maintaining your pet theory that one can say of everything, "Do it or don't do it—you will regret both."

WALTER LIPPMANN (1889—)

Sex and Birth Control

With contraception established as a more or less legitimate idea in modern society, a vast discussion has ensued as to how the practice of it can be rationalized. In this discussion the pace is set by those who accept the apparent logic of contraception and are prepared boldly to revise the sexual conventions accordingly. They take as their major premise the obvious fact that by contraception it is possible to dissociate procreation from gratification, and therefore to pursue independently what Mr. Havelock Ellis calls the primary and secondary objects of the sexual impulse. They propose, therefore, to sanction two distinct sets of conventions: one designed to protect the interests of the offspring by promoting intelligent, secure, and cheerful parenthood; the other designed to permit the freest and fullest expression of the erotic personality. They propose, in other words to distinguish between parenthood as a vocation involving public responsibility, and love as an art, pursued privately for the sake of happiness.

As a preparation for the vocation of parenthood it is proposed to educate both men and women in the care, both physical and psychological, of children. It is proposed further that mating for parenthood shall become an altogether deliberate and voluntary choice: the argument here is that the duties of parenthood cannot be successfully fulfilled except where both parents cheerfully and knowingly assume them. Therefore, it is proposed, in order to avert the dangers of love at first sight and of mating under the blind compulsion of instinct, that a period of free experimentation be allowed to precede the solemn engagement to produce and rear children. This engagement is regarded as so much a public responsibility that it is even proposed, and to some extent has been embodied in the law of certain jurisdictions, that marriage for parenthood must be sanctioned by medical authority. In order, too, that no compulsive considerations may determine what ought to be a free and intelligent choice, it is argued that women should be economically independent before and during marriage. As this may not be possible for women without property of their own during the years when they are bearing and rearing children, it is proposed in some form or other to endow motherhood. This endowment may take the form of a legal claim upon the earnings of the father, or it may mean a subsidy from the state through mothers' pensions, free medical attention, day nurseries, and kindergartens. The principle that successful parenthood must be voluntary is maintained as consistently as possible. Therefore, among those who follow the logic of their idea, it is proposed that even marriages deliberately entered into for procreation shall be dissoluble at the will of either party, the state intervening only to insure the economic security of the offspring. It is proposed, furthermore, that where women find the vocation of motherhood impracticable for one reason or another, they may be relieved of the duty of rearing their children.

Not all of the advanced reformers adopt the whole of this program, but the whole of this program is logically inherent in the conception of parenthood as a vocation deliberately undertaken, publicly pursued, and motivated solely by the parental instincts.

The separate set of conventions which it is proposed to adopt for the development of love as an art have a logic of their own. Their function is not to protect the welfare of the child but the happiness of lovers. It is very easy to misunderstand this conception. Mr. Havelock Ellis, in fact, describes it as a "divine and elusive mystery," a description which threatens to provide a rather elusive standard by which to fix a new set of sexual conventions. But baffling as this sounds, it is not wholly inscrutable, and a sufficient understanding of what is meant can be attained by clearing up the dangerous ambiguity in the phrase "love as an art."

There are two arts of love and it makes a considerable difference which one is meant. There is the art of love as Casanova, for example, practiced it. It is the art of seduction, courtship, and sexual gratification: it is an art which culminates in the sexual act. It can be repeated with the same lover and with other lovers, but it exhausts itself in the moment of ecstasy. When that moment is reached, the work of art is done, and the lover as artist "after an interval, perhaps of stupor and vital recuperation" must start all over again, until at last the rhythm is so stale it is a weariness to start at all; or the lover must find new lovers and new resistances to conquer. The aftermath of romantic love —that is, of love that is consummated in sexual ecstasy—is either tedium in middle age or the compulsive adventurousness of the libertine.

Now this is not what Mr. Ellis means when he talks about love as an art. "The act of intercourse," he says, "is only an incident, and not an essential in love." Incident to what? His answer is that it is an incident to an "exquisitely and variously and harmoniously blended" activity of "all the finer activities of the organism, physical and psychic." I take this to mean that when a man and woman are successfully in love, their whole activity is energized and victorious. They walk better, their digestion improves, they think more clearly, their secret worries drop away, the world is fresh and interesting and they can do more than they dreamed that they could do. In love of this kind sexual intimacy is not the dead end of desire as it is in romantic or promiscuous love, but periodic affirmation of the inward delight of desire pervading an active life. Love of this sort can grow; it is not, like youth itself, a moment that comes and is gone and remains only a memory of something which cannot be recovered. It can grow because it has something to grow upon and to grow with; it is not contracted and stale because it has for its object, not the mere relief of physical tension, but all the objects with which the two lovers are concerned. They desire their worlds in each other, and therefore their love is as interesting as their worlds and their worlds are as interesting as their love.

It is to promote unions of this sort that the older liberals are proposing a new set of sexual conventions. There are, however, reformers in the field who take a much less exalted view of the sexual act, who regard it, indeed, not only as without biological or social significance, but also as without any very impressive psychological significance. "The practice of birth control," says Mr. C. E. M. Joad, for example, "will profoundly modify our sexual habits. It will enable the pleasures of sex to be tasted without its penalties, and it will remove the most formidable deterrent to irregular intercourse." For birth control "offers to the young ... the prospect of shameless, harmless, and unlimited pleasure." But whether the reformers agree with Mr. Ellis that sexual intimacy is, as he says, a sacrament signifying some great spiritual reality, or with Mr. Joad that it is a harmless pleasure, they are agreed that the sexual conventions should be revised to permit such unions without penalties and without any sense of shame.

They ask public opinion to sanction what contraception has made feasible. They point out that "a large number of the men and women of to-day form sexual relationships outside marriage—whether or not they ultimately lead to marriage—which they conceal or seek to conceal from the world." These relationships, says Mr. Ellis, differ from the extramarital manifestations of the sexual life of the past in that they do not derive from prostitution or seduction. Both of these ancient practices, he adds, are diminishing, for prostitution is becoming less attractive and, with the education of women, seduction is becoming less possible. The novelty of these new relations, the prevalence of which is conceded though it cannot be measured, lies in the fact that they are entered into voluntarily, have no obvious social consequences, and are altogether beyond the power of law or opinion to control. The argument, therefore, is that they should be approved, the chief point being made that by removing all stigma from such unions, they will become candid, wholesome, and delightful. The objection of the reformers to the existing conventions is that the sense of sin poisons the spontaneous goodness of such relationships.

The actual proposals go by a great variety of fancy names such as free love, trial marriage, companionate marriage. When these proposals are examined it is evident they all take birth control as their major premise, and then deduce from it some part or all of the logical consequences. Companionate marriage, for example, is from the point of view of the law, whatever it may be subjectively, nothing but a somewhat roundabout way of saying that childless couples may be divorced by mutual consent. It is a proposal, if not to control, then at least to register publicly, all sexual unions, the theory being that this public registration will abolish shame and furtiveness and give them a certain permanence. Companionate marriage is frankly an attempt at a compromise between marriages that are difficult to dissolve and clandestine relationships which have no sanction whatever.

The uncompromising logic of birth control has been stated more clearly, I think, by Mr. Bertrand Russell than by anyone else. Writing to Judge Lindsey during the uproar about companionate marriage, Mr. Russell said:

> I go further than you do: the things which your enemies say about you would be largely true of me. My own view is that the state and the law should take no notice of sexual relations apart from children, and that no marriage ceremony should be valid unless accompanied by a medical certificate of the woman's pregnancy. But when once there are children, I think that divorce should be avoided except for very grave cause. I should not regard physical infidelity as a very grave cause and should teach people that it is to be expected and tolerated, but should not involve the begetting of illegitimate children—not because illegitimacy is bad in itself, but because a home with two parents is best for children. I do not feel that the main thing in marriage is the feeling of the parents for each other; the main thing is cooperation in bearing children.

In this admirably clear statement there is set forth a plan for that complete separation between the primary and secondary function of sexual intercourse which contraception makes possible.

It is one thing, however, to recognize the full logic of birth control and quite another thing to say that convention ought to be determined by that logic. One might as well argue that because automobiles can be driven at a hundred miles an hour the laws should sanction driving at the rate of a hundred miles an hour. Birth control is a device like the automobile, and its inherent possibilities do not fix the best uses to be made of it.

What an understanding of the logic of birth control does is to set before us the limits of coercive control of sexual relations. The law can, for example, make divorce very difficult where there are children. It could, as Mr. Bertrand Russell suggests, refuse divorce on the ground of infidelity. On the other hand the law cannot effectively prohibit infidelity, and as a matter of fact does not do so to-day. It cannot effectively prohibit fornication though there are statutes against it. Therefore, what Mr. Russell has done is to describe accurately enough the actual limits of effective legal control.

But sexual conventions are not statutes, and it is important to define quite clearly just what they are. In the older world they were rules of conduct enforceable by the family and the community through habit, coercion, and authority. In this sense of the word, convention tends to lose force and effect in modern civilization. Yet a convention is essentially a theory of conduct and all human conduct implies some theory of conduct. Therefore, although it may be that no convention is any longer coercive, conventions remain, are adopted, revised, and debated. They embody the considered results of experience: perhaps the experience of a lonely pioneer or perhaps the collective experience of the dominant members of a community. In any event they are as necessary to a society which recognizes no authority as to one which does. For the inexperienced must be offered some kind of hypothesis when they are confronted with the necessity of making choices: they cannot be so utterly open-minded that they stand inert until something collides with them. In the modern world, therefore, the function of conventions is to declare the meaning of experience. A good convention is one which will most probably show the inexperienced the way to happy experience.

Just because the rule of sexual conduct by authority is dissolving, the need of conventions which will guide conduct is increasing. That, in fact, is the reason for the immense and urgent discussion of sex throughout the modern world. It is an attempt to attain an understanding of the bewilderingly new experiences to which few men or women know how to adjust themselves. The true business of the moralist in the midst of all this is not to denounce this and to advocate that, but to see as clearly as he can into the meaning of it, so that out of the chaos of pain and happiness and worry he may help to deliver a usable insight.

It is, I think, to the separation of parenthood as a vocation from love as an end in itself that the moralist must address himself. For this is the heart of the problem: to determine whether this separation, which birth control has made feasible and which law can no longer prevent, is in harmony with the conditions of human happiness.

Among those who hold that the separation of the primary and secondary functions of the sexual impulse is good and should constitute the major premise of modern sexual conventions, there are, as I have already pointed out, two schools of thought. There are the transcendentalists who believe with Mr. Havelock Ellis that "sexual pleasure, wisely used and not abused, may prove the stimulus and liberator of our finest and most exalted activities," and there are the unpretentious hedonists who believe that sexual pleasure is pleasure and not the stimulus or liberator of anything important. Both are, as we say, emancipated: neither recognizes the legitimacy of objective control unless a child is born, and both reject as an evil the traditional subjective control exercised by the sense of sin. Where they differ is in their valuation of love.

Hedonism as an attitude toward life is, of course, not a new thing in the world, but it has never before been tested out under such favorable conditions. . . . There is now a generation in the world which is approaching middle age. They have exercised the privileges which were won by the iconoclasts who attacked what was usually called the Puritan or Victorian tradition. They have exercised the privileges without external restraint and without inhibition. Their conclusions are reported in the latest works of fiction. Do they report that they have found happiness in their freedom? Well, hardly. Instead of the gladness which they were promised, they seem, like Hegesias, to have found the wasteland. . . .

If you start with the belief that love is the pleasure of a moment, is it really surprising that it yields only a momentary pleasure? For it is the most ironical of all illusions to suppose that one is free of illusions in contracting any human desire to its primary physiological satisfaction. Does a man dine well because he ingests the requisite number of calories? Is he freer from illusions about his appetite than the man who creates an interesting dinner party out of the underlying fact that his guests and he have the need to fill their stomachs? Would it really be a mark of enlightenment if each of them filled his stomach in the solitary and solemn conviction that good conversation and pleasant companionship are one thing and nutrition is another?

This much the transcendentalists understand well enough. They do not wish to isolate the satisfaction of desire from our "finest and most exalted activities." They would make it "the stimulus and the liberator" of these activities. They would use it to arouse to "wholesome activity all the complex and interrelated systems of the organism." But what are these finest and most exalted activities which are to be stimulated and liberated? The discovery of truth, the making of works of art, meditation and insight? Mr. Ellis does not specify. If these are the activities that are meant, then the discussion applies to a very few of the men and women on earth. For the activities of most of them are necessarily concerned with earning a living and managing a household and rearing children and finding recreation. If the art of love is to stimulate and liberate activities, it is these prosaic activities which it must stimulate and liberate. But if you idealize the logic of birth control, make parenthood a separate vocation, isolate love from work and the hard realities of living, and say that it must be spontaneous and carefree, what have you done? You have separated it from all the important activities which it might stimulate and liberate. You have made love spontaneous but empty, and you have made home-building and parenthood efficient, responsible, and dull.

What has happened, I believe, is what so often happens in the first enthusiasm for a revolutionary invention. Its possibilities are so dazzling that men forget that inventions belong to man and not man to his inventions. In the discussion which has ensued since birth control became generally feasible, the central confusion has been that the reformers have tried to fix their sexual ideals in accordance with the logic of birth control instead of the logic of human nature. Birth control does make feasible this dissociation of interests which were once organically united. There are undoubtedly the best of reasons for dissociating them up to a point. But how completely it is wise to dissociate them is a matter to be determined not by saying how completely it is possible to dissociate them, but how much it is desirable to dissociate them.

All the varieties of the modern doctrine that man is a collection of separate impulses, each of which can attain its private satisfaction, are in fundamental contradiction not only with the traditional body of human wisdom but with the modern conception of the human character. Thus in one breath it is said in advanced circles that love is a series of casual episodes, and in the next it transpires that the speaker is in process of having himself elaborately psychoanalyzed in order to disengage his soul from the effects of apparently trivial episodes in his childhood. On the one hand it is asserted that sex pervades everything and on the other that sexual behavior is inconsequential. It is taught that experience is cumulative, that we are what our past has made us and shall be what we are making of ourselves now, and then with bland indifference to the significance of this we are told that all experiences are free, equal, and independent.

It is not hard to see why those who are concerned in revising sexual conventions should have taken the logic of birth control rather than knowledge of human nature as their major premise. Birth control is an immensely beneficent invention which can and does relieve men and women of some of the most tragic sorrows which afflict them: the tragedies of the unwanted child, the tragedies of insupportable economic burdens, the tragedies of excessive child-bearing and the destruction of youth and the necessity of living in an unrelenting series of pregnancies. It offers them freedom from intolerable mismating, from sterile virtue, from withering denials of happiness. These are the facts which the reformers saw, and in birth control they saw the instrument by which such freedom could be obtained.

The sexual conventions which they have proposed are really designed to cure notorious evils. They do not define the good life in sex; they point out ways of escape from the bad life. Thus companionate marriage is proposed by Judge Lindsey not as a type of union which is inherently desirable, but as an avenue of escape from corrupt marriages on the one hand and furtive promiscuity on the other. The movement for free divorce comes down to this: it is necessary because so many marriages are a failure. The whole theory that love is separate from parenthood and home-building is supported by the evidence in those cases where married couples are not lovers. It is the pathology of sexual relations which inspires the reformers of sexual conventions.

There is no need to quarrel with them because they insist upon remedies for manifest evils. Deep confusion results when they forget that these remedies are only remedies, and go on to institute them as ideals. It is better, without any doubt, that incompatible couples should be divorced and that each should then be free to find a mate who is compatible. But the frequency with which men and women have to resort to divorce because they are incompatible will be greatly influenced by the notions they have before and during marriage of what compatibility is, and what it involves. The remedies for failure are important. But what is central is the conception of sexual relations by which they expect to live successfully.

They cannot—I am, of course, speaking broadly—expect to live successfully by the conception that the primary and secondary functions of sex are in separate compartments of the soul. I have indicated why this conception is self-defeating and why, since human nature is organic and experience cumulative, our activities must, so to speak, engage and imply each other. Mates who are not lovers will not really cooperate, as Mr. Bertrand Russell thinks they should, in bearing children; they will be distracted, insufficient, and worst of all they will be merely dutiful. Lovers who have nothing to do but love each other are not really to be envied; love and nothing else very soon is nothing else. The emotion of love, in spite of the romantics, is not self-sustaining; it endures only when the lovers love many things together, and not merely each other. It is this understanding that love cannot successfully be isolated from the business of living which is the enduring wisdom of the institution of marriage. Let the law be what it may be as to what constitutes a marriage contract and how and when it may be dissolved. Let public opinion be as tolerant as it can be toward any and every kind of irregular and experimental relationship. When all the criticisms have been made, when all supernatural sanctions have been discarded, all subjective inhibitions erased, all compulsions abolished, the convention of marriage still remains to be considered as an interpretation of human experience. It is by the test of how genuinely it interprets human experience that the convention of marriage will ultimately be judged.

The wisdom of marriage rests upon an extremely unsentimental view of lovers and their passions. Its assumptions, when they are frankly exposed, are horrifying to those who have been brought up in the popular romantic tradition of the Nineteenth Century. These assumptions are that, given an initial attraction, a common social background, common responsibilities, and the conviction that the relationship is permanent, compatibility in marriage can normally be achieved. It is precisely this that the prevailing sentimentality about love denies. It assumes that marriages are made in heaven, that compatibility is instinctive, a mere coincidence, that happy unions are, in the last analysis, lucky accidents in which two people who happen to suit each other happen to have met. The convention of marriage rests on an interpretation of human nature which does not confuse the subjective feeling of the lovers that their passion is unique, with the brutal but objective fact that, had they never met, each of them would in all probability have found a lover who was just as unique. . . .

This is the reason why the popular conception of romantic love as the meeting of two affinities produces so much unhappiness. The mysterious glow of passion is accepted as a sign that the great coincidence has occurred; there is a wedding and soon, as the glow of passion cools, it is discovered that no instinctive and preordained affinity is present. At this point, the wisdom of popular romantic marriage is exhausted. For it proceeds on the assumption that love is a mysterious visitation. There is nothing left, then, but to grin and bear a miserably dull and nagging fate, or to break off and try again. The deep fallacy of the conception is in the failure to realize that compatibility is a process and not an accident, that it depends upon the maturing of instinctive desire by adaptation to the whole nature of the other person and to the common concerns of the pair of lovers.

The romantic theory of affinities rests upon an immature theory of desire. It springs from an infantile belief that the success of love is in the satisfactions which the other person provides. What this really means is that in child-like fashion the lover expects his mistress to supply him with happiness. But in the adult world that expectation is false. Because nine-tenths of the cause, as Mr. Santayana says, are in the lover for one-tenth that may be in the object, it is what the lover does about that nine-tenths which is decisive for his happiness. It is the claim, therefore, of those who uphold the ideal of marriage as a full partnership, and reject the ideal which would separate love as an art from parenthood as a vocation, that in the home made by a couple who propose to see it through, there are provided the essential conditions under which the passions of men and women are most likely to become mature, and therefore harmonious and disinterested.

They need not deny, indeed it would be foolish as well as cruel for them to underestimate, the enormous difficulty of achieving successful marriages under modern conditions. For with the dissolution of authority and compulsion, a successful marriage depends wholly upon the capacity of the man and the woman to make it successful. They have to accomplish wholly by understanding and sympathy and disinterestedness of purpose what was once in a very large measure achieved by habit, necessity, and the absence of any practicable alternative. It takes two persons to make a successful marriage in the modern world, and that fact more than doubles its difficulty. For these reasons alone the modern state ought to do what it would none the less be compelled to do: it ought to provide decent ways of retreat in case of failure.

But if it is the truth that the convention of marriage correctly interprets human experience, whereas the separatist conventions are self-defeating, then the convention of marriage will prove to be the conclusion which emerges out of all this immense experimenting. It will survive not as a rule of law imposed by force, for that is now, I think, become impossible. It will not survive as a moral commandment with which the elderly can threaten the young. They will not listen. It will survive as the dominant insight into the reality of love and happiness, or it will not survive at all. That does not mean that all persons will live under the convention of marriage. As a matter of fact in civilised ages all persons never have. It means that the convention of marriage, when it is clarified by insight into reality, is likely to be the hypothesis upon which men and women will ordinarily proceed. There will be no compulsion behind it except the compulsion in each man and woman to reach a true adjustment of his life.

It is in this necessity of clarifying their love for those who are closest to them that the normal problems of the new age come to a personal issue. It is in the realm of sexual relations that mankind is being schooled amidst pain and worry for the novel conditions which modernity imposes. It is there, rather than in politics, business, or even in religion, that the issues are urgent, vivid, and inescapable. It is there that they touch most poignantly and most radically the organic roots of human personality. And it is there, in the ordering of their personal attachments, that for most men the process of salvation must necessarily begin.

For disinterestedness in all things, as Dean Inge says, is a mountain track which the many are likely in the future as in the past to find cold, bleak, and bare: that is why "the road of ascent is by personal affection for man." By the happy ordering of their personal affections they may establish the type and the quality and the direction of their desires for all things. It is in the hidden issues between lovers, more than anywhere else, that modern men and women are compelled, by personal anguish rather than by laws and preachments or even by the persuasions of abstract philosophy, to transcend naive desire and to reach out towards a mature and disinterested partnership with their world.

JOSEPH FLETCHER (1905–)

Love and Situation Ethics

LOVE HAS NO EQUALS

In its very marrow Christian ethics is a situation ethic. The new morality, the emerging contemporary Christian conscience, separates Christian conduct from rigid creeds and rigid codes. Some of its critics, both Protestant and Catholic, seem to fear that by dropping codes it will drop its Christian commitment.[1] What it does is to treat all rules and principles and "virtues" (that is to say, all "universals") as love's servants and subordinates, to be quickly kicked out of the house if they forget their place and try to take over. Ayn Rand, the egoist and jungle-ethic writer, tersely describes the love ethic (except that it does not teach us to *scorn* a whore, only to help and redeem her): "A morality which teaches you to scorn a whore who gives her body indiscriminately to all men—this same morality demands that you surrender your soul to promiscuous love for all comers."[2]

Augustine was right to make love the source principle, the hinge principle upon which all other "virtues" hang, whether "cardinal" (natural) or "theological" (revealed). Love is not one virtue among others, one principle among equals, not even a *primus inter pares*. One theologian, Robert Gleason, S.J., in a full-dress attack on situation ethics, threw down the gauntlet most lucidly (and how different a challenge from that of Ayn Rand!) by asserting, "While the motive of love is a noble one, it is not in Christian tradition to present it as the exclusive motive for moral action."[3] This succinctly challenges the view that love has a monopoly control. It flies directly in the face of Paul's "single saying" in Gal. 5:14 and the conclusion of his hymn to love, I Cor., ch. 13. But what else can the man of law do, trapped as he

---

[1] C. B. Eavey, *Principles of Christian Ethics* (Zondervan Publishing House, 1958), p. 246; Kenneth Moore, O. Carm., *American Ecclesiastical Review*, Vol. 135 (1956), pp. 29–38.

[2] *Atlas Shrugged* (Random House, Inc., 1957), p. 1033.

[3] "Situational Morality," *Thought*, Vol. 32 (1957), pp. 533–558.

The selection is from Joseph Fletcher, *Situation Ethics: The New Morality* (Philadelphia: The Westminster Press, 1966), pp. 77-140, with omissions. Copyright © 1966 W. L. Jenkins. Used by permission of The Westminster Press and the foreign publishers: SCM Press Ltd., London; Gütersloher Verlagshaus, Gütersloh; and Llibres del Nopal, Barcelona.

is in his intrinsic rights and wrongs and his collections and systems of virtues and absolutes?

To illustrate what legalism does in the civil order, we might recall what happened a few years ago in an English court. The law reads that a marriage must be validated ("consummated") by sexual union. In the case before it, it found that a young wife had conceived a son by means of A.I.H. (artificial insemination from her husband) because he was suffering a temporary erectile failure, subsequently corrected. The court was faithful to its law, and ruled that the little boy was conceived out of wedlock, i.e., that the child was a bastard, the mother an adulteress or fornicator, the wife husbandless when her child was born, the father without a son and heir, and the child an outlaw. All of this even though their child was seed of their seed, flesh of their flesh!

Augustine was right again, as situationists see it, to reduce the whole Christian ethic to the single maxim, *Dilige et quod vis, fac* (Love with care and *then* what you will, do). It was not, by the way, *Ama et fac quod vis* (Love with desire and do what you please)![4] It was not antinomianism.

Christian love is not desire. *Agapē* is giving love—non-reciprocal, neighbor-regarding—"neighbor" meaning "everybody", even an enemy (Luke 6:32–35). It is usually distinguished from friendship love (*philia*) and romantic love (*erōs*), both of which are selective and exclusive. Erotic love and philic love have their proper place in our human affairs but they are not what is meant by *agapē*, agapeic love or "Christian love." Erotic and philic love are emotional, but the effective principle of Christian love is *will*, disposition; it is an *attitude*, not feeling.

Situationists welcome the German label for this conception, *Gesinnungs-ethik*, an attitudinal ethic rather than a legal one. "Have this mind among yourselves, which you have in Christ Jesus" (Phil. 2:5), and *then*, as Augustine says, whatever you do will be right! The mind of him whom Bonhoeffer called "the Man for others" is to be for others, for neighbors. *That* is *agapē*.

What a difference it makes when love, understood agapeically, is boss; when love is the only norm. How free and therefore responsible we are! The natural law moralists, just to cite an example of legalism, are trapped into cheating on love or even into altogether denying love's demands, in the matter of sterilizations. In the name of a "natural

[4] *Ep. Joan.*, vii. 5, in J. P. Migne, *Patralogiae cursus completus, series Latina* (Paris: Garnier Fr., 1864), Vol. 35, col. 2033. "*Semel ergo breve praeceptum tibi praecipitur, Dilige, et quod vis fac.*"

law" of procreation they have to prohibit obstetricians from tying off the tubes of a cardiac mother in delivery, for whom another pregnancy is a mortal danger. In the name of a "natural law" of secrecy they have been known to admonish a doctor to withhold from an innocent girl the fact that she is about to marry a syphilitic man. No such cut-and-dried, coldly predetermined (prejudiced) position could or would be taken by a situationist.

At this juncture we might do well to look at the question whether a situationist can agree with legalism's effort to *force* people to be good. The answer is, of course, that "it all depends." It seems impossible to see any sound reason for most of such attempts to legislate morality. Yet there was a lot of furious surprise in a California city recently when the police found a wife-swapping club and learned there were *no laws* to stop it. The District Attorney saw no cause to be alarmed, even so. "Wife-swapping just doesn't violate any section of the penal code." It is doubtful that love's cause is helped by any of the sex laws that try to dictate sexual practices for consenting adults.

The triple terrors of infection, conception, and detection, which once scared people into "Christian" sex relations (marital monopoly), have pretty well become obsolete through medicine and urbanism. There is less and less cause, on the basis of situation ethics, for the opinion that people should abide by, or pretend to, an ideal or standard that is not their own. It may well be, especially with the young, that situationists should advise continence or chastity for practical expedient reasons, but that is a situational, not a legalistic approach.

THE END OF IDEOLOGY

Political and social establishments feel safer when buttressed by an ethical establishment, a fixed code. In some circles there is a growing hunger for law; it can be seen in cultural conformism, and in the lust for both political and theological orthodoxy. Like the existentialists to an extent, situationists are in revolt against the cultural stodginess of "respectable" and traditional ethics. They rebel against the reigning ethics of American middle-class culture because of its high-flown moral laws on the one hand and its evasive shilly-shallying on the other; it is often and acutely described as "the leap from Sunday to Monday."

Nothing in the world causes so much conflict of conscience as the continual, conventional payment of lip service to moral "laws" that are constantly flouted in practice because they are too petty or too rigid to fit the facts of life. Many people prefer to fit reality to rules rather than to fit rules to reality. Legalism always bears down hard on the need for order, putting its premium on obedience to law, even statutory law. It would, if it could, immobilize Martin Luther King and the sit-in demonstrators or civil rights protesters, whereas situation ethics gives high-order value to freedom, and to that *responsibility* for free decision which is the obverse side of the coin of freedom.

In ethics as in politics we can see that ideology has come to a dead end. Doctrinaire by-the-book theory and practice is too confining, too narrow. "The point is," says Daniel Bell, "that ideologists are terrible simplifiers. Ideology makes it unnecessary for people to confront individual issues in individual situations. One simply turns to the ideological vending machine, and out comes the prepared formula."[5] Substitute "law" for ideology in Bell's statement and we have the nub of the matter. A committee set up by the late President Kennedy to deal with questions of business ethics, of which the writer of this book was a member, got nowhere at all because it was code-minded, wrote a code to cover all business, and found itself possessed of nothing but platitudes.

For real decision-making, freedom is required, an open-ended approach to situations. Imagine the plight of an obstetrician who believed he must always respirate every baby he delivered, no matter how monstrously deformed! A century ago Thomas Huxley rather thought he would prefer being accurate and correct as a moral decision maker, even if he had to be as mechanical as a clock wound up for the day, than assume the burden of mistakes entailed by freedom. What an irony to compare his opinion to Tik-Tok's in *The Wizard of Oz*! There the mechanical man had the special grace of always doing "what he was wound up to do," but wanted instead to be *human*. And what did he lack? Freedom to choose.

No wonder that Jesus, in the language of a French Catholic moralist whose concern is contemporary, "reacted particularly against code morality and against casuistry," and that his "attitude toward code morality [was] purely and simply one of reaction."[6] Modern Christians ought not to be naïve enough to accept any other view of Jesus' ethic than the situational one. When Edmund Wilson ran his famous article in *The New Yorker* some ten years ago on the Dead Sea Scrolls he made quite a splash by saying that Jesus' teaching was a copy

[5] *The End of Ideology: On the Exhaustion of Political Ideas in the Fifties*, new rev. ed. (Collier Books, 1962), p. 17.

[6] J. LeClercq, *Christ and the Modern Conscience*, pp. 59, 61.

of the Essenes' teaching at the Qumran community.[7] Actually, the quickest way to expose the error in all such uncritical comparisons is simply to point out that the legalism and code rule of the Qumran sect put even the Pharisees to shame, whereas Jesus boldly rejected all such legalisms.

As we know, for many people, sex is so much a moral problem, largely due to the repressive effects of legalism, that in newspapers and popular parlance the term "morals charge" always means a sex complaint! "Her morals are not very high" means her sex life is rather looser than the mores allow. Yet we find nothing in the teachings of Jesus about the ethics of sex, except adultery and an absolute condemnation of divorce—a correlative matter. He said nothing about birth control, large or small families, childlessness, homosexuality, masturbation, fornication or premarital intercourse, sterilization, artificial insemination, abortion, sex play, petting, and courtship. Whether any form of sex (hetero, homo, or auto) is good or evil depends on whether love is fully served.

The Christian ethic is not interested in reluctant virgins and technical chastity. What sex probably needs more than anything is a good airing, demythologizing it and getting rid of its mystique-laden and occult accretions, which come from romanticism on the one hand and puritanism on the other. People are learning that we can have sex without love, and love without sex; that baby-making can be (and often ought to be) separated from love-making. It is, indeed, for re-creation as well as for procreation. But if people do not believe it is wrong to have sex relations outside marriage, it isn't, unless they hurt themselves, their partners, or others. This is, of course, a very big "unless" and gives reason to many to abstain altogether except within the full mutual commitment of marriage. The civil lawmakers are rapidly ridding their books of statutes making unmarried sex a crime between consenting adults. All situationists would agree with Mrs. Patrick Campbell's remark that they can do what they want "as long as they don't do it in the street and frighten the horses."

Situation ethics always suspects prescriptive law of falsifying life and dwarfing moral stature, whether it be the Scripture legalism of Biblicist Protestants and Mohammedans or the nature legalism (natural law) of the Catholics and disciples of Confucius. One American theologian has complained that situation ethics fails to realize that people

---

[7] Republished as *The Scrolls from the Dead Sea* (Oxford University Press, 1955).

are unwilling to grapple with what he calls "paradoxical ambiguities" —that they want something more definite and exact than ethical relativism offers.[8] Of course; they want the Grand Inquisitor. T. S. Eliot was right to say that people cannot bear too much reality. But there is no escape for them. To learn love's sensitive tactics, such people are going to have to put away their childish rules.

PETER A. BERTOCCI (1910–)

Sex and Values

THE HUMAN EXPERIENCE OF SEX

When a person decides that he is going to get all he can out of sex *as sex*, he is driven into an almost endless progression: he must find a new fancy, a new variety of sexual experience, real or imaginary, for he soon tires of the last mode of sexual exploration. Having made sex an end in itself, as a miser makes money an end in itself, or as a glutton makes food an end in itself, there is nothing more to do but seek some more thrilling or novel sexual experience. Many sexual perverts are products of this chase for new forms of pleasure. They teach us that sexual expression for its own sake brings diminishing returns. I am not, of course, trying to say that every incontinent person becomes a sex pervert, but he invites trouble for himself and others when he tries to find in sex what sex as such cannot give him. Sex experience for its own sake, and certainly when the other person is simply "used," hardens the arteries of tender feeling. Though sexual perversion is by no means a necessary result, the loss of tenderness and sympathy, let alone self-confidence, is a tremendous price to pay for sex pleasure.

On the other hand, sex is an increasing source of personal enrichment when dedicated to objectives other than mere self-satisfaction.

---

[8] W. Burnett Easton, Jr., "Ethical Relativism and Popular Morality," *loc. cit.*

The selection is from Peter A. Bertocci, *The Human Venture in Sex, Love, and Marriage* (New York: Association Press; London: Longmans, Green and Co., Ltd., 1949), pp. 47–53. Used by permission of the publishers.

The fact of human experience seems to be that persons enjoy deeper, more lasting, and more profound satisfaction when the normal experience of sex lust is not primarily an end in itself but a symbolic expression of other values. This, after all, is true not only about sex but about other desires also. We enjoy eating at a banquet in honor of a friend more than eating in solitude. Before elaborating this theme, several remarks must be made about a counter-theme that has pervaded, sometimes quite subtly, much thinking about the functioning of sex in human life.

There is a tendency to think of sex in human experience as a continuation of the sex function in animals. Man's life, including sex, is more complicated but not essentially different from that of the higher animals. The prevalence of this view has sometimes led us to suppose that sex education is hardly necessary since at the right time the biological organism will react effectively and appropriately as it does among animals. Thinking of man as a complicated animal, we falsely reasoned that his sex behavior is as mechanical and automatic with him as it is with animals. Indeed some of us added, to expect him to control himself sexually is like expecting an animal in heat to reject sexual advances. The best we can do, according to this view, is to realize that man is a higher animal and teach him enough of the physiology of sex to avoid disease.

This line of reasoning neglects the *human* significance of sex. Sex in the human is so interwoven with his total psychological being that, once allowance is made for some physiological similarities, the contrasts are more illuminating than the likenesses. To compare the sounds an animal makes with the poetry of word symbols gives some notion of the range of differences possible. The biological transaction of sexual intercourse in animals has at its best nowhere near the possible meaning that a similar biological transaction can have in human experience. Sex education has failed to make enough of the function of sex as human experience. In consequence we have talked as if the biology of sex measures its importance as a human function.

Consequently the argument against intercourse has emphasized the physical effects of sexual promiscuity, the danger of sexual diseases and of pregnancy. These must not be minimized, but they have played such a large part in the so-called "case for chastity" that both young and old have wondered, with justification, what possible case can be made against promiscuity once knowledge of the methods of disease prevention and contraceptives has been increased and disseminated. The concern of the military during World War II did not go beyond educating young men and women for physical efficiency.

The general impression was left that sin is not in sexual intercourse but in the infection that may result from carelessness. We seemed to be bankrupt of really adequate reasons why human beings should abstain from promiscuity when they are confident that impregnation or venereal diseases can be prevented.

The situation will not be greatly changed until we become more fully aware of the conditions in human experience under which sexual intercourse makes its deepest contributions. Here we are clearly in the area of the interpretation of the value of sex as part of the meaning of life. If we cannot interpret the higher values of sex as clearly as we have explained physiological, and even psychological, details, we shall go on "expressing" sex and "avoiding frustration" when we might be finding, through sex experience, a creative human joy.

THE HUMAN CHALLENGE IN LOVE

The assumption at this stage of the argument is that love, marriage, and the home are among the supreme values of human existence; that the human beings who cannot enjoy the blessings that love, marriage, and the home bestow are relatively poverty-stricken. We shall try to show that the experience of sex may bless or endanger love, that it may bless or be a constant source of friction in marriage, that it may be a solid foundation for co-operative family life or a source of frustrating disharmony.

As already suggested, there is a "love progression" in human life. This progression is affected by the sexual progression, but it has its own laws. The love progression protects the satisfactions of sex, but sex, unless mastered, will endanger the progression of love and enslave the person. The individual in love invests his energies and abilities in joyous concern for the security and growth of another. He finds fulfillment of his own life in consecration to the needs and development of his beloved. As his love grows, his self-discipline increases with a view to insuring the happiness of his sweetheart. He rethinks and replans the goals of his life so that she may find opportunity and realization within them. "To love a person productively implies to care, to feel responsible for his life, not only for his physical existence, but for the growth and development of all his human powers."[1]

[1] Fromm, Eric. *Man for Himself.* (New York: Farrar & Rinehart)

Loving, therefore, is a kind of growing. Love inspires one to live with at least one other person in mind. The circle of self-enjoyment grows into an ellipse in which the two poles are included. But, as Plato long ago reminded us, love is a suffering yearning for what one does not possess completely. The individual must refocus his mind and body, re-form his ideas and dreams, so that the good he wants for himself and for his sweetheart may be realized. Love means growth; it means work; it means moral progress. Thus *love, inclusive of sex, needs marriage to protect and nourish its values. And marriage, to be a most fruitful and inclusive experience which protects and nourishes the values of both love and sex, must be put to work in building a family and a society.* This is the inner progression of love.

It is evident that there will be many obstacles on the way to realizing personality and character built around love. The deception in the progression of love is just the opposite of that in the sexual progression. For now the individual will be tempted to stop short of more complete fulfillment. It will be easy to think that a sexual experience enjoyed by two persons will remain an adequate source of joy, that the pleasure of sex and love without marriage will endure, that marriage without commitment to objectives greater than the union of two married lovers will maintain a challenging equilibrium. For there is no doubt that sex lust usually brings pleasure sufficiently gratifying to seem entirely satisfactory, especially to those who do not know the quality of sex love. So also with this next step in the progression of love: sex love without marriage can bring so much satisfaction, at least for a time, that two persons may be tempted to forego the more complete satisfaction of married love. Then there are some who, having reached a high level of married love, may be tempted to forfeit the more creative experience that children and a home can bring.

Let the sexual act be the expression of the conscious desire and decision to become parents, and that act reaches its zenith in human feeling, inspiration, and fulfillment. It is almost foolish to try to make this experience clear to those who have not known it. Words that receive their content from other levels of sex experience are quite inadequate for this. Let two persons extend their love for each other into the tender and responsible decision to have and care for children, and they will find the meaning of the sexual experience immeasurably enriched.

Sex, love, marriage, family, and social responsibility are human ventures all along the line. The question is: Which venture brings completeness, invites to growth in character and personality, enables the individual to feel that he has accepted the role that his abilities allow in the achievement of a dependable social order? It is our thesis that love, including sex love, is the more radiant and satisfying when it becomes a means of communicating one's concern for the wider range of values that purposeful living together makes possible. Sex without love, love without marriage, and marriage without creative commitments to children (or the equivalent) are in constant danger of vanishing away. Persons disregard the laws of growth and development in human nature only to find that they have forfeited their heritage.

Love, at its best, is the supreme victory over parasitism and egoism. It is a unique fruition of human experience, so unique and so different from anything in the physical and biological world, that it stands as the richest product of human effort. It is not, however, a fruit which just comes with maturation. It will be no greater than the person in love; it will reflect and challenge the intelligence, emotion, and discipline dedicated to its development.

THOMAS NAGEL (1937—)

Sexual Perversion

There is something to be learned about sex from the fact that we possess a concept of sexual perversion. I wish to examine the concept, defending it against the charge of unintelligibility and trying to say exactly what about human sexuality qualifies it to admit of perversions. Let me make some preliminary comments about the problem before embarking on its solution.

Some people do not believe that the notion of sexual perversion makes sense, and even those who do disagree over its application. Nevertheless I think it will be widely conceded that, if the concept is viable at all, it must meet certain general conditions. First, if there are any sexual perversions, they will have to be sexual desires or

The selection is from Thomas Nagel, "Sexual Perversion," *The Journal of Philosophy*, Vol. LXVI, Number 1, January 16, 1969, pp. 5–17. Used by permission of the Editor and Author.

practices that can be plausibly described as in some sense unnatural, though the explanation of this natural/unnatural distinction is of course the main problem. Second, certain practices will be perversions if anything is, such as shoe fetishism, bestiality, and sadism; other practices, such as unadorned sexual intercourse, will not be; about still others there is controversy. Third, if there are perversions, they will be unnatural sexual *inclinations* rather than merely unnatural practices adopted not from inclination but for other reasons. I realize that this is at variance with the view, maintained by some Roman Catholics, that contraception is a sexual perversion. But although contraception may qualify as a deliberate perversion of the sexual and reproductive functions, it cannot be significantly described as a *sexual* perversion. A sexual perversion must reveal itself in conduct that expresses an unnatural *sexual* preference. And although there might be a form of fetishism focused on the employment of contraceptive devices, that is not the usual explanation for their use.

I wish to declare at the outset my belief that the connection between sex and reproduction has no bearing on sexual perversion. The latter is a concept of psychological, not physiological interest, and it is a concept that we do not apply to the lower animals, let alone to plants, all of which have reproductive functions that can go astray in various ways. (Think of seedless oranges.) Insofar as we are prepared to regard higher animals as perverted, it is because of their psychological, not their anatomical similarity to humans. Furthermore, we do not regard as a perversion every deviation from the reproductive function of sex in humans: sterility, miscarriage, contraception, abortion.

Another matter that I believe has no bearing on the concept of sexual perversion is social disapprobation or custom. Anyone inclined to think that in each society the perversions are those sexual practices of which the community disapproves, should consider all the societies that have frowned upon adultery and fornication. These have not been regarded as unnatural practices, but have been thought objectionable in other ways. What is regarded as unnatural admittedly varies from culture to culture, but the classification is not a pure expression of disapproval or distaste. In fact it is often regarded as a *ground* for disapproval, and that suggests that the classification has an independent content.

I am going to attempt a psychological account of sexual perversion, which will depend on a specific psychological theory of sexual desire and human sexual interactions. To approach this solution I wish first to consider a contrary position, one which provides a basis for skepticism about the existence of any sexual perversions at all, and perhaps about the very significance of the term. The skeptical argument runs as follows:

"Sexual desire is simply one of the appetites, like hunger and thirst. As such it may have various objects, some more common than others perhaps, but none in any sense 'natural'. An appetite is identified as sexual by means of the organs and erogenous zones in which its satisfaction can be to some extent localized, and the special sensory pleasures which form the core of that satisfaction. This enables us to recognize widely divergent goals, activities, and desires as sexual, since it is conceivable in principle that anything should produce sexual pleasure and that a nondeliberate, sexually charged desire for it should arise (as a result of conditioning, if nothing else). We may fail to emphathize with some of these desires, and some of them, like sadism, may be objectionable on extraneous grounds, but once we have observed that they meet the criteria for being sexual, there is nothing more to be said on *that* score. Either they are sexual or they are not: sexuality does not admit of imperfection, or perversion, or any other such qualification—it is not that sort of affection."

This is probably the received radical position. It suggests that the cost of defending a psychological account may be to deny that sexual desire is an appetite. But insofar as that line of defense is plausible, it should make us suspicious of the simple picture of appetites on which the skepticism depends. Perhaps the standard appetites, like hunger, cannot be classed as pure appetites in that sense either, at least in their human versions.

Let us approach the matter by asking whether we can imagine anything that would qualify as a gastronomical perversion. Hunger and eating are importantly like sex in that they serve a biological function and also play a significant role in our inner lives. It is noteworthy that there is little temptation to describe as perverted an appetite for substances that are not nourishing. We should probably not consider someone's appetites as *perverted* if he liked to eat paper, sand, wood, or cotton. Those are merely rather odd and very unhealthy tastes: they lack the psychological complexity that we expect of perversions. (Coprophilia, being already a sexual perversion, may be disregarded.) If on the other hand someone liked to eat cookbooks, or magazines with pictures of food in them, and preferred these to ordinary food—or if when hungry he sought satisfaction by fondling a napkin or ashtray from his favorite restaurant—then the concept of perversion might seem appropriate (in fact it would be natural to describe this as a case of gastronomical fetishism). It would be natural to describe as gastronomically perverted someone who could eat only by having food forced down his throat through a funnel, or only if the meal were a living animal. What helps in such cases is the peculiarity of the desire itself, rather than the inappropriateness of its object to the biological function that the desire serves. Even an appetite, it would seem, can have perversions if in addition to its biological function it has a significant psychological structure.

In the case of hunger, psychological complexity is provided by the activities that give it expression. Hunger is not merely a disturbing sensation that can be quelled by eating; it is an attitude toward edible portions of the external world, a desire to relate to them in rather special ways. The method of ingestion: chewing, savoring, swallowing, appreciating the texture and smell, all are important components of the relation, as is the passivity and controllability of the food (the only animals we eat live are helpless mollusks). Our relation to food depends also on our size: we do not live upon it or burrow into it like aphids or worms. Some of these features are more central than others, but any adequate phenomenology of eating would have to treat it as a relation to the external world and a way of appropriating bits of that world, with characteristic affection. Displacements or serious restrictions of the desire to eat could then be described as perversions, if they undermined that direct relation between man and food which is the natural expression of hunger. This explains why it is easy to imagine gastronomical fetishism, voyeurism, exhibitionism, or even gastronomical sadism and masochism. Indeed some of these perversions are fairly common.

If we can imagine perversions of an appetite like hunger, it should be possible to make sense of the concept of sexual perversion. I do not wish to imply that sexual desire is an appetite—only that being an appetite is no bar to admitting of perversions. Like hunger, sexual desire has as its characteristic object a certain relation with something in the external world; only in this case it is usually a person rather than an omelet, and the relation is considerably more complicated. This added complication allows scope for correspondingly complicated perversions.

The fact that sexual desire is a feeling about other persons may tempt us to take a pious view of its psychological content. There are those who believe that sexual desire is properly the expression of some other attitude, like love, and that when it occurs by itself it is incomplete and unhealthy—or at any rate subhuman. (The extreme Platonic version of such a view is that sexual practices are all vain attempts to express something they cannot in principle achieve: this makes them all perversions, in a sense.) I do not believe that any such view is correct. Sexual desire is complicated enough without having to be linked to anything else as a condition for phenomenological analysis. It cannot be denied that sex may serve various functions—economic, social, altruistic—but it also has its own content as a relation between persons, and it is only by analyzing that relation that we can understand the conditions of sexual perversion.

I believe it is very important that the object of sexual attraction is a particular individual, who transcends the properties that make him attractive. When different persons are attracted to a single person for different reasons: eyes, hair, figure, laugh, intelligence—we feel that the object of their desire is nevertheless the same, namely that person. There is even an inclination to feel that this is so if the lovers have different sexual aims, if they include both men and women, for example. Different specific attractive characteristics seem to provide enabling conditions for the operation of a single basic feeling, and the different aims all provide expressions of it. We approach the sexual attitude toward the person through the features that we find attractive, but these features are not the objects of that attitude.

This is very different from the case of an omelet. Various people may desire it for different reasons, one for its fluffiness, another for its mushrooms, another for its unique combination of aroma and visual aspect; yet we do not enshrine the transcendental omelet as the true common object of their affections. Instead we might say that several desires have accidentally converged on the same object: any omelet with the crucial characteristics would do as well. It is not similarly true that any person with the same flesh distribution and way of smoking can be substituted as object for a particular sexual desire that has been elicited by those characteristics. It may be that they will arouse attraction whenever they recur, but it will be a new sexual attraction with a new particular object, not merely a transfer of the old desire to someone else. (I believe this is true even in cases where the new object is unconsciously identified with a former one.)

The importance of this point will emerge when we see how complex a psychological interchange constitutes the natural development of sexual attraction. This would be incomprehensible if its object were not a particular person, but rather a person of a certain *kind*. Attraction is only the beginning, and fulfillment does not consist merely of behavior and contact expressing this attraction, but involves much more.

The best discussion of these matters that I have seen appears in part III of Sartre's *Being and Nothingness*.[1] Since it has influenced my own views, I shall say a few things about it now. Sartre's treatment of sexual desire and of love, hate, sadism, masochism, and further attitudes toward others, depends on a general theory of consciousness and the body which we can neither expound nor assume here. He does not discuss perversion, and this is partly because he regards sexual desire as one form of the perpetual attempt of an embodied consciousness to come to terms with the existence of others, an attempt that is as doomed to fail in this form as it is in any of the others, which include sadism and masochism (if not certain of the more impersonal deviations) as well as several nonsexual attitudes. According to Sartre, all attempts to incorporate the other into my world as another subject, i.e., to apprehend him at once as an object for me and as a subject for whom I am an object, are unstable and doomed to collapse into one or other of the two aspects. Either I reduce him entirely to an object, in which case his subjectivity escapes the possession or appropriation I can extend to that object; or I become merely an object for him, in which case I am no longer in a position to appropriate his subjectivity. Moreover, neither of these aspects is stable; each is continually in danger of giving way to the other. This has the consequence that there can be no such thing as a *successful* sexual relation, since the deep aim of sexual desire cannot in principle be accomplished. It seems likely, therefore, that the view will not permit a basic distinction between successful or complete and unsuccessful or incomplete sex, and therefore cannot admit the concept of perversion.

I do not adopt this aspect of the theory, nor many of its metaphysical underpinnings. What interests me is Sartre's picture of the attempt. He says that the type of possession that is the object of sexual desire is carried out by "a double reciprocal incarnation" and that this is accomplished, typically in the form of a caress, in the following way: "I make myself flesh in order to impel the Other to realize *for-herself* and *for me* her own flesh, and my caresses cause my flesh to

[1] Translated by Hazel E. Barnes (New York: Philosophical Library: 1956).

be born for me in so far as it is for the Other *flesh causing her to be born as flesh*" (391; italics Sartre's). The incarnation in question is described variously as a clogging or troubling of consciousness, which is inundated by the flesh in which it is embodied.

The view I am going to suggest, I hope in less obscure language, is related to this one, but it differs from Sartre's in allowing sexuality to achieve its goal on occasion and thus in providing the concept of perversion with a foothold.

Sexual desire involves a kind of perception, but not merely a single perception of its object, for in the paradigm case of mutual desire there is a complex system of superimposed mutual perceptions—not only perceptions of the sexual object, but perceptions of oneself. Moreover, sexual awareness of another involves considerable self-awareness to begin with—more than is involved in ordinary sensory perception. The experience is felt as an assault on oneself by the view (or touch, or whatever) of the sexual object.

Let us consider a case in which the elements can be separated. For clarity we will restrict ourselves initially to the somewhat artificial case of desire at a distance. Suppose a man and a woman, whom we may call Romeo and Juliet, are at opposite ends of a cocktail lounge, with many mirrors on the walls which permit unobserved observation, and even mutual unobserved observation. Each of them is sipping a martini and studying other people in the mirrors. At some point Romeo notices Juliet. He is moved, somehow, by the softness of her hair and the diffidence with which she sips her martini, and this arouses him sexually. Let us say that X *senses* Y whenever X regards Y with sexual desire. (Y need not be a person, and X's apprehension of Y can be visual, tactile, olfactory, etc., or purely imaginary; in the present example we shall concentrate on vision.) So Romeo senses Juliet, rather than merely noticing her. At this stage he is aroused by an unaroused object, so he is more in the sexual grip of his body than she of hers.

Let us suppose, however, that Juliet now senses Romeo in another mirror on the opposite wall, though neither of them yet knows that he is seen by the other (the mirror angles provide three-quarter views). Romeo then begins to notice in Juliet the subtle signs of sexual arousal: heavy-lidded stare, dilating pupils, faint flush, et cetera. This of course renders her much more bodily, and he not only notices but senses this as well. His arousal is nevertheless still solitary. But now, cleverly calculating the line of her stare without actually looking her in the eyes, he realizes that it is directed at him through the mirror on the opposite wall. That is, he notices, and moreover senses, Juliet sensing him. This is definitely a new development, for it gives him a sense of embodiment not only through his own reactions but through the eyes and reactions of another. Moreover, it is separable from the initial sensing of Juliet; for sexual arousal might begin with a person's sensing that he is sensed and being assailed by the perception of the other person's desire rather than merely by the perception of the person.

But there is a further step. Let us suppose that Juliet, who is a little slower than Romeo, now senses that he senses her. This puts Romeo in a position to notice, and be aroused by, her arousal at being sensed by him. He senses that she senses that he senses her. This is still another level of arousal, for he becomes conscious of his sexuality through his awareness of its effect on her and of her awareness that this effect is due to him. Once she takes the same step and senses that he senses her sensing him, it becomes difficult to state, let alone imagine, further iterations, though they may be logically distinct. If both are alone, they will presumably turn to look at each other directly, and the proceedings will continue on another plane. Physical contact and intercourse are perfectly natural extensions of this complicated visual exchange, and mutual touch can involve all the complexities of awareness present in the visual case, but with a far greater range of subtlety and acuteness.

Ordinarily, of course, things happen in a less orderly fashion—sometimes in a great rush—but I believe that some version of this overlapping system of distinct sexual perceptions and interactions is the basic framework of any full-fledged sexual relation and that relations involving only part of the complex are significantly incomplete. The account is only schematic, as it must be to achieve generality. Every real sexual act will be psychologically far more specific and detailed, in ways that depend not only on the physical techniques employed and on anatomical details, but also on countless features of the participants' conceptions of themselves and of each other, which become embodied in the **act**. (It is a familiar enough fact, for example, that people often take their social roles and the social roles of their partners to bed with them.)

The general schema is important, however, and the proliferation of levels of mutual awareness it involves is an example of a type of complexity that typifies human interactions. Consider aggression, for example. If I am angry with someone, I want to make him feel it, either to produce self-reproach by getting him to see himself through the eyes of my anger, and to dislike what he sees—or else to produce reciprocal anger or fear, by getting him to perceive my anger as a threat or attack. What I want will depend on the details of my anger, but in either case it will involve a desire that the object of that anger be aroused. This accomplishment constitutes the fulfillment of my emotion, through domination of the object's feelings.

Another example of such reflexive mutual recognition is to be found in the phenomenon of meaning, which appears to involve an intention to produce a belief or other effect in another by bringing about his recognition of one's intention to produce that effect. (That result is due to H. P. Grice,[2] whose position I shall not attempt to reproduce in detail.) Sex has a related structure: it involves a desire that one's partner be aroused by the recognition of one's desire that he or she be aroused.

It is not easy to define the basic types of awareness and arousal of which these complexes are composed, and that remains a lacuna in this discussion. I believe that the object of awareness is the same in one's own case as it is in one's sexual awareness of another, although the two awarenesses will not be the same, the difference being as great as that between feeling angry and experiencing the anger of another. All stages of sexual perception are varieties of identification of a person with his body. What is perceived is one's own or another's *subjection* to or *immersion* in his body, a phenomenon which has been recognized with loathing by St. Paul and St. Augustine, both of whom regarded "the law of sin which is in my members" as a grave threat to the dominion of the holy will.[3] In sexual desire and its expression the blending of involuntary response with deliberate control is extremely important. For Augustine, the revolution launched against him by his body is symbolized by erection and the other involuntary physical components of arousal. Sartre too stresses the fact that the penis is not a prehensile organ. But mere involuntariness characterizes other bodily processes as well. In sexual desire the involuntary responses are combined with submission to spontaneous impulses: not only one's pulse and secretions but one's actions are taken over by the body; ideally, deliberate control is needed only to guide the expression of those impulses. This is to some extent also true of an appetite like hunger, but the takeover there is more localized,

[2] "Meaning," *Philosophical Review*, LXVI, 3 (July 1957): 377–388.
[3] See Romans, VII, 23; and the *Confessions*, Book 8, v.

less pervasive, less extreme. One's whole body does not become saturated with hunger as it can with desire. But the most characteristic feature of a specifically sexual immersion in the body is its ability to fit into the complex of mutual perceptions that we have described. Hunger leads to spontaneous interactions with food; sexual desire leads to spontaneous interactions with other persons, whose bodies are asserting their sovereignty in the same way, producing involuntary reactions and spontaneous impulses in *them*. These reactions are perceived, and the perception of them is perceived, and that perception is in turn perceived; at each step the domination of the person by his body is reinforced, and the sexual partner becomes more possessible by physical contact, penetration, and envelopment.

Desire is therefore not merely the perception of a preexisting embodiment of the other, but ideally a contribution to his further embodiment which in turn enhances the original subject's sense of himself. This explains why it is important that the partner be aroused, and not merely aroused, but aroused by the awareness of one's desire. It also explains the sense in which desire has unity and possession as its object: physical possession must eventuate in creation of the sexual object in the image of one's desire, and not merely in the object's recognition of that desire, or in his or her own private arousal. (This may reveal a male bias: I shall say something about that later.)

To return, finally, to the topic of perversion: I believe that various familiar deviations constitute truncated or incomplete versions of the complete configuration, and may therefore be regarded as perversions of the central impulse.

In particular, narcissistic practices and intercourse with animals, infants, and inanimate objects seem to be stuck at some primitive version of the first stage. If the object is not alive, the experience is reduced entirely to an awareness of one's own sexual embodiment. Small children and animals permit awareness of the embodiment of the other, but present obstacles to reciprocity, to the recognition by the sexual object of the subject's desire as the source of his (the object's) sexual self-awareness.

Sadism concentrates on the evocation of passive self-awareness in others, but the sadist's engagement is itself active and requires a retention of deliberate control which impedes awareness of himself as a bodily subject of passion in the required sense. The victim must recognize him as the source of his own sexual passivity, but only as the active source. De Sade claimed that the object of sexual desire was to evoke involuntary responses from one's partner, especially audible ones. The infliction of pain is no doubt the most efficient way to accomplish this, but it requires a certain abrogation of one's own exposed spontaneity. All this, incidentally, helps to explain why it is tempting to regard as sadistic an excessive preoccupation with sexual technique, which does not permit one to abandon the role of agent at any stage of the sexual act. Ideally one should be able to surmount one's technique at some point.

A masochist on the other hand imposes the same disability on his partner as the sadist imposes on himself. The masochist cannot find a satisfactory embodiment as the object of another's sexual desire, but only as the object of his control. He is passive not in relation to his partner's passion but in relation to his nonpassive agency. In addition, the subjection to one's body characteristic of pain and physical restraint is of a very different kind from that of sexual excitement: pain causes people to contract rather than dissolve.

Both of these disorders have to do with the second stage, which involves the awareness of oneself as an object of desire. In straight forward sadism and masochism other attentions are substituted for desire as a source of the object's self-awareness. But it is also possible for nothing of that sort to be substituted, as in the case of a masochist who is satisfied with self-inflicted pain or of a sadist who does not insist on playing a role in the suffering that arouses him. Greater difficulties of classification are presented by three other categories of sexual activity: elaborations of the sexual act; intercourse of more than two persons; and homosexuality.

If we apply our model to the various forms that may be taken by two-party heterosexual intercourse, none of them seem clearly to qualify as perversions. Hardly anyone can be found these days to inveigh against oral-genital contact, and the merits of buggery are urged by such respectable figures as D. H. Lawrence and Norman Mailer. There may be something vaguely sadistic about the latter technique (in Mailer's writings it seems to be a method of introducing an element of rape), but it not obvious that this has to be so. In general, it would appear that any bodily contact between a man and a woman that gives them sexual pleasure is a possible vehicle for the system of multi-level interpersonal awareness that I have claimed is the basic psychological content of sexual interaction. Thus a liberal platitude about sex is upheld.

About multiple combinations, the least that can be said is that they are bound to be complicated. If one considers how difficult it is to carry on two conversations simultaneously, one may appreciate the problems of multiple simultaneous interpersonal perception that can arise in even a small-scale orgy. It may be inevitable that some of the component relations should degenerate into mutual epidermal stimulation by participants otherwise isolated from each other. There may also be a tendency toward voyeurism and exhibitionism, both of which are incomplete relations. The exhibitionist wishes to display his desire without needing to be desired in return; he may even fear the sexual attentions of others. A voyeur, on the other hand, need not require any recognition by his object at all: certainly not a recognition of the voyeur's arousal.

It is not clear whether homosexuality is a perversion if that is measured by the standard of the described configuration, but it seems unlikely. For such a classification would have to depend on the possibility of extracting from the system a distinction between male and female sexuality; and much that has been said so far applies equally to men and women. Moreover, it would have to be maintained that there was a natural tie between the type of sexuality and the sex of the body, and also that two sexualities of the same type could not interact properly.

Certainly there is much support for an aggressive-passive distinction between male and female sexuality. In our culture the male's arousal tends to initiate the perceptual exchange, he usually makes the sexual approach, largely controls the course of the act, and of course penetrates whereas the woman receives. When two men or two women engage in intercourse they cannot both adhere to these sexual roles. The question is how essential the roles are to an adequate sexual relation. One relevant observation is that a good deal of deviation from these roles occurs in heterosexual intercourse. Women can be sexually aggressive and men passive, and temporary reversals of role are not uncommon in heterosexual exchanges of reasonable length. If such conditions are set aside, it may be urged that there is something irreducibly perverted in attraction to a body anatomically like one's own. But alarming as some people in our culture may find such attraction, it remains psychologically unilluminating to class it as perverted. Certainly if homosexuality is a perversion, it is so in a very different sense from that in which shoe-fetishism is a perversion, for some version of the full range of interpersonal perceptions seems perfectly possible between two persons of the same sex.

In any case, even if the proposed model is correct, it remains implausible to describe as perverted every deviation from it. For example, if the partners in heterosexual intercourse indulge in private heterosexual fantasies, that obscures the recognition of the real partner and so, on the theory, constitutes a defective sexual relation. It is not, however, generally regarded as a perversion. Such examples suggest that a simple dichotomy between perverted and unperverted sex is too crude to organize the phenomena adequately.

I should like to close with some remarks about the relation of perversion to good, bad, and morality. The concept of perversion can hardly fail to be evaluative in some sense, for it appears to involve the notion of an ideal or at least adequate sexuality which the perversions in some way fail to achieve. So, if the concept is viable, the judgment that a person or practice or desire is perverted will constitute a sexual evaluation, implying that better sex, or a better specimen of sex, is possible. This in itself is a very weak claim, since the evaluation might be in a dimension that is of little interest to us. (Though, if my account is correct, that will not be true.)

Whether it is a moral evaluation, however, is another question entirely—one whose answer would require more understanding of both morality and perversion than can be deployed here. Moral evaluation of acts and of persons is a rather special and very complicated matter, and by no means all our evaluation of persons and their activities are moral evaluations. We make judgments about people's beauty or health or intelligence which are evaluative without being moral. Assessments of their sexuality may be similar in that respect.

Furthermore, moral issues aside, it is not clear that unperverted sex is necessarily *preferable* to the perversions. It may be that sex which receives the highest marks for perfection *as sex* is less enjoyable than certain perversions; and if enjoyment is considered very important, that might outweigh considerations of sexual perfection in determining rational preference.

That raises the question of the relation between the evaluative content of judgments of perversion and the rather common *general* distinction between good and bad sex. The latter distinction is usually confined to sexual acts, and it would seem, within limits, to cut across the other: even someone who believed, for example, that homosexuality was a perversion could admit a distinction between better and worse homosexual sex, and might even allow that good homosexual sex could be better *sex* than not very good unperverted sex.

If this is correct, it supports the position that, if judgments of perversion are viable at all, they represent only one aspect of the possible evaluation of sex, even *qua sex*. Moreover it is not the only important aspect: certainly sexual deficiencies that evidently do not constitute perversions can be the object of great concern.

Finally, even if perverted sex is to that extent not so good as it might be, bad sex is generally better than none at all. This should not be controversial: it seems to hold for other important matters, like food, music, literature, and society. In the end, one must choose from among the available alternatives, whether their availability depends on the environment or on one's own constitution. And the alternatives have to be fairly grim before it becomes rational to opt for nothing.

ALIENATION

The general theme of alienation is now widely known and developed. Introduced in its modern form by Hegel, it has been utilized and exploited in a number of fields. The literature and drama of two continents—if not the world—have pictured alienated man in a variety of contexts; and social scientists, especially sociologists and psychologists, have found the concept of alienation to be an important explanatory tool. Philosophers and theologians too have taken alienation as a clue to man's situation in the modern world.

What is alienation? In their important anthology on the subject,[1] Eric and Mary Josephson write that

in modern terms . . . 'alienation' has been used by philosophers, psychologists and sociologists to refer to an extraordinary variety of psychosocial disorders, including loss of self, anxiety states, anomie, despair, depersonalization, rootlessness, apathy, social disorganization, loneliness, atomization, powerlessness, meaninglessness, isolation, pessimism, and the loss of beliefs or values.

[1] *Man Alone* (New York: Dell Publishing Co., Inc., 1962). This introduction, together with some of its references, owes much to the Josephsons' book.

In a similar vein, the philosopher F. H. Heinemann has written that

> the facts to which the term 'alienation' refers are, objectively, different kinds of dissociation, break or rupture between human beings and their objects, whether the latter be other persons, or the natural world, or their own creations in art, science and society: and subjectively, the corresponding states of disequilibrium, disturbance, strangeness and anxiety.

Together these statements suggest that the root meaning of alienation is man's loss of identity or selfhood through the breakdown of those relations that constitute and maintain personal identity.

It is also to be noted that alienation is a term used primarily in descriptions of modern man. This is not to deny that many of the experiences—despair, loneliness, loss of belief—were experienced by earlier generations. But the emergence of the individual, of the solitary human atom, together with a technological and mass society, has made alienation a critical modern problem. These two—individualism and mass society—are peculiarly related in reference to alienation: mass society tends to destroy traditional human groupings such as the family, thus isolating individuals; and the alienated individual finds it impossible to appropriate meaningfully the culture maintained by mass society. Indeed, a vicious circle results which for many can be broken only by revolt, rejection, and even a choice of estrangement as the basic mode of relating to the world.

As can be expected, the self-division of alienation has been discussed and analyzed in a variety of ways. The selections that follow reflect this variety: Hegel finds alienation in man's self-consciousness and the crises in his spiritual life, Marx finds it in the economic conditions of capitalistic societies, Simmel concentrates on the rise of metropolitan life, Weiss explores psychological aspects of alienation, Jaspers accuses technology, and Arendt finds alienation produced by the totality of conditions in modern mass society. For students of ethics, much of this literature will seem only descriptive. The problems of normative ethics (acceptable judgments of obligation and value, it will be remembered) and meta-ethics (the meaning and justification of such moral judgments) are more implicit than explicit, though they are surely present. But the literature on alienation may be taken as posing a more radical problem, namely, that of the very existence any longer of ethical behavior and of reflective ethical theory. The fact of alienation is not the only basis for such a question—some

students, for example, may wonder about the implications of scientific
determinism for ethics—but it is certainly one of them.

Because the problem of alienation involves both individuals
and society, it serves as an important transition from topics in individual ethics to those in social ethics. Very much an individual
experience, alienation has deep social roots and origins as well. Some
observers would in fact treat alienation as primarily a problem for
social ethics. A firm decision about classifying the concept need not
be made here, however; far more important are the ethical issues it
raises on individual and social levels. The following materials discuss
alienation with both these levels in mind.

G. W. F. HEGEL (1770-1831)

The Unhappy Consciousness

In Scepticism consciousness gets, in truth, to know itself as a
consciousness containing contradiction within itself. From the experience of this proceeds a new attitude which brings together the two
thoughts which Scepticism holds apart. The want of intelligence
which Scepticism manifests regarding itself is bound to vanish, because
it is in fact *one* consciousness which possesses these two modes within
it. This new attitude consequently is one which is *aware* of being the
double consciousness of itself as self-liberating, unalterable, self-
identical, and as utterly self-confounding, self-perverting; and this
new attitude is the consciousness of this contradiction within itself.

In Stoicism, self-consciousness is the bare and simple freedom
of itself. In Scepticism, it realizes itself, negates the other side of
determinate existence, but, in so doing, really doubles itself, and is
itself now a duality. In this way the duplication, which previously
was divided between two individuals, the lord and the bondsman, is
concentrated into one. Thus we have here that dualizing of self-
consciousness within itself; which lies essentially in the notion of

The selection is from G. W. F. Hegel, *The Phenomenology of Mind,* 2nd ed., trans. J. B.
Baillie (New York: The Macmillan Company; London: George Allen & Unwin, Ltd.,
1931)., pp. 250–259. Reprinted by permission of Harper & Row, Publishers, Inc.

mind; but the unity of the two elements is not yet present. Hence the *Unhappy Consciousness.*[1] Alienated Soul which is the consciousness of self as a divided nature, a doubled and merely contradictory being.

This unhappy consciousness, divided and at variance within itself, must, because this contradiction of its essential nature is felt to be a single consciousness, always have in the one consciousness the other also; and thus must be straightway driven out of each in turn, when he thinks it has therein attained to the victory and rest of unity. Its true return into itself, or reconciliation with itself, will, however, display the notion of mind endowed with a life and existence of its own, because it implicitly involves the fact that, while being an undivided consciousness, it is a double-consciousness. It is itself the gazing of one self-consciousness into another, and itself is both, and the unity of both is also its own essence; but objectively and consciously it is not yet this essence itself—is not yet the unity of both.

Since, in the first instance, it is the immediate, the implicit unity of both, while for it they are not one and the same, but opposed, it takes one, namely, the simple unalterable, as essential, the other, the manifold and changeable as the unessential. For it, both are realities foreign to each other. Itself, because consciousness of this contradiction, assumes the aspect of changeable consciousness and is to itself the unessential; but as consciousness of unchangeableness, of the ultimate essence, it must, at the same time, proceed to free itself from the unessential, i.e., to liberate itself from itself. For though in its own view it is indeed only the changeable, and the unchangeable is foreign and extraneous to it, yet itself is simple, and therefore unchangeable consciousness, of which consequently it is conscious as its essence, but still in such wise that itself is again in its own regard not this essence. The position, which it assigns to both, cannot, therefore, be an indifference of one to the other, i.e., cannot be an indifference of itself towards the unchangeable. Rather it is immediately both itself; and the relation of both assumes for it the form of a relation of essence to the non-essential, so that this latter has to be cancelled; but since both are to it equally essential and are contradictory, it is only the conflicting contradictory process in which opposite does not come to

---

[1] The term "ungluckliches Bowusstsein" is designed as a summary expression for the following movement, there being no recognized general term for this purpose, as in the case of "Stoicism." The term hardly seems fortunate: with the following analysis should be read Hegel's *Philosophy of History*, part 4, sec. 2, c. 1 and 2. (Eng. tr. pp. 380–415) and *History of Philosophy*, part 2, Introduction. *Tr.*

rest in its own opposite, but produces itself therein afresh merely as an opposite.

Here, then, there is a struggle against an enemy, victory over whom really means being worsted, where to have attained one result is really to lose it in the opposite. Consciousness of life, of its existence and action, is merely pain and sorrow over this existence and activity; for therein consciousness finds only consciousness of its opposite as its essence—and of its own nothingness. Elevating itself beyond this, it passes to the unchangeable. But this elevation is itself this same consciousness. It is, therefore, immediately consciousness of the opposite, viz. of itself as single, individual, particular. The unchangeable, which comes to consciousness, is in that very fact at the same time affected by particularity, and is only present with this latter. Instead of particularly having been abolished in the consciousness of immutability, it only continues to appear there still.

In this process, however, consciousness experiences just this appearance of particularity in the unchangeable, and of the unchangeable in particularity. Consciousness becomes aware of particularity *in general* in the immutable essence, and at the same time it there finds its own particularity. For the truth of this process is precisely that the double consciousness is one and single. This unity becomes a fact to it, but in the first instance the unity is one in which the diversity of both factors is still the dominant feature. Owing to this, consciousness has before it the threefold way in which particularity is connected with unchangeableness. In one form it comes before itself as opposed to the unchangeable essence, and is thrown back to the beginning of that struggle, which is, from first to last, the principle constituting the entire situation. At another time it finds the unchangeable appearing in the form of particularity; so that the latter is an embodiment of unchangeableness, into which, in consequence, the entire form of existence passes. In the third case, it discovers *itself* to be this particular fact in the unchangeable. The first unchangeable is taken to be merely the alien, external Being,[2] which passes sentence on particular existence; since the second unchangeable is a form or mode of particularity like itself,[3] it, i.e., the consciousness, becomes in the third place spirit (*Geist*), has the joy of finding itself therein, and becomes aware within itself that its particularity has been reconciled with the universal.[4]

[2] God as Judge *Tr.*
[3] Christ. *Tr.*
[4] The religious communion. *Tr.*

What is set forth here as a mode and relation of the unchangeable, came to light as the experience through which self-consciousness passes in its unhappy state of diremption. This experience is now doubtless not its own onesided process; for it is itself unchangeable consciousness; and this latter, consequently, is a particular consciousness as well; and the process is as much a process of that unchangeable consciousness, which makes its appearance there as certainly as the other. For that movement is carried on in these moments: an unchangeable now opposed to the particular in general, then, being itself particular, opposed to the other particular, and finally at one with it. But this consideration, so far as it is our affair,[5] is here out of place, for thus far we have only had to do with unchangeableness as unchangeableness of *consciousness*, which, for that reason, is not true immutability, but is still affected with an opposite; we have not had before us the unchangeable *per se* and by itself; we do not, therefore, know how this latter will conduct itself. What has here so far come to light is merely this, that to consciousness, which is our object here, the determinations above indicated appear in the unchangeable.

For this reason, then, the unchangeable consciousness also preserves, in its very form and bearing, the character and fundamental features of diremption and separate self-existence, as against the particular consciousness. For the latter it is thus altogether a contingency, a mere chance event, that the unchangeable receives the form of particularity; just as the particular consciousness merely happens to find itself opposed to the unchangeable, and therefore has this relation *per naturam.* Finally that it *finds itself* in the unchangeable appears to the particular consciousness to be brought about partly, no doubt, by itself, or to take place for the reason that itself is particular; but this union, both as regards its origin as well as in its being, appears partly also due to the unchangeable; and the opposition remains within this unity itself. In point of fact, through the unchangeable assuming a definite form, the "beyond," as a moment, has not only remained, but really is more securely established. For if the remote "beyond" seems indeed brought closer to the individual by this particular form of realization, on the other hand, it is henceforward fixedly opposed to the individual, a sensuous, impervious unit, with all the hard resistance of what is actual. The hope of becoming one therewith must remain a hope, i.e., without fulfilment, without present fruition; for between the hope and fulfilment there stands

[5] I.e. the philosophical observer. *Tr.*

precisely the absolute contingency, or immovable indifference, which is involved in the very assumption of determinate shape and form, the basis and foundation of the hope. By the nature of this existent unit, through the particular reality it has assumed and adopted, it comes about of necessity that it becomes a thing of the past, something that has been somewhere far away, and absolutely remote it remains.

If, at the beginning, the bare notion of the sundered consciousness involved the characteristic of seeking to cancel it, *qua* particular consciousness, and become the unchangeable consciousness, the direction its effort henceforth takes is rather that of cancelling its relation to the pure unchangeable, without shape or embodied form, and of adopting only the relation to the unchangeable which has form and shape.[6] For the oneness of the particular consciousness with the unchangeable is henceforth its object and the essential reality for it, just as in the mere notion of it the essential object was merely the formless abstract unchangeable: and the relation found in this absolute disruption, characteristic of its notion, is now what it has to turn away from. The external relation, however, primarily adopted to the formed and embodied unchangeable, as being an alien extraneous reality, must be transmuted and raised to that of complete and thoroughgoing fusion and identification.

The process through which the unessential consciousness strives to attain this oneness, is itself a triple process, in accordance with the threefold character of the relation which this consciousness takes up to its transcendent and remote reality embodied in specific form. In one it is a pure consciousness; at another time a particular individual who takes up towards actuality the attitude characteristic of desire and labour; and in the third place it is a consciousness of its self-existence, its existence for itself. We have now to see how these three modes of its being are found and are constituted in that general relation.

In the first place, then, regarded as pure consciousness, the unchangeable embodied in definite historical form seems, since it is an object for pure consciousness, to be established as it is in its self-subsistent reality. But this, its reality in and for itself, has not yet come to light, as we already remarked. Were it to be in consciousness as it is in itself and for itself, this would certainly have to come about not from the side of consciousness, but from the unchangeable. But, this being so, its presence here is brought about through consciousness

---

[6] The historic Christ as worshipped, e.g. in the mediæval church. *Tr.*

only in a onesided way to begin with, and just for that reason is not found in a perfect and genuine form, but constantly weighted and encumbered with imperfection, with an opposite.

But although the "unhappy consciousness" does not possess this actual presence, it has, at the same time, transcended pure thought, so far as this is the abstract thought of Stoicism, which turns away from particulars altogether, and again the merely restless thought of Scepticism—so far, in fact, as this is merely particularity in the sense of aimless contradiction and the restless process of contradictory thought. It has gone beyond both of these; it brings and keeps together pure thought and particular existence, but has not yet risen to that level of thinking where the particularity of consciousness is harmoniously reconciled with pure thought itself. It rather stands midway, at the point where abstract thought comes in contact with the particularity of consciousness *qua* particularity. Itself *is* this act of contact; it is the union of pure thought and individuality; and this thinking individuality or pure thought also exists as object for it, and the unchangeable is essentially itself an individual existence. But that this its object, the unchangeable, which assumes essentially the form of particularity, is *its own self*, the self which is particularity of consciousness—this is *not* established *for it*.

In this first condition, consequently, in which we treat it as pure consciousness, it takes up towards its object an attitude which is not that of thought; but rather (since it is indeed in itself pure thinking particularity and its object is just this pure thought, but pure thought is not their relation to one another as such), it, so to say, merely gives itself up to thought, devotes itself to thinking (*geht an das Denken'hin*), and is the state of Devotion (*Andacht*). Its thinking as such is no more than the discordant clang of ringing bells, or a cloud of warm incense, a kind of thinking in terms of music, that does not get the length of notions, which would be the sole, immanent, objective mode of thought. This boundless pure inward feeling comes to have indeed its object; but this object does not make its appearance in conceptual form, and therefore comes on the scene as something external and foreign. Hence we have here the inward movement of pure emotion (*Gemüth*) which feels itself, but feels itself in the bitterness of soul-diremption. It is the movement of an infinite Yearning, which is assured that its nature is a pure emotion of this kind, a pure thought which thinks itself as particularity—a yearning that is certain of being known and recognized by this object, for the very reason that this object thinks itself as particularity. At the same time, however, this nature is the unattainable "beyond" which, in being seized, escapes or rather has already escaped. The "beyond" has already escaped, for it is in part the unchangeable, thinking itself as particularity, and consciousness, therefore, attains itself therein immediately,—attains itself, but as something opposed to the unchangeable; instead of grasping the real nature consciousness merely *feels*, and has fallen back upon itself. Since, in thus attaining itself, consciousness cannot keep itself at a distance as this opposite, it has merely laid hold of what is unessential instead of having seized true reality. Thus, just as, on one side, when striving to find itself in the essentially real, it only lays hold of its own divided state of existence, so, too, on the other side, it cannot grasp that other [the essence] as particular or as concrete. That "other" cannot be found where it is sought; for it is meant to be just a "beyond", that which can *not* be found. When looked for as a particular it is not universal, a thought-constituted particularity, not notion, but particular in the sense of an object, or a concrete actual, an object of immediate sense-consciousness of sense certainty; and just for that reason it is only one which has disappeared. Consciousness, therefore, can only come upon the *grave* of its life. But because this is itself an actuality, and since it is contrary to the nature of actuality to afford a lasting possession, the presence even of that tomb is merely the source of trouble, toil, and struggle, a fight which must be lost.[7] But since consciousness has found out by experience that the grave of its actual unchangeable Being has no concrete *actuality*, that the vanished particularity *qua* vanished is not true particularity, it will give up looking for the unchangeable particular existence as something actual, or will cease trying to hold on to what has thus vanished. Only so is it capable of finding particularity in a true form, a form that is universal.

---

[7] Cp. The Crusades. *Tr.*

KARL MARX (1818–1883)

Alienated Labor

We have proceeded from the presuppositions of political economy. We have accepted its language and its laws. We presupposed private property, the separation of labor, capital and land, hence of wages, profit of capital and rent, likewise the division of labor, competition, the concept of exchange value, etc. From political economy itself in its own words, we have shown that the worker sinks to the level of a commodity, the most miserable commodity; that the misery of the worker is inversely proportional to the power and volume of his production; that the necessary result of competition is the accumulation of capital in a few hands and thus the revival of monopoly in a more frightful form; and finally that the distinction between capitalist and landowner, between agricultural laborer and industrial worker, disappears and the whole society must divide into the two classes of *proprietors* and propertyless *workers*.

Political economy proceeds from the fact of private property. It does not explain private property. It grasps the actual, *material* process of private property in abstract and general formulae which it then takes as *laws*. It does not *comprehend* these laws, that is, does not prove them as proceeding from the nature of private property. Political economy does not disclose the reason for the division between capital and labor, between capital and land. When, for example, the the relation of wages to profits is determined, the ultimate basis is taken to be the interest of the capitalists; that is, political economy assumes what it should develop. Similarly, competition is referred to at every point and explained from external circumstances. Political economy teaches us nothing about the extent to which these external, apparently accidental circumstances are simply the expression of a necessary development. We have seen how political economy regards exchange itself as an accidental fact. The only wheels which political economy puts in motion are *greed* and the *war among the greedy, competition*.

Just because political economy does not grasp the interconnections within the movement, the doctrine of competition could stand opposed

From *Writings of the Young Marx on Philosophy and Society,* edited and translated by Loyd D. Easton and Kurt H. Guddat. Copyright © 1967 by Loyd D. Easton and Kurt H. Guddat. Reprinted by permission of Doubleday & Company, Inc.

to the doctrine of monopoly, the doctrine of freedom of craft to that of the guild, the doctrine of the division of landed property to that of the great estate. Competition, freedom of craft, and division of landed property were developed and conceived only as accidental, deliberate, forced consequences of monopoly, the guild, and feudal property, rather than necessary, inevitable, natural consequences.

We now have to grasp the essential connection among private property, greed, division of labor, capital and land-ownership, and the connection of exchange with competition, of value with the devaluation of men, of monopoly with competition, etc., and of this whole alienation with the *money*-system.

Let us not put ourselves in a fictitious primordial state like a political economist trying to clarify things. Such a primordial state clarifies nothing. It merely pushes the issue into a gray, misty distance. It acknowledges as a fact or event what it should deduce, namely, the necessary relation between two things, for example, between division of labor and exchange. In such a manner theology explains the origin of evil by the fall of man. That is, it asserts as a fact in the form of history what it should explain.

We proceed from a *present* fact to a political economy.

The worker becomes poorer the more wealth he produces, the more his production increases in power and extent. The worker becomes a cheaper commodity the more commodities he produces. The *increase in value* of the world of things is directly proportional to the *decrease in value* of the human world. Labor not only produces commodities. It also produces itself and the worker as a *commodity*, and indeed in the same proportion as it produces commodities in general.

This fact simply indicates that the object which labor produces, its product, stands opposed to it as an *alien thing*, as a *power independent* of the producer. The product of labor is labor embodied and made objective in a thing. It is the *objectification* of labor. The realization of labor is its objectification. In the viewpoint of political economy this realization of labor appears as the *diminution* of the worker, the objectification as the *loss of and subservience to the object*, and the appropriation as *alienation [Entfremdung]*, as externalization *[Entäusserung]*.

So much does the realization of labor appear as diminution that the worker is diminished to the point of starvation. So much does objectification appear as loss of the object that the worker is robbed of the most essential objects not only of life but also of work. Indeed, work itself becomes a thing of which he can take possession only with the greatest effort and with the most unpredictable interruptions. So much does the appropriation of the object appear as alienation that the more objects the worker produces, the fewer he can own and the more he falls under the domination of his product, of capital.

All these consequences follow from the fact that the worker is related to the *product of his labor* as to an *alien* object. For it is clear according to this premise: The more the worker exerts himself, the more powerful becomes the alien objective world which he fashions against himself, the poorer he and his inner world become, the less there is that belongs to him. It is the same in religion. The more man attributes to God, the less he retains in himself. The worker puts his life into the object; then it no longer belongs to him but to the object. The greater this activity, the poorer is the worker. What the product of his work is, he is not. The greater this product is, the smaller he is himself. The *externalization* of the worker in his product means not only that his work becomes an object, an *external* existence, but also that it exists *outside him* independently, alien, an autonomous power, opposed to him. The life he has given to the object confronts him as hostile and alien.

Let us now consider more closely the *objectification*, the worker's production and with it the *alienation* and *loss* of the object, his product.

The worker can make nothing without *nature*, without the *sensuous external world*. It is the material wherein his labor realizes itself, wherein it is active, out of which and by means of which it produces.

But as nature furnishes to labor the *means of life* in the sense that labor cannot *live* without objects upon which labor is exercised, nature also furnishes the *means of life* in the narrower sense, namely, the means of physical subsistence of the *worker* himself.

The more the worker *appropriates* the external world and sensuous nature through his labor, the more he deprives himself of the *means of life* in two respects: first, that the sensuous external world gradually ceases to be an object belonging to his labor, a *means of life* of his work; secondly, that it gradually ceases to be a *means of life* in the immediate sense, a means of physical subsistence of the worker.

In these two respects, therefore, the worker becomes a slave to his objects; first, in that he receives an *object of labor*, that is, he receives *labor*, and secondly that he receives the *means of subsistence*. The first enables him to exist as a *worker* and the second as a *physical subject*. The terminus of this slavery is that he can only maintain himself as a *physical subject* so far as he is a *worker*, and only as a *physical subject* is he a worker.

(The alienation of the worker in his object is expressed according to the laws of political economy as follows: the more the worker produces, the less he has to consume; the more values he creates the more worthless and unworthy he becomes; the better shaped his product, the more misshapen is he; the more civilized his product, the more barbaric is the worker; the more powerful the work, the more powerless becomes the worker; the more intelligence the work has, the more witless is the worker and the more he becomes a slave of nature.)

Political economy conceals the alienation in the nature of labor by ignoring the direct relationship between the worker (labor) *and production.* To be sure, labor produces marvels for the wealthy but it produces deprivation for the worker. It produces palaces, but hovels for the worker. It produces beauty, but mutilation for the worker. It displaces labor through machines, but it throws some workers back into barbarous labor and turns others into machines. It produces intelligence, but for the worker it produces imbecility and cretinism.

The direct relationship of labor to its products is the relationship of the worker to the objects of his production. The relationship of the rich to the objects of production and to production itself is only a *consequence* of this first relationship and confirms it. Later we shall observe the latter aspect.

Thus, when we ask, What is the essential relationship of labor? we ask about the relationship of the *worker* to production.

Up to now we have considered the alienation, the externalization of the worker only from one side: his *relationship to the products of his labor.* But alienation is shown not only in the result but also in the *process of production,* in the *producing activity* itself. How could the worker stand in an alien relationship to the product of his activity if he did not alienate himself from himself in the very act of production? After all, the product is only the résumé of activity, of production. If the product of work is externalization, production itself must be active externalization, externalization of activity, activity of externalization. Only alienation—and externalization in the activity of labor itself —is summarized in the alienation of the object of labor.

What constitutes the externalization of labor?

First is the fact that labor is *external* to the laborer—that is, it is not part of his nature—and that the worker does not affirm himself in his work but denies himself, feels miserable and unhappy, develops no free physical and mental energy but mortifies his flesh and ruins his mind. The worker, therefore feels at ease only outside work, and during work he is outside himself. He is at home when he is not working and when he is working he is not at home. His work, therefore, is not voluntary, but coerced, *forced labor*. It is not the satisfaction of a need but only a *means* to satisfy other needs. Its alien character is obvious from the fact that as soon as no physical or other pressure exists, labor is avoided like the plague. External labor, labor in which man is externalized, is labor of self-sacrifice, of penance. Finally, the external nature of work for the worker appears in the fact that it is not his own but another person's, that in work he does not belong to himself but to someone else. In religion the spontaneity of human imagination, the spontaneity of the human brain and heart, acts independently of the individual as an alien, divine or devilish activity. Similarly, the activity of the worker is not his own spontaneous activity. It belongs to another. It is the loss of his own self.

The result, therefore, is that man (the worker) feels that he is acting freely only in his animal functions—eating, drinking, and procreating, or at most in his shelter and finery—while in his human functions he feels only like an animal. The animalistic becomes the human and the human the animalistic.

To be sure, eating, drinking, and procreation are genuine human functions. In abstraction, however, and separated from the remaining sphere of human activities and turned into final and sole ends, they are animal functions.

We have considered labor, the act of alienation of practical human activity, in two aspects: (1) the relationship of the worker to the *product of labor* as an alien object dominating him. This relationship is at the same time the relationship to the sensuous external world, to natural objects as an alien world hostile to him; (2) the relationship of labor to the *act of production in labor*. This relationship is that of the worker to his own activity as alien and not belonging to him, activity as passivity, power as weakness, procreation as emasculation, the worker's *own* physical and spiritual energy, his personal life—for what else is life but activity—as an activity turned against him, independent of him, and not belonging to him. *Self-alienation*, as against the alienation of the *object*, stated above.

We have now to derive a third aspect of *alienated labor* from the two previous ones.

Man is a species-being [*Gattungswesen*] not only in that he practically and theoretically makes his own species as well as that of other things his object, but also—and this is only another expression for the same thing—in that as present and living species he considers himself to be a *universal* and consequently free being.

The life of the species in man as in animals is physical in that man, (like the animal) lives by inorganic nature. And as man is more universal than the animal, the realm of inorganic nature by which he lives is more universal. As plants, animals, minerals, air, light, etc., in theory form a part of human consciousness, partly as objects of natural science, partly as objects of art—his spiritual inorganic nature or spiritual means of life which he first must prepare for enjoyment and assimilation—so they also form in practice a part of human life and human activity. Man lives physically only by these products of nature; they may appear in the form of food, heat, clothing, housing, etc. The universality of man appears in practice in the universality which makes the whole of nature his *inorganic* body: (1) as a direct means of life, and (2) as the matter, object, and instrument of his life activity. Nature is the *inorganic body* of man, that is, nature insofar as it is not the human body. Man *lives* by nature. This means that nature is his *body* with which he must remain in perpetual process in order not to die. That the physical and spiritual life of man is tied up with nature is another way of saying that nature is linked to itself, for man is a part of nature.

In alienating (1) nature from man, and (2) man from himself, his own active function, his life activity, alienated labor also alienates the *species* from him; it makes *species-life* the means of individual life. In the first place it alienates species-life and the individual life, and secondly it turns the latter in its abstraction into the purpose of the former, also in its abstract and alienated form.

For labor, *life activity*, and *productive life* appear to man at first only as a *means* to satisfy a need, the need to maintain physical existence. Productive life, however, is species-life. It is life begetting life. In the mode of life activity lies the entire character of a species, its species-character; and free conscious activity is the species-character of man. Life itself appears only as a *means of life*.

The animal is immediately one with its life activity, not distinct from it. The animal is *its life activity*. Man makes his life activity itself into an object of will and consciousness. He has conscious life activity. It is not a determination with which he immediately identifies. Conscious life activity distinguishes man immediately from the life activity of the animal. Only thereby is he a species-being. Or rather, he is only a conscious being—that is, his own life is an object for him—since he is a species-being. Only on that account is his activity free activity. Alienated labor reverses the relationship in that man, since he is a conscious being, makes his life activity, his *essence*, only a means for his *existence*.

The practical creation of an *objective world*, the *treatment* of inorganic nature, is proof that man is a conscious species-being, that is, a being which is related to its species as to its own essence or is related to itself as a species-being. To be sure animals also produce. They build themselves nests, dwelling places, like the bees, beavers, ants, etc. But the animal produces only what is immediately necessary for itself or its young. It produces in a one-sided way while man produces universally. The animal produces under the domination of immediate physical need while man produces free of physical need and only genuinely so in freedom from such need. The animal only produces itself while man reproduces the whole of nature. The animal's product belongs immediately to its physical body while man is free when he confronts his product. The animal builds only according to the standard and need of the species to which it belongs while man knows how to produce according to the standard of any species and at all times knows how to apply an intrinsic standard to the object. Thus man creates also according to the laws of beauty.

In the treatment of the objective world, therefore, man proves himself to be genuinely a *species-being*. This production is his active species-life. Through it nature appears as *his* work and his actuality. The object of labor is thus the *objectification of man's species-life:* he produces himself not only intellectually, as in consciousness, but also actively in a real sense and sees himself in a world he made. In taking from man the object of his production, alienated labor takes from his *species-life*, his actual and objective existence as a species. It changes his superiority to the animal to inferiority, since he is deprived of nature, his inorganic body.

By degrading free spontaneous activity to the level of a means, alienated labor makes the species-life of man a means of his physical existence.

The consciousness which man has from his species is altered through alienation, so that species-life becomes a means for him.

(3) Alienated labor hence turns the *species-existence of man*, and also nature as his mental species-capacity, into an existence *alien* to him, into the *means* of his *individual existence*. It alienates his spiritual nature, his *human essence*, from his own body and likewise from nature outside him.

(4) A direct consequence of man's alienation from the product of his work, from his life activity, and from his species-existence, is the *alienation of man* from *man*. When man confronts himself, he confronts *other* men. What holds true of man's relationship to his

work, to the product of his work, and to himself, also holds true of man's relationship to other men, to their labor, and the object of their labor.

In general, the statement that man is alienated from his species-existence means that one man is alienated from another just as each man is alienated from human nature.

The alienation of man, the relation of man to himself, is realized and expressed in the relation between man and other men.

Thus in the relation of alienated labor every man sees the others according to the standard and the relation in which he finds himself as a worker.

We began with an economic fact, the alienation of the worker and his product. We have given expression to the concept of this fact: *alienated, externalized* labor. We have analyzed this concept and have thus analyzed merely a fact of political economy.

Let us now see further how the concept of alienated, externalized labor must express and represent itself in actuality.

If the product of labor is alien to me, confronts me as an alien power, to whom then does it belong?

If my own activity does not belong to me, if it is an alien and forced activity, to whom then does it belong?

To a being *other* than myself.

Who is this being?

Gods? To be sure, in early times the main production, for example, the building of temples in Egypt, India, and Mexico, appears to be in the service of the gods, just as the product belongs to the gods. But gods alone were never workmasters. The same is true of *nature*. And what a contradiction it would be if the more man subjugates nature through his work and the more the miracles of gods are rendered superfluous by the marvels of industry, man should renounce his joy in producing and the enjoyment of his product for love of these powers.

The *alien* being who owns labor and the product of labor, whom labor serves and whom the product of labor satisfies can only be *man* himself.

That the product of labor does not belong to the worker and an alien power confronts him is possible only because this product belongs to *a man other than the worker*. If his activity is torment for him, it must be the *pleasure* and the life-enjoyment for another. Not gods, not nature, but only man himself can be this alien power over man.

Let us consider the statement previously made, that the relationship of man to himself is *objective* and *actual* to him only through his relationship to other men. If man is related to the product of his labor, to his objectified labor, as to an *alien*, hostile, powerful object independent of him, he is so related that another alien, hostile, powerful man independent of him is the lord of this object. If he is unfree in relation to his own activity, he is related to it as bonded activity, activity under the domination, coercion, and yoke of another man.

Every self-alienation of man, from himself and from nature, appears in the relationship which he postulates between other men and himself and nature. Thus religious self-alienation appears necessarily in the relation of laity to priest, or also to a mediator, since we are here now concerned with the spiritual world. In the practical real world self-alienation can appear only in the practical real relationships to other men. The means whereby the alienation proceeds is a *practical* means. Through alienated labor man thus not only produces his relationship to the object and to the act of production as an alien man at enmity with him. He also creates the relation in which other men stand to his production and product, and the relation in which he stands to these other men. Just as he begets his own production as loss of his reality, as his punishment; just as he begets his own product as a loss, a product not belonging to him, so he begets the domination of the non-producer over production and over product. As he alienates his own activity from himself, he confers upon the stranger an activity which is not his own.

Up to this point, we have investigated the relationship only from the side of the worker and will later investigate it also from the side of the non-worker.

Thus through *alienated externalised labor* does the worker create the relation to this work of man alienated to labor and standing outside it. The relation of the worker to labor produces the relation of the capitalist to labor, or whatever one wishes to call the lord of labor. *Private property* is thus product, result and necessary consequence of *externalized labor*, of the external relation of the worker to nature and to himself.

Private property thus is derived, through analysis, from the concept of *externalized labor*, that is, *externalized man*, alienated labor, alienated life, and *alienated* man.

We have obtained the concept of *externalized labor* (*externalized life*) from political economy as a result of the *movement of private property*. But the analysis of this idea shows that though private property appears to be the ground and cause of externalized labor, it is rather a consequence of externalized labor, just as gods are *originally* not the cause but the effect of an aberration of the human mind. Later this relationship reverses.

Only at the final culmination of the development of private property does this, its secret, reappear—namely, that on the one hand it is the *product* of externalized labor and that secondly it is the *means* through which labor externalizes itself, the *realization of this externalization.*

This development throws light on several conflicts hitherto unresolved.

(1) Political economy proceeds from labor as the very soul of production and yet gives labor nothing, private property everything. From this contradiction Proudhon decided in favor of labor and against private property. We perceive, however, that this apparent contradiction is the contradiction of *alienated labor* with itself and that political economy has only formulated the laws of alienated labor.

Therefore we also perceive that *wages* and *private property* are identical: for when the product, the object of labor, pays for the labor itself, wages are only a necessary consequence of the alienation of labor. In wages labor appears not as an end in itself but as the servant of wages. We shall develop this later and now only draw some conclusions.

An enforced *raising of wages* (disregarding all other difficulties, including that this anomaly could only be maintained forcibly) would therefore be nothing but a *better slave-salary* and would not achieve either for the worker or for labor human significance and dignity.

Even the *equality of wages*, as advanced by Proudhon, would only convert the relation of the contemporary worker to his work into the relation of all men to labor. Society would then be conceived as an abstract capitalist.

Wages are a direct result of alienated labor, and alienated labor is the direct cause of private property. The downfall of one is necessarily the downfall of the other.

(2) From the relation of alienated labor to private property it follows further that the emancipation of society from private property, etc., from servitude, is expressed in its *political* form as the *emancipation of workers*, not as though it is only a question of their emancipation but because in their emancipation is contained universal human emancipation. It is contained in their emancipation because the whole of human servitude is involved in the relation of worker to production, and all relations of servitude are only modifications and consequences of the worker's relation to production.

As we have found the concept of *private property* through *analysis* from the concept of *alienated, externalized labor*, so we can develop all the *categories* of political economy with the aid of these two factors, and we shall again find in each category—for example, barter, competition, capital, money—only a *particular* and *developed expression* of these primary foundations.

Before considering this configuration, however, let us try to solve two problems.

(1) To determine the general *nature of private property* as a result of alienated labor in its relation to *truly human* and *social property*.

(2) We have taken the *alienation of labor* and its *externalization* as a fact and analyzed this fact. How, we ask now, does it happen that *man externalizes* his *labor*, alienates it? How is this alienation rooted in the nature of human development? We have already achieved much in resolving the problem by *transforming* the question concerning the *origin of private property* into the question concerning the relationship of *externalized labor* to evolution of humanity. In talking about *private property* one believes he is dealing with something external to man. Talking of labor, one is immediately dealing with man himself. This new formulation of the problem already contains its solution.

On (1) *The general nature of private property and its relation to truly human property.*

We have resolved alienated labor into two parts which mutually determine each other or rather are only different expressions of one and the same relationship. *Appropriation* appears as *alienation*, as *externalization; externalization* as *appropriation; alienation* as the true *naturalization*.

We considered the one side, *externalized* labor, in relation to the *worker* himself, that is, the *relation of externalized labor to itself.* We have found the *property relation of the non-worker* to the *worker* and *labor* to be the product, the necessary result, of this relationship. *Private property* as the material, summarized expression of externalized labor embraces both relationships—the *relationship of worker to labor, the product of his work, and the nonworker*; and the relationship of the *non-worker to the worker* and *the product of his labor.*

As we have seen that in relation to the worker who *appropriates* nature through his labor the appropriation appears as alienation—self-activity as activity for another and of another, living as the sacrifice of life, production of the object as loss of it to an alien power, an *alien* man—we now consider the relationship of this *alien* man to the worker, to labor and its object.

It should be noted first that everything which appears with the worker as an *activity of externalization* and an *activity of alienation* appears with the non-worker as a *condition of externalization,* a *condition of alienation.*

Secondly, that the *actual, practical attitude* of the worker in production and to his product (as a condition of mind) appears as a *theoretical* attitude in the non-worker confronting him.

Thirdly, the non-worker does everything against the worker which the worker does against himself, but he does not do against his own self what he does against the worker.

Let us consider more closely these three relationships.
[Here the manuscript breaks off, unfinished.]

GEORG SIMMEL (1858–1918)

The Metropolis and Mental Life

The deepest problems of modern life derive from the claim of the individual to preserve the autonomy and individuality of his existence in the face of overwhelming social forces, of historical heritage, of external culture, and of the technique of life. The fight with nature which primitive man has to wage for his *bodily* existence attains in this modern form its latest transformation. The eighteenth century called upon man to free himself of all the historical bonds in the state and in religion, in morals and in economics. Man's nature, originally good and common to all, should develop unhampered. In addition to more liberty, the nineteenth century demanded the functional specialization of man and his work; this specialization makes one individual incomparable to another, and each of them indispensable to the highest possible extent. However, this specialization makes each man the more directly dependent upon the supplementary activities of all others. Nietzsche sees the full development of the individual conditioned by the most ruthless struggle of individuals; socialism believes in the suppression of all competition for the same reason. Be that as it may,

The selection is from Georg Simmel, "The Metropolis and Mental Life" trans. H. H. Gerth and C. Wright Mills, in Kurt H. Wolff, ed., *The Sociology of Georg Simmel* (New York: The Free Press, 1950), pp. 409–424. Used by permission of the publisher.

in all these positions the same basic motive is at work: the person, resists being leveled down and worn out by a social-technological mechanism. An inquiry into the inner meaning of specifically modern life and its products, into the soul of the cultural body, so to speak, must seek to solve the equation which structures like the metropolis set up between the individual and the superindividual contests of life. Such an inquiry must answer the question of how the personality accomodates itself in the adjustments to external forces.

The psychological basis of the metropolitan type of individuality consists in the *intensification of nervous stimulation* which results from the swift and uninterrupted change of outer and inner stimuli. Man is a differentiating creature. His mind is stimulated by the difference between a momentary impression and the one which preceded it. Lasting impressions, impressions which differ only slightly from one another, impressions which take a regular and habitual course and show regular and habitual contrasts—all these use up, so to speak, less consciousness than does the rapid crowding of changing images, the sharp discontinuity in the grasp of a single glance, and the unexpectedness of onrushing impressions. These are the psychological conditions which the metropolis creates. With each crossing of the street, with the tempo and multiplicity of economic, occupational and social life, the city sets up a deep contrast with small town and rural life with reference to the sensory foundations of psychic life. The metropolis exacts from man as a discriminating creature a different amount of consciousness than does rural life. Here the rhythm of life and sensory mental imagery flows more slowly, more habitually, and more evenly. Precisely in this connection the sophisticated character of metropolitan psychic life becomes understandable—as over against small town life which rests more upon deeply felt and emotional relationships. These latter are rooted in the more unconscious layers of the psyche and grow most readily in the steady rhythm of uninterrupted habituations. The intellect, however, has its locus in the transparent, conscious, higher layers of the psyche; it is the most adaptable of our inner forces. In order to accommodate to change and to the contrast of phenomena, the intellect does not require any shocks and inner upheavals; it is only through such upheavals that the more conservative mind could accommodate to the metropolitan rhythm of events. Thus the metropolitan type of man—which, of course, exists in a thousand individual variants—develops an organ protecting him against the threatening currents and discrepancies of his external environment which would uproot him. He reacts with his head instead of his heart. In this an increased awareness assumes the psychic prerogative. Metropolitan life, thus, underlies a heightened awareness and a predominance of intelligence in metropolitan man. The reaction to metropolitan phenomena is shifted to that organ which is least sensitive and quite remote from the depth of the personality. Intellectuality is thus seen to preserve subjective life against the overwhelming power of metropolitan life, and intellectuality branches out in many directions and is integrated with numerous discrete phenomena.

The metropolis has always been the seat of the money economy. Here the multiplicity and concentration of economic exchange gives an importance to the means of exchange which the scantiness of rural commerce would have not allowed. Money economy and the dominance of the intellect are intrinsically connected. They share a matter-of-fact attitude in dealing with men and with things; and, in this attitude, a formal justice is often coupled with an inconsiderate hardness. The intellectually sophisticated person is indifferent to all genuine individuality, because relationships and reactions result from it which cannot be exhausted with logical operations. In the same manner, the individuality of phenomena is not commensurate with the pecuniary principle. Money is concerned only with what is common to all: it asks for the exchange value, it reduces all quality and individuality to the question: How much? All intimate emotional relations between persons are founded in their individuality, whereas in rational relations man is reckoned with like a number, like an element which is in itself indifferent. Only the objective measurable achievement is of interest. Thus metropolitan man reckons with his merchants and customers, his domestic servants and often even with persons with whom he is obliged to have social intercourse. These features of intellectuality contrast with the nature of the small circle in which the inevitable knowledge of individuality as inevitably produces a warmer tone of behavior, a behavior which is beyond a mere objective balancing of service and return. In the sphere of the economic psychology of the small group it is of importance that under primitive conditions production serves the customer who orders the goods, so that the producer and the consumer are acquainted. The modern metropolis, however, is supplied almost entirely by production for the market, that is, for entirely unknown purchasers who never personally enter the producer's actual field of vision. Through this anonymity the interests of each party acquire an unmerciful matter-of-factness; and the intellectually calculating economic egoisms of both parties need not fear any deflection because of the imponderables of personal relationships. The money economy dominates the metropolis; it has displaced the last survivals of domestic production and the direct barter of goods; it minimizes, from day to day the amount of work ordered by customers. The matter-of-fact attitude is obviously so intimately interrelated with the money economy, which is dominant in the metropolis, that nobody can say whether the intellectualistic mentality first promoted the money economy or whether the latter determined the former. The metropolitan way of life is certainly the most fertile soil for this reciprocity, a point which I shall document merely by citing the dictum of the most eminent English constitutional historian: throughout the whole course of English history, London has never acted as England's heart but often as England's intellect and always as her moneybag!

In certain seemingly insignificant traits, which lie upon the surface of life, the same psychic currents characteristically unite. Modern mind has become more and more calculating. The calculative exactness of practical life which the money economy had brought about corresponds to the ideal of natural science: to transform the world into an arithmetic problem, to fix every part of the world by mathematical formulas. Only money economy has filled the days of so many people with weighing, calculating, with numerical determinations, with a reduction of qualitative values to quantitative ones. Through the calculative nature of money a new precision, a certainty in the definition of identities and differences, an unambiguousness in agreements and arrangements has been brought about in the relations of life-elements—just as externally this precision has been effected by the universal diffusion of pocket watches. However, the conditions of metropolitan life are at once cause and effect of this trait. The relationships and affairs of the typical metropolitan usually are so varied and complex that without the strictest punctuality in promises and services the whole structure would break down into an inextricable chaos. Above all, this necessity is brought about by the aggregation of so many people with such differentiated interests, who must integrate their relations and activities into a highly complex organism. If all clocks and watches in Berlin would suddenly go wrong in different ways, even if only by one hour, all economic life and communication of the city would be disrupted for a long time. In addition an apparently mere external factor—long distances—would make all waiting and broken appointments result in an ill-afforded waste of time. Thus, the technique of metropolitan life is unimaginable without the most punctual integration of all activities and mutual relations into a stable and impersonal time schedule. Here again the general conclusions of this entire task of reflection become obvious, namely, that from each point on the surface of existence—however closely attached to the surface alone—one may drop a sounding into the depth of the psyche so that all the most banal externalities of life finally are connected with the ultimate decisions concerning the meaning and style of life. Punctuality, calculability, exactness are forced upon life by the complexity and extension of metropolitan existence and are not only most intimately connected with its money economy and intellectualistic character. These traits must also color the contents of life and favor the exclusion of those irrational, instinctive, sovereign traits and impulses which aim at determining the mode of life from within, instead of receiving the general and precisely schematized form of life from without. Even though sovereign types of personality, characterized by irrational impulses, are by no means impossible in the city, they are, nevertheless, opposed to typical city life. The passionate hatred of men like Ruskin and Nietzsche for the metropolis is understandable in these terms. Their nature discovered the value of life alone in the unschematized existence which cannot be defined with precision for all alike. From the same source of this hatred of the metropolis surged their hatred of money economy and of the intellectualism of modern existence.

The same factors which have thus coalesced into the exactness and minute precision of the form of life have coalesced into a structure of the highest impersonality; on the other hand, they have promoted a highly personal subjectivity. There is perhaps no psychic phenomenon which has been so unconditionally reserved to the metropolis as has the blasé attitude. The blasé attitude results first from the rapidly changing and closely compressed contrasting stimulations of the nerves. From this, the enhancement of metropolitan intellectuality, also, seems originally to stem. Therefore, stupid people who are not intellectually alive in the first place usually are not exactly blasé. A life in boundless pursuit of pleasure makes one blasé because it agitates the nerves to their strongest reactivity for such a long time that they finally cease to react at all. In the same way, through the rapidity and contradictoriness of their changes, more harmless impressions force such violent responses, tearing the nerves so brutally hither and thither that their last reserves of strength are spent; and if one remains in the same milieu they have no time to gather new strength. An incapacity thus emerges to react to new sensations with the appropriate energy. This constitutes that blasé attitude which, in fact, every metropolitan child shows when compared with children of quieter and less changeable milieus.

This physiological source of the metropolitan blasé attitude is joined by another source which flows from the money economy. The essence of the blasé attitude consists in the blunting of discrimination.

This does not mean that the objects are not perceived, as is the case with the half-wit, but rather that the meaning and differing values of things, and thereby the things themselves, are experienced as insubstantial. They appear to the blasé person in an evenly flat and gray tone; no one object deserves preference over any other. This mood is the faithful subjective reflection of the completely internalized money economy. By being the equivalent to all the manifold things in one and the same way, money becomes the most frightful leveler. For money expresses all qualitative differences of things in terms of "how much?" Money, with all its colorlessness and indifference, becomes the common denominator of all values; irreparably it hollows out the core of things, their individuality, their specific value, and their incomparability. All things float with equal specific gravity in the constantly moving stream of money. All things lie on the same level and differ from one another only in the size of the area which they cover. In the individual case this coloration, or rather discoloration, of things through their money equivalence may be unnoticeably minute. However, through the relations of the rich to the objects to be had for money, perhaps even through the total character which the mentality of the contemporary public everywhere imparts to these objects, the exclusively pecuniary evaluation of objects has become quite considerable. The large cities the main seats of the money exchange, bring the purchasability of things to the fore much more impressively than do smaller localities. That is why cities are also the genuine locale of the blasé attitude. In the blasé attitude the concentration of men and things stimulates the nervous system of the individual to its highest achievement so that it attains its peak. Through the mere quantitative intensification of the same conditioning factors this achievement is transformed into its opposite and appears in the peculiar adjustment of the blasé attitude. In this phenomenon the nerves find in the refusal to react to their stimulation the last possibility of accommodating to the contents and forms of metropolitan life. The self-preservation of certain personalities is bought at the price of devaluating the whole objective world, a devaluation which in the end unavoidably drags one's own personality down into a feeling of the same worthlessness.

Whereas the subject of this form of existence has to come to terms with it entirely for himself, his self preservation in the face of the large city demands from him a no less negative behavior of a social nature. This mental attitude of metropolitans toward one another we may designate, from a formal point of view, as reserve. If so many inner reactions were responses to the continuous external contacts with

innumerable people as are those in the small town, where one knows
almost everybody one meets and where one has a positive relation to
almost everyone, one would be completely atomized internally and
come to an unimaginable psychic state. Partly this psychological fact,
partly the right to distrust which men have in the face of the touch-and
go elements of metropolitan life, necessitates our reserve. As a result
of this reserve we frequently do not even know by sight those who have
been our neighbors for years. And it is this reserve which in the eyes
of the small-town people makes us appear to be cold and heartless.
Indeed, if I do not deceive myself, the inner aspect of this outer reserve
is not only indifference but, more often than we are aware, it is a slight
aversion, a mutual strangeness and repulsion, which will break into
hatred and fight at the moment of a closer contact, however caused.
The whole inner organization of such an extensive communicative life
rests upon an extremely varied hierarchy of sympathies, indifferences,
and aversions of the briefest as well as of the most permanent nature.
The sphere of indifference in this hierarchy is not as large as might
appear on the surface. Our psychic activity still responds to almost
every impression of somebody else with a somewhat distinct feeling.
The unconscious, fluid and changing character of this impression
seems to result in a state of indifference. Actually this indifference
would be just as unnatural as the diffusion of indiscriminate mutual
suggestion would be unbearable. From both these typical dangers of
the metropolis, indifference and indiscriminate suggestibility, antipathy
protects us. A latent antipathy and the preparatory stage of practical
antagonism effect the distances and aversions without which this mode
of life could not at all be led. The extent and the mixture of this style
of life, the rhythm of its emergence and disappearance, the forms in
which it is satisfied—all these, with the unifying motives in the narrower
sense, form the inseparable whole of the metropolitan style of life.
What appears in the metropolitan style of life directly as dissociation
is in reality only one of its elemental forms of socialization.

This reserve with its overtone of hidden aversion appears in
turn as the form or the cloak of a more general mental phenomenon
of the metropolis: it grants to the individual a kind and an amount
of personal freedom which has no analogy whatsoever under other
conditions. The metropolis goes back to one of the large develop-
mental tendencies of social life as such, to one of the few tendencies
for which an approximately universal formula can be discovered.
The earliest phase of social formations found in historical as well as in
contemporary social structures is this: a relatively small circle firmly

closed against neighboring, strange, or in some way antagonistic circles. However, this circle is closely coherent and allows its individual members only a narrow field for the development of unique qualities and free, self-responsible movements. Political and kinship groups, parties and religious associations begin in this way. The self-preservation of very young associations requires the establishment of strict boundaries and a centripetal unity. Therefore they cannot allow the individual freedom and unique inner and outer development. From this stage social development proceeds at once in two different, yet corresponding, directions. To the extent to which the group grows—numerically, spatially, in significance and in content of life—to the same degree the group's direct, inner unity loosens, and the rigidity of the original demarcation against others is softened through mutual relations and connections. At the same time, the individual gains freedom of movement, far beyond the first jealous delimitation. The individual also gains a specific individuality to which the division of labor in the enlarged group gives both occasion and necessity. The state and Christianity, guilds and political parties, and innumerable other groups have developed according to this formula, however much, of course, the special conditions and forces of the respective groups have modified the general scheme. This scheme seems to me distinctly recognizable also in the evolution of individuality within urban life. The small-town life in Antiquity and in the Middle Ages set barriers against movement and relations of the individual toward the outside, and it set up barriers against individual independence and differentiation within the individual self. These barriers were such that under them modern man could not have breathed. Even today a metropolitan man who is placed in a small town feels a restriction similar, at least, in kind. The smaller the circle which forms our milieu is, and the more restricted those relations to others are which dissolve the boundaries of the individual, the more anxiously the circle guards the achievements, the conduct of life, and the outlook of the individual, and the more readily a quantitative and qualitative specialization would break up the framework of the whole little circle.

The ancient *polis* in this respect seems to have had the very character of a small town. The constant threat to its existence at the hands of enemies from near and afar effected strict coherence in political and military respects, a supervision of the citizen by the citizen, a jealousy of the whole against the individual whose particular life was suppressed to such a degree that he could compensate only by acting as a despot in his own household. The tremendous agitation and excitement, the unique colorfulness of Athenian life, can perhaps be understood in terms of the fact that a people of incomparably individualized personalities struggled against the constant inner and outer pressure of a deindividualizing small town. This produced a tense atmosphere in which the weaker individuals were suppressed and those of stronger natures were incited to prove themselves in the most passionate manner. This is precisely why it was that there blossomed in Athens what must be called, without defining it exactly, "the general human character" in the intellectual development of our species. For we maintain factual as well as historical validity for the following connection: the most extensive and the most general contents and forms of life are most intimately connected with the most individual ones. They have a preparatory stage in common, that is, they find their enemy in narrow formations and groupings the maintenance of which places both of them into a state of defense against expanse and generality lying without and the freely moving individuality within. Just as in the feudal age, the "free" man was the one who stood under the law of the land, that is, under the law of the largest social orbit, and the unfree man was the one who derived his right merely from the narrow circle of a feudal association and was excluded from the larger social orbit—so today metropolitan man is "free" in a spiritualized and refined sense, in contrast to the pettiness and prejudices which hem in the small-town man. For the reciprocal reserve and indifference and the intellectual life conditions of large circles are never felt more strongly by the individual in their impact upon his independence than in the thickest crowd of the big city. This is because the bodily proximity and narrowness of space makes the mental distance only the more visible. It is obviously only the obverse of this freedom if, under certain circumstances, one nowhere feels as lonely and lost as in the metropolitan crowd. For here as elsewhere it is by no means necessary that the freedom of man be reflected in his emotional life as comfort.

It is not only the immediate size of the area and the number of persons which, because of the universal historical correlation between the enlargement of the circle and the personal inner and outer freedom, has made the metropolis the locale of freedom. It is rather in transcending this visible expanse that any given city becomes the seat of cosmopolitanism. The horizon of the city expands in a manner comparable to the way in which wealth develops; a certain amount of property increases in a quasi-automatical way in ever more rapid progression. As soon as a certain limit has been passed, the economic, personal, and intellectual relations of the citizenry, the sphere of intellectual predominance of the city over its hinterland, grow as in geometrical progression. Every gain in dynamic extension becomes a step, not for an equal, but for a new and larger extension. From every thread spinning out of the city, ever new threads grow as if by themselves, just as within the city the unearned increment of ground rent, through the mere increase in communication, brings the owner automatically increasing profits. At this point, the quantitative aspect of life is transformed directly into qualitative traits of character. The sphere of life of the small town is, in the main, self-contained and autarchic. For it is the decisive nature of the metropolis that its inner life overflows by waves into a far-flung national or international area. Weimar is not an example to the contrary, since its significance was hinged upon individual personalities and died with them; whereas the metropolis is indeed characterized by its essential independence even from the most eminent individual personalities. This is the counterpart to the independence, and it is the price the individual pays for the independence, which he enjoys in the metropolis. The most significant characteristic of the metropolis is this functional extension beyond its physical boundaries. And this efficacy reacts in turn and gives weight, importance, and responsibility to metropolitan life. Man does not end with the limits of his body or the area comprising his immediate activity. Rather is the range of the person constituted by the sum of effects emanating from him temporally and spatially. In the same way, a city consists of its total effects which extend beyond its immediate confines. Only this range is the city's actual extent in which its existence is expressed. This fact makes it obvious that individual freedom, the logical and historical complement of such extension, is not to be understood only in the negative sense of mere freedom of mobility and elimination of prejudices and petty philistinism. The essential point is that the particularity and incomparability, which ultimately every human being possesses, be somehow expressed in the working-out of a way of life. That we follow the laws of our own nature—and this after all is freedom—becomes obvious and convincing to ourselves and to others only if the expressions of this nature differ from the expressions of others. Only our unmistakability proves that our way of life has not been superimposed by others.

Cities are, first of all, seats of the highest economic division of labor. They produce thereby such extreme phenomena as in Paris the remunerative occupation of the *quartorzième*. They are persons who identify themselves by signs on their residences and who are ready at the dinner hour in correct attire, so that they can be quickly called upon if a dinner party should consist of thirteen persons. In the measure of its expansion, the city offers more and more the decisive conditions of the division of labor. It offers a circle which through its size can absorb a highly diverse variety of services. At the same time, the concentration of individuals and their struggle for customers compel the individual to specialize in a function from which he cannot be readily displaced by another. It is decisive that city life has transformed the struggle with nature for livelihood into an inter-human struggle for gain, which here is not granted by nature but by other men. For specialization does not flow only from the competition for gain but also from the underlying fact that the seller must always seek to call forth new differentiated needs of the lured customer. In order to find a source of income which is not yet exhausted, and to find a function which cannot readily be displaced, it is necessary to specialize in one's services. This process promotes differentiation, refinement, and the enrichment of the public's needs, which obviously must lead to growing personal differences within this public.

All this forms the transition to the individualization of mental and psychic traits which the city occasions in proportion to its size. There is a whole series of obvious causes underlying this process. First, one must meet the difficulty of asserting his own personality within the dimensions of metropolitan life. Where the quantitative increase in importance and the expense of energy reach their limits, one seizes upon qualitative differentiation in order somehow to attract the attention of the social circle by playing upon its sensitivity for differences. Finally, man is tempted to adopt the most tendentious peculiarities, that is, the specifically metropolitan extravagances of mannerism, caprice, and preciousness. Now, the meaning of these extravagances does not at all lie in the contents of such behavior, but rather in its form of "being different," of standing out in a striking manner and thereby attracting attention. For many character types, ultimately the only means of saving for themselves some modicum of self-esteem and the sense of filling a position is indirect, through the awareness of others. In the same sense a seemingly insignificant factor is operating, the cumulative effects of which are, however, still noticeable. I refer to the brevity and scarcity of the interhuman contacts granted to the metropolitan man, as compared with social intercourse in the small town. The temptation to appear "to the point," to appear concentrated and strikingly characteristic, lies much closer to the individual in brief metropolitan contacts than in an atmosphere in which frequent and prolonged association assures the personality of an unambiguous image of himself in the eyes of the other.

The most profound reason, however, why the metropolis conduces to the urge for the most individual personal existence—no matter whether justified and successful—appears to me to be the following: the development of modern culture is characterized by the preponderance of what one may call the "objective spirit" over the "subjective spirit." This is to say, in language as well as in law, in the technique of production as well as in art, in science as well as in the objects of the domestic environment, there is embodied a sum of spirit. The individual in his intellectual development follows the growth of this spirit very imperfectly and at an ever increasing distance. If, for instance, we view the immense culture which for the last hundred years has been embodied in things and in knowledge, in institutions and in comforts, and if we compare all this with the cultural progress of the individual during the same period—at least in high status groups—a frightful disproportion in growth between the two becomes evident. Indeed, at some points we notice a retrogression in the culture of the individual with reference to spirituality, delicacy, and idealism. This discrepancy results essentially from the growing division of labor. For the division of labor demands from the individual an ever more one-sided accomplishment, and the greatest advance in a one-sided pursuit only too frequently means dearth to the personality of the individual. In any case, he can cope less and less with the overgrowth of objective culture. The individual is reduced to a negligible quantity, perhaps less in his consciousness than in his practice and in the totality of his obscure emotional states that are derived from this practice. The individual has become a mere cog in an enormous organization of things and powers which tear from his hands all progress, spirituality, and value in order to transform them from their subjective form into the form of a purely objective life. It needs merely to be pointed out that the metropolis is the genuine arena of this culture which outgrows all personal life. Here in buildings and educational institutions, in the wonders and comforts of space-conquering technology, in the formations of community life, and in the visible institutions of the state, is offered such an overwhelming fullness of crystallized and impersonalized spirit that the personality, so to speak, cannot maintain itself under its impact. On the one hand, life is made infinitely easy for the personality in that stimulations, interests, uses of time and consciousness are offered to it from all sides. They carry the person as if in a stream, and one needs hardly to swim for oneself. On the other hand, however, life is composed more and more of these impersonal contents and offerings which tend to displace the genuine personal colorations and incomparabilities. This results in the individual's summoning the utmost in uniqueness and particularization, in order to preserve his most personal core. He has to exaggerate this personal element in order to remain audible even to himself. The atrophy of individual culture through the hypertrophy of objective culture is one reason for the bitter hatred which the preachers of the most extreme individualism, above all Nietzsche, harbor against the metropolis. But it is, indeed, also a reason why these preachers are so passionately loved in the metropolis and why they appear to the metropolitan man as the prophets and saviors of his most unsatisfied yearnings.

If one asks for the historical positions of these two forms of individualism which are nourished by the quantitative relation of the metropolis, namely, individual independence and the elaboration of individuality itself, then the metropolis assumes an entirely new rank order in the world history of the spirit. The eighteenth century found the individual in oppressive bonds which had become meaningless —bonds of a political, agrarian, guild, and religious character. They were restraints which, so to speak, forced upon man an unnatural form and outmoded, unjust inequalities. In this situation the cry for liberty and equality arose, the belief in the individual's full freedom of movement in all social and intellectual relationships. Freedom would at once permit the noble substance common to all to come to the fore, a substance which nature had deposited in every man and which society and history had only deformed. Besides this eighteenth-century ideal of liberalism, in the nineteenth century, through Goethe and Romanticism, on the one hand, and through the economic division of labor, on the other hand, another ideal arose; individuals liberated from historical bonds now wished to distinguish themselves from one another. The carrier of man's values is no longer the "general human being" in every individual, but rather man's qualitative uniqueness and irreplaceability. The external and internal history of our time takes its course within the struggle and in the changing entanglements of these two ways of defining the individual's role in the whole of society. It is the function of the metropolis to provide the arena for this struggle and its reconciliation. For the metropolis presents the peculiar conditions which are revealed to us as the opportunities and the stimuli for the development of both these ways of allocating roles to men. Therewith these conditions gain a unique place, pregnant with inestimable meanings for the development of psychic existence. The metropolis reveals itself as one of those great historical formations in which opposing streams which enclose life unfold, as well as join one another with equal right. However, in this process the currents of life, whether their individual phenomena touch us sympathetically or antipathetically, entirely transcend the sphere for which the judge's attitude is appropriate. Since such forces of life have grown into the roots and into the crown of the whole of the historical life in which we, in our fleeting existence, as a cell, belong only as a part, it is not our task either to accuse or to pardon, but only to understand.

FREDERICK A. WEISS (1899–1967)

Self-Alienation

During the past decade, psychoanalytic therapy has become more difficult because more patients show an increasing degree of inner dissociation and emotional withdrawal. The age of hysteria was followed by the age of psychosomatics in which anxiety and conflict were mainly expressed in physical symptoms. In our times this has been followed by the age of alienation. The main characteristic of today's patient is his estrangement from himself. I am referring here not only to the extreme: the ambulatory schizophrenic so common today, whose automatized and mechanized shell personality enables him to function and survive surprisingly well in our present automatized and mechanized society. I am thinking of the majority of our neurotic patients. Here the alienation reveals itself—to use Horney's description—in "the remoteness of the neurotic from his own feelings, wishes, beliefs and energies. It is a loss of the feeling of being an active determining force in his own life. It is a loss of feeling himself as an organic whole . . . an alienation from the real self."

Alienation has social and individual aspects which can be found in the two original meanings of the term. With emphasis on the social

The selection is from Frederick A. Weiss, "Self-Alienation: Dynamics and Therapy." Reprinted by permission of *The American Journal of Psychoanalysis*. Vol. XXI, No. 2 (1961), and of Mrs. Gertrude Weiss.

aspect, the estrangement from others and the environment, the concept of alienation was created by Hegel and later by Marx, who saw man become estranged from others and from his work under the impact of the Industrial Revolution. With emphasis on the individual aspect, the estrangement from the self, the concept of alienation was used in the last century and is being used now in some countries as connoting mental illness *per se.*

The pathogenic effect of social and cultural factors which reinforce ano perpetuate the process of self-alienation is evidenced by comparative cross-cultural anthropological studies. However, to find the primary roots and the dynamics of self-alienation we have to study the early phases of human development and the "inner life history" of alienated patients. We have to use the methods of psychoanalysis.

The term "alienation" is not used by Freud. But in a letter to Romain Rolland, written in 1936, Freud reports about an *Entremdungsgefuehl*, a feeling of alienation, which he had experienced on the Acropolis. He sees it as an aspect of depersonalization. "The subject feels that . . . a piece of his own self is strange to him . . . The phenomenon is seen as serving the purpose of defense . . . at keeping something away from the ego."

Fenichel sees the alienation of one's own feelings as characteristic of compulsive neurotics and generally as the result of a long development, but it may also originate in specific traumatic experiences. He considers alienation as the effect of a reactive withdrawal of libido which serves as a defense against objectionable feelings.

Paul Schilder, as early as 1914, described the alienated patient as a person who observes his behavior from the point of view of a spectator. His "central ego does not live in his present and previous experiences. The self appears without soul." Later he stated that alienation can be not only part of depressive and schizophrenic psychoses, but that to some extent it occurs in almost all neuroses as an "unspecific result of the general shock of the psychic conflict. . . . The individual does not dare to place his libido either in the body or in the outside world."

While still using the mechanistic concept of the libido theory in saying "the individual does not *dare,*" Schilder already speaks in terms of motivation, of courage—or rather, lack of courage, the avoidance of anxiety and conflict and resignation, which we consider today basic aspects of self-alienation.

Schilder also states that the "amount of interest an individual receives in his early childhood is of great importance." This view is confirmed by my clinical experience, which shows that the most severe forms of self-alienation occur in patients whose early relationships were characterized either by lack of physical and emotional closeness, the fatal effects of which Spitz has convincingly demonstrated, or by symbiotic relationships fostered by anxious or over-powering mothers who deprive the child of the chance of growing up as an individual, and particularly by open or hidden over-expectations of compulsively ambitious parents who condition their love and make "shoulds" of performance or behavior a prerequisite for full acceptance of the child.

W. H. Auden describes this utterly destructive process in his poem, "The Average":

> *His peasant parents killed themselves with toil*
> *To let their darling leave a stingy soil*
> *For any of those smart professions which*
> *Encourage shallow breathing, and grow rich.*
>
> *The pressure of their fond ambition made*
> *Their shy and country-loving child afraid.*
> *No sensible career was good enough,*
> *Only a hero could deserve such love.*
>
> *So here he was without maps or supplies*
> *A hundred miles from any decent town;*
>
> *The desert glared into his blood-shot eyes;*
> *The silence roared displeasure: looking down,*
> *He saw the shadow of an Average Man,*
> *Attempting the Exceptional, and ran.*

This is the soil in which rebellious resignation grows. Here also grows compulsive non-conformism which, while it contains constructive strivings for freedom, distorts its meaning and perpetuates self-alienation as much as does compulsive conformism. The "beatnik" often is as alienated from himself as is "the man in the gray flannel suit."

The alienated patient is not born alienated, nor does he choose alienation. Lacking genuine acceptance, love, and concern for his individuality in childhood, he experiences basic anxiety. Early he begins to move away from his self, which seems not good enough to be loved. He moves away from what he is, what he feels, what he wants. If one is not loved for what one is, one can at least be safe—safe perhaps by being very good and perfect and being loved for it, or by being very strong and being admired or feared for it, or by learning not to feel, not to want, not to care. Therefore, one has to free oneself from any need for others, which means first their love and affection, and, later on, in many instances, sex. Why feel, why want, if there is no response? So the person puts all his efforts into becoming what he *should* be. Later, he idealizes his self-effacement as goodness, his aggression as strength, his withdrawal as freedom. Instead of developing in the direction of increasing freedom, self-expression, and self-realization, he moves toward safety, self-elimination, and self idealization.

The alienated patient often is a good observer of himself. Together with the therapist, he looks at himself as though he were a third person in the empty chair. He seems not to care about anything, not to desire anything, particularly anything to which he could get attached. Experiences are dissociated from feelings, feelings do not reach awareness. Events "happen" to him, as they happen to Camus' *Stranger:* the death of his mother, the love of a girl, the fight, the murder. "It's all the same to me," he says again and again. No feeling is experienced, no joy, no longing, no love, no anger, no despair, no continuity of time and life, no self.

He has no active relation to life. This may be connected with an observation I have made several times. These patients often go first to an opthalmologist with complaints about visual disturbances for which no organic basis is found. Erwin Straus showed that in seeing we relate actively to the world around us, while hearing involves awareness of something which comes toward us. Physical symptoms, such as tiredness, dizziness, a general or localized numbness, various degrees of sexual anesthesia, headaches, or gastric disturbances, often are the only clinical evidence of a deeper emotional problem. The loss of primary feelings may be extreme, as in a patient who did not know how he felt until he had looked at his bowel movement in the morning. Such a patient often does not even experience his own feelings in a most intimate situation: when he has a date with his girl, or when he goes to a funeral. What matters to him is only whether he has the "right" attitude toward the girl or at the funeral—"right" meaning the attitude he is expected to have.

The absence of manifest anxiety, rage, or conflict in the clinical picture—Oberndorf spoke of "playing dead"—has led some psychoanalysts to diagnose this condition as an emotional or even constitutional defect, or as an irreversible end-stage of the neurotic process. Clinical experience, however, shows that below the apparently insensitive, frozen surface of these patients is a highly sensitive self, weakened and paralyzed by violent conflict. Underground there exist strong longings and feelings.

The alienated patient is by no means simply the other-directed radar type of Riesman.[1] He is much more deeply blocked. He is dissociated from the active, spontaneous core of himself and his feelings and, therefore, from his incentives and his capacity for making decisions. Recently, a patient said: "I am color-blind until somebody reveals the colors to me. Only when plugged into the wall-socket of 'the other' do I get the light, the energy, the reality of myself." He could have added, ". . . and the feeling of being alive."

This explains the existence of what I call "*echo phenomenon*" in the alienated patient. His own inner voice often is so weak and unconvincing that he hardly hears it. A pertinent statement, a creative idea, a promising plan on which he has been working for weeks remains unreal and meaningless to him until, with much hesitation, he expresses it to another person. When, however, "the other," whom he experiences as an insider of life, repeats his statement, his idea, or his plan, this echo suddenly sounds real and convincing to him, while his own—usually much better—formulation of the same thought remains unreal. In his inner experience he does not count. He does not exist as an individual on his own.

He may say, "Nothing moves me," or "I cannot make any move." But should one follow his limited movements in life, one will notice that he moves for short spurts, like a car with a dead battery, which must be pushed by another car. It stops, however, not simply due to lack of power, but due to the action of an automatic built-in brake. The patient seems to say in a non-verbal way: "I *will* not move on."

The patient's paralysis reveals itself in psychoanalytic therapy in free associations, and particularly in dreams, as a "sit-down strike" against life. This is motivated in a passive way by feelings of deprivation and resignation, such as, "I don't want anything. If I don't want I cannot be hurt," or, in an active way, by violent feelings of bitterness, frustration, resentment, and rage against life and the world which has withheld love or recognition.

In both forms we find the same powerful, unconscious premise: "I shall not participate in the game of life, get emotionally involved,

---

[1 The reference is to David Reisman's work, *The Lonely Crowd* (New Haven: Yale University Press, 1950). *Eds.*]

or make a move on my own, until there is a guarantee for the fulfillment of my needs." These by now have become "just" claims for
total love or unique success which form part of the unconscious
idealized image that has to be actualized.

The apparently static condition of self-alienation reveals itself
as a dynamic and comprehensive attempt to avoid the painful experience of severe inner conflict, particularly between strong dependency
needs and co-existing violent and hostile aggression. By remaining
alienated from himself and detached from others, the patient avoids
the anxiety connected with emotional involvement in conflict. But
he pays for this with a steadily increasing restriction of his life, his
feelings, and his wants; he pays with a loss of his self.

Self-alienation is an unavoidable result of the neurotic process.
Simultaneously, however, it is an active move away from—or, rather,
against—the real self:

1) Alienation prevents disturbing self-awareness. The alienated
patient often complains of being "in a fog," but unconsciously he
wants to stay in it. He welcomes *self-anesthesia.*

2) Alienation, in the sense of conforming like an automaton,
protects him from the burden and the responsibility of commitment
to himself and his identity. It permits *self-elimination.*

3) Alienation, in its most active form, is the rejection of being
oneself and the attempt to become the other, ideal self. It means
escape from the hated self through *self-idealization.*

These three ways, in which the "despair at not being willing to be
oneself" finds expression, were already described by Kierkegaard, who
gained insight from the experience of his own anxiety and conflict.
He called loss of the self "sickness unto death." The first way is to
avoid consciousness of the self:

> By diversions or in other ways, e.g., by work and busy occupations
> as means of distractions, he seeks to preserve an obscurity about
> his condition, yet again in such a way that it does not become
> quite clear to him that he does it for this reason (that he does
> what he does in order to bring about obscurity).

This is the overbusy persons whom Tennessee Williams describes
so well:

> Mrs. Stone pursued the little diversions, the hairdresser at four
> o'clock, the photographer at 5:00, the Colony at 6:00, the theatre

at 7:30, Sardi's at midnight . . . she moved in the great empty circle. But she glanced inward from the periphery and saw the void enclosed there. She saw the emptiness . . . but the way that centrifugal force prevents a whirling object from falling inward, she was removed for a long time from the void she circled.

This void, the "existential vacuum," as Victor Frankl calls it, is a main aspect of the neuroses of our time. Our culture is continuously providing new means for self-anesthesia through "shallow living" (Horney): social drinking, late and late-late shows on television, never-ending double features at the movies, Miltown taken like candy.

The second way "to avoid willing to be oneself?" is "willing to be simply the conventional self":

> By becoming wise about how things go in this world, such a man forgets himself . . . finds it too venturesome to think, to be himself, far easier and safer to be like the others, to become an imitation, a number, a cipher in the crowd. This form of despair is hardly ever noticed in the world. Such a man, precisely by losing himself in this way, has gained perfectability in adjusting.

Kierkegaard here anticipates what today has become a mass phenomenon: self-elimination through conforming "adjustment."

The third, most radical way "to avoid willing to be oneself" is "willing to be someone else." Binswanger emphasized the central role of this motivation for the schizophrenic in the "Case of Ellen West." I find the wish "to be someone else," in a decisive though modified way, also in most neurotic patients. They want to free themselves from the burden they experience their actual self to be, escape into fantasy, and try to become that ideal other self they feel they should be.

This process leads, in two ways, to steadily increasing atrophy and paralysis of the self and interference with its further growth. The first factor is the result of a kind of "inner deprivation." All available energy is used in the compulsive attempt to actualize the other, the ideal, self. Too little energy is left for the developing of the real potentials of the self. The second, much more active factor is the destructive force of contempt and hate which is generated incessantly by the omnipotent, idealized self-image and directed against the despicable, actual "self that failed." Early self-rejection and active self-alienation are the roots of masochistic and compulsive homosexual trends.

To get rid of his hated self is the pervasive motivation of the masochist. In Maugham's *Of Human Bondage:*

> Philip would imagine that he was some boy whom he had a particular fancy for. He would throw his soul, as it were, into the other's body, talk with his voice and laugh with his heart; he would imagine himself doing all the things the other did. It was so vivid that he seemed for a moment to be *no longer himself.* In this way he enjoyed many intervals of fantastic happiness.

This self-elimination and identification with somebody else gives Philip "fantastic happiness" because he is temporarily freed from his hated self; but it also drives him into the self-destructive morbid-dependency relationship with Mildred.

Freud was right when he observed the close relationship between narcissism and homosexuality. The dynamics of compulsive homosexuality, however, become clear only when we recognize with Horney that "narcissism is an expression not of self love, but of alienation from the self. . . . A person clings to illusions about himself because and as far as he has lost himself."

The narcissist lost vital aspect of himself due to early rejection which he internalized. He defends himself against this self-rejection by compulsive self-idealization. If the early rejection is experienced as directed particularly against aspects of the self connected with the sexual role, no clear sense of sexual identity can develop. It is a desperate search for a self and identity which drives him into the homosexual relationship. "I don't want to be me. I want to have his balls. I want to be him," a patient recently said.

Symbiosis seems to provide the solution in two ways: by merging with the partner he hopes to become the other, the ideal, self. This partner often is the externalized symbol of the lost, the repressed part of his own self, for example, of his "masculinity." The second function of the symbiotic relationship is what I have called the "*magic mirror symbiosis.*"

The alienated person exists, becomes at least partially alive, only in the mirror image reflected by others. Without it he feels emotionally dead, as Sartre shows in *No Exit.* A patient says it well: "I searched a way to me by drawing pieces of myself out of their eyes."

In the symbiotic relationship each partner functions as a mirror of the other's image. His "love" has to neutralize the acid of destructive self-hate in the other. The relationship immediately breaks when the mirror-function stops.

Phenomena such as so-called "penis envy," or a man's wish to be a woman, have to be seen as symbols of a partial or total rejection of personal and sexual identity. "If I had the chance of being myself, I would not be myself," a woman said. "I would be a boy. As a boy you are in control. You can do what you want; it is very depressing not to be a man." Such statements have to be analyzed as an expression of the total attitude the patient has toward himself and his life, as a characteristic of his very specific being in the world.

The wish not to be oneself often focuses on the body, fostering a negative body-image which may crystallize around tallness or shortness, overweight or underweight, face, skin, sex—and color. If self-rejection selects the focus on color or nationality, distorting attitudes not only of the parents but of the community have been in operation. We may well ask whether segregation does not foster as much self-alienation in the segregating person who glorifies body aspects, as in the victim.

Only when the unconscious attempts fail—be they self-anesthesia, self-elimination through conforming adjustment, or escape from the self through identification with the other, the ideal self—does the patient come to us. Something has "happened" to him which shows that his safety system is not so safe, his solution not so perfect as he expected. He hopes that the therapist will help him to correct his mistake, to improve his solution.

Thus a paradox is inherent in the therapy of such patients. In the beginning, patient and therapist seem to move in opposite directions. The therapist wants to help the patient to move in a "centripetal" direction, to reconnect him with the vital roots and the creative potential in him. But the patient is unconsciously divided. From the very beginning of therapy he is in search of his self and longs for a genuine relationship. But he still feels driven to accelerate his centrifugal move away from his self, which means to perfect his alienation. Or at least he expects to be freed from anxiety. He wants reassurance. Reassurance removes anxiety. But in so doing, it blocks awareness and destroys the patient's chance for growth and change. All too often the patient gets what he wants: the therapist complies with his expectations for a painless (because changeless) "cure."

The task of the psychoanalyst is not to remove anxiety and thereby to perpetuate alienation. He has to help the patient find the way back to himself. He has to help him face the anxiety generated on this road by self-confrontation and the surrender of cherished illusions. This can rarely be done by analysis in the orthodox manner, with the therapist sitting behind the couch taking notes and giving interpretations. The alienated, "shut-up" patient has all his life used words not to express but to hide his feelings.

Psychoanalysis has to outgrow alienated concepts of personality as well as alienating techniques in therapy. The image of man as an id harboring only libidinous, aggressive, and destructive drives, but no constructive forces; as a super-ego, functioning as an inner police force, not as a healthy human conscience; and as a more or less passive ego, which reminds one of a rather sick self—such an image of man in itself appears fragmented and alienated. The concept of a doctor-patient relationship which is seen as determined by the transference of a neurotic past but disregards the constructive impact of the creative "meeting" in the present is in itself alienating. Instead of lessening the patient's alienation, it is likely to prolong it.

Psychoanalysis, born as a child of the age of enlightenment, overestimated the therapeutic effect of knowledge in itself. Making the unconscious conscious is not, in itself, therapeutically effective. To know, for example, that I harbor strong, compulsive dependency needs, may increase rather than lessen my self-alienation. Self-knowledge becomes therapeutically active only when it is experientially owned, and generates the emotional shock which is inherent in the process of self-confrontation. Only such experience has the power to lead to change, choice, and commitment. Kierkegaard was aware of this:

> '*gnothi seauton*' (know yourself) has been seen as the goal of all human endeavor . . . but it cannot be the goal if it is not at the same time the beginning. The ethical individual knows himself, but this knowledge is not a mere contemplation . . . it is a reflection upon himself which itself is an action and therefore I have deliberately preferred to use the expression 'choose oneself' instead of 'know oneself' . . . when the individual knows himself and has chosen himself he is about to realize himself.

Frequently at the end of an orthodox analysis, the patient has gained much knowledge. He could easily "present his own case." He looks with some interest at that stranger who happens to be himself. He may even reflect the image which the therapist expects. But he has not changed. The patient needs, as Ferenczi, Franz Alexander, and Fromm-Reichmann have emphasized, not explanations but emotional experience. To break through his alienation he needs to begin to feel himself and to permit himself more and more to be. The first step involves helping him to stop hating himself. "Any true psychotherapy," Binswanger states—and this is particularly true for the alienated patient—"is reconciliation of man with himself and thereby with the world, is a transformation of hostility against himself into friendship with himself and thereby with the world."

In the beginning of therapy, the patient who refuses participation in life will also refuse true participation in psychoanalysis, even though he may lie down on the couch or sit down on the chair with a compliant smile. He is deeply convinced that nobody cares, nobody understands him, and that communicating his true feelings, his sufferings, and his rage to anybody, including the analyst, is sheer waste.

To "defrost," to open up, to experience and to accept himself become possible for the patient only in a warm, mutually trusting relationship in which, often for the first time in his life, he feels fully accepted as he is, accepted *with* those aspects of himself which early in life he had felt compelled to reject or repress. Only this enables the patient gradually to drop his defenses. He will test the reliability of this acceptance again and again before he risks emotional involvement. He will need this basic trust especially when he begins to experience the "dizziness of freedom" (Kierkegaard). The road from self-alienation and self-rejection to self-acceptance and self-realization leads through steadily growing self-awareness, which is made possible by the new creative experience of acceptance and meeting. Thus, the main therapeutic factor becomes the doctor-patient relationship itself. Very much limited in the beginning by the patient's passive and active distrust, the relationship gradually becomes spontaneous and mutual. Binswanger expresses it like this:

> The communication must under no circumstances be considered mere repetition, as orthodox analysts believe, that is to say, as transference and counter-transference in the positive case, as resistance and counter-resistance in the negative one; rather, the relationship between patient and doctor invariably constitutes an autonomous communicative novum, a new existential bond.

In the beginning of therapy, questions such as, "What do you feel now?" or "What would you really want?" may bring the patient close to panic. He becomes aware for a moment how deeply his capacity for spontaneous feeling or wanting is impaired.

The patient needs "emotional insight." Such insight is rarely verbalized. The patient may be silent or cry or laugh or do both at the same time. He may perspire, have palpitations, or breathe heavily. If he could verbalize his insight—it is characteristic that he cannot usually do it—he might say, "Yes, now I see: it is me, not they. It is me, not fate." In Kierkegaard's terms this changes the "aesthetical" person who experiences everything as coming from without to the "ethical" person, who, transparent to himself, knows that everything depends upon what *he* sees, feels, and does. In psychoanalytic terms it is the change from the feeling of being a victim of fate, constitution, the environment or "the unconscious," to experiencing one's conflicts within oneself, and oneself as an active force in one's life. It is a prerequisite for moving in the direction of freedom, choice, and responsibility.

Kretschmer compared alienated patients to Italian villas that have closed their shutters against the glaring sun. Inside, however, in subdued light exciting events are happening. It often is the dream that opens the shutters for a moment. As the pupil widens in the dark, the dream widens the scope of our self-awareness which, during the daytime, is restricted by compulsive focusing on emergencies, action, and defense. Self-alienation is temporarily lessened. The dream becomes a door to the larger self. It has access to aspects of our selves, neurotic as well as healthy, which we are rejecting or repressing.

With progress in therapy, the dreams of the alienated patient who appears emotionally dead often begin to reveal surprising aliveness and depth, passionate longings, strong feelings of loss and sadness, and conflict between moving into life and resignation. They may confront him with his emotional deadness, his unlived life, as in Ingmar Bergman's "Wild Strawberries," with the neglect of the growth of his real self, which may be symbolized by a plant that needs water, a kitten that needs shelter, a baby that needs food.

On the other hand, early in therapy—earlier than memories or free associations which here are often sparse—dreams reconnect the alienated patient, who is disconnected from his past and his roots, with his childhood when his feelings were more spontaneous and genuine, with his adolescence when he faced the conflicts of growing up, with times in his life when he was closer to his real self, when his heart was alive, and when he took a stand for himself. The past here enters the dream as a symbol of the potential present, as a symbol of the dreamer's own spontaneity, genuineness, and capacity for commitment. Originating in himself, such dreams often convince the patient that there is more strength, more courage, more "self" available in him than he was aware of.

Dreams may help him to move from alienation and self-rejection to genuine self-acceptance: acceptance of the self with its human limitations but with awareness of the potentiality as well as the responsibility for further growth. The patient may experience in a dream a new feeling of love and responsibility for a growing child that resembles him. Or he may meet and accept a person who symbolizes an aspect of himself he had violently rejected before. A Jewish immigrant, proud of his successful Americanization, met in his dream a strange-looking Ghetto inmate who reminded him of his father and, after initial hesitation, welcomed him warmly. A girl who had left the South, rebelling against parents and home, in her dream saw herself, to her own surprise, welcome cordially a girl whose Southern drawl revealed her own identity.

Therapy often is seen in dreams first as a molding procedure, a threat, a humiliation, an invasion of privacy. The patient experiences himself as a passive object resenting and rejecting the procedure. Whatever has to be done, he feels, will be done *on* him, *to* him, *for* or *against* him by the therapist. An alienated patient, unable to experience an intimate sexual relationship, saw himself on an operating table, anesthetized from the waist down. He felt nothing, but joined the surgeon in an intellectual discussion of the interesting operation. Later dreams reflect the patient more and more as an active partner in the analytic relationship. Medard Boss showed the lessening of alienation in a patient whose dreams first dealt only with inanimate objects, such as machines and cars. Then a plant appeared, and only much later, after many animals had entered the dreams, the first human being was encountered. I have seen the dreaming pattern in alienated patients change from dreams in which the dreamer himself is not seen—except perhaps as the symbol of a statue, a skeleton, or brain—to dreams in which the patient often appears, first, as a detached onlooker. Later, when the ice-wall of alienation is slowly beginning to melt, violent "split-image" dreams may occur, which show symbols of the emerging larger self in violent struggle with the old neurotic self, which often is idealized. Such dreams, if they are experientially "owned" by the patient, often are accompanied by that feeling of explosive rage and the sudden eruption of the long repressed hunger for life that Camus shows in the final crisis of *The Stranger:* "I started yelling at the top of my voice. I hurled insults. . . . It was as if that great rush of anger had washed me clean—I felt ready to start life all over again." Total emotional involvement in rage and conflict often precedes acceptance of self.

This explains why, when the alienated patient first begins to "relate," there often are violent outbursts of rage. The therapist has to take hostility and contempt until the patient realizes that he has externalized his self-contempt onto the therapist.

An alienated patient whose key childhood memory was waiting in the rain for mother, in his first dream misses the boat—of life. Later dreams show him turning his back on life, running away from home where his parents are fighting, to follow his dog on a lonely road through the woods; living underground in a cellar, absorbed in monotonous, meaningless labor, trying to repair broken clocks (time has stopped for him), while upstairs in the daylight his wife, his life, are waiting. In a subsequent dream he is attracted to a warm, giving woman, but feels, "If I let myself be touched by her, I will get so involved that I will lose myself." Relating closely often contains for the alienated patient the threat of losing his weak identity. This is a fear that, in its greatest intensity, I occasionally have found expressed in fear of orgasm; emotional surrender, giving up control, here is experienced, as "*la petite mort*," the small death.

Finally, the patient is shocked by a dream in which he sees himself actually touched by the therapist without being aware of it, an experience which he had fought but secretly wanted. Toward the end of his analysis, this patient said: "What helped me? Not so much your interpretations. It was the process of getting in touch, being touched by you, very much against my will, touching you, which I first did not like, and often disagreeing with you, during which I began to feel my own identity."

In such a patient, who is frightened of contact and longing for contact at the same time, the usual psychoanalytic technique often results only in a series of negative therapeutic reactions because for a long time the maintenance of the alienation appears to the patient as the only way to survive as an individual. Healing—to use Hans Trueb's words—here occurs mainly through meeting. But not just any meeting will be healing. The patient will misuse the relationship and the therapist for the satisfaction of his neurotic needs for love, for power, or for uniqueness. Only very slowly will the relationship change from what Martin Buber calls an "I-It" relationship to a truly mutual "I-Thou" relationship.

The therapist must have achieved in his analysis a lessening of his own alienation, which often is hidden behind a professional pseudo-identity. He must have gained a high tolerance for anxiety and hostility in the patient and in himself, an immunity against getting seduced by and neurotically involved with the patient. The authoritarian therapist fosters the development of a passive-rebellious pseudo-identity. The over-protective therapist fosters a weak, unconsciously still symbiotic pseudo-identity. The detached therapist often has the "meeting" with the patient so far out in the all that the boundaries between the self of the patient, the self of the therapist, and the cosmos become blurred. Here the patient has little chance to lessen his alienation and to gain true personal and sexual identity. Such a therapist, who himself is often afraid of a truly close and mutual relationship, deprives the patient of the experience of a genuine person-to-person meeting, which alone has the power of healing. Required is a truly mutual bipolar relationship. No "I" can develop without encountering a clearly defined, solid, but warm and spontaneous "Thou" in the therapist.

In the words of Buber, who wrote a beautiful introduction to Trueb's *Healing Through Meeting*:

> If the psychotherapist is satisfied to 'analyze' the patient . . . at best he may help a soul which is diffused and poor in structure to collect and order itself to some extent. But the real matter, the regeneration of an atrophied personal center will not be achieved . . . This can only be attained in the person-to-person attitude of a partner.

SUMMARY

1. Self-alienation originates in an early childhood situation which deprives the child of the vital experience of feeling genuinely accepted as an individual. (Lack of physical and emotional closeness, symbiotic parent-child relationships, over-expectations of compulsively ambitious parents). Basic anxiety fosters compulsive needs for safety which deflect the development of the child from spontaneity, self-expression, and self-realization to self-rejection, self-elimination, and escape into the fantasy of self-idealization. Cultural factors reinforce trends toward self-alienation.

2. Self-alienation is a result of the neurotic process. Simultaneously, however, by providing self-anesthesia and self-elimination, it becomes a dynamic and comprehensive unconscious attempt to avoid disturbing self-awareness, anxiety, and interpersonal and intrapsychic conflict.

3. Active alienation from the self, unconscious rejection of

personal and sexual identity, and the wish to be the other—the ideal self—are basic aspects of the neurotic personality of our time. They foster self-destructive masochistic and homosexual trends and compulsive symbiotic relationships.

4. To help the alienated patient, psychoanalysis has to outgrow alienated concepts of personality and alienating techniques in therapy. The basic change from alienation and self-rejection to self-acceptance and self-realization requires steadily growing self-awareness gained in emotional experience and emotional insight.

5. Dreams occur during a period of lessened self-alienation and become, therefore, an important mobilizing force in the therapy of the alienated patient. They move him closer to his real self and reconnect him with the vital roots in his past and with the constructive potential he will strive to realize in the future.

6. Therapeutic goals are genuine acceptance of self and others, growing autonomy, a stronger sense of personal and sexual identity, and commitment to further self-realization. The main therapeutic factor is the new creative experience of acceptance and "meeting" in a warm, truly mutual, trusting doctor-patient relationship.

KARL JASPERS (1883–1969)

The Present Situation

More urgent than ever has become the problem concerning the present situation of mankind as the upshot of past developments and in view of the possibilities of the future. On the one hand we see possibilities of decay and destruction, and on the other hand we see possibilities that a truly human life is now about to begin, but as between these conflicting alternatives, the prospect is obscure.

The achievements that transformed the pre-human being into man were effected, not only before the days of recorded history, but even before tradition began. What lifted our forefathers above the

The selection is from Karl Jaspers, *Man in the Modern Age*, trans. Eden and Cedar Paul (London: Routledge and Kegan Paul, Ltd., 1957), pp. 15–23 and 62–64. Used by permission of the publisher.

animal world was the persistent and not merely fortuitous use of tools, the making and utilisation of fire, the birth of language, and a control of sexual jealousy sufficient to render possible comradeship and the foundation of durable societies. Recorded history, extending back for only six thousand years, is but a brief span in comparison with the hundreds of thousands of years of inaccessible pre-history during which these decisive steps in the making of man were being taken. In those long ages, men existed in various forms, widespread over the surface of the globe, knowing naught of one another. From among them western man (who has conquered the world, brought men of all parts into contact with one another, and made them aware of their common humanity) would seem to have developed in virtue of the consistent application of three great principles.

The first is an unflinching *rationalism*, grounded upon Hellenic science, weighing and measuring the data of experience, and achieving their technical mastery. Universally valid scientific research, predictability of legal decisions thanks to the systematisation of Roman law, calculation applied to economic enterprise and pushed to the extent of rationalising all activity (even such as is arrested through being rationalised). These were the outcome of complete submission to the dominion of logical thought and empirical actuality as they disclose themselves to all persons and at all times.

The second principle is the *subjectivity of selfhood* which became explicit in the teachings of the Jewish prophets, in the wisdom of the Greek philosophers, and in the activities of the statesmen of classical Rome. What we term individuality developed along these lines in the men of the western world and was from the outset correlated with rationalism.

Coming to the third principle, we find in western man a firm conviction that *the world is a tangible reality in time*, this conviction being contraposed to the 'unworldliness' of the East, which is the outcome of a sentiment that not-being is perhaps the essential reality of what presents itself to us as being. Assurance is assurance of this tangible reality and cannot arise independently thereof. Selfhood and rationalism are the twin sources of assurance, which cognises reality and seeks to master it.

Only during recent centuries have these three principles been developed, and not until the nineteenth century did they enter into their own. The surface of the world became universally accessible; space capitulated. For the first time man was enabled to dwell wherever he would on our planet. All things are interrelated. The technical mastery of space, time, and matter advances irresistibly, and no longer through casual and isolated discoveries, but by organised collaboration, in the course of which discovery itself has been systematised and subjected to purposive endeavour.

After thousands of years during which civilisation progressed along detached and even divergent roads, the last four and a half centuries have witnessed the European conquest of the world, which the last hundred years have completed. During the acceleration of this concluding phase there was an abundance of independent and outstanding personalities; of persons animated by the pride of leadership, the delight of the master-craftsman, the fervour of the discoverer, venturesomeness tempered with discretion, the contentment of those who reach uttermost bourns: and there arose a sense of close kinship with the world thus revealed. To-day, however, we feel that for us this century of expansion is over and done with. There has been a reversal of mood, owing to which, though the positive achievements remain, we have come to recognise the persistence of vast and wellnigh insuperable difficulties. The movement of objective conquest seems to have attained its term; we no longer advance, but are inclined rather to retreat.

The guiding principles of western mankind are incompatible with the notion that a mere circular recurrence can be stable. Our reason tells us that every new cognition implies further possibilities. Reality does not exist as such, but has to be grasped by a cognition which is an active seizure. From decade to decade the rapidity of the relevant movements has increased. No longer is anything fixed. All things are put to the question and as far as possible transformed; and of late this has been effected at the cost of internal frictions which were unknown in the nineteenth century.

The feeling of a breakaway from previous history is widespread. The innovation, however, is something more than a mere revolutionising of society in the sense of shattering it to bits, a change in property relationships, the overthrow of aristocracy. An ancient Egyptian papyrus dating from more than four thousand years ago contains the following passages:

> Robbers abound. ... No one ploughs the land. People are saying: "We do not know what will happen from day to day." ... Dirt prevails everywhere, and no longer does any one wear clean raiment. ... The country is spinning round and round like a potter's wheel. ... Slave-women are wearing necklaces of gold

and lapis lazuli. . . . No more do we hear any one laugh . . . Great men and small agree in saying: "Would that I had never been born." . . . Well-to-do persons are set to turn mill-stones. . . . Ladies have to demean themselves to the tasks of serving-women. . . . People are so famished that they snatch what falls from the mouths of swine. . . . The offices where records are kept have been broken into and plundered . . . and the documents of the scribes have been destroyed. . . . Moreover, certain foolish persons have bereft the country of the monarchy; . . . the officials have been driven hither and thither; . . . no public office stands open where it should, and the masses are like timid sheep without a shepherd. . . . Artists have ceased to ply their art. . . . The few slay the many. . . . One who yesterday was indigent is now wealthy, and the sometime rich overwhelm him with adulation. . . . Impudence is rife. . . . Oh that man could cease to be, that women should no longer conceive and give birth. Then, at length the world would find peace.[1]

We see from the foregoing that the feeling that social conditions are hopelessly disordered, and that no firm abiding-place remains, is not new to history. Thucydides' account of conditions in Hellas during the Peloponnesian war is another testimony from the ancient world.

But to strike home in the new times the notion must be more penetrating than can be a general conception of the possibilities of revolution, disorder, a loosening of moral ties. Since the days of Schiller, the modern mind has become aware of the loss of the sense of a divine presence in the world—a loss characteristic of recent centuries. In the West this process has been carried to a far greater extreme than elsewhere. Doubtless there were sceptics in ancient India and in the classical world, men for whom nothing but the immediate present, as it discloses itself to our senses, counted for anything—the immediate present, inexorably grasped, and itself accounted as null. But, even so, for them the world as a whole was still a spiritualised entity. In the West, as a sequel of the spread of Christianity, scepticism of another kind became possible. The idea of a transcendental creator, existing before, after, and apart from the world he had fashioned out of chaos, reduced that world to the level of a mere creature. The demons known to paganism vanished from the realm of nature, and the world became a godless world. All that had been created was now the object of human cognition, rethinking (as it were) God's thoughts. Protestant

[1] Selections from Erman, *Die Literatur der Aegypten*, 1923, pp. 130–48.

Christianity took the matter very seriously. The natural sciences, with their rationalisation, mathematicisation, and mechanisation of the world, were closely akin to this form of Christianity. The great scientific investigators of the seventeenth and eighteenth centuries were pious Christians. But when, finally, advancing doubt made an end of God the Creator, there was left in being no more than the mechanical world-system recognised by the natural sciences—a world-system which would never have been so crudely denuded of spirit but for its previous degradation to the status of a creature.

The despiritualisation of the world is not the outcome of the unfaith of individuals, but is one of the possible consequences of a mental development which here has actually led to Nothingness. We feel the unprecedented vacancy of existence, a sense of vacancy against which even the keenest scepticism of classical times was safeguarded by the richly-peopled fullness of an undecayed mythical reality, with which the *De rerum natura* of Lucretius the Epicurean is instinct. Such a development is not, indeed, absolutely inevitable to the human consciousness, for it presupposes a misunderstanding of the true significance of natural science and an unduly rigid application of its categories to all being. But, as aforesaid, it is possible; and it has actually occurred, having been promoted by the overwhelming successes of science in the technical and practical fields. What, in all the millenniums of human history and pre-history, no god had been able to do for man, man has done for himself. It is natural enough that in these achievements of his he should discern the true inwardness of being—until he shrinks back in alarm from the void he has made for himself.

Moderns are inclined to compare the present situations with that which prevailed during the decline of the classical systems, with the fall of the Greek States and the decay of Hellenism, or with the third century of the Christian era when ancient culture was collapsing. Yet there are more important differences. Classical civilisation was the civilisation of no more than a small part of the world, in an area which did not comprise within its bounds all the factors of the future of mankind. To-day, when communications are world-wide, the whole human race must enter the domain of western civilisation. At the beginning of the Dark Ages, population was declining; now it has increased and is still increasing beyond measure. Then the menace to civilisation came from without, now it comes from within. But the most conspicuous difference between our own time and the third century A.D. is that then technique was stationary or retrograde, whereas now it is advancing with giant strides. The favourable and unfavourable chances lie outside the range of possible prediction.

The objectively conspicuous new factor which cannot fail henceforward to modify the foundations of human existence, and thus provide it with new conditions, is this development of the world of technique. For the first time an effective control of nature has begun. If we think of our world as being buried, subsequent excavators would not bring to light any such beautiful objects as those which have come down to us from classical days, whose street-pavement, even, is a delight to us. They would, however, discover such vast quantities of iron and concrete as to make it plain that during the last few decades (as contrasted with all previous ages) man had begun to enwrap the planet in a mesh of apparatus. The step thus taken has been as momentous as that taken when our forefathers first began to use tools; and we can already look forward to the day when the world will become one vast factory for the utilisation of its matter and energy. For the second time man has broken away from nature to do work which nature would never have done for herself, and which rivals nature in creative power. This work becomes actualised for us, not only in its visible and tangible products, but also in its functioning; and our hypothetical excavator would not be able, from the vestiges of wireless masts and antennae, for instance, to infer the universality of the diffusion of news over the earth's surface.

The novelty of our century, the changes whose completion will set it so utterly apart from the past, are not, however, exhaustively comprised within the limits of the despiritualisation of the world and its subjection to a regime of advanced technique. Even those who lack clear knowledge of the subject are becoming decisively aware that they are living in an epoch when the world is undergoing a change so vast as to be hardly comparable to any of the great changes of past millenniums. The mental situation of our day is pregnant with immense dangers and immense possibilities; and it is one which, if we are inadequate to the tasks which await us, will herald the failure of mankind.

Is it an end that draws near, or a beginning? Is it perhaps a beginning as significant as that when man first became man, but now enriched by newly acquired means, and the capacity for experience upon a new and higher level?

DREAD OF LIFE

In the rationalisation and universalisation of the life-order there has grown contemporaneously with its fantastic success an awareness of imminent ruin tantamount to a dread of the approaching end of all that makes life worth living. Not only does the apparatus seem, by its perfectionment, to threaten the annihilation of everything; even the apparatus itself is menaced. A paradox results. Man's life has become dependent upon the apparatus which proves ruinous to mankind at one and the same time by its perfectionment and by its breakdown.

The prospect of so disastrous a future inspires the individual with dread, seeing that he cannot be content to become a simple function detached from his origin. A dread of life perhaps unparalleled in its intensity is modern man's sinister companion. He is alarmed at the likelihood that he will in the near future become unable to obtain the vital necessaries. Seeing their supply thus imperilled, his attention becomes riveted on them more strongly than ever before; and he is also inspired with a very different dread, namely that concerning his selfhood, which he cannot face up to.

Dread attaches itself to everything. All uncertainties are tinged by it unless we succeed in forgetting it. Care makes us unable to protect our lives adequately. The cruelties that used to abound everywhere without remark are less frequent than of yore, but we have become aware of those that remain and they seem more terrible than ever. He who wants to keep himself alive must strain his labour power to the uttermost; must work unrestingly, and subject to ever more intensive compulsion. Every one knows that a man who is left behind in the race will fall and remain untended; and he who has passed the age of forty feels that the world has no longer any use for him. True, we have our social-welfare institutions, our systems of social insurance, savings banks, and what not; but what public assistance and private charity can supply, falls more and more below what is regarded as the standard of a decent existence, even though people are no longer allowed to starve to death.

The dread of life attaches itself to the body. Although what statisticians term the expectation of life is considerably increased, we all have a growing sense of vital insecurity. People demand medical treatment far beyond what is regarded as reasonable from the medical and scientific point of view. If a man comes to look upon his life as spiritually unacceptable, as intolerable were it merely because he can no longer understand its significance, he takes flight into illness, which envelops him like a visible protector. For in those limitary situations which (as mere life-experiences) crush him inwardly, man needs, either the selfhood of freedom, or else some objective point of support.

Dread or anxiety increases to such a pitch that the sufferer may feel himself to be nothing more than a lost point in empty space, inasmuch as all human relationships appear to have no more than a temporary validity. The work that binds human beings into a community is of fleeting duration. In erotic relationships, the question of duty is not even raised. The sufferer from anxiety has confidence in no one; he will not enter into absolute ties with any other person. One who fails to participate in what others are doing is left alone. The threat of being sacrificed arouses the sense of having been utterly forsaken, and this drives the sufferer out of his frivolous ephemeralness into cynical hardness and then into anxiety. In general, life seems full of dread.

Anxiety interferes with the working of the various institutions which exist, as part of the life-order, to tranquilise people and make them forget. The organisations in question are designed to arouse a sense of membership. The apparatus promises safety to its members. Doctors try and talk the sick or those who believe themselves sick out of the fear of death. But these institutions function effectively only when things are going well with the individual. The life-order cannot dispel the dread which is part of every individual's lot. This anxiety can only be controlled by the more exalted dread felt by existence threatened with the loss of its selfhood, which induces an overriding religious or philosophical exaltation. When existence is paralysed, the dread of life cannot fail to grow. The all-embracing dominion of the life-order would destroy man as existence without ever being able to free him from the dread of life. It is, indeed, the tendency of the life-order to become absolute which arouses an uncontrollable dread of life.

HANNAH ARENDT (1906—)

World Alienation

Three great events stand at the threshold of the modern age and determine its character: the discovery of America and the ensuing exploration of the whole earth; the Reformation, which by expropriating ecclesiastical and monastic possessions started the twofold process of individual expropriation and the accumulation of social wealth; the invention of the telescope and the development of a new science that considers the nature of the earth from the viewpoint of the universe. These cannot be called modern events as we know them since the French Revolution, and although they cannot be explained by any chain of causality, because no event can, they are still happening in an unbroken continuity, in which precedents exist and predecessors can be named. None of them exhibits the peciliar character of an explosion of undercurrents which, having gathered their force in the dark, suddenly erupt. The names we connect with them, Galileo Galilei and Martin Luther and the great seafarers, explorers, and adventurers in the age of discovery, still belong to a premodern world. Moreover, the strange pathos of novelty, the almost violent insistence of nearly all the great authors, scientists, and philosophers since the seventeenth century that they saw things never seen before, thought thoughts never thought before, can be found in none of them, not even in Galileo.[1] These precursors are not revolutionists, and their motives and intentions are still securely rooted in tradition.

In the eyes of their contemporaries, the most spectacular of these events must have been the discoveries of unheard-of continents and

---

[1] The term *scienza nuova* seems to occur for the first time in the work of the sixteenth-century Italian mathematician Niccolò Tartaglia, who designed the new science of ballistics which he claimed to have discovered because he was the first to apply geometrical reasoning to the motion of projectiles. (I owe this information to Professor Alexandre Koyré.) Of greater relevance in our context is that Galileo, in the *Sidereus Nuncius* (1610), insists on the "absolute novelty" of his discoveries, but this certainly is a far cry from Hobbes's claim that political philosophy was "no older than my own book *De Cive*" (*English Works*, ed. Molesworth [1839], I, ix) or Descartes' conviction that no philosopher before him had succeeded in philosophy ("Lettre au traducteur pouvant servir de préface" for *Les principes de la philosophie*). From the seventeenth century on, the insistence on absolute novelty and the rejection of the whole tradition became commonplace. Karl Jaspers (*Descartes und die Philosophie* [2d ed.; 1948], pp. 61 ff.) stresses the difference between Renaissance philosophy, where "Drang nach Geltung der originalen Persönlichkeit ... das Neusein als Auszeichnung verlangte," and modern science, where "sich das Wort 'neu' als sachliches Wertpraedikat verbreitet." In the same context, he shows how different in significance the claim to novelty is in science and philosophy. Descartes certainly presented his philosophy as a scientist may present a new scientific discovery. Thus, he writes as follows about his "considérations": "Je ne mérite point plus de gloire de les avoir trouvées, que ferait un passant d'avoir rencontré par bonheur à ses pieds quelque riche trésor, que la diligence de plusieurs aurait inutilement cherché longtemps auparavant" (*La recherche de la vérité* [Pléiade ed.], p. 669).

undreamed-of oceans; the most disturbing might have been the Refor mation's irremediable split of Western Christianity, with its inherent challenge to orthodoxy as such and its immediate threat to the tran quillity of men's souls; certainly the least noticed was the addition of a new implement to man's already large arsenal of tools, useless except to look at the stars, even though it was the first purely scientific instru ment ever devised. However, if we could measure the momentum of history as we measure natural processes, we might find that what originally had the least noticeable impact, man's first tentative steps toward the discovery of the universe, has constantly increased in momen tousness as well as speed until it has eclipsed not only the enlargement of the earth's surface, which found its final limitation only in the limitations of the globe itself, but also the still apparently limitless economic accumulation process.

But these are mere speculations. As a matter of fact, the discovery of the earth, the mapping of her lands and the charting of her waters, took many centuries and has only now begin to come to an end. Only now has man taken full possession of his mortal dwelling place and gathered the infinite horizons, which were temptingly and forbiddingly open to all previous ages, into a globe whose majestic outlines and detailed surface he knows as he knows the lines in the palm of his hand. Precisely when the immensity of available space on earth was discovered, the famous shrinkage of the globe began, until eventually in our world (which, though the result of the modern age, is by no means identical with the modern age's world) each man is as much an inhabitant of the earth as he is an inhabitant of his country. Men now live in an earth-wide continuous whole where even the notion of distance, still inherent in the most perfectly unbroken contiguity of parts, has yielded before the onslaught of speed. Speed has conquered space; and though this conquering process finds its limit at the unconquerable boundary of the simultaneous presence of one body at two different places, it has made distance meaningless, for no significant part of a human life— years, months, or even weeks—is any longer necessary to reach any point on the earth.

Nothing, to be sure, could have been more alien to the purpose of the explorers and circumnavigators of the early modern age than this closing-in process; they went to enlarge the earth, not shrink her into a ball, and when they submitted to the call of the distant, they had no intention of abolishing distance. Only the wisdom of hindsight sees the obvious, that nothing can remain immense if it can be measured, that every survey brings together distant parts and therefore establishes closeness where distance ruled before. Thus the maps and navigation charts of the early stages of the modern age anticipated the technical inventions through which all earthly space has become small and close at hand. Prior to the shrinkage of space and the abolition of distance through railroads, steamships, and airplanes, there is the infinitely greater and more effective shrinkage which comes about through the surveying capacity of the human mind, whose use of numbers, symbols, and models can condense and scale earthly physical distance down to the size of the human body's natural sense and understanding. Before we knew how to circle the earth, how to circumscribe the sphere of human habitation in days and hours, we had brought the globe into our living rooms to be touched by our hands and swirled before our eyes.

There is another aspect of this matter which, as we shall see, will be of greater importance in our context. It is in the nature of the human surveying capacity that it can function only if man disentangles himself from all involvement in and concern with the close at hand and withdraws himself to a distance from everything near him. The greater the distance between himself and his surroundings, world or earth, the more he will be able to survey and to measure and the less will worldly, earth-bound space be left to him. The fact that the decisive shrinkage of the earth was the consequence of the invention of the airplane, that is, of leaving the surface of the earth altogether, is like a symbol for the general phenomenon that any decrease of terrestrial distance can be won only at the price of putting a decisive distance between man and earth, of alienating man from his immediate earthly surroundings.

The fact that the Reformation, an altogether different event, eventually confronts us with a similar phenomenon of alienation, which Max Weber even identified, under the name of "innerworldly asceticism," as the innermost spring of the new capitalist mentality, may be one of the many coincidences that make it so difficult for the historian not to believe in ghosts, demons, and *Zeitgeists*. What is so striking and disturbing is the similarity in utmost divergence. For this innerworldly alienation has nothing to do, either in intent or content, with the alienation from the earth inherent in the discovery and taking possession of the earth. Moreover, the innerworldly alienation whose historical factuality Max Weber demonstrated in his famous essay is not only present in the new morality that grew out of Luther's and Calvin's attempts to restore the uncompromising otherworldliness of the Christian faith; it is equally present, albeit on an altogether different level, in the expropriation of the peasantry, which was the unforeseen consequence of the expropriation of church property and, as such, the greatest single factor in the breakdown of the feudal system.[2] It is, of course, idle to speculate on what the course of our economy would have been without this event, whose impact propelled Western mankind into a development in which all property was destroyed in the process of its appropriation, all things devoured in the process of their production, and the stability of the world undermined in a constant process of change. Yet, such speculations are meaningful to the extent that they remind us that history is a story of events and not of forces or ideas with predictable courses. They are idle and even dangerous when used as arguments against reality and when meant to point to positive potentialities and alternatives, because their number is not only indefinite by definition but they also lack the tangible unexpectedness of the event, and compensate for it by mere plausibility. Thus, they remain sheer phantoms no matter in how pedestrian a manner they may be presented.

In order not to underestimate the momentum this process has reached after centuries of almost unhindered development, it may be well to reflect on the so-called "economic miracle" of postwar Germany, a miracle only if seen in an outdated frame of reference. The German example shows very clearly that under modern conditions the expropriation of people, the destruction of objects, and the devastation of cities will turn out to be a radical stimulant for a process, not of mere recovery, but of quicker and more efficient accumulation of wealth—if only the country is modern enough to respond in terms of the production process. In Germany, outright destruction took the place of the relentless process of depreciation of all worldly things, which is the hallmark of the waste economy in which we now live. The result is almost the same: a booming prosperity which, as postwar Germany illustrates, feeds not on the abundance of material goods or on anything stable and given but on the process of production and consumption itself. Under modern conditions, not destruction but conservation spells ruin because the very durability of conserved objects is the greatest

[2] This is not to deny the greatness of Max Weber's discovery of the enormous power that comes from an other-worldliness directed toward the world (see "Protestant Ethics and the Spirit of Capitalism," in *Religionssoziologie* [1920], Vol. I). Weber finds the Protestant work ethos preceded by certain traits of monastic ethics, and one can indeed see a first germ of these attitudes in Augustine's famous distinction between *uti* and *frui*, between the things of this world which one may use but not enjoy and those of the world to come which may be enjoyed for their own sake. The increase in power of man over the things of this world springs in either case from the distance which man puts between himself and the world, that is, from world alienation.

impediment to the turnover process, whose constant gain in speed is the only constancy left wherever it has taken hold.[3]

We saw before that property, as distinguished from wealth and appropriation, indicates the privately owned share of a common world and therefore is the most elementary political condition for man's worldliness. By the same token, expropriation and world alienation coincide, and the modern age, very much against the intentions of all the actors in the play, began by alienating certain strata of the population from the world. We tend to overlook the central importance of this alienation for the modern age because we usually stress its secular character and identify the term secularity with worldliness. Yet secularization as a tangible historical event means no more than separation of Church and State, of religion and politics, and this, from a religious viewpoint, implies a return to the early Christian attitude of "Render unto Caesar the things that are Caesar's and unto God the things that are God's" rather than a loss of faith and transcendance or a new and emphatic interest in the things of this world.

Modern loss of faith is not religious in origin—it cannot be traced to the Reformation and Counter Reformation, the two great religious movements of the modern age—and its scope is by no means restricted to the religious sphere. Moreover, even if we admitted that the modern age began with a sudden, inexplicable eclipse of transcendence, of belief in a hereafter, it would by no means follow that this loss threw man back upon the world. The historical evidence, on the contrary, shows that modern men were not thrown back upon this world but upon themselves. One of the most persistent trends in modern philosophy since Descartes and perhaps its most original contribution to philosophy had been an exclusive concern with the self, as distinguished from the soul or person or man in general, an attempt to reduce all experiences, with the world as well as with other human beings, to experiences between man and himself. The greatness of Max Weber's discovery

[3] The reason most frequently given for the surprising recovery of Germany—that she did not have to carry the burden of a military budget—is inconclusive on two accounts: first, Germany had to pay for a number of years the costs of occupation, which amounted to a sum almost equal to a full-fledged military budget, and second, war production is held in other economies to be the greatest single factor in the postwar prosperity. Moreover, the point I wish to make could be equally well illustrated by the common and yet quite uncanny phenomenon that prosperity is closely connected with the "useless" production of means of destruction, of goods produced to be wasted either by using them up in destruction or—and this is the more common case—by destroying them because they soon become obsolete.

about the origins of capitalism lay precisely in his demonstration that an enormous, strictly mundane activity is possible without any care for or enjoyment of the world whatever, an activity whose deepest motivation, on the contrary, is worry and care about the self. World alienation and not self-alienation as Marx thought,[4] has been the hallmark of the modern age.

Expropriation, the deprivation for certain groups of their place in the world and their naked exposure to the exigencies of life, created both the original accumulation of wealth and the possibility of transforming this wealth into capital through labor. These together constituted the conditions for the rise of a capitalist economy. That this development, started by expropriation and fed upon it, would result in an enormous increase in human productivity was manifest from the beginning, centuries before the industrial revolution. The new laboring class, which literally lived from hand to mouth, stood not only directly under the compelling urgency of life's necessity[5] but was at the same time

[4] There are several indications in the writings of the young Marx that he was not altogether unaware of the implications of world alienation in capitalist economy. Thus, in the early article of 1842, "Debatten über das Holzdiebstahlsgesetz" (see *Marx-Engels Gesamtausgabe* [Berlin, 1932], Part 1, Vol. 1, pp. 266 ff.) he criticizes a law against theft not only because the formal opposition of owner and thief leaves "human needs" out of account—the fact that the thief who uses the wood needs it more urgently than the owner who sells it—and therefore dehumanizes men by equating wood-user and wood-seller as wood proprietors, but also that the wood itself is deprived of its nature. A law which regards men only as property-owners considers things only as properties and properties only as exchange objects, not as use things. That things are denatured when they are used for exchange was probably suggested to Marx by Aristotle, who pointed out that though a shoe may be wanted for either usage or exchange, it is against the nature of a shoe to be exchanged, "for a shoe is not made to be an object of barter" (*Politics* 1257a8). (Incidentally the influence of Aristotle on the style of Marx's thought seems to me almost as characteristic and decisive as the influence of Hegel's philosophy.) However, such occasional considerations play a minor role in his work, which remained firmly rooted in the modern age's extreme subjectivism. In his ideal society, where men will produce as human beings, world alienation is even more present than it was before; for then they will be able to objectify (*vergegenständlichen*) their individuality, their peculiarity, to confirm and actualize their true being: "Unsere Produktionen wären ebensoviele Spiegel, woraus unser Wesen sich entgegen leuchtete" ("Aus den Exzerptheften" [1844–45], in *Gesamtausgabe*, Part 1, Vol. III, pp. 546–47).

[5] This of course is markedly different from present conditions, where the day laborer has already become a weekly wage-earner; in a probably not very distant future the guaranteed annual wage will do away with these early conditions altogether.

alienated from all cares and worries which did not immediately follow from the life process itself. What was liberated in the early stages of the first free laboring class in history was the force inherent in "labor power," that is, in the sheer natural abundance of the biological process, which like all natural forces—of procreation no less than of laboring—provides for a generous surplus over and beyond the reproduction of young to balance the old. What distinguishes this development at the beginning of the modern age from similar occurrences in the past is that expropriation and wealth accumulation did not simply result in new property or lead to a new redistribution of wealth, but were fed back into the process to generate further expropriations, greater productivity, and more appropriation.

In other words, the liberation of labor power as a natural process did not remain restricted to certain classes of society, and appropriation did not come to an end with the satisfaction of wants and desires; capital accumulation, therefore, did not lead to the stagnation we know so well from rich empires prior to the modern age, but spread throughout the society and initiated a steadily increasing flow of wealth. But this process, which indeed is the "life process of society," as Marx used to call it, and whose wealth-producing capacity can be compared only with the fertility of natural processes where the creation of one man and one woman would suffice to produce by multiplication any given number of human beings, remains bound to the principle of world alienation from which it sprang; the process can continue only provided that no worldly durability and stability is permitted to interfere, only as long as all worldly things, all end products of the production process are fed back into it at an ever increasing speed. In other words, the process of wealth accumulation, as we know it, stimulated by the life process and in turn stimulating human life, is possible only if the world and the very worldliness of man are sacrificed.

The first stage of this alienation was marked by its cruelty, the misery and material wretchedness it meant for a steadily increasing number of "labouring poor," whom expropriation deprived of the twofold protection of family and property, that is, of a family-owned private share in the world, which until the modern age had housed the individual life process and the laboring activity subject to its necessities. The second stage was reached when society became the subject of the new life process, as the family had been its subject before. Membership in a social class replaced the protection previously offered by membership in a family, and social solidarity became a very efficient substitute for the earlier, natural solidarity ruling the family unit. Moreover, society as a whole, the "collective subject" of the life process, by no means remained an intangible entity, the "communist fiction" needed by classical economics; just as the family unit had been identified with a privately owned piece of the world, its property, society was identified with a tangible, albeit collectively owned piece of property, the territory of the nation-state, which until its decline in the twentieth century offered all classes a substitute for the privately owned home of which the class of the poor had been deprived.

The organic theories of nationalism, especially in its Central European version, all rest on an identification of the nation and the relationships between its members with the family and family relationships. Because society becomes the substitute for the family, "blood and soil" is supposed to rule the relationships between its members; homogeneity of population and its rootedness in the soil of a given territory become the requisites for the nation-state everywhere. However while this development undoubtedly mitigated cruelty and misery, it hardly influenced the process of expropriation and world alienation, since collective ownership, strictly speaking, is a contradiction in terms.

The decline of the European nation-state system; the economic and geographic shrinkage of the earth, so that prosperity and depression tend to become world-wide phenomena; the transformation of mankind, which until our own time was an abstract notion or a guiding principle for humanists only, into a really existing entity whose members at the most distant points of the globe need less time to meet than the members of a nation needed a generation ago—these mark the beginning of the last stage in this development. Just as the family and its property were replaced by class membership and national territory, so mankind now begins to replace nationally bound societies, and the earth replaces the limited state territory. But whatever the future may bring, the process of world alienation, started by expropriation and characterized by an ever-increasing progress in wealth, can only assume even more radical proportions if it is permitted to follow its own inherent law. For men cannot become citizens of the world as they are citizens of their countries, and social men cannot own collectively as family and household men own their private property. The rise of society brought about the simultaneous decline of the public as well as the private realm. But the eclipse of a common public world, so crucial to the formation of the lonely mass man and so dangerous in the formation of the wordless mentality of modern ideological mass movements, began with the much more tangible loss of a privately owned share in the world.

Part II

Studies in Social Ethics

PROPERTY AND WELFARE

It is difficult to imagine an issue that is more emotionally flammable than property rights. Many observers of the civil rights movement, for example, argue that it was the suburb's intransigence in the 1960s over open housing and economic opportunity that made violence inevitable, and others report, somewhat cynically, that the American public is much more easily aroused by the destruction of private property than by the destruction of human lives. Certainly the battle to protest or erode "the rights of private property" is the most divisive factor currently on the American scene.

It is also difficult to imagine an issue where argument has become more routine, at least at the level of popular political discussion. Discussion usually ignores the astonishingly diverse character of property in the American economy, which ranges from pension funds (whose ownership is obscure indeed) to the bundle of rights granted to corporations by state charter, to the proprietory functions of industry's management, to stock certificates which often invest their owners with only diluted and indirect management powers, to the small plot of land owned by the bank but administered by the so-called homeowner, to the relatively stable succession of welfare subsidies. Discussion also ignores changing political, social, and economic situations which alter the relations of the various forms of property and which give to these forms an evolving identity. In fact, popular argument about property rights seldom moves beyond positions developed in the eighteenth and nineteenth centuries, and even these have been considerably vitiated by the sloganizing tendencies of twentieth-century politics.

The eighteenth and nineteenth centuries were preoccupied with the origin of property rights, which was taken to be a means of understanding the nature of political man. As Pierre-Joseph Proudhon suggests, the classical doctrines viewed property variously as a civil right, defined by law, or as an inherent right, "originating in labor" or in the nature of man himself. The pragmatic spirit of John Stuart Mill leads to considerable flexibility in determining the form, control, and distribution of property conducive to the general welfare. For Mill, the question of property is always open—it is part of the continuing political problem of engineering the social structure for the broadest distribution of the greatest amount of happiness. On the other hand, John Locke establishes the property right on man's habit of identifying himself with the products of his own labor, on divine creation, and ultimately, on the right which man has to the conditions required for being fully human. The selection from Proudhon's *What Is Property?* is an appeal to the theory of anarchy—an attempt to show the paucity of classical doctrines of poverty, such as those developed by Locke and Mill.

What should not be missed, in spite of the disagreements represented by Locke, Mill, and Proudhon, is the implicit consensus that property is a significant form of social power, a weapon of defense or of aggression. The myths that account for the origin of property are, in part, interpreted as endeavors to make legitimate the distributions of power approved by various theorists. Even John Locke's image of a relatively harmonious state of nature as the seedbed of property rights was a consciously honed instrument in his effort to extend parliamentary reform. Thus, in dealing with theories of property, the perceptive critic will inquire about whose privileges are being legitimated, which forms of coercive enforcement are approved, and who is suffering a loss. In short, he will inquire about how the definition of property affects power within a particular configuration of social conflict.

Oswald Spengler's selection is an interesting alternative in the ethical analysis of money and property. His style is largely descriptive rather than prescriptive. It proceeds on the basis of Spengler's well known judgments about the "decline of the West," but it also serves his desire to observe what actually happens in the relationship of the possessor and his money. The classification Spengler uses is suggestive of insight, especially in relation to some confusions in traditional arguments about property (for example, Proudhon's dictum: "Property is theft!") But more important, and apart from Spengler's usual abstract theorizing, the locus of discussion is shifted to experiential grounds, and a basis is provided for a relational doctrine of money and property, growing from an awareness of the ideal events which shape the existence of persons in their relation to self, others, and to objects.

Frankel broadens the discussion of property into a consideration of public welfare in general. He is appalled by the inability of theorists to provide a livable rationale for a more just distribution of goods in Western society, and by the degree to which Americans, through default, draw upon Locke's dated notion that the right to possession is created in the act of labor. In this selection, he attempts to be more experimental in finding a satisfactory frame of reference within which problems of welfare can be considered.

Erich Fromm is of the same concern, except that he is speaking on behalf of a particular proposal—a universally guaranteed income. Fromm's comments were initially published as a psychological essay, but his interests are deeply ethical, partly because of his belief about the ethical foundations of the psychological sciences. The selection constitutes a prototype for the synthesis of descriptive and prescriptive material in the logic of moral argument. When placed in relation to Frankel's selection, Fromm's essay also demonstrates the process whereby a broad theory of commitment to general welfare becomes particularized in terms of actual policy recommendations. Do you believe that the logic of Frankel's argument can validly be extended into support for the guaranteed income? Could other policies be as easily justified in Frankel's terms?

JOHN LOCKE (1632–1704)

On Property

Whether we consider natural reason, which tells us, that men, being once born, have a right to their preservation, and consequently to meat and drink, and such other things as nature affords for their subsistence; or revelation, which gives us an account of those grants God made of the world to Adam, and to Noah, and his sons; it is very clear, that God, as king David says, Psal. cxv. 16. "has given the earth to the children of men;" given it to mankind in common. But this being supposed, it seems to some a very great difficulty how any one should ever come to have a property in any thing: I will not content myself to answer, that if it be difficult to make out property, upon a supposition, that God gave the world to Adam, and his posterity in common, it is impossible that any man, but one universal monarch, should have any property upon a supposition, that God gave the world to Adam, and his heirs in succession, exclusive of all the rest of his posterity. But I shall endeavour to show, how men might come to have a property in several parts of that which God gave to mankind in common, and that without any express compact of all the commoners.

God, who hath given the world to men in common, hath also given them reason to make use of it to the best advantage of life, and convenience. The earth, and all that is therein, is given to men for the support and comfort of their being. And though all the fruits it naturally produces, and beasts it feeds, belong to mankind in common, as they are produced by the spontaneous hand of nature; and nobody has originally a private dominion, exclusive of the rest of mankind, in any of them, as they are thus in their natural state; yet being given for the use of men, there must of necessity be a means to appropriate them some way or other, before they can be of any use, or at all beneficial to any particular man. The fruit, or venison, which nourishes the wild Indian, who knows no enclosure, and is still a tenant in common, must be his, and so his, i.e. a part of him, that another can no longer have any right to it, before it can do him any good for the support of his life.

Though the earth, and all inferior creatures, be common to all men, yet every man has a property in his own person: this nobody has any right to but himself. The labour of his body, and the work of his

The selection is from John Locke, *The Works of John Locke,* Vol. V (London: T. Davison, 1812).

hands, we may say, are properly his. Whatsoever then he removes out of the state that nature hath provided, and left it in, he hath mixed his labour with, and joined to it something that is his own, and thereby makes it his property. It being by him removed from the common state nature hath placed it in, it hath by this labour something annexed to it, that excludes the common right of other men. For this labour being the unquestionable property of the labourer, no man but he can have a right to what that is once joined to, at least where there is enough, and as good, left in common for others.

He that is nourished by the acorns he picked up under an oak, or the apples he gathered from the trees in the wood, has certainly appropriated them to himself. Nobody can deny but the nourishment is his. I ask then, when did they begin to be his? when he digested? or when he eat? or when he boiled? or when he brought them home? or when he picked them up? and it is plain, if the first gathering made them not his, nothing else could. That labour put a distinction between them and common: that added something to them more than nature, the common mother of all, had done; and so they became his private right. And will any one say, he had no right to those acorns or apples he thus appropriated, because he had not the consent of all mankind to make them his? was it a robbery thus to assume to himself what belonged to all in common? If such a consent as that was necessary, man had starved, notwithstanding the plenty God had given him. We see in commons, which remain so by compact, that it is the taking any part of what is common, and removing it out of the state nature leaves it in, which begins the property; without which the common is of no use. And the taking of this or that part does not depend on the express consent of all the commoners. Thus the grass my horse has bit; the turfs my servant has cut; and the ore I have digged in any place, where I have a right to them in common with others; become my property, without the assignation or consent of any body. The labour that was mine, removing them out of that common state they were in, hath fixed my property in them.

By making an explicit consent of every commoner necessary to any one's appropriating to himself any part of what is given in common, children or servants could not cut the meat, which their father or master had provided for them in common, without assigning to every one his peculiar part. Though the water running in the fountain be every one's, yet who can doubt, but that in the pitcher is his only who drew it out? His labour hath taken it out of the hands of nature, where it was common, and belonged equally to all her children, and hath thereby appropriated it to himself.

222 STUDIES IN SOCIAL ETHICS

Thus this law of reason makes the deer that Indian's who hath killed it; it is allowed to be his goods, who hath bestowed his labour upon it, though before it was the common right of every one. And amongst those who are counted the civilized part of mankind, who have made and multiplied positive laws to determine property, this original law of nature, for the beginning of property, in what was before common, still takes place; and by virtue thereof, what fish any one catches in the ocean, that great and still remaining common of mankind; or what ambergrise any one takes up here, is by the labour that removes it out of that common state nature left it in, made his property, who takes that pains about it. And even amongst us, the hare that any one is hunting, is thought his who pursues her during the chace: for being a beast that is still looked upon as common, and no man's private posession; whoever has employed so much labour about any of that kind, as to find and pursue her, has thereby removed her from the state of nature, wherein she was common, and hath begun a property.

It will perhaps be objected to this, that "if gathering the acorns, or other fruits of the earth, &c. makes a right to them, then any one may engross as much as he will." To which I answer, Not so. The same law of nature, that does by this means give us property, does also bound that property too. "God has given us all things richly," I Tim. vi. 17. is the voice of reason confirmed by inspiration. But how far has he given it us? To enjoy. As much as any one can make use of to any advantage of life before it spoils, so much he may by his labour fix a property in: whatever is beyond this, is more than his share, and belongs to others. Nothing was made by God for man to spoil or destroy. And thus, considering the plenty of natural provisions there was a long time in the world, and the few spenders; and to how small a part of that provision the industry of one man could extend itself, and engross it to the prejudice of others; especially keeping within the bounds, set by reason, of what might serve for his use; there could be then little room for quarrels or contentions about property so established.

But the chief matter of property being now not the fruits of the earth, and the beasts that subsist on it, but the earth itself; as that which takes in, and carries with it all the rest; I think it is plain, that property in that too is is acquired as the former. As much land as a man tills, plants, improves, cultivates, and can use the product of, so much is his property. He by his labour does, as it were, enclose it from the common. Nor will it invalidate his right, to say everybody else has an equal title to it, and therefore he cannot appropriate, he cannot enclose, without the consent of all his fellow commoners, all mankind. God, when he gave the world in common to all mankind, commanded man also to labour, and the penury of his condition required it of him. God and his reason commanded him to subdue the earth, i.e. improve it for the benefit of life, and therein lay out something upon it that was his own, his labour. He that, in obedience to this command of God, subdued, tilled, and sowed any part of it, thereby annexed to it something that was his property, which another had no title to, nor could without injury take from him.

Nor was this appropriation of any parcel of land, by improving it, any prejudice to any other man, since there was still enough, and as good left; and more than the yet unprovided could see. So that, in effect, there was never the less left for others because of his enclosure for himself: for he that leaves as much as another can make use of, does as good as take nothing at all. Nobody could think himself injured by the drinking of another man, though he took a good draught, who had a whole river of the same water left him to quench his thirst; and the case of land and water, where there is enough for both, is perfectly the same.

God gave the world to men in common; but since he gave it them for their benefit, and the greatest conveniencies of life they were capable to draw from it, it cannot be supposed he meant it should always remain common and uncultivated. He gave it to the use of the industrious and rational, (and labour was to be his title to it) not to the fancy or covetousness of the quarrelsome and contentious. He that had as good left for his improvement, as was already taken up, needed not complain, ought not to meddle with what was already improved by another's labour: if he did, it is plain he desired the benefit of another's pains, which he had no right to, and not the ground which God had given him in common with others to labour on, and whereof there was as good left, as that already possessed, and more than he knew what to do with, or his industry could reach to.

It is true, in land that is common in England, or any other country, where there is plenty of people under government, who have money and commerce, no one can enclose or appropriate any part, without the consent of all his fellow-commoners; because this is left common by compact, i.e. by the law of the land, which is not to be violated. And though it be common, in respect of some men, it is not so to all mankind, but is the joint property of this country, or this parish. Besides, the remainder, after such enclosure, would not be as good to the rest of the commoners, as the whole was when they could all make use of the whole; whereas in the beginning and first peopling of the great common of the world, it was quite otherwise. The law man was under, was rather for appropriating. God commanded, and his wants forced him to labour. That was his property which could not be taken from him wherever he had fixed it. And hence subduing or cultivating the earth, and having dominion, we see are joined together. The one gave title to the other. So that God, by commanding to subdue, gave authority so far to appropriate: and the condition of human life, which requires labour and materials to work on, necessarily introduces private possessions.

The measure of property nature has well set by the extent of men's labour, and the conveniencies of life: no man's labour could subdue, or appropriate all; nor could his enjoyment consume more than a small part; so that it was impossible for any man, this way, to intrench upon the right of another, or acquire to himself a property, to the prejudice of his neighbour, who would still have room for as good, and as large a possession (after the other had taken out his) as before it was appropriated. This measure did confine every man's possession to a very moderate proportion, and such as he might appropriate to himself, without injury to any body, in the first ages of the world, when men were more in danger to be lost, by wandering from their company, in the then vast wilderness of the earth, than to be straitened for want of room to plant in. And the same measure may be allowed still without prejudice to any body, as full as the world seems: for supposing a man, or family, in the state they were at first peopling of the world by the children of Adam, or Noah; let him plant in some inland, vacant places of America, we shall find that the possessions he could make himself, upon the measures we have given, would not be very large, nor, even to this day, prejudice the rest of mankind, or give them reason to complain, or think themselves injured by this man's encroachment; though the race of men have now spread themselves to all the corners of the world, and do infinitely exceed the small number was at the beginning. Nay, the extent of ground is of so little value, without labour, that I have heard it affirmed, that in Spain itself a man may be permitted to plough, sow, and reap, without being disturbed, upon land he has no other title to, but only his making use of it. But, on the contrary, the inhabitants think themselves beholden to him, who, by his industry on neglected, and consequently waste land, has increased the stock of corn, which they wanted. But be this as it will, which I lay no stress on; this I dare boldly affirm, that the same rule of propriety, (viz.) that every man should have as much as he could make use of, would hold still in the world, without straitening any body; since there is land enough in the world to suffice double the inhabitants, had not the invention of money, and the tacit agreement of men to put a value on it, introduced (by consent) larger possessions, and a right to them; which, how it has done, I shall by and by show more at large.

This is certain, that in the beginning, before the desire of having more than man needed had altered the intrinsic value of things, which depends only on their usefulness to the life of man; or had agreed, that a little piece of yellow metal, which would keep without wasting or decay, should be worth a great piece of flesh, or a whole heap of corn; though men had a right to appropriate, by their labour, each one to himself as much of the things of nature as he could use: yet this could not be much, nor to the prejudice of others, where the same plenty was still left to those who would use the same industry. To which let me add, that he who appropriates land to himself by his labour, does not lessen, but increase the common stock of mankind: for the provisions serving to the support of human life, produced by one acre of enclosed and cultivated land, are (to speak much within compass) ten times more than those which are yielded by an acre of land of an equal richness lying waste in common. And therefore he that encloses land, and has a greater plenty of the conveniences of life from ten acres, than he could have from an hundred left to nature, may truly be said to give ninety acres to mankind: for his labour now supplies him with provisions out of ten acres, which were by the product of an hundred lying in common. I have here rated the improved land very low, in making its product but as ten to one, when it is much nearer an hundred to one: for I ask, whether in the wild woods and uncultivated waste of America, left to nature, without any improvement, tillage, or husbandry, a thousand acres yield the needy and wretched inhabitants as many conveniencies of life, as ten acres equally fertile land do in Devonshire, where they are well cultivated.

Before the appropriation of land, he who gathered as much of the wild fruit, killed, caught, or tamed, as many of the beasts as he could; he that so employed his pains about any of the spontaneous products of nature, as any way to alter them from the state which nature put them in, by placing any of his labour on them, did thereby acquire a propriety in them: but if they perished, in his possession, without their due use; if the fruits rotted, or the venison putrified, before he could spend it; he offended against the common law of nature, and was liable to be punished: he invaded his neighbour's share, for he had no right, farther than his use called for any of them, and they might serve to afford him conveniencies of life. . . .

Thus labour, in the beginning, gave a right of property, wherever any one was pleased to employ it upon what was common, which remained a long while the far greater part, and is yet more than mankind makes use of. Men, at first, for the most part, contented themselves with what unassisted nature offered to their necessities: and though afterwards, in some parts of the world, (where the increase of people and stock, with the use of money, had made land scarce, and so of some value) the several communities settled the bounds of their distinct territories, and by laws within themselves regulated the properties of the private men of their society, and so, by compact and agreement, settled the property which labour and industry began: and the leagues that have been made between several states and kingdoms, either expressly or tacitly disowning all claim and right to the land in the others possession, have, by common consent, given up their pretences to their natural common right, which originally they had to those countries, and so have, by positive agreement, settled a property amongst themselves, in distinct parts and parcels of the earth; yet there are still great tracts of ground to be found, which (the inhabitants thereof not having joined with the rest of mankind, in the consent of the use of their common money) lie waste, and are more than the people who dwell on it do, or can make use of, and so still lie in common; though this can scarce happen amongst that part of mankind that have consented to the use of money.

The greatest part of things really useful to the life of man, and such as the necessity of subsisting made the first commoners of the world look after, as it doth the Americans now, are generally things of short duration; such as, if they are not consumed by use, will decay and perish of themselves: gold, silver, and diamonds, are things that fancy or agreement hath put the value on, more than real use, and the necessary support of life. Now of those good things which nature hath provided in common, every one had a right, (as hath been said) to as much as he could use, and property in all that he could effect with his labour; all that his industry could extend to, to alter from the state nature had put it in, was his. He that gathered a hundred bushels of acorns or apples, had thereby a property in them, they were his goods as soon as gathered. He was only to look, that he used them before they spoiled, else he took more than his share, and robbed others. And indeed it was a foolish thing, as well as dishonest, to hoard up more than he could make use of. If he gave away a part to any body else, so that it perished not uselessly in his possession, these he also made use of. And if he also bartered away plums, that would have rotted in a week, for nuts that would last good for his eating a whole year, he did no injury; he wasted not the common stock; destroyed no part of the portion of the goods that belonged to others, so long as nothing perished uselessly in his hands. Again, if he would give his nuts for a piece of metal, pleased with its colour; or exchange his sheep for shells, or wool for a sparkling pebble or a diamond, and keep those by him all his life, he invaded not the right of others, he might heap as much of these durable things as he pleased; the exceeding of the bounds of his just property not lying in the largeness of his possession, but the perishing of any thing uselessly in it.

And thus came in the use of money, some lasting thing that men might keep without spoiling, and that by mutual consent men would take in exchange for the truly useful, but perishable supports of life.

And as different degrees of industry were apt to give men possessions in different proportions, so this invention of money gave them the opportunity to continue and enlarge them: for supposing an island, separate from all possible commerce with the rest of the world, wherein there were but an hundred families, but there were sheep, horses, and cows, with other useful animals, wholesome fruits, and land enough for corn for a hundred thousand times as many, but nothing in the island, either because of its commonness, or perishableness, fit to supply the place of money; what reason could any one have there to enlarge his possessions beyond the use of his family and a plentiful supply to its consumption, either in what their own industry produced, or they could barter for like perishable, useful commodities with others? Where there is not something, both lasting and scarce, and so valuable to be hoarded up, there men will not be apt to enlarge their possessions of land, were it ever so rich, ever so free for them to take: for I ask, what would a man value ten thousand, or an hundred thousand acres of excellent land, ready cultivated and well stocked too with cattle, in the middle of the inland parts of America, where he had no hopes of commerce with other parts of the world, to draw money to him by the sale of the product? It would not be worth the enclosing, and we should see him give up again to the wild common of nature, whatever was more than would supply the conveniencies of life to be had there for him and his family.

Thus in the beginning all the world was America, and more so than that is now; for no such thing as money was any where known. Find out something that hath the use and value of money amongst his neighbours, you shall see the same man will begin presently to enlarge his possessions.

But since gold and silver, being little useful to the life of man in proportion to food, raiment, and carriage, has its value only from the consent of men, whereof labour yet makes, in great part, the measure; it is plain, that men have agreed to a disproportionate and unequal possession of the earth, they having, by a tacit and voluntary consent, found out a way how a man may fairly possess more land than he himself can use the product of, by receiving in exchange for the overplus, gold and silver, which may be hoarded up without injury to any one; these metals not spoiling or decaying in the hands of the possessor. This partage of things in an inequality of private possessions, men have made practicable out of the bounds of society, and without compact; only by putting a value on gold and silver, and tacitly agreeing in the use of money: for in governments, the laws regulate the right of property, and the possession of land is determined by positive constitutions.

And thus, I think, it is very easy to conceive, "how labour could at first begin a title of property" in the common things of nature, and how the spending it upon our uses bounded it. So that there could then be no reason of quarrelling about title, nor any doubt about the largeness of possession it gave. Right and conveniency went together; for as a man had a right to all he could employ his labour upon, so he had no temptation to labour for more than he could make use of. This left no room for controversy about the title, nor for encroachment on the right of others; what portion a man carved to himself, was easily seen; and it was useless, as well as dishonest, to carve himself too much, or take more than he needed.

PIERRE-JOSEPH PROUDHON (1809–1865)

What is Property?

WHAT PROPERTY IS

If I were asked to answer the following question: *What is slavery?* and I should answer in one word, *It is murder*, my meaning would be understood at once. No extended argument would be required to show that the power to take from a man his thought, his will, his personality,

The selection is from Pierre-Joseph Proudhon, *What Is Property?*, trans. Benjamin R. Tucker (Princeton, Massachusetts: Benjamin R. Tucker, 1876).

is a power of life and death; and that to enslave a man is to kill him. Why, then, to this other question: *What is property?* may I not likewise answer, *It is robbery*, without the certainty of being misunderstood; the second proposition being no other than a transformation of the first?

I undertake to discuss the vital principle of our government and our institutions, property: I am in my right. I may be mistaken in the conclusion which shall result from my investigations: I am in my right. I think best to place the last thought of my book first: still am I in my right.

Such an author teaches that property is a civil right, born of occupation and sanctioned by law; another maintains that it is a natural right, originating in labor,—and both of these doctrines, totally opposed as they may seem, are encouraged and applauded. I contend that neither labor, nor occupation, nor law, can create property; that is is an effect without a cause: am I censurable?

But murmurs arise!

Property is robbery! That is the war-cry of '93! That is the signal of revolutions!

Reader, calm yourself: I am no agent of discord, no firebrand of sedition. I anticipate history by a few days; I disclose a truth whose development we may try in vain to arrest; I write the preamble of our future constitution. This proposition which seems to you blasphemous —*property is robbery*—would, if our prejudices allowed us to consider it, be recognized as the lightning-rod to shield us from the coming thunderbolt; but how many interests, how many prejudices, stand in the way!... Alas! philosophy will not change the course of events: destiny will fulfill itself regardless of prophecy. Besides, must not justice be done and our education be finished?

Property is robbery!... What a revolution in human ideas! *Proprietor* and *robber* have been at all times expressions as contradictory as the beings whom they designate are hostile; all languages have perpetuated this opposition. On what authority, then, do you venture to attack universal consent, and give the lie to the human race? Who are you, that you should question the judgment of the nations and the ages?

Of what consequence to you, reader, is my obscure individuality? I live, like you, in a century in which reason submits only to fact and to evidence. My name, like yours, is TRUTH-SEEKER. My mission is written in these words of the law: *Speak without hatred and without fear; tell all that which thou knowest....*

Others offer you the spectacle of genius wresting Nature's secrets from her, and unfolding before you her sublime messages; you will find here only a series of experiments upon *justice* and *right*, a sort of verification of the weights and measures of your conscience. The operations shall be conducted under your very eyes; and you shall weigh the result.

Nevertheless I build no system. I ask an end to privilege, the abolition of slavery, equality of rights, and the reign of law. Justice, nothing else; that is the alpha and omega of my argument; to others I leave the business of governing the world. . . .

THE JUSTIFICATION OF PROPERTY

The Declaration of Rights has placed property on its list of the natural and inalienable rights of man, four in all: *liberty, equality, property, security*. What rule did the legislators of '93 follow in compiling this list? None. They laid down principles, just as they discussed sovereignty and the laws; from a general point of view, and according to their own opinion. They did everything in their own blind way. . . .

Nevertheless, if we compare these three or four rights with each other, we find that property bears no resemblance whatever to the others; that for the majority of citizens it exists only potentially, and as a dormant faculty without exercise; that for the others, who do enjoy it, it is susceptible of certain compromises and modifications which do not harmonize with the idea of a natural right, that, in practice, governments, tribunals, and laws do not respect it; and finally that everybody, spontaneously and with one voice, regards it as chimerical. . . .

Liberty is an absolute right, because it is to man what impenetrability is to matter,—a *sine qua non* of existence; equality is an absolute right, because without equality there is no society; security is an absolute right, because in the eyes of every man his own liberty and life are as precious as another's. These three rights are absolute; that is, susceptible of neither increase or diminution; because in society each associate receives as much as he gives—liberty for liberty, equality for equality, body for body, soul for soul, in life and in death.

But property, in its derivative sense, and by the definitions of law, is a right outside of society; for it is clear that, if the wealth of each was social wealth, the conditions would be equal for all, and it would be a contradiction to say: *Property is a man's right to dispose at will of social property.* Then if we are associated for the sake of liberty, equality, and security, we are not associated for the sake of property; then if property is a *natural* right, this natural right is not social, but *anti-social*. Property and society are utterly irreconcilable institutions. It is as impossible to associate two proprietors as to join two magnets by their similar poles. Either society must perish, or it must destroy property.

If property is a natural, absolute, imprescriptible, and inalienable right, why, in all ages, has there been so much speculation as to its origin?—for this is one of its distinguishing characteristics. The origin of a natural right! Good God! who ever inquired into the origin of the rights of liberty, security, or equality? They exist by the same right that we exist; they are born with us, they live and die with us. With property it is very different, indeed. By law, property can exist without a proprietor, like a quality without a subject. It exists for the human being who as yet is not, and for the octogenarian who is no more. And yet, in spite of these wonderful prerogatives which savor of the eternal and the infinite, they have never found the origin of property; the doctors still disagree. In one point only are they in harmony: namely, that the validity of the right of property depends upon the authenticity of its origin. But this harmony is their condemnation. Why have they acknowledged the right before settling the question of origin?

Certain classes do not relish investigations into the pretended titles to property, and its fabulous and perhaps scandalous history. They wish to hold to this proposition: that property is a fact; that it always has been, and always will be. . . .

The titles on which they pretend to base the right of property are two in number: *occupation* and *labor*. I shall examine them successively, under all their aspects and in detail; and I remind the reader that, to whatever authority we appeal, I shall prove beyond a doubt that property, to be just and possible, must necessarily have equality for its condition. . . .

OCCUPATION AS A BASIS FOR PROPERTY RIGHTS

Not only does occupation lead to equality, it *prevents* property. For, since every man, from the fact of his existence, has the right of occupation, and, in order to live, must have material for cultivation on which he may labor; and since, on the other hand, the number of occupants varies continually with the births and deaths,—it follows that the quantity of material which each laborer may claim varies with the number of occupants; consequently, that occupation is always subordinate to population. Finally, that, inasmuch as possession, in right, can never remain fixed, it is impossible, in fact, that it can ever become property.

Every occupant is, then, necessarily a possessor or usufructuary;

he cannot therefore be a proprietor; he is responsible for the thing entrusted to him; he must use it in conformity with general utility, with a view to its preservation and development; he has no power to transform it, to diminish it, or to change its nature, he cannot so divide the usufruct that another shall perform the labor while he receives the product. In a word, the usufructuary is under the supervision of society, submitted to the condition of labor and the law of equality.

Thus is annihilated the Roman definition of property—*the right of use and abuse*—an immorality born of violence, the most monstrous pretension that the civil laws ever sanctioned. Man receives his usufruct from the hands of society, which alone is the permanent possessor. The individual passes away, society is deathless.

What a profound disgust fills my soul while discussing such simple truths! Do we doubt these things to-day? Will it be necessary to again take up arms for their triumph? And can force, in default of reason, alone introduce them into our laws?

All have equal right of occupancy.

The amount occupied being measured, not by the will, but by the variable conditions of space and number, property cannot exist.

This no code has ever expressed; this no consititution can admit! These are axioms which the civil law and the law of nations deny! ...

LABOR AS A BASIS FOR PROPERTY RIGHTS

But I hear the exclamations of the partisans of another system: "Labor, labor! that is the basis of property!"

Reader, do not be deceived. This new basis of property is worse than the first, and I shall soon have to ask your pardon for having demonstrated things clearer, and refuted pretensions more unjust, than any which we have yet considered. ...

Admit, however, that labor gives a right of property in material. Why is not this principle universal? Why is the benefit of this pretended law confined to a few and denied to the mass of laborers? A philosopher, arguing that all animals sprang up formerly out of the earth warmed by the rays of the sun, almost like mushrooms, on being asked why the earth no longer yielded crops of that nature, replied: "Because it is old, and has lost its fertility." Has labor, once so fecund, likewise become sterile? Why does the tenant no longer acquire through his labor the land which was formerly acquired by the labor of the proprietor?

"Because," they say, "it is already appropriated." That is no answer. A farm yields fifty bushels per *hectare*; the skill and labor of the tenant double this product: the increase is created by the tenant. Suppose the owner, in a spirit of moderation rarely met with, does not go to the extent of absorbing this product by raising the rent, but allows the cultivator to enjoy the results of his labor; even then justice is not satisfied. The tenant, by improving the land, has imparted a new value to the property; he, therefore, has a right to a part of the property. If the farm was originally worth 100,000 francs, and if by the labor of the tenant its value has risen to 150,000 francs, the tenant, who produced this extra value, is the legitimate proprietor of one-third of the farm. M. Ch. Comte could not have pronounced this doctrine false, for it was he who said:—"Men who increase the fertility of the earth are no less useful to their fellow-men, than if they create new land."

Why, then, is not this rule applicable to the man who improves the land, as well as to him who clears it? The labor of the former makes the land worth 1; that of the latter makes it worth 2: both create equal values. Why not accord to both equal property? I defy any one to refute this argument, without again falling back on the right of first occupancy.

"But," it will be said, "even if your wish should be granted, property would not be distributed much more evenly than it is now. Land does not go on increasing in value forever; after two or three seasons it attains its maximum fertility. That which is added by the agricultural art results rather from the progress of science and the diffusion of knowledge, than from the skill of the cultivator. Consequently, the addition of a few laborers to the mass of proprietors would be no argument against property."

This discussion would, indeed, prove a well-nigh useless one, if our labors culminated in simply extending land-privilege and industrial monopoly; in emancipating only a few hundred laborers out of the millions of proletarians. But this also is a misconception of our real thought, and does but prove the general lack of intelligence and logic.

If the laborer, who adds to the value of a thing, has a right of property in it, he who maintains this value acquires the same right. For what is maintenance? It is incessant addition,—continuous creation. What is it to cultivate? It is to give the soil its value every year: it is, by annually renewed creation, to prevent the diminution or destruction of the value of a piece of land. Admitting, then, that property is rational and legitimate,—admitting that rent is equitable and just,—I say that he who cultivates acquires property by as good a title as he who clears, or he who improves; and that every time a tenant pays his rent, he obtains a fraction of property in the land entrusted to his care, the denominator of which is equal to the proportion of rent paid. Unless you admit this, you fall into absolutism and tyranny; you recognize class privileges; you sanction slavery.

Whoever labors becomes a proprietor—this is an inevitable deduction from the acknowledged principles of political economy and jurisprudence. And when I say proprietor, I do not mean simply (as do our hypocritical economists) proprietor of his allowance, his salary, his wages,—I mean proprietor of the value which he creates, and by which the master alone profits.

As all this relates to the theory of wages and of the distribution of products,—and as this matter never has been even partially cleared up,—I ask permission to insist on it: this discussion will not be useless to the work in hand. Many persons talk of admitting working-people to a share in the products and profits; but in their minds this participation is pure benevolence: they have never shown—perhaps never suspected—that it was a natural, necessary right, inherent in labor, and inseparable from the function of producer, even in the lowest forms of his work.

This is my proposition: *The laborer retains, even after he has received his wages, a natural right of property in the thing which he has produced.* . . .

The labor of the workers has created a value; now this value is their property. But they have neither sold nor exchanged it; and you, capitalist, you have not earned it. That you should have a partial right to the whole, in return for the materials that you have furnished and the provisions that you have supplied is perfectly just. You contributed to the productions, you ought to share in the enjoyment. But your right does not annihilate that of the laborers, who, in spite of you, have been your colleagues in the work of production. Why do you talk of wages? The money with which you pay the wages of the laborers remunerates them for only a few years of the perpetual possession which they have abandoned to you. Wages is the cost of the daily maintenance and refreshment of the laborer. You are wrong in calling it the price of a sale. The workingman has sold nothing; he knows neither his right, nor the extent of the concession which he has made to you, nor the meaning of the contract which you pretend to have made with him. On his side, utter ignorance; on yours, error and surprise, not to say deceit and fraud. . . .

In this century of bourgeois morality, in which I have had the honor to be born, the moral sense is so debased that I should not be at all surprised if I were asked, by many a worthy proprietor, what I see in this that is unjust and illegitimate. Debased creature! galvanized corpse! how can I expect to convince you, if you cannot tell robbery when I show it to you? A man, by soft and insinuating words, discovers the secret of taxing others that he may establish himself; then, once enriched by their united efforts, he refuses, on the very conditions which he himself dictated, to advance the well-being of those who made his fortune for him: and you ask how such conduct is fraudulent! Under the pretext that he has paid his laborers, that he owes them nothing more, that he has nothing to gain by putting himself at the service of others, while his own occupations claim his attention,—he refuses, I say, to aid others in getting a foothold, as he was aided in getting his own; and when, in the impotence of their isolation, these poor laborers are compelled to sell their birthright, he—this ungrateful proprietor, this knavish upstart—stands ready to put the finishing touch to their deprivation and ruin. And you think that just? Take care! I read in your startled countenance the reproach of a guilty conscience, much more clearly than the innocent astonishment of involuntary ignorance....

FALLACIOUS METHODS OF ESTABLISHING EQUALITY

But, some half-converted proprietor will observe, "Would it not be possible, by suppressing the bank, incomes, farm-rent, house-rent, usury of all kinds, and finally property itself, to proportion products to capacities? That was Saint-Simon's idea; it was also Fourier's; it is the desire of the human conscience; and no decent person would dare maintain that a minister of state should live no better than a peasant."

O Midas! your ears are long! What! will you never understand that disparity of wages and the right of increase are one and the same? Certainly, Saint-Simon, Fourier, and their respective flocks committed a serious blunder in attempting to unite, the one, inequality and communism; the other, inequality and property: but you, a man of figures, a man of economy,—you, who know by heart your logarithmic tables,—how can you make so stupid a mistake? Does not political economy itself teach you that the product of a man, whatever be his individual capacity, is never worth more than his labor, and that a man's labor is worth no more than his consumption?...

Listen, proprietor. Inequality of talent exists in fact; in right it is inadmissible, it goes for nothing, it is not thought of. One Newton in a century is equal to 30 millions of men; the psychologist admires the rarity of so fine a genius, the legislator sees only the rarity of the function. Now, rarity of function bestows no privilege upon the functionary; and that for several reasons, all equally forcible.

1. Rarity of genius was not, in the Creator's design, a motive to compel society to go down on its knees before the man of superior talents, but a providential means for the performance of all functions to the greatest advantage of all.

2. Talent is a creation of society rather than a gift of Nature; it is an accumulated capital, of which the receiver is only the guardian. Without society,—without the education and powerful assistance which it furnishes,—the finest nature would be inferior to the most ordinary capacities in the very respect in which it ought to shine. The more extensive a man's knowledge, the more luxuriant his imagination, the more versatile his talent,—the more costly has his education been, the more remarkable and numerous were his teachers and his models, and the greater is his debt. The farmer produces from the time that he leaves his cradle until he enters his grave: the fruits of art and science are late and scarce; frequently the tree dies before the fruit ripens. Society, in cultivating talent, makes a sacrifice to hope.

3. Capacities have no common standard of comparison: the conditions of development being equal, inequality of talent is simply speciality of talent.

4. Inequality of wages, like the right of increase, is economically impossible. Take the most favorable case,—that where each laborer has furnished his maximum production; that there may be an equitable distribution of products, the share of each must be equal to the quotient of the total production divided by the number of laborers. This done, what remains wherewith to pay the higher wages? Nothing whatever.

Will it be said that all laborers should be taxed? But, then, their consumption will not be equal to their production, their wages will not pay for their productive service, they will not be able to purchase their product, and we shall once more be afflicted with the calamities of property. I do not speak of the injustice done to the defrauded laborer, of rivalry, of excited ambition, and burning hatred,—these may all be important considerations, but they do not hit the point.

On the one hand, each laborer's task being short and easy, and the means for its successful accomplishment being equal in all cases, how could there be large and small producers? On the other hand, all functions being equal, either on account of the equivalence of talents and capacities, or on account of social cooperation, how could a functionary claim a salary proportional to the worth of his genius?

But, what do I say? In equality wages are always proportional to talents. What is the economical meaning of wages? The reproductive consumption of the laborer. The very act by which the laborer produces constitutes, then, this consumption, exactly equal to his production, of which we are speaking. When the astronomer produces observations, the poet verses, or the *savant* experiments, they consume instruments, books, travels, &c., &c.; now, if society supplies this consumption, what more can the astronomer, the *savant*, or the poet demand? We must conclude, then, that in equality, and only in equality, Saint-Simon's adage—*To each according to his capacity, to each capacity according to its results*—finds its full and complete application. . . .

Here my task should end. I have proved the right of the poor; I have shown the usurpation of the rich. I demand justice; it is not my business to execute the sentence. If it should be argued—in order to prolong for a few years an illegitimate privilege—that it is not enough to demonstrate equality, that it is necessary also to organize it, and above all to establish it peacefully, I might reply: The welfare of the oppressed is of more importance than official composure. Equality of conditions is a natural law upon which public economy and jurisprudence are based. The right to labor, and the principle of equal distribution of wealth, cannot give way to the anxieties of power. It is not for the proletarian to reconcile the contradictions of the codes, still less to suffer for the errors of the government. On the contrary, it is the duty of the civil and administrative power to reconstruct itself on the basis of political equality. An evil, when known, should be condemned and destroyed. The legislator cannot plead ignorance as an excuse for upholding a glaring iniquity. Restitution should not be delayed. Justice, justice! recognition of right! Reinstatement of the proletarian!—when these results are accomplished, then, judges and consuls, you may attend to your police, and provide a government for the Republic! . . .

ANARCHISM THE SOLUTION

By means of self-instruction and the acquisition of ideas, man finally acquires the idea of *science*,—that is, of a system of knowledge in harmony with the reality of things, and inferred from observation. He searches for the science, or the system, of inanimate bodies,—the system of organic bodies, the system of the human mind, and the system of the universe: why should he not also search for the system of society? But, having reached this height he comprehends that political truth, or the science of politics, exists quite independently of the will of sovereigns, the opinion of majorities, and popular beliefs,—that kings, ministers, magistrates, and nations, as wills, have no connection with the science, and are worthy of no consideration. He comprehends, at the same time, that if man is born a sociable being, the authority of his father over him ceases on the day when, his mind being formed and his education finished, he becomes the associate of his father; that his true chief and his king is the demonstrated truth; that politics is a science, not a stratagem; and that the function of the legislator is reduced, in the last analysis, to the methodical search for truth.

Thus, in a given society, the authority of man over man is inversely proportional to the stage of intellectual development which that society has reached; and the probable duration of that authority can be calculated from the more or less general desire for a true government, —that is, for a scientific government. And just as the right of force and the right of artifice retreat before the steady advance of justice, and must finally be extinguished in equality, so the sovereignty of the will yields to the sovereignty of the reason, and must at last be lost in scientific socialism. Property and royalty have been crumbling to pieces ever since the world began. As man seeks justice in equality, so society seeks order in anarchy.

Anarchy,—the absence of a master, of a sovereign[1]—such is the form of government to which we are every day approximating, and which our accustomed habit of taking man for our rule, and his will for law, leads us to regard as the height of disorder and the expression of chaos. The story is told, that a citizen of Paris, in the seventeenth century, having heard it said that in Venice there was no king, the good man could not recover from his astonishment, and nearly died from laughter at the mere mention of so ridiculous a thing. So strong is our prejudice. As long as we live, we want a chief or chiefs; and at this very moment I hold in my hand a brochure, whose author—a zealous communist—dreams, like a second Marat—of the dictatorship. The most advanced among us are those who wish the greatest possible number of sovereigns,—their most ardent wish is for the royalty of the National Guard. Soon, undoubtedly, some one, jealous of the citizen militia, will say, "Everybody is king." But, when he has spoken, I will say, in my turn, "Nobody is king; we are, whether we will or no, associated." Every question of domestic politics must be decided by departmental statistics; every question of foreign politics is an affair of

---

[1] The meaning ordinarily attached to the word "anarchy" is absence of principle, absence of rule; consequently it has been regarded as synonymous with disorder. [Proudhon's note.]

international statistics. The science of government rightly belongs to one of the sections of the Academy of Sciences, whose permanent secretary is necessarily prime minister; and, since every citizen may address a memoir to the Academy, every citizen is a legislator. But, as the opinion of no one is of any value until its truth has been proven, no one can substitute his will for reason,—nobody is king.

All matters of legislation and politics are matters of science, not of opinion. The legislative power belongs only to the reason, methodically recognized and demonstrated. To attribute to any power whatever the right of veto or of sanction, is the last degree of tyranny. Justice and legality are two things as independent of our approval as is mathematical truth. To compel, they need only to be known; to be known, they need only to be considered and studied. What, then, is the nation, if it is not the sovereign,—if it is not the source of the legislative power? The nation is the guardian of the law—the nation is the *executive power*. Every citizen may assert: "This is true; that is just;" but his opinion controls no one but himself. That the truth which he proclaims may become a law, it must be recognized. Now, what is it to recognize a law? It is to verify a mathematical or a metaphysical calculation; it is to repeat an experiment, to observe a phenomenon, to establish a fact. Only the nation has the right to say, "Be it known and decreed."

I confess that this is an overturning of received ideas, and that I seem to be attempting to revolutionize our political system; but I beg the reader to consider that, having begun with a paradox, I must, if I reason correctly, meet with paradoxes at every step, and must end with paradoxes. For the rest, I do not see how the liberty of citizens would be endangered by entrusting to their hands, instead of the pen of the legislator, the sword of the law. The executive power, belonging properly to the will, cannot be confided to too many proxies. That is the true sovereignty of the nation.

JOHN STUART MILL (1806–1873)

The Distribution of Welfare

DISTRIBUTION OF WEALTH CONTROLLABLE BY SOCIETY

The principles which have been set forth in the first part of this treatise, are, in certain respects, strongly distinguished from those on the consideration of which we are now about to enter. The laws and conditions of the Production of wealth partake of the character of physical truths. There is nothing optional or arbitrary in them. Whatever mankind produce, must be produced in the modes, and under the conditions, imposed by the constitution of external things, and by the inherent properties of their own bodily and mental structure. Whether they like it or not, their productions will be limited by the amount of their previous accumulation, and, that being given, it will be proportional to their energy, their skill, the perfection of their machinery, and their judicious use of the advantages of combined labour. Whether they like it or not, a double quantity of labour will not raise, on the same land, a double quantity of food, unless some improvement takes place in the processes of cultivation. Whether they like it or not, the unproductive expenditure of individuals will *pro tanto* tend to impoverish the community, and only their productive expenditure will enrich it. The opinions, or the wishes, which may exist on these different matters, do not control the things themselves. . . .

It is not so with the Distribution of wealth. That is a matter of human institution solely. The things once there, mankind, individually or collectively, can do with them as they like. They can place them at the disposal of whomsoever they please, and on whatever terms. Further, in the social state, in every state except total solitude, any disposal whatever of them can only take place by the consent of society, or rather of those who dispose of its active force. Even what a person has produced by his individual toil, unaided by any one, he cannot keep, unless by the permission of society. Not only can society take it from him, but individuals could and would take it from him, if society only remained passive; if it did not either interfere *en masse*, or employ and pay people for the purpose of preventing him from being disturbed

---

The selection is from John Stuart Mill, *Principles of Political Economy* (London: Longman, Green, Longman, Roberts and Green, 1865).

in the possession. The distribution of wealth, therefore, depends on the laws and customs of society. The rules by which it is determined are what the opinions and feelings of the ruling portion of the community make them, and are very different in different ages and countries; and might be still more different, if mankind so chose. . . .

PRIVATE PROPERTY AND ITS CRITICS

We proceed, then, to the consideration of the different modes of distributing the produce of land and labour, which have been adopted in practice, or may be conceived in theory. Among these, our attention is first claimed by that primary and fundamental institution, on which, unless in some exceptional and very limited cases, the economical arrangements of society have always rested, though in its secondary features it has varied, and is liable to vary. I mean, of course, the institution of individual property.

Private property, as an institution, did not owe its origin to any of those considerations of utility, which plead for the maintenance of it when established. Enough is known of rude ages, both from history and from analogous states of society in our own time, to show that tribunals (which always precede laws) were originally established, not to determine rights, but to repress violence and terminate quarrels. With this object chiefly in view, they naturally enough gave legal effect to first occupancy, by treating as the aggressor the person who first commenced violence, by turning, or attempting to turn, another out of possession. The preservation of the peace, which was the original object of civil government, was thus attained: while by confirming, to those who already possessed it, even what was not the fruit of personal exertion, a guarantee was incidentally given to them and others that they would be protected in what was so. . . .

Private property, in every defence made of it, is supposed to mean the guarantee to individuals of the fruits of their own labour and abstinence. The guarantee to them of the fruits of the labour and abstinence of others, transmitted to them without any merit or exertion of their own, is not of the essence of the institution, but a mere incidental consequence which, when it reaches a certain height, does not promote, but conflicts with, the ends which render private property legitimate. To judge of the final destination of the institution of property, we must suppose everything rectified which causes the institution to work in a manner opposed to that equitable principle, of proportion between remuneration and exertion, on which in every vindication of it that will bear the light it is assumed to be grounded. We must also suppose two conditions realized, without which neither Communism nor any other laws or institutions could make the condition of the mass of mankind other than degraded and miserable. One of these conditions is universal education; the other, a due limitation of the numbers of the community. With these there could be no poverty, even under the present social institutions: and these being supposed, the question of Socialism is not, as generally stated by Socialists, a question of flying to the sole refuge against the evils which now bear down humanity; but a mere question of comparative advantages, which futurity must determine. We are too ignorant either of what individual agency in its best form, or Socialism in its best form, can accomplish, to be qualified to decide which of the two will be the ultimate form of human society.

If a conjecture may be hazarded, the decision will probably depend mainly on one consideration, viz. which of the two systems is consistent with the greatest amount of human liberty and spontaneity. After the means of subsistence are assured, the next in strength of the personal wants of human beings is liberty; and (unlike the physical wants, which as civilization advances become more moderate and more amenable to control) it increases instead of diminishing in intensity as the intelligence and the moral faculties are more developed. The perfection both of social arrangements and of practical morality would be, to secure to all persons complete independence and freedom of action, subject to no restriction but that of not doing injury to others: and the education which taught or the social institutions which required them to exchange the control of their own actions for any amount of comfort or affluence, or to renounce liberty for the sake of equality, would deprive them of one of the most elevated characteristics of human nature. . . .

PROSPECTS AND METHODS OF SOCIAL IMPROVEMENT

It must always have been seen, more or less distinctly, by political economists, that the increase of wealth is not boundless: that at the end of what they term the progressive state lies the stationary state, that all progress in wealth is but a postponement of this, and that each step in advance is an approach to it. We have now been led to recognise that this ultimate goal is at all times near enough to be fully in view; that we are always on the verge of it, and that if we have not reached it long ago, it is because the goal itself flies before us. The richest and most prosperous countries would very soon attain the stationary state, if no further improvements were made in the productive arts, and if there were a suspension of the overflow of capital from those countries into the uncultivated or ill-cultivated regions of the earth.

This impossibility of ultimately avoiding the stationary state—this irresistible necessity that the stream of human industry should finally spread itself out into an apparently stagnant sea—must have been, to the political economists of the last two generations, an unpleasing and discouraging prospect; for the tone and tendency of their speculations goes completely to identify all that is economically desirable with the progressive state, and with that alone. . . .

The doctrine that, to however distant a time incessant struggling may put off our doom, the progress of society must "end in shallows and in miseries," far from being, as many people still believe, a wicked invention of Mr. Malthus, was either expressly or tacitly affirmed by his most distinguished predecessors, and can only be successfully combated on his principles. Before attention had been directed to the principle of population as the active force in determining the remuneration of labour, the increase of mankind was virtually treated as a constant quantity; it was, at all events, assumed that in the natural and normal state of human affairs population must constantly increase, from which it followed that a constant increase of the means of support was essential to the physical comfort of the mass of mankind. The publication of Mr. Malthus' *Essay* is the era from which better views of this subject must be dated; and notwithstanding the acknowledged errors of his first edition, few writers have done more than himself, in the subsequent editions, to promote these juster and more hopeful anticipations.

Even in a progressive state of capital, in old countries, a conscientious or prudential restraint on population is indispensable, to prevent the increase of numbers from outstripping the increase of capital, and the condition of the classes who are at the bottom of society from being deteriorated. Where there is not, in the people, or in some very large proportion of them, a resolute resistance to this deterioration—a determination to preserve an established standard of comfort—the condition of the poorest class sinks, even in a progressive state, to the lowest point which they will consent to endure. The same determination would be equally effectual to keep up their condition in the stationary state, and would be quite as likely to exist. Indeed, even now, the countries in which the greatest prudence is manifested in the regulating of population are often those in which capital increases least rapidly. Where there is an indefinite prospect of employment for increased numbers, there is apt to appear less necessity for prudential restraint. If it were evident that a new hand could not obtain employment but by displacing, or succeeding to, one already employed, the combined influences of prudence and public opinion might in some measure be relied on for restricting the coming generation within the numbers necessary for replacing the present. . . .

Those who do not accept the present very early stage of human improvement as its ultimate type, may be excused for being comparatively indifferent to the kind of economical progress which excites the congratulations of ordinary politicians; the mere increase of production and accumulation. For the safety of national independence it is essential that a country should not fall much behind its neighbours in these things. But in themselves they are of little importance, so long as either the increase of population or anything else prevents the mass of the people from reaping any part of the benefit of them. I know not why it should be matter of congratulation that persons who are already richer than any one needs to be, should have doubled their means of consuming things which give little or no pleasure except as representative of wealth; or that numbers of individuals should pass over, every year, from the middle classes into a richer class, or from the class of the occupied rich to that of the unoccupied. It is only in the backward countries of the world that increased production is still an important object: in those most advanced, what is economically needed is a better distribution, of which one indispensable means is a stricter restraint on population. Levelling institutions, either of a just or of an unjust kind, cannot alone accomplish it; they may lower the heights of society, but they cannot, of themselves, permanently raise the depths.

On the other hand, we may suppose this better distribution of property attained, by the joint effect of the prudence and frugality of individuals, and of a system of legislation favouring equality of fortunes, so far as is consistent with the just claim of the individual to the fruits, whether great or small, of his or her own industry. We may suppose, for instance . . ., a limitation of the sum which any one person may acquire by gift or inheritance to the amount sufficient to constitute a moderate independence. Under this twofold influence society would exhibit these leading features: a well-paid and affluent body of labourers; no enormous fortunes, except what were earned and accumulated during a single lifetime; but a much larger body of persons than at present, not only exempt from the coarser toils, but with sufficient leisure, both physical and mental, from mechanical details, to cultivate freely the graces of life, and afford examples of them to the classes less favourably circumstanced for their growth. . . .

Whether the aggregate produce [of industry] increases absolutely or not, is a thing in which, after a certain amount has been obtained, neither the legislator nor the philanthropist need feel any strong interest: but, that it should increase relatively to the number of those who share in it, is of the utmost possible importance; and this (whether the wealth of mankind be stationary, or increasing at the most rapid rate ever known in an old country), must depend on the opinions and habits of the most numerous class, the class of manual labourers.

When I speak, either in this place or elsewhere, of "the labouring classes," or of labourers as a "class," I use those phrases in compliance with custom, and as descriptive of an existing, but by no means a necessary or permanent, state of social relations. I do not recognise as either just or salutary, a state of society in which there is any "class" which is not labouring; any human beings, exempt from bearing their share of the necessary labours of human life, except those unable to labour, or who have fairly earned rest by previous toil. So long, however, as the great social evil exists of a non-labouring class, labourers also constitute a class, and may be spoken of, though only provisionally, in that character.

Considered in its moral and social aspect, the state of the labouring people has latterly been a subject of much more speculation and discussion than formerly; and the opinion that it is not now what it ought to be, has become very general. The suggestions which have been promulgated, and the controversies which have been excited, on detached points rather than on the foundations of the subject, have put in evidence the existence of two conflicting theories, respecting the social position desirable for manual labourers. The one may be called the theory of dependence and protection, the other that of self-dependence.

According to the former theory, the lot of the poor, in all things which affect them collectively, should be regulated *for* them, not *by* them. They should not be required or encouraged to think for themselves, or give to their own reflection or forecast an influential voice in the determination of their destiny. It is supposed to be the duty of the higher classes to think for them, and to take the responsibility of their lot, as the commander and officers of an army take that of the soldiers composing it. This function, it is contended, the higher classes should prepare themselves to perform conscientiously, and their whole demeanour should impress the poor with a reliance on it, in order that, while yielding passive and active obedience to the rules prescribed for them, they may resign themselves in all other respects to a trustful *insouciance*, and repose under the shadow of their protectors. The relation between rich and poor, according to this theory (a theory also applied to the relation between men and women) should be only partly authoritative; it should be amiable, moral, and sentimental: affectionate tutelage on the one side, respectful and grateful deference on the other. The rich should be *in loco parentis* to the poor, guiding and restraining them like children. Of spontaneous action on their part there should be no need. They should be called on for nothing but to do their day's work, and to be moral and religious. Their morality and religion should be provided for them by their superiors, who should see them properly taught it, and should do all that is necessary to ensure their being, in return for labour and attachment, properly fed, clothed, housed, spiritually edified, and innocently amused.

This is the ideal of the future, in the minds of those whose dissatisfaction with the Present assumes the form of affection and regret towards the Past.[1] Like other ideals, it exercises an unconscious influence on the opinions and sentiments of numbers who never consciously guide themselves by any ideal. It has also this in common with other ideals, that it has never been historically realised. It makes its appeal to our imaginative sympathies in the character of a restoration of the good times of our forefathers. But no times can be pointed out in which the higher classes of this or any other country performed a part even distantly resembling the one assigned to them in this theory. It is an idealization, grounded on the conduct and character of here and there an individual. All privileged and powerful classes, as such, have used their power in the interest of their own selfishness, and have indulged their self-importance in despising, and not in lovingly caring for, those who were, in their estimation, degraded, by being under the necessity of working for their benefit. I do not affirm that what has always been must always be, or that human improvement has no tendency to correct the intensely selfish feelings engendered by power; but though the evil may be lessened, it cannot be eradicated, until the power itself is withdrawn. This, at least, seems to me undeniable, that long before the superior classes could be sufficiently improved to govern in the tutelary manner supposed, the inferior classes would be too much improved to be so governed. . . .

It is on a far other basis that the well-being and well-doing of the labouring people must henceforth rest. The poor have come out of

[1 Cf. Thomas Carlyle's *Past and Present*, which appeared in 1843. *Eds.*]

leading-strings, and cannot any longer be governed or treated like children. To their own qualities must now be commended the care of their destiny. . . .

It appears to me impossible but that the increase of intelligence, of education, and of the love of independence among the working classes, must be attended with the corresponding growth of the good sense which manifests itself in provident habits of conduct, and that population, therefore, will bear a gradually diminishing ratio to capital and employment. This most desirable result would be much accelerated by another change, which lies in the direct line of the best tendencies of the time; the opening of industrial occupations freely to both sexes. The same reasons which make it no longer necessary that the poor should depend on the rich, make it equally unnecessary that women should depend on men; and the least which justice requires is that law and custom should not enforce dependence (when the correlative protection has become superfluous) by ordaining that a woman, who does not happen to have a provision by inheritance, shall have scarcely any means open to her of gaining a livelihood, except as a wife and mother. Let women who prefer that occupation, adopt it; but that there should be no option, no other *carrière* possible for the great majority of women, except in the humbler departments of life, is a flagrant social injustice. The ideas and institutions by which the accident of sex is made the groundwork of an inequality of legal rights, and a forced dissimilarity of social functions, must ere long be recognized as the greatest hindrance to moral, social, and even intellectual improvement. On the present occasion I shall only indicate, among the probable consequences of the industrial and social independence of women, a great diminution of the evil of over-population. It is by devoting one-half of the human species to that exclusive function, by making it fill the entire life of one sex, and interweave itself with almost all the objects of the other, that the animal instinct in question is nursed into the disproportionate preponderance which it has hitherto exercised in human life. . . .

Hitherto there has been no alternative for those who lived by their labour, but that of labouring either each for himself alone, or for a master. But the civilizing and improving influences of association, and the efficiency and economy of production on a large scale, may be obtained without dividing the producers into two parties with hostile interests and feelings, the many who do the work being mere servants under the command of the one who supplies the funds, and having no interests of their own in the enterprise except to earn their wages with as little labour as possible. The speculations and discussions of the last fifty years and the events of the last thirty, are abundantly conclusive on this point. If the improvement which even triumphant military despotism has only retarded, not stopped, shall continue its course, there can be little doubt that the *status* of hired labourers will gradually tend to confine itself to the description of work-people whose low moral qualities render them unfit for anything more independent: and that the relation of masters and work-people will be gradually superseded by partnership, in one of two forms: in some cases, association of the labourers with the capitalist; in others, and perhaps finally in all, association of labourers among themselves.

The first of these forms of association has long been practised, not indeed as a rule, but as an exception. In several departments of industry there are already cases in which every one who contributes to the work, either by labour or by pecuniary resources, has a partner's interest in it, proportional to the value of his contribution. It is already a common practice to remunerate those in whom peculiar trust is reposed, by means of a percentage on the profits: and cases exist which the principle is, with excellent success, carried down to the class of mere manual labourers. . . .

The form of association, however, which if mankind continue to improve, must be expected in the end to predominate, is not that which can exist between a capitalist as chief, and work-people without a voice in the management, but the association of the labourers themselves on terms of equality, collectively owning the capital with which they carry on their operations, and working under managers elected and removable by themselves. So long as this idea remained in a state of theory, in the writings of [Robert] Owen or of Louis Blanc, it may have appeared, to the common modes of judgment, incapable of being realized, and not likely to be tried unless by seizing on the existing capital, and confiscating it for the benefit of the labourers; which is even now imagined by many persons, and pretended by more, both in England and on the Continent, to be the meaning and purpose of Socialism. But there is a capacity of exertion and self-denial in the masses of mankind, which is never known but on the rare occasions on which it is appealed to in the name of some great idea or elevated sentiment. Such an appeal was made by the French Revolution of 1848. For the first time it then seemed to the intelligent and generous of the working classes of a great nation that they had obtained a government who sincerely desired the freedom and dignity of the many, and who did not look upon it as their natural and legitimate state to be instruments of production, worked for the benefit of the possessors of capital. Under this encouragement, the ideas sown by Socialist writers, of an emancipation of labour to be effected by means of association, throve and fructified; and many working people came to the resolution, not only that they would work for one another, instead of working for a master tradesman or manufacturer, but that they would also free themselves, at whatever cost of labour or privation, from the necessity of paying, out of the produce of their industry, a heavy tribute for the use of capital; that they would extinguish this tax, not by robbing the capitalists of what they or their predecessors had acquired by labour and preserved by economy, but by honestly acquiring capital for themselves. If only a few operatives had attempted this arduous task, or if, while many attempted it, a few only had succeeded, their success might have been deemed to furnish no argument for their system as a permanent mode of industrial organization. But, excluding all the instances of failure, there exist, or existed a short time ago, upwards of a hundred successful, and many eminently prosperous, associations of operatives in Paris alone, besides a considerable number in the departments. . . .

It is not in France alone that these associations have commenced a career of prosperity. To say nothing at present of Germany, Piedmont, and Switzerland (where the Konsum-Verein of Zürich is one of the most prosperous cooperative associations in Europe), England can produce cases of success rivalling even those which I have cited from France. Under the impulse commenced by Mr. Owen, and more recently propagated by the writings and personal efforts of a band of friends, chiefly clergymen and barristers, to whose noble exertions too much praise can scarcely be given, the good seed was widely sown; the necessary alterations in the English law of partnership were obtained from Parliament, on the benevolent and public-spirited initiative of Mr. Slaney; many industrial associations, and a still greater number of cooperative stores for retail purchases, were founded. Among these are already many instances of remarkable prosperity, the most signal of which are the Leeds Flour Mill, and the Rochdale Society of Equitable Pioneers. Of this last association, the most successful of all, the history has been written in a very interesting manner by Mr. Holyoake; and the notoriety which by this and other means has been given to facts so encouraging, is causing a rapid extension of associations with similar objects in Lancashire, Yorkshire, London, and elsewhere. . . .

Associations like those which we have described, by the very process of their success, are a course of education in those moral and active qualities by which alone success can be either deserved or attained. As associations multiplied, they would tend more and more to absorb all work-people, except those who have too little understanding, or too little virtue, to be capable of learning to act on any other system than that of narrow selfishness. As this change proceeded, owners of capital would gradually find it to their advantage, instead of maintaining the struggle of the old system with work-people of only the worst description, to lend their capital to the associations; to do this at a diminishing rate of interest, and at last, perhaps, even to exchange their capital for terminable annuities. In this or some such mode, the existing accumulations of capital might honestly, and by a kind of spontaneous process, become in the end the joint property of all who participate in their productive employment: a transformation which, thus effected, (and assuming of course that both sexes participate equally in the rights and in the government of the association,) would be the nearest approach to social justice, and the most beneficial ordering of industrial affairs for the universal good, which it is possible at present to foresee.

I agree, then, with the Socialist writers in their conception of the form which industrial operations tend to assume in the advance of improvement; and I entirely share their opinion that the time is ripe for commencing this transformation, and that it should by all just and effectual means be aided and encouraged. But while I agree and sympathize with Socialists in this practical portion of their aims, I utterly dissent from the most conspicuous and vehement part of their teaching, their declamations against competition. With moral conceptions in many respects far ahead of the existing arrangments of society, they have in general very confused and erroneous notions of its actual working; and one of their greatest errors, as I conceive, is to charge upon competition all the economical evils which at present exist. They forget that wherever competition is not, monopoly is; and that monopoly, in all its forms, is the taxation of the industrious for the support of indolence, if not of plunder. They forget, too, that with the exception of competition among labourers, all other competition is for the benefit of the labourers, by cheapening the articles they consume; that competition even in the labour market is a source not of low but of high wages, wherever the competition *for* labour exceeds the competition *of* labour, as in America, in the colonies, and in the skilled trades; and never could be a cause of low wages, save by the overstocking of the labour market through the too great numbers of the labourers' families; while, if the supply of labourers is excessive, not even Socialism can prevent their remuneration from being low. Besides, if association were universal, there would be no competition between labourer and labourer; and that between association and association would be for the benefit of the consumers, that is, of the associations; of the industrious classes generally.

I do not pretend that there are no inconveniences in competition, or that the moral objections urged against it by Socialist writers, as a source of jealousy and hostility among those engaged in the same occupation, are altogether groundless. But if competition has its evils, it prevents greater evils. . . . .

Instead of looking upon competition as the baneful and anti-social principle which it is held to be by the generality of Socialists, I conceive that, even in the present state of society and industry, every restriction of it is an evil, and every extension of it, even if for the time injuriously affecting some class of labourers, is always an ultimate good. To be protected against competition is to be protected in idleness, in mental dulness; to be saved the necessity of being as active and as intelligent as other people; and if it is also to be protected against being underbid for employment by a less highly paid class of labourers, this is only where old custom, or local and partial monopoly, has placed some particular class of artizans in a privileged position as compared with the rest; and the time has come when the interest of universal improvement is no longer promoted by prolonging the privileges of a few. If the slop-sellers and others of their class have lowered the wages of tailors, and some other artizans, by making them an affair of competition instead of custom, so much the better in the end. What is now required is not to bolster up old customs, whereby limited classes of labouring people obtain partial gains which interest them in keeping up the present organization of society, but to introduce new general practices beneficial to all; and there is reason to rejoice at whatever makes the privileged classes of skilled artizans feel that they have the same interests, and depend for their remuneration on the same general causes, and must resort for the improvement of their condition to the same remedies, as the less fortunately circumstanced and comparatively helpless multitude.

OSWALD SPENGLER (1880–1936)

Appollinian and Faustian Money

As every Culture has its own mode of thinking in money, so also it has its proper money-symbol through which it brings to visible expression its principle of valuation in the economic field. This something, a sense-actualizing of the thought, is in importance fully the equal of the spoken, written, or drawn figures and other symbols of the mathematic. Here lies a deep and fruitful domain of inquiry, so far almost unexplored. Not even the basic notions have been correctly enunciated, and it is therefore quite impossible to-day to translate intelligibly the money-idea that underlay the barter and the bill business of Egypt, the banking of Babylonia, the book-keeping of China, and the capitalism of the Jews, Parsees, Greeks, and Arabs from Haroun-al-Raschid's day. All that is possible is to set forth the essential opposition of Apollinian and Faustian money—the one, *money as magnitude*, and the other, *money as function*.

Economically, as in other ways, Classical man saw his world-around as a sum of bodies that changed their place, travelled, drove or hit or annihilated one another, as in Democritus's description of Nature. Man was a body among bodies, and the Polis as sum thereof a body of higher order. All the needs of life consisted in corporeal quantities, and money, too, therefore represented such a body, in the same way as an Apollo-statue represented a god. About 650 [B.C.], simultaneously with the stone body of the Doric temple and the free statue true-modelled in the round, appeared the *coin*, a metal weight of beautiful impressed form. Value as a magnitude had long existed—in fact as long as this Culture itself. In Homer, a talent is a little aggregate of gold, in bullion and decorative objects, of a definite total weight. The Shield of Achilles represents "two talents" of gold, and even as late as Roman times it was usual to specify silver and gold vessels by weight.

The discovery of the Classically formed money-body, however, is so extraordinary that we have not even yet grasped it in its deep and purely Classical significance. We regard it as one of the "achievements of humanity," and so we strike these coinages everywhere, just as we put statues in our streets and squares. So much and no more it is within our power to do; we can imitate the shape, but we cannot impart the same economic significance thereto. The coin *as money* is a purely Classical phenomenon—only possible in an environment conceived wholly on Euclidean ideas, but there creatively dominant over all economic life. Notions like income, resources, debt, capital, meant in the Classical cities something quite different from what they mean to us. They meant, not economic energy radiating from a point, but a sum of valuable objects in hand. Wealth was always a mobile *cash-supply*, which was altered by addition and subtraction of valuable objects and had nothing at all to do with possessions in land—for in Classical thinking the two were completely separate. Credit consisted in the lending of cash in the expectation that the loan would be repaid in cash. Catiline was poor because, in spite of his wide estates, he could find nobody to lend him the cash that he needed for his political aims; and the immense debts of Roman politicians had for their ultimate security, not their equivalent in land, but the definite prospect of a province to be plundered of its movable assets.

In the light of this, and only in the light of this, we begin to understand certain phenomena such as the mass-execution of the wealthy under the Second Tyrannis, and the Roman proscriptions (with the object of seizing a large part of the cash current in the community), and the melting down of the Delphian temple-treasure by the Phocians in the Sacred War, of the art-treasures of Corinth by Mummius, and the the last votive offerings in Rome by Caesar, in Greece by Sulla, in Asia Minor by Brutus and Cassius, without regard to artistic value when the noble stuffs and metals and ivory were needed. The captured statues and the vessels borne in the triumphs were, in the eyes of the spectators, sheer cash, and Mommsen[1] could attempt to determine the site of Varus's disaster by the places in which coin-hoards were unearthed—for the Roman veteran carried his whole property in precious metal on his person. Classical wealth does not consist in having possessions, but piling money; a Classical money-market was not a centre of credit like the bourses of our world and of ancient Thebes, but a city in which an important part of the world's cash was actually collected. It may be taken that in Caesar's time much more than half of the Classical world's gold was in Rome.

But when, from about Hannibal's time, this world advanced into the state of unlimited plutocracy, the naturally limited mass of precious

[1] Theodor Mommsen, 1817–1903. German classical scholar and historian. *Eds.*]

metals and materially valuable works of art in its sphere of control became hopelessly inadequate to cover needs, and a veritable craving set in for new bodies capable of being used as money. Then it was that men's eyes fell upon the slave, who was another sort of body, but a thing and not a person and capable, therefore, of being thought of as money. From that point Classical slavery became unique of its kind in all economic history. The properties of the coin were extended to apply to living objects, and the stock of men in the regions "opened up" to the plunderings of proconsuls, and tax-farmers became as interesting as the stock of metal. A curious sort of double valuation developed. The slave had a market price, although ground and soil had not. He served for the accumulation of great uninvested fortunes, and hence the enormous slave-masses of the Roman period, which are entirely inexplicable by any other sort of necessity. So long as man needed only as many slaves as he could gainfully employ, their number was small and easily covered by the prisoners of war and judgment-debtors. It was in the sixth century that Chios made a beginning with the importation of bought slaves (Argyronetes). The difference between these and the far more numerous paid labourers was originally of a political and legal, not an economic kind. As the Classical economy was static and not dynamic, and was ignorant of the systematic opening-up of energy-sources, the slaves of the Roman age did not exist to be exploited in work, but were employed—more or less—so that the greatest possible number of them could be maintained. Specially presentable slaves possessing particular qualifications of one sort or another were preferred, because for equal cost of maintenance they represented a better asset; they were loaned as cash was loaned; and they were allowed to have businesses on their account, so that they could become rich; free labour was undersold—all this so as to cover at any rate the upkeep of this capital. The bulk of them cannot have been employed at all. They answered their purpose by simply existing, as a stock of money in hand which was not bound up to a natural limit like the stock of metal available in those days. And through that very fact the need of slaves grew and grew indefinitely and led, not only to wars that were undertaken simply for slave-getting, but to slave-hunting by private entrepreneurs all along the Mediterranean coasts (which Rome winked at) and to a new way of making the proconsuls' fortunes, which consisted in bleeding the population of a region and then selling it into slavery for debt. The market of Delos must have dealt with ten thousand slaves a day. When Caesar went to Britain, the disappointment caused in Rome by the money-poverty of the Britons was compensated by the prospect of rich booty in slaves.

When, for example, Corinth was destroyed, the melting-down of the statues for coinage and the auctioning of the inhabitants at the slave-mart were, for Classical minds, one and the same operation—the transformation of corporeal objects into money.

In extremest contrast to this stands the symbol of Faustian money—money as Function, the value of which lies in its effect and not its mere existence. The specific style of this economic thinking appears already in the way in which the Normans of A.D. 1000 organized their spoils of men and land into an economic force. Compare the pure book-valuation of these ducal officials (commemorated in our words "cheque," "account," and "checking") with the "contemporary" gold talent of the Iliad, one meets at the very outset of the Culture the rudiments of its modern credit-system, which is the outcome of confidence in the force and durability of its economic mode, and with which the idea of money in our sense is almost identical. These financial methods, transplanted to the Roman Kingdom of Sicily by Roger II, were developed by the Hohenstaufen Emperor Frederick II (about A.D. 1230) into a powerful system far surpassing the original in dynamism and making him the "first capitalist power of the world"; and while this fraternization of mathematical thinking-power and royal will-to-power made its way from Normandy into France and was applied on the grand scale to the exploitation of conquered England (to this day English soil is nominally royal demesne) its Sicilian side was imitated by the Italian city-republics, and (as their ruling patricians soon took the methods of the civic economy into use for their private book-keeping,) spread over the commercial thought and practice of the whole Western world. A little later, the Sicilian methods were adopted by the Order of the Teutonic Knights and by the dynasty of Aragon, and it is probably to these origins that we should assign the model accountancy of Spain in the days of Philip II, and of Prussia in those of Frederick William I.

The decisive event, however, was the invention—"contemporary" with that of the Classical coin about 650 B.C.—of double-entry book-keeping by Fra Luca Pacioli in 1494. Goethe calls this in *Wilhelm Meister* "one of the finest discoveries of the human intellect," and indeed its author may without hesitation be ranked with his contemporaries Columbus and Copernicus. To the Normans we owe our modes of reckoning and to the Lombards our book-keeping. These, be it observed, were the same two Germanic stocks which created the two most suggestive juristic works of the early Gothic, and whose longing into distant seas gave the impulses for the two discoveries of America. "Double-entry book-keeping is born of the same spirit as the system of

Galileo and Newton. . . . With the same means as these, it orders the phenomenon into an elegant system, and it may be called the first Cosmos built up on the basis of a mechanistic thought. Double-entry book-keeping discloses to us the Cosmos of the economic world by the same method as later the Cosmos of the stellar universe was unveiled by the great investigation of natural philosophy. . . . Double-entry book-keeping rests on the basic principle, logically carried out, of comprehending all phenomena purely as quantities."

Double-entry book-keeping is a pure Analysis of the space of values, referred to a co-ordinate system, of which the origin is the "Firm." The coinage of the Classical world had only permitted of arithmetical compilations with value-*magnitudes.* Here, as ever, Pythagoras and Descartes stand opposed. It is legitimate for us to talk of the "integration" of an undertaking, and the graphic curve is the same optical auxiliary to economics as it is to science. The Classical economy-world was ordered, like the cosmos of Democritus, according to *stuff and form.* A stuff, in the form of a coin, carries the economic movement and presses against the demand-unit of equal value-quantity at the place of use. *Our* economy-world is ordered by *force and mass.* A field of money-tensions lies in space and assigns to every object, irrespective of its specific kind, a positive or negative effect-value, which is represented by a book-entry. "*Quod non est in libris, non est in mundo.*" But the symbol of the functional money thus imagined, that which *alone* may be compared with the Classical coin, is not the actual book-entry, not yet the share-voucher, cheque, or note, *but the act by which the function is fulfilled in writing,* and the role of the value-paper is merely to be the *generalized historical evidence* of this act.

Yet side by side with this the West, in its unquestioning admiration of the Classical, has gone on striking coins, not merely as tokens of sovereignty, but in the belief that this evidenced money was money corresponding in reality to the economics in thought. In just the same way, ever within the Gothic age, we took over Roman law with its equating of things to bodily magnitudes, and the Euclidean mathematic, which was built upon the concept of number as magnitude. And so it befell that the evolution of these three intellectual form-worlds of ours proceeded, not like the Faustian music in a pure and flowerlike unfolding, but in the shape of a *progressive emancipation from the notion of magnitude.* The mathematic had already achieved this by the close of the Baroque age. The jurisprudence, on the other hand, has not yet even recognized its coming task, but this century is going to set it, and to demand that which for Roman jurists was the self-evident basis of law, namely, the inward congruence of economic and legal thought and an equal practical familiarity with both. The conception of money that was symbolized in the coin agreed precisely with the Classical thing-law, but with us there is nothing remotely like such an agreement. Our whole life is disposed dynamically, not statically and Stoically; therefore our essentials are forces and performances, relations and capacities—organizing talents and intuitive intellects, credit, ideas, methods, energy-sources—and not mere existence of corporeal things. The "Romanist" thing-thought of our jurists, and the theory of money that consciously or unconsciously starts from the coin, are equally alien to our life. The vast metallic hoard to which, in imitation of the Classical, we were continually adding till the World War came, has indeed made a role for itself off the main road, but with the inner form, tasks, and aims of modern economy it has *nothing* to do; and if as the result of the war it were to disappear from currency altogether, nothing would be altered thereby.

Unhappily, the modern national economics were founded in the age of Classicism. Just as statues and vases and stiff dramas alone counted as true art, so also finely stamped coins alone counted as true money. What Josiah Wedgwood (1758) aimed at with his delicately toned reliefs and cups, that also, at bottom, Adam Smith aimed at in his theory of value—namely, the pure present of tangible magnitudes. For it is entirely consonant with the illusion that money and pieces of money are the same, to measure the value of a thing against the magnitude of a quantity of work. Here work is no longer an *effecting* in a world of effects, a working which can differ infinitely from case to case as to inward worth and intensity and range, which propagates itself in wider and wider circles and like an electric field may be measured but not marked off—but the *result* of the effecting, considered entirely materially, *that which is worked-up*, a tangible thing showing nothing noteworthy about it except just its extent.

In reality, the economy of the European-American Civilization is built up on work of a kind in which distinctions go entirely according to the inner quality—more so than ever in China or Egypt, let alone the Classical World. It is not for nothing that we live in a world of economic dynamism, where the works of the individual are not addictive in the Euclidean way, but functionally related to one another. The purely executive work (which alone Marx takes into account) is in reality nothing but the function of an inventive, ordering, and organizing work; it is from this that the other derives its meaning, relative value, and even possibility of being done at all. The whole world-economy since the discovery of the steam-engine has been the creation of a quite small number of superior heads, without whose high-grade work everything else would never have come into being. But this achievement is of creative thinking, not a quantum, and its value is not to be weighed against a certain number of coins. Rather it *is* itself money—Faustian money, namely, which is not minted, but *thought of as an efficient centre* coming up out of a life—and it is the inward quality of that life which elevates the thought to the significance of a fact. *Thinking in money generates money*—that is the secret of the world-economy. When an organizing magnate writes down a million on paper, that million exists, for the personality as an economic centre vouches for a corresponding heightening of the economic energy of his field. This, and nothing else, is the meaning of the word "Credit" for us. But all the gold pieces in the world would not suffice to invest the actions of the manual worker with a meaning, and therefore a value, if the famous "expropriation of the expropriators" were to eliminate the superior capacities from their creations; were this to happen, these would become soulless, will-less, empty shells. Thus, in fact, Marx is just as much a Classical, just as truly a product of the Romanist law-thought as Adam Smith; he sees only the completed magnitude, not the function and he would like to separate the means of production from those whose minds, by the discovery of methods, the organization of efficient industries, and the acquisition of outlet-markets, alone turn a mass of bricks and steel into a factory, and who, if their forces find no field of play, do not occur.

If anyone seeks to enunciate a theory of modern work, let him begin by thinking of this trait of all life. There are subjects and objects in every kind of life as lived, and the more important, the more rich in form, the life is, the clearer the distinction between them. As every stream of Being consists of a minority of leaders and a huge majority of led, so *every sort of economy consists in leader-work and executive work*. The frog's perspective of Marx and the social-ethical ideologues shows only the aggregate of last small things, but these only exist at all in virtue of the first things, and the spirit of this world of work can be grasped only through a grasp of its highest possibilities. The inventor of the steam-engine and not its stoker is the determinant. The *thought* is what matters.

And, similarly, thinking in money has subjects and objects: those who by force of their personality generate and guide money, and those who are maintained by money. Money of the Faustian brand is the *force* distilled from economy-dynamics of the Faustian brand, and it appertains to the destiny of the individual (on the economic side of his life-destiny) that he is inwardly constituted to represent a part of this force, or that he is, on the contrary, nothing but mass to it.

CHARLES FRANKEL (1917–)

The Transformation of Welfare

The concept of welfare as it functions today in social work and social assistance has of course undergone changes, but its intellectual source, I believe, lies here. Welfare is the child of charity—it is associated with the notion of unearned relief from distress. It is something that cannot be brought within the sphere of the controlling doctrine that work is the sole justification for receiving any benefits from others. Welfare activities, accordingly, have been regarded as essentially exceptional in character; they deal with boundary-line conditions; there is a stigma attached to them; the recipients of welfare, if they are not always beyond the pale, are not quite within the pale either. Seen from the point of view of its seventeenth-century origins, the concept of welfare is what might be called a "waste-basket" concept. It is where we file the problems that fall outside strict considerations of property and of justice....

... While we have, until recently, been talking in one way in Western society, we have been acting in a different way more often, perhaps, than we have realized. Under the rubric of free contracts, we have developed collective procedures for taking care of the needs of people in certain types of situation or position. Whether we take care of these needs well or badly is not for the moment to the point. But we take care of these needs not as an exercise in philanthropy, nor as part of a system or charity, nor as a last-ditch defense in emergency. We take care of them in consequence of an organized projection of the probable needs of different categories of individuals, and on the basis of the at least implicit hypothesis that general social regulation and control are

The selection is from Charles Frankel, "The Transformation of Welfare," in John S. Morgan, ed., *Welfare and Wisdom* (Toronto: University of Toronto Press, 1966), pp. 168–184, with omissions. Used by permission of the publisher.

necessary if these needs are to be served. And it seems to me that in such arrangements another idea of welfare besides the minimal, residual concept we have discussed can be discerned—an idea that is more relevant to the world in which we live. It is a concept of social welfare whose content would come from forecasting the needs of individuals in different positions in society, and undertaking within the limits of available and probable resources, to provide securely for these needs.

Why should such a concept, an extension of what has been implicit in much past practice, be systematically adopted as a guide to welfare policy? Let us recall that we are dealing with a moral ideal offered as an hypothesis, and let us see what some of its consequences might be. If we take the so-called "problems of youth" as examples, welfare, so conceived, would not focus on issues such as "school dropouts" or "the prevention of delinquency." Welfare policy would be based on the recognition that "youth," so-called, is primarily a social category, a social status, created by law and convention. The status of "youth" is assigned to all those individuals who, though biologically mature, are nevertheless, for a variety of reasons, kept in a socially dependent or apprentice position. A transformed concept of welfare would promote inquiry into whether all the reasons normally given for maintaining this state of dependency were justified, the probable categories into which different kinds of "youth" would fall, and the size of the groups concerned—for example, those who would stay in school for ten years, those who would stay for twelve, those who would seek vocational training, those for whom on-the-job training would be best, etc. And it would undertake to provide appropriate environments to meet the needs of all these different categories of young people. Whether the problems of youth would be better dealt with—whether procedures would be more humane, more effective, and, yes, more economical—when approached from this point of view is precisely the hypothesis that would be under examination.

That we have reason to think it an hypothesis worth testing may be suggested by comparing it with our present approach. What this transformed concept of welfare would not encourage would be what, I fear, we mainly do now. This consists, first, in employing definitions that rest more on social ignorance and insularity than on careful inquiry, and which establish some one set of conditions and one type of youth as normal and respectable. It consists, second, in treating those who do not conform to these definitions as special cases calling for philanthropy, therapy, or punishment. It is instructive how quickly, given existing modes of thought, the public mind has come to associate "school drop-out" with "juvenile delinquent" and to regard the former as though it were a mild case of the latter. But the phrase "school drop-out" stands, in general, for a category of person in potential trouble only because there is so little organized social provision apart from schools, for a large number of young people, who, it can be predicted, will not want to be in school or should not be in school. And I cannot help but note that when such organized provision is not made, schools themselves are forced to a function not theirs. They become in large part custodial institutions. The deformation of the contemporary school in large cities is a consequence of the purely residual notion of welfare we still employ.

As this example may suggest, the transformed view of welfare I am describing would presumably have a number of general consequences. It would remove the stigma from welfare. It would transform welfare from a peripheral function at the fringes of society to the central object of organized social planning. And it would turn reflection away from the problem of helping those who cannot help themselves, and towards the problem of creating conditions in which fewer people will need others' help. The attitude that now keeps us in a mental bind is reflected in the question which is, of all questions, the principal one affecting current discussion of welfare issues. This is the question: How can welfare programmes be controlled and regulated so that they do not reward shiftlessness, and do not collide with the primary principle that individuals should seek to support themselves by work? The question is part and parcel of the traditional attitude which, on one side, dwells on the sanctity of work, and, on the other, on the sad necessity for welfare. It is unlikely that such an approach will be able to deal effectively with the conditions that make for chronic shiftlessness, and the inbred disposition to avoid work. The hypothesis implicit in the concept of welfare that is here proposed is that these problems would be met more effectively by an approach that focussed not on punitive sanctions, but on the provision of positive capacities and motivations to work. This is an essentially long-range process. It would stress education; it would invite inquiry into the character and environment of the process of work itself; it would require creative imagination aimed at organizing work so that it offered to those who now fear or resent it ampler opportunities for satisfaction and achievement. Not occupational therapy but the joys of interesting occupation would be at the centre of attention. That there are limits to what such an approach could accomplish with regard to making all kinds of work pleasurable goes without saying. But that it would be more effective in dealing with the problem of voluntary idleness in an era of abundance than our present methods is surely an hypothesis worth trying.

Such a concept of welfare, it should be stressed, has a dimension which the received, residual concept of welfare does not have. The received concept concentrates on aid to individuals. The transformed concept calls attention as well to social needs. As the remarks that I have just made may suggest, problems like delinquency, chronic poverty, and unemployment are generally associated with structural deficiencies in the environment of those most affected. They go with inadequate schools, bad health, dispiriting broken-down neighbourhoods, boredom and its anodyne, violence, and public attitudes of distrust and hostility that every child can detect in the glances of the policeman or the indifference of his teachers.

Problems that also affect the more fortunate members of society ..the degrading ugliness and inconvenience of cities, the deterioration of large sections of the countryside, the absence of reasonable opportunities to lift one's intellectual sights if one wishes, the domination of the aesthetic and moral landscape by the art or the craft of the advertiser and the press agent—are problems of a similar sort. They exist in their present degree and intensity because the sector of our economy which is rationalized by the traditional philosphy of free contract has neither the will nor the way to do what is necessary to deal with them. Social needs exist which it is romantic to expect that private enterprise will or can serve. A reasonable balance between the public and private sectors is a prerequisite to the adequate recognition and satisfaction of such general social needs.[1] This is why a transformed and enlarged conception of social welfare—a conception which does not draw its content only from the behaviour of individuals in the market system—is urgently needed, and is, indeed, overdue. . . .

It is natural enough . . . that there should be serious concern about the expansion of the concept of welfare, and that the view should still exist that it is imperative that we draw a sharp line between the welfare activities in which the State may properly engage and those in which it attempts to redesign a society in the light of a moral vision. "It is essential," says Professor Hayek

> that we become clearly aware of the line that separates a state of affairs in which the community accepts the duty of preventing

[1] Readers of Mr. Galbraith's works will recognize my debt to him in these paragraphs. See especially his recent article. "Economics and the Quality of Life," *Science*, July 10, 1964.

destitution and of providing a minimum level of welfare from that in which it assumes the power to determine the "just" position of everybody and allocates to each what it thinks he deserves. Freedom is critically threatened when the government is given exclusive powers to provide certain services—powers which, in order to achieve its purpose, it may use for the discretionary coercion of individuals.[2]

But can this sharp line be drawn between an idea of a "minimum level of welfare" and larger conceptions of social justice? The hypothesis that we would do better to adopt a transformed conception of welfare turns on the merits of the arguments pro and con with regard to this issue.

Obviously, no man and no government can say what any individual really deserves, and the thought of drawing up a scale of merit and assigning each person his rightful place in accordance with it would be a form of madness. Nevertheless, a tangle of questionable assumptions is involved, it seems to me, in the notion that a liberal state, bound by the rule of law, can make no substantive judgments about distributive justice, but must accept the results decreed by the impersonal market-place. For it is surely a function of such a state at least to protect the fairness and purity of competition in this market-place. But if that is so, it has to determine, for example, whether monopoly is "fair" and whether labour unions are "fair." It is difficult to see how these judgments can be made on purely procedural grounds. They involve deciding whether or not there are significant inequalities at issue, and whether or not such inequalities should be rectified. This cannot be done purely by appeal to a formal principle of "equality before the law."

The same is true when we consider what must surely be a fundamental function of the liberal state from Professor Hayek's point of view—namely, the safeguarding of the system of free contract. It is only at the boundaries—in relatively exceptional circumstances—that the judicial and executive powers of government are used to enforce contracts between individuals. The State is there to ensure the performance of contracts, but that is not its most normal function. Its more usual function is to make up for human imprecision and inexactness, and for the remarkable capacity of nature and society to produce novel situations that the contracting parties could not have foreseen. To take a simple

[2] F. V. Hayek, *The Constitution of Liberty* (Chicago: University of Chicago Press, 1960), pp. 289–90.

example, if goods are put on a freight train that never reaches its destination, which of the contracting parties shall take the loss—the seller or the buyer? In such ambiguous or unforeseen circumstances, where the contract itself offers no answer, the courts have to decide what constitutes performance, and how the burdens accruing to non-performance shall be distributed. In effect, the courts are deciding how the risks incident to contracts shall be distributed. If this can be done without appeal to substantive notions of distributive justice some wholly unforeseen changes in the laws of logic have taken place.

Similar considerations apply to the notion that a liberal government will not take it upon itself to be the moral arbiter of the community. If a free society exists, the government will surely not be the only arbiter. But it cannot escape being an arbiter, and an influential one, whatever its view of welfare. Liberal states engage in education; they encourage patriotism; they honour noble men; and even when they are neutral with regard to religion, they generally give religious establishments indirect subsidies by exempting them from taxation. All of these would seem to involve value-judgments. There is, indeed, a certain disingenuousness in the argument that political officials have no right to impose their personal moral or aesthetic preferences on others. The argument suggests that nobody else is making the attempt. But the effort to cut the tastes of the citizenry to the pattern of one's own tastes—or, at any rate, one's own economic advantage—is a major industry in modern societies and absorbs a good part of the national wealth.

Nor is it true that governments that restrict themselves to a minimal conception of welfare do not engage in the discretionary coercion of individuals. In many parts of the United States, intrusions into private life including midnight visits by officials on private citizens are normal elements in the supervision and enforcement of welfare laws. These invasions of the privacy of the poor constitute one of the most widespread and serious threats to the right to privacy with which we are now confronted. Yet they are commonly condoned by precisely those people who argue that any enlargement of the conception of welfare beyond relief from destitution entails grave threats to private rights, and threatens the growth of a moralistic, Big Brotherly officialdom. Our welfare activities, under their existing rationale, are in fact wholly governed by an antecedent moral ideal. Their intent is to encourage people to wish to work and to live decently. I could not agree with that intent more wholeheartedly. I permit myself some reservations, however, about the effectiveness of the pedagogical methods that are employed, and about their congruences with regard to the protection of elementary rights that all citizens of free societies should presumably possess.

In sum, there would be more force to the charge that an enlarged welfare state must necessarily impose a special moral vision on the citizenry if those who made the objection could themselves plead innocent to the charge. But if the arguments I offered in my first lecture have any validity, we have already seen that the concept of welfare which treats welfare as a matter of relief from destitution, and attempts to extrude all questions of a larger social justice, nevertheless makes some considerable moral commitments. It reflects and accepts certain definite ways of recruiting and rewarding labour, certain definite arrangements for the distribution of the penalties and rewards of economic production, and certain unmistakably class-angled views about the moral obligations to earn one's living by the sweat of one's brow. The conception of social justice that emerges from these commitments may not always be either articulate or defensible, but it is a conception of social justice just the same.

But I would add a most important cautionary note. If there is confusion on this side, there should not be a parallel error on the other. It is an hypothesis that the conception of welfare I have adumbrated could be adopted as a programme of action without sacrificing fundamental liberties. That hypothesis should not be certified a priori by playing tricks with words. What gives pause to partisans of liberty when they contemplate the enlargements of the ideal of welfare is a point of view that has become increasingly widespread. It consists in the total identification of welfare and freedom. The adoption of this way of thinking is ruinous to the conception of welfare within freedom for which I am attempting to make a case.

It is tempting to think that "welfare" is really all that we can seriously mean by "freedom." In a famous passage in *Equality*, Tawney wrote

There is no such thing as freedom in the abstract, divorced from the realities of a particular time and place. Whatever else the conception may imply, it involves a power of choice between alternatives, a choice which is real, not merely nominal, between alternatives which exist in fact, not only on paper. . . . It means the ability to do, or to refrain from doing, definite things, at a definite moment, in definite circumstances, or it means nothing at all.

The intent of this argument is both clear and laudable. If young Peter is free to attend any school of his choice in the sense that the law says he may and promises to support him against anyone who tries to prevent him from doing so, but if there simply is no school within fifty miles of his home, Peter's freedom is an abstraction and it is a cruel joke to tell him that he has the right to choose his school. To give freedom meaning and substance it has to be associated with power and opportunity. Otherwise, it is a mere formalism, an empty, indeed a cynical, word. There is a long tradition, which includes liberal philosophers from T. H. Green to John Dewey, that has taken this view. Indeed, the tendency to see welfare as an integral part of freedom has been enshrined in the Atlantic Charter, which places "freedom from want" among the four freedoms. Still, despite its distinguished intellectual pedigree, this view of freedom spreads confusion. It mixes up quite distinguishable things. "Freedom" and "welfare" both stand for desirable goals of human endeavour, but they are not the same goal. I have freedom when, in a given situation, no man or law prevents or prohibits me from doing a given thing if I wish to do it. My welfare is something else—it is a matter of my physical and mental health, of the resources at my disposal, of my powers and opportunities.

Of course, there is very often little or no value in my possessing a freedom unless I have the ability and opportunity to act on it. But this does not mean that the ability and opportunity are the same as the freedom. I may have the ability and opportunity to study, to travel, or to refute the nonsense I hear from the leaders of governments, but I may still not have the freedom to do any of these things. And if it is true that the ability and opportunity to do something is generally necessary if the freedom to do it is to be important to a man, the reverse is also true: with regard to a great many things, the freedom to do them is necessary if the ability and opportunity to do them are to emerge.

To be sure, Tawney, in the statement I have quoted, speaks of freedom as "the ability to do or to refrain from doing," and thereby indicates that he thinks there can be no freedom without choice. Still, it is important from the point of view of social policy to keep clearly separate the question whether a man has the ability and opportunity to do something and the question whether he has the freedom to do it. Otherwise we may find ourselves saying odd things such as that the citizens of Country X are freer than they used to be because they have more medical care these days. It ought to be possible at least to raise the question whether there is a conflict between better medical care and freedom. To do this we have to avoid defining our terms so that the question is answered a priori.

Indeed, the habit of identifying welfare and freedom can lead us to say, as many have indeed said, that we are really free precisely when, and only when, we have reached a stage of such utter well-being and moral self-realization that it does not occur to us ever to want to do anything that we ought not to do. It is intelligible that there should be a long tradition, going back to Saint Paul and beyond, in which people speak of freedom in this way. Most of us know what it is to struggle against irresolution or plain laziness, against inner divisions and constraints, against odd blockages inside us, or against perverse drives to do what, soberly, we would not wish to do. And in such circumstances, we often speak quite naturally of wishing somehow to be "free." We mean that we wish to be whole, to be in unimpeded command of ourselves, and it is natural to call this state "freedom" because if we were whole, if we were in command of ourselves, we should have got rid of these strange drives and restraints and weaknesses that we feel are somehow external to our real selves, and that do not belong with what we are and are trying to be. And from this it is very easy to move on, and to say that we are not our real selves when we are tempted to do wrong, or when, in our blindness, we choose the wrong only because we did not know the right. And then freedom becomes the same thing as complete moral well-being. It is nothing but our welfare, full and complete.

This way of speaking about "freedom" dissolves freedom into welfare. To the extent that we adopt it, we must be prepared to grant to the State, or to whatever institution knows what is really good for us, supreme and unchallenged authority to promote our well-being. But the satisfaction of our needs, even our highest needs, is not freedom unless we retain the right to choose, including the right to make the wrong choices. It is possible—it is necessary—to say that freedom of choice is an integral part of what we shall choose to mean by "the good life"; it is not possible, without dire confusion, to say that freedom is nothing more than our welfare.

Accordingly, in suggesting that any conception of human welfare has a moral bias written into it, and in urging that the State undertake a commitment to human welfare just the same, I have very much in mind a necessary limiting condition. I should not wish liberal governments to adopt the broad conception of welfare that I have described if they were the only centres of power or the only sources of employment and benefits in the community. If they were the only centres of power in the community, indeed, they would not be liberal states. For the older conception of welfare that I have rejected nevertheless performed an indispensable function. It served as a support of a philosophy that put individual choice at the centre of the stage, and that helped guide and regulate the struggle in the West to free individuals from irrevocable dependence on any particular group. The assumption that there will be choice, that a pluralistic society will exist and that individuals will have some opportunity to say "yes" or "no" where official notions of human welfare are concerned, is central to what I have said.

The transformed concept of welfare thus retains an essential element of the older concept. Its heart is the right to choose. It merely goes further than the older concept in its concern for freedom. It proposes to ensure that the beneficiaries of welfare measures have not only the right but the intelligent power to choose. That, it seems to me, is what "welfare," in the end, is all about. It stands for the effort to create a society in which individuals will have significant choices, and will have sufficient knowledge and ability and resources so that, when they make the choices, they can reasonably be held responsible for what they have done.

Is it possible for governments to undertake so large a responsibility without becoming tyrannical? It is possible, I think, though it is obvious that we should not take the safety of freedom for granted. There is much that should legitimately concern us in the growth of so many bureaus, forms, regulations, committees, and committees to co-ordinate committees, and in the steady increase in the number of official and semi-official interventions in daily and personal life. However, there is no evidence that a conscious moral vision is the cause of this state of affairs. On the contrary, all this has come about in the absence of order and plan, and may well be its product. We ought at least to examine the alternative possibility that organized planning directed by a co-ordinated idea of welfare could reduce the daily weight and cost of the governmental presence.

In practice, then, an enlightened public welfare policy need not consist in the coercive imposition on a community of a point of view. It need not consist in this even where it concerns itself explicitly, as I believe it should, with aesthetic issues or with the protection and projection of standards of taste and achievement cherished only by a minority. Such a policy is simply an effort to restore perspective and balance; it is an effort to ensure that the better will not suffer because few know that it exists. For you cannot be said to know what you are choosing unless you know the alternatives, and there is no way of escaping Philistia unless you know there are other countries. A decent amplitude of genuine choice for all citizens is a reasonable and necessary objective of liberal government. I am inclined to think that in this objective we sum up most of what we mean by "welfare."

ERICH FROMM (1900–)

Guaranteed Income and Expanded Freedom

Until now, man's freedom to act has been limited by two factors: the use of force on the part of the rulers (essentially their capacity to kill the dissenters); and, more important, the threat of starvation against all who were unwilling to accept the imposed conditions of work.

Whoever rebelled against these conditions, even if no other force was used against him, was confronted with hunger. The principle prevailing throughout most of human history (in capitalism as well as in the Soviet Union) is: "He who does not work shall not eat." This threat forced man not only to act in accordance with what was demanded of him, but also to think and to feel in such a way that he would not even be tempted to act differently.

The reason that past history is based on the threat of starvation has its source in the fact that, with the exception of certain primitive societies, man has lived at a level of scarcity. There were never sufficient material goods to satisfy the needs of all; usually a small group of "directors" took for themselves all that their hearts desired, and the many who could not sit at the table were told it was God's or Nature's law that this should be so. But it must be noted that the main factor in this was not the greed of the "directors" but the low level of material productivity.

A guaranteed income, which becomes possible in the era of economic abundance, could for the first time free man from the threat of starvation, and thus make him truly free and independent economically

The selection is from Erich Fromm, "Psychology of a Guaranteed Income," *The Nation*, December 6, 1965, pp. 439–442. Used by permission of the publisher.

and psychologically. Nobody would have to accept conditions of work merely because he feared hunger; a talented or ambitious man or woman could learn new skills in preparation for a different kind of occupation. A woman could leave her husband, an adolescent his family. People would no longer learn to be afraid, if they did not have to fear for their bread. (This holds true, of course, only if no political threat inhibits man's free thought, speech and action.)

A guaranteed income would not only establish freedom as a reality rather than a slogan; it would also establish a principle deeply rooted in Western religious and humanist traditions: man has the right to live, regardless! This right to live—to have food, shelter, medical care, education, etc.—is an intrinsic human right that cannot be restricted by any condition, not even the one that the individual must be socially "useful."

The shift from a psychology of scarcity to that of abundance is one of the most important steps in human development. A psychology of scarcity produces anxiety, envy, egotism (to be seen most drastically in peasant cultures the world over). A psychology of abundance produces initiative, faith in life, solidarity. The fact is that most men are still geared psychologically to the economic facts of scarcity, when the industrial world is in the process of entering a new era of economic abundance. Because of this psychological "lag," many people cannot even understand the new ideas implicit in the concept of a guaranteed income.

A further effect of a guaranteed income, coupled with greatly diminished working hours for all, would be to make the spiritual and religious problems of human existence real and imperative. Until now, most men have been too much occupied with work (or too tired after work) to be seriously concerned with such problems as "What is the meaning of life?" "What do I believe in?" "What are my values?" "Who am I?" If work ceases to be the main concern, man will either be free to confront these problems seriously—or he will be driven half mad by boredom. It should follow that economic abundance, liberation from fear of starvation, would mark the transition from a pre-human to a truly human society.

To balance this picture, one must raise some objections against, or at least questions about, the concept of a guaranteed income. The most obvious question is whether it would not reduce the incentive for work.

It is a fact that even now there is no work for an ever-increasing sector of the population, and that for these people the question of incentive is irrelevant. Nevertheless, the objection is a serious one. I believe, however, that it can be demonstrated that material necessity is by no means the only incentive for work and effort. Pride, social recognition, pleasure in work itself—examples of the force of such alternate incentives are not lacking. An obvious one is the work of scientists, artists, et al., whose achievements were not principally motivated by the need for money but by a mixture of factors: interest in the work, satisfaction in the achievement, or the wish for fame. But obvious though this example may be, it is not entirely convincing, because it can be said that such outstanding people will make extraordinary efforts precisely because they are extraordinarily gifted; hence they give no clue to the reactions of the citizenry at large. This objection may be overcome, however, if we consider the incentives for people who are not notably creative. What prodigious effort is expended on sports, on recreation, on hobbies, from which no material rewards are to be expected! The extent to which interest in the work process itself can be an incentive for working was closely demonstrated for the first time by Prof. Elton Mayo in his classic study at the Chicago Hawthorne works of the Western Electric Company. The very fact that unskilled women workers were drawn into the experiment of work productivity of which they were the subjects, the fact that they became interested and active participants in the experiment, resulted in increased productivity. As a corollary, their physical health improved.

The situation becomes even clearer from the study of older forms of society. The efficiency and incorruptibility of the traditional Prussian civil service were famous, despite the fact that wages were very low. In this case such concepts as honor, loyalty, duty were the determining motivations for excellent work. Still another motivation appears in pre-industrial societies (like medieval Europe or the half-feudal Latin-American states at the beginning of this century). In these societies the carpenter, for instance, wanted to earn enough to satisfy the needs of his traditional standard of living, and would refuse more work when he had reached that point.

Aside from the multiple nature of the incentives to work it is a fact that man, by nature, is not lazy. On the contrary, he suffers from the results of inactivity. People might enjoy loafing for one or two months, but the vast majority (except for the very sick or the most philosophic) would after that beg to work, even without pay. The fields of child development and mental illness offer abundant data in this connection; what is needed is a systematic investigation in which the available facts are organized and analyzed from the standpoint of "laziness as disease." Modern, alienated man is deeply bored (usually unconsciously) and hence has a yearning for laziness, rather than for activity. This yearning, however, is itself a symptom of our "pathology of normalcy." Presumably, misuse of the guaranteed income would disappear after a short time, just as the new clerk in the candy store ceases to filch caramels after a few weeks of gorging.

Skepticism as to the benefits of the guaranteed income is also expressed in the observation that those who earn a comfortable living are probably just as afraid to lose a job that gives them, say, $15,000 a year, as are those who might go hungry if they were to lose their jobs. If this objection is valid, the guaranteed income would still increase the freedom of the large majority, but would do little for the middle and upper classes.

In order to deal responsibly with this objection we must consider the spirit of contemporary industrial society. Man has transformed himself into a homo consumens. He is voracious and passive, and tries to compensate for his inner emptiness by continuous and ever-increasing consumption (there are many clinical examples for this mechanism in cases of overeating, overbuying, overdrinking, as a reaction to depression and anxiety); he consumes cigarettes, liquor, sex, movies, travel, as well as education, books, lectures and art. He appears to be active, "thrilled," yet deep down he is anxious, lonely, depressed and bored (boredom can be defined as that type of chronic depression that can successfully be compensated by consumption). Twentieth-century industrialism has created this new psychological type, homo consumens, primarily for economic reasons, i.e., the need for mass consumption, which is stimulated and manipulated by advertising. But the character type, once created, also influences the economy and makes the principles of ever-increasing satisfaction appear rational and realistic.

Contemporary man, thus, has an unlimited hunger for more and more consumption. From this follow several consequences: if there is no limit to the greed for consumption, and since in the foreseeable future no economy can produce enough for unlimited consumption by everybody, there can never be true "abundance" (psychologically speaking) as long as the character structure of the homo consumens remains dominant. For the greedy person there is always scarcity—he never has enough, however much he has. Furthermore, he feels covetous and competitive toward everybody else. Hence he is basically isolated and frightened. He cannot really enjoy art or other cultural stimulations, since he remains basically greedy.

It follows that persons so oriented who lived on the guaranteed-income level would feel frustrated and worthless, and those who earned more would remain prisoners of circumstances, because they were frightened and had lost the possibility for maximum consumption. For those reasons I believe that guaranteed income without a change from the principle of maximal consumption would take care of only certain problems (economic and social) and would not have the radical effect possible from its implications.

What, then, must be done to implement the guaranteed income? Generally speaking, we must change our system from one of maximal to one of optimal consumption. This would mean a vast change in industry from the production of commodities for individual consumption to the production of commodities for public use: schools, theatres, libraries, parks, hospitals, public transportation, housing; in other words an emphasis on the production of those things that encourage the unfolding of the individual's inner productiveness and activity. It can be shown that the voraciousness of homo consumens is directed mainly toward the things he "eats" (incorporates); the free public services, which enable the individual to enjoy life, do not evoke greed. Such a change from maximal to optimal consumption would require drastic changes in production patterns, and also a drastic reduction of the appetite-whetting techniques of advertising.

These considerations lead to other problems that require further study: Are there objectively valid criteria to distinguish between rational and irrational, between good and bad needs, or is any subjectively felt need of the same value? (Good is defined here as enhancing human aliveness, awareness, productivity, sensitivity; bad as weakening or paralyzing these human potentials.) In the case of drug addiction, overeating, alcoholism, we all make such a distinction. Study in this area should lead to the following practical consideration: what are the minimum legitimate needs of an individual? (For instance: one room per person, so much clothing, so many calories, so many culturally valuable commodities such as radio, books, etc.) In a society as abundant as the United States today, it should be easy to figure the cost for a decent subsistence minimum and also what the limits for maximal consumption might be. Progressive taxation on consumption beyond a certain threshold could be considered. All this would mean the combination of the principles of a guaranteed income, with transformation of our society from maximal to optimal individual consumption, and a drastic shift from production for individual needs to production for public needs.

I believe it is important to consider along with the idea of a guaranteed income the concept of free consumption of certain commodities.

One example would be that of bread, then milk and vegetables. Let us assume that everyone could go into any bakery and take as much bread as he liked (the state would pay the bakery for all bread produced). The greedy would at first take more than they could use, but after a short time this "greed consumption" would wear itself out and people would take only what they really needed. Such free consumption would, in my opinion, create a new dimension in human life (unless we look at it as the repetition on a much higher level of the consumption pattern in certain primitive societies). Man would feel freed from the principle, "he who does not work shall not eat." Even this beginning of free consumption might consitute a novel experience of freedom. It is obvious even to the non-economist that the provision of free bread for all could be easily paid for by the state, which would cover this disbursement by a corresponding tax. However, we can go a step further. Assume that not only all minimal needs for food were obtained free—bread, milk, vegetables, fruit—but that everybody could obtain, without paying, say one suit, three shirts, six pairs of socks, etc., per year; that transportation was free (requiring, of course, vastly improved systems of public transportation), while private cars became much more expensive. Eventually, one imagines, housing could be solved in the same way, by big housing projects with sleeping halls for the young, one small room for older, or married couples, to be used without cost by anybody who chose.

This leads me to the suggestion that a way of solving the guaranteed-income problem would be by free minimal consumption of all necessities, instead of through cash payments. The production of these minimum necessities, together with highly improved public services, would keep production going, just as would guaranteed-income payments.

It may be objected that this method is more radical, and hence less acceptable than the proposal to guarantee everyone an income for life; but it must be noted that free minimal services could theoretically be installed within the present system, while the idea of guaranteed income will not be acceptable to many not because it is not feasible but because of the psychological resistance against the abolishment of the principle: "he who does not work shall not eat."

One other philosophical, political and psychological problem to be studied is that of freedom. The Western concept of freedom was to a large extent based on the freedom to own property, and to exploit it, as long as other legitimate interests were not threatened. This principle has actually been punctured in many ways in Western industrial societies by taxation, which is a form of expropriation, and by state intervention in agriculture, trade and industry. At the same time, private property in the means of production is becoming increasingly replaced by the semi-public property typical of giant corporations. While the guaranteed-income concept would mean some additional state regulations, it must be remembered that today the concept of freedom for the average individual lies not so much in his freedom to own and exploit property (capital) as in his freedom to consume whatever he likes. Many people today consider it an interference with their freedom if unlimited consumption is restricted, although only those on top are really free to choose what they want. The competition between different brands of the same commodities and different kinds of commodities creates the illusion of personal freedom, when in reality the individual wants what he is conditioned to want. A new approach to the problem of freedom is necessary; only with the transformation of homo consumens into a productive, active person will man experience freedom as the opportunity to do what is most fulfilling and not as an unlimited choice of commodities.

The full effect of the principle or the guaranteed income is to be expected only in conjunction with:

(1) A change in habits of consumption, the transformation of homo consumens into the productive, active man (in Spinoza's sense).

(2) The creation of a new spiritual attitude, that of humanism (in theistic or nontheistic forms).

(3) A renaissance of truly democratic methods (for instance, a new lower house of Congress in which would be integrated decisions arrived at by hundreds of thousands of face-to-face groups).

The danger that a state that nourishes all could become a mother goddess with dictatorial qualities can be overcome only by a simultaneous, drastic increase of democratic procedure in all spheres of social activities. The fact is that even today the state is extremely powerful, without giving these benefits.

In sum, together with economic research in the field of the guaranteed income, other study must search out the psychological, philosophical, religious and educational parallel effects. And it must not be forgotten that the guaranteed income can succeed only if we stop spending 10 percent of our total resources on economically useless and dangerous armaments, if we can halt the spread of senseless violence by systematic help to the underdeveloped countries, and if we find methods to contain the population explosion. Without such changes, no plan for the future will succeed, because there will be no future.

VIOLENCE

In the seventeenth century, Thomas Hobbes argued that violence is simply a dimension of the order of human relations. When not restrained, individuals act violently because they must compete for the prizes of life, even for life itself, their weapons ranging from shrewdly chosen words to lethal strategies. So "solitary, poor, nasty, brutish, and short" is the natural state of man's war "against every man" that the most arrogantly exercised authority of Leviathan stands as a welcome alternative. Law and order rest upon political violence or the threat of violence, but such is the price that warring man pays to escape the agonies of anarchy. Thus, Thomas Hobbes—whom the political philosopher A. D. Lindsay calls "the father of them all," arch conservatives and radicals alike—concludes that there is little point in arguing about the goodness or badness of violence in general. It is a given, part of the warp and woof of human existence. What is appropriate is a calculating consideration of the particular forms and occasions when violence can be made to serve the common welfare.

The selections taken from the writings of Aristotle and Reinhold Niebuhr agree with the rather foreboding analysis of Hobbes, at least with his point that violence does not represent a radical threat to the continuum of human events but is inevitably an element in that continuum. Aristotle shows that various forms of government generate forces conducive to their own violent destruction. Reinhold Niebuhr, drawing heavily on St. Augustine and on Reformation theologians, sees violence as one expression of man's original sin—his propensity to radical evil. Both resist the notion that violence ought to drive us to despair about the mortal sickness of mankind, but both see it as a factor that must be considered by anyone who wants to be politically effective. In sharp contrast to their point of view is the position of Leo Tolstoy, who finds grounds in the Law of Christ for viewing violence as a tragic intrusion within God's harmonious order.

The choice of violence as a tactic for social reconstruction, however, does raise serious problems of justification. Under what circumstances does violence become creative, and under what circumstances should violence become the tool of a broad commitment to revolution?

Answers to these questions depend to some extent on how bad the existing order appears to be. Such a judgment may finally rest on arbitrary grounds—how the potential revolutionary feels about the abuses and possibilities of his social environment. But arbitrary as this judgment may be, important conceptual errors may be committed. One ought carefully to separate his valuation of the social system itself from his valuation of what happens to be the equilibrium within that system at a given moment. For example, the potential revolutionary ought to decide whether his disillusionment is with democratic pluralism or with imbalances of power that make for colonialist-imperialist relations among various social and racial groups. When revolutionary tactics are chosen to rectify imbalances of power, social militants may soon discover that they are destroying the very framework which allowed for their goals.

The choice of violence as a tactic for social reconstruction also depends on whether one believes that it is possible to create an order that is substantially better. Do all protest movements evolve into establishments? Do all establishments become the instruments of the strong against the weak? Can we even conceive of an alternative social system that avoids imbalances of power, and therefore the impetus to unjust uses of law and inequitable distributions of burdens and benefits? In the selections that follow, Hobbes argues the negative position, because he is convinced that violent revolution cannot produce a more just political order. Herbert Marcuse, however, believes that modern political revolutions have contributed to "the enlargement of the social range of freedom and the enlargement of the satisfaction of needs." He is able to argue that the pain of violent revolution is at times justified, if it can be shown that violence ultimately can become the means for the extension of the social good.

Is there an ethic of violence? Are there criteria according to which the morality of violent acts can be measured—apart from an appeal to a vision of the revolution's end, the Just Society? Georges Sorel's *Reflection on Violence* is an attempt to free violence from all ethical considerations. He compares revolutionary tactics to military tactics, and therefore makes the relationship of means and ends into a technical one. The issue he raises is a haunting one: is it possible to develop an ethic, similar to the Just War theory, that might suggest appropriate limits for violence, while not condemning as always evil the use of violence?

ARISTOTLE (384–322 B.C.)

On Revolution

Speaking broadly then of politics in general, we may say that these are the causes which have resulted in revolutions. We have now to take the various kinds of polity severally and by the light of the principles at which we have arrived consider the actual results in detail.

The main cause of revolutions in Democracies is the intemperate conduct of the demagogues who force the propertied class to combine partly by instituting malicious prosecutions against individuals—for the worst enemies are united by a common fear—and partly by inciting the masses against them as a body. We may see this actually occurring in many cases. At Cos e.g. the democracy was revolutionized through the appearance of unscrupulous demagogues in the State and the consequent combination of the nobles. At Rhodes the demagogues were in the habit of supplying the people with fees *for their attendance in the public Assembly and the Courts of Law* and of preventing the payment of dues to the trierarchs, so that they were compelled by fear of the lawsuits with which they were threatened *by their creditors* to form a conspiracy and abolish the Democracy. It was the fault of the demagogues again that the Democracy of Heracleia was abolished immediately after the foundation of the colony; for the nobles fled one after another from the oppression to which they were subjected, until at a later date the exiles collected in a body, returned home and abolished

The selection is from Aristotle, *The Politics,* trans. J. E. C. Weldon (London: Macmillan and Company, 1883).

the Democracy. It was much in the same way that the Democracy at Megara was overthrown. The demagogues in order to have an opportunity of confiscation ejected large numbers of the nobles from the State, until they had swelled the ranks of the exiles to such an extent that they returned home, conquered the Democrats in a pitched battle and established the Oligarchy. The same was the case at Cyme with the Democracy overthrown by Thrasymachus. And if we look at the generality of other States, we may discover the same characteristics in their revolutions. The demagogues drive the nobles to combine sometimes by direct oppression in the hope of currying favour with the people, whether they make an actual re-distribution of their properties *among the lower orders or cripple* their incomes by heavy public burdens, and at other times by vexatious prosecutions intended to afford an opportunity of confiscating the possessions of the wealthy.

It usually happened in ancient times, whenever the functions of demagogue and general were united in the same person, that Democracies were revolutionized into Tyrannies. The great majority of an cient tyrants had been demagogues. The reason why this was the case in those days and is not so now is that the demagogues of that age belonged to the class of active generals, as at that early date there were no practised rhetoricians *to become popular leaders*, whereas in our own day, when Rhetoric has become so important, it is able speakers who play the part of demagogues, and their ignorance of military matters prevents them from attempting to seize supreme power, although there may have been some trifling exceptions to this rule. One reason for the creation of Tyrannies in former times rather than in our own day was the importance of the official positions intrusted to individuals. Thus at Miletus a Tyranny was the outcome of the Presidency owing to the wide and important jurisdiction of the President. Another reason is that, as States were not large in those days, and the people lived in the country busily engaged in their occupations, the popular leaders, whenever they were men of military genius, attempted to make themselves tyrants. They were enabled to do so in all cases by possessing the confidence of the commons, the ground of this confidence being their detestation of the wealthy classes. . . .

Yet another species of revolution is from the traditional to the most modern form of Democracy. Where the offices of State are elective, but there is no requisite property qualification, and the election is in the hands of the commons, candidates who are eager for office go so far in their desire of popularity as to invest the commons with an authority superior even to the laws. The means of preventing or at least mitigating this evil would be to place the appointment of the executive officers in the hands of the tribes instead of the whole body of commons.

The causes which I have specified are practically productive of all the various revolutions in Democracies.

Revolutions in Oligarchies on the other hand generally assume two most conspicious forms.

The first is the case where the Oligarchs oppress the masses. For any champion of the people is good enough at such a time, especially when it happens that the leader is taken from the ranks of the Oligarchs themselves, like Lygdamis at Naxos who subsequently made himself tyrant of the Naxians.

But secondly when the sedition arises among the actual Oligarchs, it may take a variety of forms.

Sometimes the destruction of the polity is effected by persons who are members of the propertied class, although not of the official body, when the honours of State are in the hands of a narrow clique. This has been the case at Massalia, at Istros, at Heracleia and in other States where the members of the propertied class who were excluded from office kept up an agitation until first the elder and at a later date the younger brothers obtained admission. It must be explained that there are some States in which a father and a son and others in which an elder and a younger brother are not allowed to hold office simultaneously. And while at Massalia the Oligarchy assumed more the character of a Polity, at Istros it ended eventually in a Democracy and at Heracleia was transferred from the hands of a smaller body to a body of Six Hundred. Again, the revolution of the Oligarchy at Cnidos was due to an internal quarrel among the nobles arising from the fact that the admission to office was confined to a few persons and, as has been said, if a father was a member of the official class, the son was excluded, and if there were several brothers in a family, it was only the eldest who was admitted. For the commons seizing the opportunity of these feuds and finding a champion in the ranks of the nobles rose in insurrection and overcame the Oligarchs; for a house divided against itself can never stand. It was the same at Erythrae with the Oligarchy of the Basilidae in olden times. The strict limitation of the official class, despite the wise administration of the persons who possessed political privileges, produced such a feeling of indignation in the commons that they revolutionized the polity.

Another occasion of disturbance in Oligarchies arising within the oligarchical body itself is when personal rivalry induces the Oligarchs to assume the rôle of demagogues. But this demagogy may take two forms. It may be within the oligarchical body itself. The appearance of a demagogue is possible even in a narrow clique of Oligarchs. Thus it was within the ranks of the Thirty at Athens that the party of Charicles rose to power by courting like demagogues the other members of the Thirty, and it was within the ranks of the Four Hundred that the party of Phrynichus rose to power in the same manner. It may be the mob on the other hand to whom the members of the Oligarchy pay court, as at Larisa where the Guardians of the citizens were always toadying the mob upon whom they were dependent for election. This is liable to occur in any Oligarchy where it is not the class from which the officers of State are taken that constitutes the body of electors but, while eligibility to office is conditional upon a high property qualification or upon membership in a political club, the electing body consists of the heavy-armed soldiers or of the whole body of commons, as was long the case at Abydos. It is the same where the Courts of Law are not constituted of members of the governing class. The result of the court paid to the people in order to secure favourable verdicts is a revolution of the polity, as actually happened at Heracleia upon the Pontus. Another occasion of revolution is when an effort is made by a certain party to narrow the Oligarchy still further, as the advocates of equality *among all the members of the oligarchical body* are then obliged to invite the assistance of the commons.

Again, revolutions occur in an Oligarchy when *some of the Oligarchs* have wasted all their private means in riotous living, as in this case they are eager for innovation and either affect a Tyranny themselves or set up somebody else as tyrant. It was thus that Hipparinus helped to place Dionysius on the throne of Syracuse, that at Amphipolis a man named Cleotimus introduced the Chalcidian settlers and upon their arrival arrayed them in opposition to the rich, and that at Ægina the person who conducted the negotiation with Chares attempted for a similar reason to effect a revolution of the polity. The spendthrifts in question sometimes make a direct attempt at political innovation and at other times plunder the Treasury; and in the latter case the result is that an attack is made upon the Government either by the offenders, *if it offers a resistance to their proceedings*, or, *if it is favourable to them*, by the opponents of their malversation, as was the case at Apollonia upon the Pontus.

Another occasion of seditions *arising within the oligarchical body itself* is when some of the actual Oligarchs suffer a repulse at the hands of others or are the victims of party violence in matrimonial or legal cases. We may instance as the results of a matrimonial question the seditious disturbances which have been already described as well as the overthrow of the Oligarchy of the Knights at Eretria by Diagoras in consequence of the wrong done him in an affair of marriage. A judicial sentence was the motive cause of the sedition at Heracleia and at Thebes, where Euetion in the one case and Archias in the other were subjected on a charge of adultery to a punishment which no doubt was merited but was prompted by a spirit of factious partisanship; for their enemies carried the vindictiveness of rivalry to such an extent as to have them confined in open market in the pillory.

It has frequently happened too that the over-despotic character of Oligarchies has led to their overthrow by exciting a sentiment of indignation in the breasts of some members of the governing class. Such was the case of the oligarchies in Cnidos and Chios.

But where harmony prevails among the Oligarchs an Oligarchy is not easily destroyed. This we may infer from the case of the Pharsalian polity in which the Oligarchs, although they form only a small minority of the population, are able to retain authority over the Many by being on good terms among themselves.

Oligarchies are sometimes destroyed on the other hand by the creation of a second Oligarchy within the first; and this is liable to occur when the entire governing class is numerically small, and yet the highest offices of State are not open to all the members of this small body. Such was once the case at Elis where the polity was in the hands of a Few, and it was only a small fraction of the Few who were admitted to the Senate, as the Senators who were always ninety in number held office for life and the method of election was dynastic, *i.e. characteristic of a narrow Oligarchy*, and similar to the election of the Senate at Lacedaemon.

A revolution in an Oligarchy may take place in time either of war or of peace. The occasion in the former case is sometimes that the Oligarchs from distrust of the commons are obliged to employ mercenary troops, and thus the individual in whose hands they place the command not infrequently makes himself tyrant like Timophanes at Corinth or, if there are several commanders, they found a dynastic government in their own interest, and at other times that the fear of this induces the Oligarchs to admit the masses to full political privileges, as they cannot dispense with the assistance of the commons. The circumstances in which an Oligarchy is revolutionized in time of peace are when the mutual distrustfulness of the Oligarchs is so great that they put the police of the city into the hands of mercenary troops and an arbiter between the factions who sometimes succeeds in making himself master of both, as happened in the case of Simus at Larisa during the reign of the Alcuadac and at Abydos in the era of the political clubs, among which the club of Iphiades was one.

Lastly, accidental circumstances may be the cause of revolutions whether in the so-called Polity or in Oligarchies, i.e. in all governments where a certain property assessment is requisite for the Council, the Courts of Law and the offices of State. If we take e.g. the property qualification originally fixed with reference to existing conditions, admitting a Few only in an Oligarchy and the middle class in a Polity to the enjoyment of political privileges, it often happens that a season of prosperity due to *long-continued* peace or some other fortunate circumstance multiplies so greatly the value of the same estates as to admit the entire body of citizens to full privileges, sometimes gradually by a slow and imperceptible process of revolution and at other times with an excessive rapidity.

We have now enumerated the causes of revolutions and seditions in Oligarchies. It is to be observed as a general rule applicable both to Democracies and Oligarchies that they are sometimes altered not to the antagonistic polities but to other polities of the same kind, e.g. from the restricted forms of Democracy and Oligarchy to the absolute forms and *vice versa.*

Coming to Aristocracies, we find that one cause of sedition is the limitation in the number of persons admitted to the honours of State, a cause which has been already described as an element of disturbance in Oligarchies. (For an Aristocracy itself is in a certain sense an Oligarchy, as in both the ruling class is numerically limited. But the ground of the limitation is different; in fact it is only in appearance that Aristocracy, as being so limited, is an Oligarchy.) This cause of political disturbance is necessarily most operative when there is a considerable body *of unprivileged persons* within the State who have a proud feeling that they are the equals *of the privileged class* in virtue, like the so-called Partheniae at Lacedaemon on the strength of their descent from the Peers *or fully enfranchised citizens;* for the Partheniae were detected in a conspiracy and sent away out of the country to be the colonists of Tarentum. Again, *sedition is apt to occur* when a stigma is put upon persons of consequence who are fully the equals of any citizen in virtue by other citizens who hold a position of greater dignity, as e.g. upon Lysander by the Lacedaemonian kings. *Other occasions of sedition in an Aristocracy are* when there is an individual of strong character who is excluded from the honours of State like Cinadon the author of the conspiracy and insurrection against the Spartiates in the reign of Agesilaus, or again when there is excessive poverty on one side and excessive wealth on the other within the State—a condition of things which is especially incident to warlike times and actually occurred at Lacedaemon about the time of the Messenian war, as appears from the poem of Tyrtaeus called Eunomia (Good Order); for it was under pressure of the war that a certain number of the citizens demanded a re-distribution of the soil—or lastly if there is an individual already powerful and capable of extending his power, *who heads a sedition* in the hope of making himself monarch, as according to the popular view was the case of Pausanias the commander-in-chief in the Persian war at Lacedaemon and of Annon at Carthage.

But the main cause of the dissolution of Polities and Aristocracies alike is a deviation from their proper principles of justice in the constitution of the polity itself. Its origin is the unsuccessful fusion of the democratical and oligarchical elements in the Polity and of these elements with virtue added in the Aristocracy, but especially of the first two, as it is a fusion of these elements only that is attempted in the majority of so-called Aristocracies as well as in Polities. For the difference between Aristocracies and Polities in the limited sense of the word and the reason why the latter are more permanent than the former is that all constitutions of the kind *we are considering* which incline to Oligarchy are called Aristocracies, while those which incline to popular government are called Polities. And thus the comparative stability of all such Polities is due to the fact that in them the numerical majority have the upper hand, and they are sooner satisfied with mere equality, while the propertied class, if invested with superiority by the political constitution, is eager to display an insolent and aggressive spirit. It is a general rule however that, whatever may be the bias of a polity, it is in that direction that it is usually revolutionized, as the two parties in the State, *the rich and the poor*, respectively extend their power, viz. Polity in the direction of Democracy and Aristocracy in the direction of Oligarchy. It may happen on the other hand that these polities are revolutionized to their opposites, viz. Aristocracy to Democracy, when the poorer classes feeling aggrieved effect a violent circumvolution of the government, and Polity to Oligarchy. For the only conditions of permanence are proportional equality and security of rights. There was an instance of a polity being changed to its opposite at Thurii where the excessive amount of the property assessment requisite for office led to its reduction and to an increase in the number of the official boards, and the illegal acquisition of the entire soil by the nobles—an encroachment facilitated by the excessively oligarchical character of the Polity—resulted in the commons who had been disciplined in the war getting the upper hand of the Guards *or military force maintained by the Oligarchs and never resting* until a surrender had been made by all who were in actual possession of an exorbitant amount of land. Another cause of revolution is that the tendency of all aristocratical polities to be oligarchical affords the nobles an opportunity of self-aggrandisement. At Lacedaemon e.g. the wealth of the country is gradually falling into the hands of a Few, and the nobles enjoy a greater freedom of action and *especially* of matrimonial alliance. And while we are upon this point, it was the marriage connexion with Dionysius, *we may remark,* that led to the destruction of the Locrian State; which would never have happened in a Democracy or in an Aristocracy where there was a successful fusion of the different elements.

But an imperceptible revolution in Aristocracies is effected principally by a gradual process of dissolution. It is a remark which has been already made in this work, as applicable to all forms of polity generally that insignificant change is one cause of revolutions. For no sooner has some one constitutional point been surrendered than it is easier to introduce another slightly more important innovation, *and so on* until an innovation has been effected in the whole existing system. This was the case with the polity at Thurii among others. There was a law there that nobody should be general a second time except after an interval of five years. Upon this some of the younger generation, who had displayed military talents and were in the enjoyment of a high popularity among the masses, in contempt of the executive authorities and in the expectation of an easy success, began by making an attempt to abrogate this law so as to allow the same people to be generals continuously, as they saw that the commons would be only too glad to vote for them. The officers appointed to watch innovations in the laws, the Councillors as they were called, although eager at first to resist the proposition, were prevailed upon to acquiesce in it under the impression that the young citizens, if they succeeded in altering this law, would leave the rest of the polity undisturbed; but at a later date their desire to prevent further innovation proved absolutely ineffectual, and the entire system of the polity was revolutionized to a dynastic government in the hands of the party who had originated the revolution.

Polities generally are liable to dissolution not only from within but from without, when there is *a State having* an antagonistic polity either near to them or distant but possessed of considerable power.

This is a truth that was continually verified in the case of the Athenians and Lacedaemonians, the former of whom abolished the Oligarchies and the latter the Democracies wherever they found them.

THOMAS HOBBES (1588–1679)

On the State of Men Without Civil Society

The greatest part of those men who have written aught concerning commonwealths, either suppose, or require us or beg us to believe, that man is a creature born fit for society. The Greeks call him $\zeta\omega\nu\ \pi o\lambda\iota\tau\iota\kappa o\nu$; and on this foundation they so build up the doctrine of civil society, as if for the preservation of peace, and the government of mankind, there were nothing else necessary than that men should agree to make certain covenants and conditions together, which themselves should then call laws. Which axiom, though received by most, is yet certainly false; and an error proceeding from our too slight contemplation of human nature. For they who shall more narrowly look into the causes for which men come together, and delight in each other's company, shall easily find that this happens not because naturally it could happen no otherwise, but by accident. For if by nature one man should love another, that is, as man, there could no reason be returned why every man should not equally love every man, as being equally man; or why he should rather frequent those, whose society affords him honour or profit. We do not therefore by nature seek society for its own sake, but that we may receive some honour or profit from it; these we desire primarily, that secondarily. How, by what advice, men do meet, will be best known by observing those things which they do when they are met. For if they meet for traffic, it is plain every man regards not his fellow, but his business; if to discharge some office, a certain market-friendship is begotten, which hath more of jealousy in it than true love, and whence factions sometimes may arise, but good will never; if for pleasure and recreation of mind, every man is wont to please himself most with those things which stir up laughter, whence he may, according to the nature of

The selection is from Thomas Hobbes, *The English Works of Thomas Hobbes,* ed. William Molesworth (London: John Bohn, 1841).

that which is ridiculous, by comparison of another man's defects and infirmities, pass the more current in his own opinion. And although this be sometimes innocent and without offence, yet it is manifest they are not so much delighted with the society, as their own vain glory. But for the most part, in these kinds of meeting we wound the absent; their whole life, sayings, actions are examined, judged, condemned. Nay, it is very rare but some present receive a fling as soon as they part; so as his reason was not ill, who was wont always at parting to go out last. And these are indeed the true delights of society, unto which we are carried by nature, that is, by those passions which are incident to all creatures, until either by sad experience or good precepts it so fall out, which in many it never happens, that the appetite of present matters be dulled with the memory of things past: without which the discourse of most quick and nimble men on this subject, is but cold and hungry.

But if it so happen, that being met they pass their time in relating some stories, and one of them begins to tell one which concerns himself; instantly every one of the rest most greedily desires to speak of himself too; if one relate some wonder, the rest will tell you miracles, if they have them; if not, they will feign them Lastly, that I may say somewhat of them who pretend to be wiser than others: if they meet to talk of philosophy, look, how many men, so many would be esteemed masters, or else they not only love not their fellows, but even persecute them with hatred. So clear is it by experience to all men who a little more narrowly consider human affairs, that all free congress ariseth either from mutual poverty, or from vain glory, whence the parties met endeavour to carry with them either some benefit, or to leave behind them that same ἐνδοκιμεῖν, some esteem and honour with those, with whom they have been conversant. The same is also collected by reason out of the definitions themselves of *will, good, honour, profitable.* For when we voluntarily contract society, in all manner of society we look after the object of the will, that is, that which every one of those who gather together, propounds to himself for good. Now whatsoever seems good, is pleasant, and relates either to the senses, or the mind. But all the mind's pleasure is either glory, (or to have a good opinion of one's self), or refers to glory in the end; the rest are sensual, or conducing to sensuality, which may be all comprehended under the word *conveniences.* All society therefore is either for gain, or for glory; that is, not so much for love of our fellows, as for the love of ourselves. But no society can be great or lasting, which begins from vain glory. Because that glory is like honour; if all men have it no man hath it, for they consist in comparison and precellence. Neither doth the society of others advance any whit the cause of my glorying in myself; for every man must account himself, such as he can make himself without the help of others. But though the benefits of this life may be much furthered by mutual help; since yet those may be better attained to by dominion than by the society of others, I hope no body will doubt, but that men would much more greedily be carried by nature, if all fear were removed, to obtain dominion, than to gain society. We must therefore resolve, that the original of all great and lasting societies consisted not in the mutual good will men had towards each other, but in the mutual fear they had of each other.

The cause of mutual fear consists partly in the natural equality of men, partly in their mutual will of hurting: whence it comes to pass, that we can neither expect from others, nor promise to ourselves the least security. For if we look on men full-grown, and consider how brittle the frame of our human body is, which perishing, all its strength, vigour, and wisdom itself perisheth with it; and how easy a matter it is, even for the weakest man to kill the strongest: there is no reason why any man, trusting to his own strength, should conceive himself made by nature above others. They are equals, who can do equal things one against the other; but they who can do the greatest things, namely, kill, can do equal things. All men therefore among themselves are by nature equal; the inequality we now discern, hath its spring from the civil law.

All men in the state of nature have a desire and will to hurt, but not proceeding from the same cause, neither equally to be condemned. For one man, according to that natural equality which is among us, permits as much to others as he assumes to himself; which is an argument of a temperate man, and one that rightly values his power. Another, supposing himself above others, will have a license to do what he lists, and challenges respect and honour, as due to him before others; which is an argument of a fiery spirit. This man's will to hurt ariseth from vain glory, and the false esteem he hath of his own strength; the other's from the necessity of defending himself, his liberty, and his goods, against this man's violence.

Furthermore, since the combat of wits is the fiercest, the greatest discords which are, must necessarily arise from this contention. For in this case it is not only odious to contend against, but also not to consent. For not to approve of what a man saith, is no less than tacitly to accuse him of an error in that thing which he speaketh: as in very many things to dissent, is as much as if you accounted him a fool whom you dissent from. Which may appear hence, that there are no wars so sharply waged as between sects of the same religion, and factions of the same commonweal, where the contestation is either concerning doctrines or politic prudence. And since all the pleasure and jollity of the mind consists in this, even to get some, with whom comparing, it may find somewhat wherein to triumph and vaunt itself; it is impossible but men must declare sometimes some mutual scorn and contempt, either by laughter, or by words, or by gesture, or some sign or other; than which there is no greater vexation of mind, and than from which there cannot possibly arise a greater desire to do hurt.

But the most frequent reason why men desire to hurt each other, ariseth hence, that many men at the same time have an appetite to the same thing; which yet very often they can neither enjoy in common, nor yet divide it; whence it follows that the strongest must have it, and who is strongest must be decided by the sword.

Among so many dangers therefore, as the natural lusts of men do daily threaten each other withal, to have a care of one's self is so far from being a matter scornfully to be looked upon, that one has neither the power nor wish to have done otherwise. For every man is desirous of what is good for him, and shuns what is evil, but chiefly the chiefest of natural evils, which is death; and this he doth by a certain impulsion of nature, no less than that whereby a stone moves downward. It is therefore neither absurd nor reprehensible, neither against the dictates of true reason, for a man to use all his endeavours to preserve and defend his body and the members thereof from death and sorrows. But that which is not contrary to right reason, that all men account to be done justly, and with right. Neither by the word *right* is anything else signified, than that liberty which every man hath to make use of his natural faculties according to right reason. Therefore the first foundation of natural right is this, that *every man as much as in him lies endeavour to protect his life and members.*

But because it is in vain for a man to have a right to the end, if the right to the necessary means be denied him, it follows, that since every man hath a right to preserve himself, he must also be allowed a right *to use all the means, and do all the actions, without which he cannot preserve himself.*

Now whether the means which he is about to use, and the action he is performing, be necessary to the preservation of his life and members or not, he himself, by the right of nature, must be judge. For if it be contrary to right reason that I should judge of mine own peril, say, that another man is judge. Why now, because he judgeth of what concerns me, by the same reason, because we are equal by nature, will I judge also of things which do belong to him. Therefore it agrees with right reason, that is, it is the right of nature that I judge of his opinion, that is, whether it conduce to my preservation or not.

Nature hath given to *every one a right to all;* that is, it was lawful for every man, in the bare state of nature, or before such time as men had engaged themselves by any covenants or bonds, to do what he would, and against whom he thought fit, and to possess, use, and enjoy all what he would, or could get. Now because whatsoever a man would, it therefore seems good to him because he wills it, and either it really doth, or at least seems to him to contribute towards his preservation, (but we have already allowed him to be judge, in the foregoing article, whether it doth or not, insomuch as we are to hold all for necessary whatsoever he shall esteem so), and by the 7th article it appears that by the right of nature those things may be done, and must be had, which necessarily conduce to the protection of life and members, it follows, that in the state of nature, to have all, and do all, is lawful for all. And this is that which is meant by that common saying, *nature hath given all to all.* From whence we understand likewise, that in the state of nature profit is the measure of right.

But it was the least benefit for men thus to have a common right to all things. For the effects of this right are the same, almost, as if there had been no right at all. For although any man might say of every thing, *this is mine,* yet could he not enjoy it, by reason of his neighbour, who having equal right and equal power, would pretend the same thing to be his.

If now to this natural proclivity of men, to hurt each other, which they derive from their passions, but chiefly from a vain esteem of themselves, you add, the right of all to all, wherewith one by right invades, the other by right resists, and whence arise perpetual jealousies and suspicions on all hands, and how hard a thing it is to provide against an enemy invading us with an intention to oppress and ruin, though he come with a small number, and no great provision; it cannot be denied but that the natural state of men, before they entered into society, was a mere war, and that not simply, but a war of all men against all men. For what is WAR, but that same time in which the will of contesting by force is fully declared, either by words or deeds? The time remaining is termed PEACE.

But it is easily judged how disagreeable a thing to the preservation either of mankind, or of each single man, a perpetual war is. But it is perpetual in its own nature; because in regard of the equality of those that strive, it cannot be ended by victory. For in this state the conqueror is subject to so much danger, as it were to be accounted a miracle if any, even the most strong, should close up his life with many years and old age. They of America are examples hereof, even in this present age: other nations have been in former ages; which now indeed are become civil and flourishing, but were then few, fierce, short-lived, poor, nasty, and deprived of all that pleasure and beauty of life, which peace and society are wont to bring with them. Whosoever therefore holds, that it had been best to have continued in that state in which all things were lawful for all men, he contradicts himself. For every man by natural necessity desires that which is good for him: nor is there any that esteems a war of all against all, which necessarily adheres to such a state, to be good for him. And so it happens, that through fear of each other we think it fit to rid ourselves of this condition, and to get some fellows; that if there needs must be war, it may not yet be against all men, nor without some helps.

Fellows are gotten either by constraint, or by consent; by constraint, when after fight the conqueror makes the conquered serve him, either through fear of death, or by laying fetters on him: by consent, when men enter into society to help each other, both parties consenting without any constraint. But the conqueror may by right compel the conquered, or the strongest the weaker, (as a man in health may one that is sick, or he that is of riper years a child), unless he will choose to die, to give caution of his future obedience. For since the right of protecting ourselves according to our own wills, proceeded from our danger, and our danger from our equality, it is more consonant to reason, and more certain for our conservation, using the present advantage to secure ourselves by taking caution, than when they shall be full grown and strong, and got out of our power, to endeavour to recover that power again by doubtful fight. And on the other side, nothing can be thought more absurd, than by discharging whom you already have weak in your power, to make him at once both an enemy and a strong one. From whence we may understand likewise as a corollary in the natural state of men, that *a sure and irresistible power confers the right of dominion and ruling over those who cannot resist;* insomuch, as the right of all things that can be done, adheres essentially and immediately unto this omnipotence hence arising.

Yet cannot men expect any lasting preservation, continuing thus in the state of nature, that is, of war, by reason of that equality of power, and other human faculties they are endued withal. Wherefore to seek peace, where there is any hopes of obtaining it, and where there is none, to enquire out for auxiliaries of war, is the dictate of right reason, that is, the law of nature; as shall be showed in the next chapter.

GEORGES SOREL (1847–1922)

Reflections on Violence

So little are we prepared to understand pessimism, that we generally employ the word quite incorrectly: we call pessimists people who are in reality only disillusioned optimists. When we meet a man who, having been unfortunate in his enterprises, deceived in his most legitimate ambitions, humiliated in his affections, expresses his griefs in the form of a violent revolt against the duplicity of his associates, the stupidity of society, or the blindness of destiny, we are disposed to look upon him as a pessimist; whereas we ought nearly always to regard him as a disheartened optimist who has not had the courage to start afresh, and who is unable to understand why so many misfortunes have befallen him, contrary to what he supposes to be the general law governing the production of happiness.

The optimist in politics is an inconstant and even dangerous man, because he takes no account of the great difficulties presented by his projects; these projects seem to him to possess a force of their own, which tends to bring about their realisation all the more easily as they are, in his opinion, destined to produce the happiest result. He frequently thinks that small reforms in the political constitution, and, above all, in the personnel of the government, will be sufficient to direct social development in such a way as to mitigate those evils of the contemporary world which seem so harsh to the sensitive mind. As soon as his friends come into power, he declares that it is necessary to let things alone for a little, not to hurry too much, and to learn how to be content with whatever their own benevolent intentions prompt them to do. It is not always self-interest that suggests these expressions of satisfaction, as people have often believed; self-interest is strongly aided by vanity and by the illusions of philosphy. The optimist passes with remarkable facility from revolutionary anger to the most ridiculous social pacificism.

If he possesses an exalted temperament, and if unhappily he finds himself armed with great power, permitting him to realise the ideal he has fashioned, the optimist may lead his country into the worst disasters. He is not long in finding out that social transformations are not

The selection is taken from Georges Sorel, *Reflections on Violence,* trans. T. E. Hulme and J. Roth (New York: Collier Books, 1967), pp. 31–37, 41–50, and 90–92, with omissions. Reprinted with permission of the Macmillan Company. Copyright 1950 by The Free Press, a Corporation.

brought about with the ease that he had counted on; he then supposes that this is the fault of his contemporaries, instead of explaining what actually happens by historical necessities; he is tempted to get rid of people whose obstinacy seems to him to be so dangerous to the happiness of all. During the Terror, the men who spilt most blood were precisely those who had the greatest desire to let their equals enjoy the golden age they had dreamt of, and who had the most sympathy with human wretchedness: optimists, idealists, and sensitive men, the greater desire they had for universal happiness the more inexorable they showed themselves.

Pessimism is quite a different thing from the caricatures of it which are usually presented to us; it is a philosophy of conduct rather than a theory of the world; it considers the *march towards deliverance* as narrowly conditioned, on the one hand, by the experimental knowledge that we have acquired from the obstacles which oppose themselves to the satisfaction of our imaginations (or, if we like, by the feeling of social determinism), and, on the other, by a profound conviction of our natural weakness. These two aspects of pessimism should never be separated, although, as a rule, scarcely any attention is paid to their close connection.

1. The conception of pessimism springs from the fact that literary historians have been very much struck with the complaints made by the great poets of antiquity on the subject of the griefs which constantly threaten mankind. There are few people who have not, at one time or another, experienced a piece of good fortune; but we are surrounded by malevolent forces always ready to spring out on us from some ambuscade and overwhelm us. Hence the very real sufferings which arouse the sympathy of nearly all men, even of those who have been more favourably treated by fortune; so that the literature of grief has always had a certain success throughout the whole course of history. But a study of this kind of literature would give us a very imperfect idea of pessimism. It may be laid down as a general rule, that in order to understand a doctrine it is not sufficient to study it in an abstract manner, nor even as it occurs in isolated people: it is necessary to find out how it has been manifested in historical groups; it is for this reason that I am here led to add the two elements that were mentioned earlier.

2. The pessimist regards social conditions as forming a system bound together by an iron law which cannot be evaded, so that the system is given, as it were, in one block, and cannot disappear except in a catastrophe which involves the whole. If this theory is admitted, it then becomes absurd to make certain wicked men responsible for

the evils from which society suffers; the pessimist is not subject to the sanguinary follies of the optimist, infatuated by the unexpected obstacles that his projects meet with; he does not dream of bringing about the happiness of future generations by slaughtering existing egoists.

3. The most fundamental element of pessimism is its method of conceiving the paths towards deliverance. A man would not go very far in the examination either of the laws of his own wretchedness or of fate, which so much shock the ingenuousness of our pride, if he were not borne up by the hope of putting an end to these tyrannies by an effort, to be attempted with the help of a whole band of companions. The Christians would not have discussed original sin so much if they had not felt the necessity of justifying the deliverance (which was to result from the death of Jesus) by supposing that this sacrifice had been rendered necessary by a frightful crime, which could be imputed to humanity. If the people of the West were much more occupied with original sin than those of the East, it was not solely, as Taine thought, owing to the influence of Roman law, but also because the Latins, having a more elevated conception of the imperial majesty than the Greeks, regarded the sacrifice of the Son of God as having realised an extraordinarily marvellous deliverance; from this proceeded the necessity of intensifying human wretchedness and of destiny.

It seems to me that the optimism of the Greek philosophers depended to a great extent on economic reasons; it probably arose in the rich and commercial urban populations who were able to regard the universe as an immense shop full of excellent things with which they could satisfy their greed. I imagine that Greek pessimism sprang from poor warlike tribes living in the mountains, who were filled with an enormous aristocratic pride, but whose material conditions were correspondingly poor; their poets charmed them by praising their ancestors and made them look forward to triumphal expeditions conducted by superhuman heroes; they explained their present wretchedness to them by relating catastrophes in which semi-divine former chiefs had succumbed to fate or the jealousy of the gods; the courage of the warriors might for the moment be unable to accomplish anything, but it would not always be so; the tribe must remain faithful to the old customs in order to be ready for great and victorious expeditions, which might very well take place in the near future.

Oriental asceticism has often been considered the most remarkable manifestation of pessimism; Hartmann is certainly right when he regards it as having only the value of an anticipation, which was useful, since it reminded men how much there is that is illusory in vulgar riches; he was wrong, however, in saying that asceticism taught men that the "destined end to all their efforts" was the annihilation of will, for in the course of history deliverance has taken quite other forms than this.

In primitive Christianity we find a fully developed and completely armed pessimism: man is condemned to slavery from his birth— Satan is the prince of the world—the Christian, already regenerate by baptism, can render himself capable of obtaining the resurrection of the body by means of the Eucharist; he awaits the glorious second coming of Christ, who will destroy the rule of Satan and call his comrades in the fight to the heavenly Jerusalem. The Christian life of that time was dominated by the necessity of membership in the holy army which was constantly exposed to the ambuscades set by the accomplices of Satan; this conception produced many heroic acts, engendered a courageous propaganda, and was the cause of considerable moral progress. The deliverance did not take place, but we know by innumerable testimonies from that time what great things the march towards deliverance can bring about.

Sixteen-century Calvinism presents a spectacle which is perhaps even more instructive; but we must be careful not to confuse it, as many authors have done, with contemporary Protestantism; these two doctrines are the antipodes of each other. I cannot understand how Hartmann came to say that Protestantism "is a halting place in the journey of true Christianity," and that it "allied itself with the renaissance of ancient paganism." These judgments only apply to recent Protestantism, which has abandoned its own principles in order to adopt those of the Renaissance. Pessimism, which formed no part of the current of ideas which characterised the Renaissance, has never been so strongly affirmed as it was by the Reformers. The dogmas of sin and predestination which correspond to the two first aspects of pessimism, the wretchedness of the human species, and social determinism, were pushed to their most extreme consequences. Deliverance was conceived under a very different form to that which had been given it by primitive Christianity; Protestants organised themselves into a military force wherever possible; they made expeditions into Catholic countries, expelled the priests, introduced the reformed cult, and promulgated laws of proscription against papists. They no longer borrowed from the apocalypses the idea of a great final catastrophe, of which the brothers-in-arms who had for so long defended themselves against the attacks of Satan would only be spectators; the Protestants, nourished on the reading of the Old

Testament, wished to imitate the exploits of the conquerors of the Holy Land; they took the offensive, and wished to establish the kingdom of God by force. In each locality they conquered the Calvinists brought about a real catastrophic revolution, which changed everything from top to bottom.

Calvinism was finally conquered by the Renaissance; it was full of theological prejudices derived from medieval traditions, and there came a time when it feared to be thought too far behind the times; it wished to be on the level of modern culture, and it finished by becoming simply a lax Christianity. To-day very few people suspect what the reformers of the sixteenth century meant by "free examination," the Protestants of to-day apply the same method to the Bible that philologist's apply to any profane text; Calvin's exegesis has been replaced by the criticisms of the humanists.

The annalist who contents himself with recording facts is tempted to regard the conception of deliverance as a dream or an error, but the true historian considers things from a different point of view; whenever he endeavours to find out what has been the influence of the Calvinist spirit on morals, law, or literature, he is always driven back to a consideration of the way in which former Protestant thought was dominated by the conception of the path to deliverance. The experience of this great epoch shows quite clearly that in this warlike excitement which accompanies this *will-to-deliverance* the courageous man finds a satisfaction which is sufficient to keep up his ardour. I am convinced that in the history of that time you might find excellent illustrations of the idea that you once expressed to me—that the Wandering Jew may be taken as a symbol of the highest aspirations of mankind, condemned as it is to march for ever without knowing rest. . . .

In the course of this study one thing has always been present in my mind, which seemed to me so evident that I did not think it worth while to lay much stress on it—that men who are participating in a great social movement always picture their coming action as a battle in which their cause is certain to triumph. These constructions, knowledge of which is so important for historians, I propose to call myths; the syndicalist "general strike" and Marx's catastrophic revolution are such myths. As remarkable examples of such myths, I have given those which were constructed by primitive Christianity, by the Reformation, by the Revolution and by the followers of Mazzini. I now wish to show that we should not attempt to analyse such groups of images in the way that we analyse a thing into its elements, but that they must be taken as a whole, as historical forces, and that we should be especially careful not to make any comparison between accomplished fact and the picture people had formed for themselves before action.

I could have given one more example which is perhaps still more striking: Catholics have never been discouraged even in the hardest trials, because they have always pictured the history of the Church as a series of battles between Satan and the hierarchy supported by Christ; every new difficulty which arises is only an episode in a war which must finally end in the victory of Catholicism. . . .

In employing the term myth I believed that I had made a happy choice, because I thus put myself in a position to refuse any discussion whatever with the people who wish to submit the idea of a general strike to a detailed criticism, and who accumulate objections against its practical possibility. It appears, on the contrary, that I had made a most unfortunate choice, for while some told me that myths were only suitable to a primitive state of society, others imagined that I thought the modern world might be moved by illusions analogous in nature to those which Renan thought might usefully replace religion. But there has been a worse misunderstanding than this even, for it has been asserted that my theory of myths was only a kind of lawyer's plea, a falsification of the real opinions of the revolutionaries, the *sophistry of an intellectualist.* . . .

As long as there are no myths accepted by the masses, one may go on talking of revolts indefinitely, without ever provoking any revolutionary movement; this is what gives such importance to the general strike and renders it so odious to socialists who are afraid of a revolution; they do all they can to shake the confidence felt by the workers in the preparations they are making for the revolution; and in order to succeed in this they cast ridicule on the idea of the general strike—the only idea that could have any value as a motive force. One of the chief means employed by them is to represent it as a Utopia; this is easy enough, because there are very few myths which are perfectly free from any Utopian element.

The revolutionary myths which exist at the present time are almost free from any such mixture; by means of them it is possible to understand the activity, the feelings and the ideas of the masses preparing themselves to enter on a decisive struggle; the myths are not descriptions of things, but expressions of a determination to act. A Utopia is, on the contrary, an intellectual product; it is the work of theorists who, after observing and discussing the known facts, seek to establish a model to which they can compare existing society in order to estimate the amount of good and evil it contains. It is a combination of imaginary institutions having sufficient analogies to real institutions for the jurist to be able to reason about them; it is a construction which can be taken to pieces, and certain parts of it have been shaped in such a way that they can (with a few alterations by way of adjustment) be fitted into approaching legislation. Whilst contemporary myths lead men to prepare themselves for a combat which will destroy the existing state of things, the effect of Utopias has always been to direct men's minds towards reforms which can be brought about by patching up the existing system; it is not surprising, then, that so many makers of Utopias were able to develop into able statesmen when they had acquired a greater experience of political life. A myth cannot be refuted, since it is, at bottom, identical with the convictions of a group, being the expression of these convictions in the language of movement; and it is, in consequence, unanalysable into parts which could be placed on the plane of historical descriptions. A Utopia, on the contrary, can be discussed like any other social constitution; the spontaneous movements it presupposes can be compared with the movements actually observed in the course of history, and we can in this way evaluate its verisimilitude; it is possible to refute Utopias by showing that the economic system on which they have been made to rest is incompatible with the necessary conditions of modern production. . . .

For a long time Socialism was scarcely anything but a Utopia; the Marxists were right in claiming for their master the honour of bringing about a change in this state of things; Socialism has now become the preparation of the masses employed in great industries for the suppression of the State and property; and it is no longer necessary, therefore, to discuss how men must organise themselves in order to enjoy future happiness; everything is reduced to the *revolutionary apprenticeship* of the proletariat. Unfortunately Marx was not acquainted with facts which have now become familiar to us; we know better than he did what strikes are, because we have been able to observe economic conflicts of considerable extent and duration; the myth of the "general strike" has become popular, and is now firmly established in the minds of the workers; we possess ideas about violence that it would have been difficult for him to have formed; we can then complete his doctrine, instead of making commentaries on his text, as his unfortunate disciples have done for so long.

In this way Utopias tend to disappear completely from Socialism; Socialism has no longer any need to concern itself with the organisation of industry since capitalism does that. I think, moreover, that I have shown that the general strike corresponds to a kind of feeling which is so closely related to those which are necessary to promote production in any very progressive state of industry, that a revolutionary apprenticeship may at the same time be considered as an apprenticeship which will enable the workmen to occupy a high rank among the best workmen of his own trade.

I believe also that it may be useful to thrash the orators of democracy and the representatives of the Government, for in this way you insure that none shall retain any illusions about the character of acts of violence. But these acts can have historical value only if they are the *clear and brutal expression of the class war:* the middle classes must not be allowed to imagine that, aided by cleverness, social science, or highflown sentiments, they might find a better welcome at the hands of the proletariat.

The day on which employers perceive that they have nothing to gain by works which promote social peace, or by democracy, they will understand that they have been ill-advised by the people who persuaded them to abandon their trade of creators of productive forces for the noble profession of educators of the proletariat. Then there is some chance that they may get back a part of their energy, and that moderate or conservative economics may appear as absurd to them as they appeared to Marx. In any case, the separation of classes being more clearly accentuated, the proletarian movement will have some chance of developing with greater regularity than to-day.

The two antagonistic classes therefore influence each other in a partly indirect but decisive manner. Capitalism drives the proletariat into revolt, because in daily life the employers use their force in a direction opposed to the desire of their workers; but the future of the proletariat is not entirely dependent on this revolt; the working classes are organised under the influence of other causes, and Socialism, inculcating in them the revolutionary idea, prepares them to suppress the hostile class. Capitalist force is at the base of all this process, and its action is automatic and inevitable. Marx supposed that the middle class had no need to be incited to employ force, but we are to-day faced with a new and very unforeseen fact—a middle class which seeks to weaken its own strength. Must we believe that the Marxian conception is dead? By no means, for proletarian violence comes upon the scene just at the moment when the conception of social peace is being held up as a means of moderating disputes; proletarian violence confines employers to their rôle of producers, and tends to restore the separation of the classes, just when they seemed on the point of intermingling in the democratic marsh.

Proletarian violence not only makes the future revolution certain, but it seems also to be the only means by which the European nations—at present stupefied by humanitarianism—can recover their former energy. This kind of violence compels capitalism to restrict its attentions solely to its material rôle and tends to restore to it the warlike qualities which it formerly possessed. A growing and solidly organised working class can compel the capitalist class to remain firm in the industrial war; if a united and revolutionary proletariat confronts a rich middle class, eager for conquest, capitalist society will have reached its historical perfection.

Thus proletarian violence has become an essential factor of Marxism. Let us add once more that, if properly conducted, it will suppress the Parliamentary Socialists, who will no longer be able to pose as the leaders of the working classes and the guardians of order.

LEO TOLSTOY (1828–1910)

The State and Violence

The efforts which the educated men of the upper classes are making to silence the growing consciousness that the present system of life must be changed, are constantly on the increase, while life itself, continuing to develop and to become more complex without changing its direction, as it increases the incongruities and suffering of human existence, brings men to the extreme limit of this contradiction. An example of this uttermost limit is found in the general military conscription.

It is usually supposed that this conscription, together with the increasing armaments and the consequent increase of the taxes and national debts of all countries, are the accidental results of a certain crisis in European affairs, which might be obviated by certain political combinations, without change of the interior life.

This is utterly erroneous. The general conscription is nothing but an internal contradiction which has crept into the social life-conception, and which has only become evident because it has arrived at its utmost

The selection is from Leo Tolstoy, *The Kingdom of God is Within You* (New York: T. Y. Crowell Company, 1899).

limits at a period when men have attained a certain degree of material development.

The social life-conception transfers the significance of life from the individual to mankind in general, through the unbroken continuity of the family, the tribe, and the State. . . .

The advocates of the social life-conception usually attempt to combine the idea of authority, otherwise violence, with that of moral influence; but such a union is utterly impossible.

The result of moral influence upon man is to change his desires, so that he willingly complies with what is required of him. A man who yields to moral influence takes pleasure in conforming his actions to its laws; whereas authority, as the word is commonly understood, is a means of coercion, by which a man is forced to act in opposition to his wishes. A man who submits to authority does not do as he pleases, he yields to compulsion, and in order to force a man to do something for which he has an aversion, the threat of physical violence, or violence itself, must be employed: he may be deprived of his liberty, flogged, mutilated, or he may be threatened with these punishments. And this is what constitutes power both in the past and in the present. . . .

"Were it not for the State," we are told, "we should be subjected to violence and to the attacks of evil men in our own land."

But who are these evil men from whose violence and attacks the government and the army saves us? If such men existed three or four centuries ago, when men prided themselves on their military skill and strength of arm, when a man proved his valor by killing his fellow men, we find none such at the present time: men of our time neither use nor carry weapons, and, believing in the precepts of humanity and pity for their neighbors, they are as desirous for peace and a quiet life as we are ourselves. Hence this extraordinary class of marauders, against whom the State might defend us, no longer exists. But if, when they speak of the men from whose attacks the government defends us, we understand that they mean the criminal classes, in that case we know that they are not extraordinary beings, like beasts of prey among sheep, but are men very much like ourselves, who are naturally just as reluctant to commit crimes as those against whom they commit them. We know now that threats and punishments are powerless to decrease the numbers of such men, but that their numbers may be decreased by change of environment and by moral influence. Hence the theory of the necessity of State violence in order to protect mankind against evil-doers, if it had any foundation three or four centuries ago, has none whatever at the present time. One might say quite the reverse nowadays, for the activity of governments, with their antiquated and merciless methods of punishment, their galleys, prisons, gallows, and guillotines, so far below the general plane of morality, tends rather to lower the standard of morals than to elevate it, and therefore rather to increase than to lessen the number of criminals.

It is said that "without the State there would be no institutions, educational, moral, religious, or international; there would be no means of communication. Were it not for the State, we should be without organizations necessary to all of us."

An argument like this could only have had a basis several centuries ago. If there ever was a time when men had so little international communication, and were so unused to intercourse or interchange of thought that they could not come to an agreement on matters of general interest—commercial, industrial, or economical—without the assistance of the State, such is not the case at present. The widely diffused means of communication and transmission of thought have achieved this result—that when the modern man desires to found societies, assemblies, corporations, congresses, scientific, economical, or political institutions, not only can he easily dispense with the assistance of governments, but in the majority of cases governments are more of a hindrance than a help in the pursuit of such objects.

Since the end of the last century almost every progressive movement on the part of mankind has been not only discouraged, but invariably hampered, by governments. Such was the case with the abolition of corporal punishment, torture, and slavery; with the establishment of freedom of the press and liberty of meeting. Furthermore, State authorities and governments nowadays not only do not coöperate, but they directly hinder the activity by means of which men work out new forms of life. The solution of labour and land questions, of political and religious problems, is not only unencouraged, but distinctly opposed, by the government authority. . . .

But the question concerning the State, whether its continued existence is a necessity, or whether it would be wiser to abolish it, cannot be decided by discussion on its usefulness for the men who are required to support it by taking part in the military service, and still less by weighing the comparative advantages and disadvantages of submission or non-submission for the individual himself. It is decided irrevocably and without appeal by the religious consciousness, by the conscience of each individual, to whom no sooner does military conscription become a question than it is followed by that of the necessity or non-necessity of the State. . . .

The question of resistance or non-resistance of evil by violence arose with the first contest among men, for every contest is simply the resistance by violence of something which each combatant believes to be an evil. But before the time of Christ men did not understand that resistance by violence of whatever the individual believed to be evil— only the same action which seems evil to one man may seem good to another—is simply one mode of settling the difficulty, and that the other method consists in not resisting evil by violence.

Before the appearance of the doctrine of Christ men believed that there could be but one way of deciding the contest, that of resisting evil by violence, and acted accordingly, while each combatant strove to persuade himself and others that what he regarded as evil was in fact the actual and absolute evil. For this purpose, dating from the oldest times, men began to invent certain definitions of evil which should be obligatory for all, and for the purpose of establishing definitions which should be thus binding, were issued, either certain laws supposed to have been received in a supernatural manner, or commands of individuals or of bodies of men to whom an infallible wisdom was ascribed. Men used violence against their fellow-men and assured themselves and others that they were but using such violence against an evil acknowledged by all.

This was the custom from the most ancient times, particularly among men who had usurped authority, and men have been long in seeing its baselessness.

But the longer mankind existed the more complex grew its mutual relations, and the more evident it became that to resist by violence everything that is considered evil is unwise; that the struggle is not diminished thereby, and that no human wisdom can ever define an infallible standard of evil. . . .

Thus matters went on for eighteen centuries, and at last arrived at their present condition, which is, that no man can dispute the fact that an infallible definition of evil will never be made. We have reached the point when men have ceased not only to believe in the possibility of finding a universal definition which all men will admit, but they have even ceased to believe in the necessity of such a definition. We have reached the point when men in authority no longer seek to prove that that which they consider evil is evil, but candidly acknowledge that they consider that to be evil which does not please them, and those who are subject to authority obey, not because they believe that the definitions of evil made by authority are just, but only because they have no power to resist. . . .

CHRISTIANITY AND NON-RESISTANCE

A man needs but to realize that the object of his life is the fulfil-ment of God's law; then the preeminence of that law, claiming as it does its entire allegiance, will of necessity invalidate the authority and restrictions of all human laws.

The Christian who contemplates that law of love implanted in every human soul, and quickened by Christ, the only guide for all man-kind, is set free from human authority.

A Christian may suffer from external violence, may be deprived of his personal freedom, may be a slave to his passions,—the man who commits sin is the slave of the sin,—but he cannot be controlled or coerced by threats into committing an act contrary to his consciousness. He cannot be forced to this, because the privations and sufferings that are so powerful an influence over men who hold the social life-concep-tion have no influence whatever over him. The privations and sufferings that destroy the material welfare which is the object of the social life-conception produce no effect upon the welfare of the Christian's life, which rests on the consciousness that he is doing God's will—nay, they may even serve to promote that welfare when they are visited upon him for fulfilling that will. . . .

A Christian enters into no dispute with his neighbor, he neither attacks nor uses violence; on the contrary, he suffers violence himself without resistance, and by his very attitude toward evil not only sets himself free, but helps to free the world at large from all outward authority.

"And ye shall know the truth, and the truth shall make you free." If there were any doubt of the truth of Christianity there could be no more indubitable proof of its authenticity than the complete freedom, recognizing no fetters, which a man feels as soon as he assimilates the Christian life-conception.

Human beings in their present condition may be likened to bees in the act of swarming, as we see them clinging in a mass to a single bough. Their position is a temporary one, and must inevitably be changed. They must rise and find themselves a new abode. Every bee knows this, and is eager to shift its own position, as well as that of the others, but not one of them will do so until the whole swarm rises. The swarm cannot rise, because one bee clings to the other and prevents it from separating itself from the swarm, and so they all continue to hang. It might seem as if there were no deliverance from this position, precisely as it seems to men of the world who have become entangled in the social net. Indeed, there would be no outlet for the bees if each one were not a living creature possessed of a pair of wings. Neither would there be any issue for men if each one were not a living individual, being gifted with a capacity for assimilating the Christian life-conception.

If among these bees who are able to fly not one could be found willing to start, the swarm would never change its position. And it is the same among men. If the man who has assimilated the Christian life-conception waits for others before he proceeds to live in accordance with it, mankind will never change its attitude. And as all that is needed to change a solid mass of bees into a flying swarm is for one bee to spread its wings and fly away, when the second, the third, the tenth, and the hundredth will follow suit; so all that is needed to break through the magic circle of social life, deliverance from which seems so hopeless, is, that one man should view life from a Christian standpoint and begin to frame his own life accordingly, whereupon others will follow in his footsteps.

But men think that the deliverance of mankind by this method is too slow a process, and that a simultaneous deliverance might be effected by some other method. Just as if bees, when the swarm was ready to rise, were to decide that it would be too long a process if they waited for each bee to spread its wings and rise separately, and that some means must be devised whereby the swarm may rise all at once, whenever it pleases. But that is impossible. Not until the first, second, third, and hundredth bee has unfolded its wings and flown away can the swarm take flight and find for itself a new home. Not until each individual man adopts the Christian life-conception, and begins to live in conformity with its precepts, will the contradictions of human life be solved, and new forms of life become established.

REINHOLD NIEBUHR (1895–1962)

Illusions about Violence

The confidence of modern secular idealism in the possibility of an easy resolution of the tension between individual and community, or between classes, races and nations is derived from a too optimistic view of human nature. This too generous estimate of human virtue is intimately related to an erroneous estimate of the dimensions of the human stature. The conception of human nature which underlies the social and political attitudes of a liberal democratic culture is that of an essentially harmless individual. The survival impulse, which man shares with the animals, is regarded as the normative form of his egoistic drive. If this were a true picture of the human situation man might be, or might become, as harmless as seventeenth- and eighteenth-century thought assumed. Unfortunately for the validity of this picture of man, the most significant distinction between the human and the animal world is that the impulses of the former are "spiritualized" in the human world. Human capacities for evil as well as for good are derived from this spiritualization. There is of course always a natural survival impulse at the core of all human ambition. But this survival impulse cannot be neatly disentangled from two forms of its spiritualization. The one form is the desire to fulfill the potentialities of life and not merely to maintain its existence. Man is the kind of animal who cannot merely live. If he lives at all he is bound to seek the realization of his true nature; and to his true nature belongs his fulfillment in the lives of others. The will to live is thus transmuted into the will to self-realization; and self-realization involves self-giving in relations to others. When this desire for self-realization is fully explored it becomes apparent that it is subject to the paradox that the highest form of self-realization is the consequence of self-giving, but that it cannot be the intended consequence of self-giving, but that it cannot be the intended consequence without being prematurely limited. Thus the will to live is finally transmuted into its opposite in the sense that only in self-giving can the self be fulfilled, for: "He that findeth his life shall lose it: and he that loseth his life for my sake shall find it."[1]

[1] Matthew 10:39.

Reprinted with the permission of Charles Scribner's Sons from *The Children of Light and the Children of Darkness,* pages 18–24, 33–36 and 40–41, by Reinhold Niebuhr. Copyright 1944 Charles Scribner's Sons. And by permission of James Nisbet & Co., Ltd., London, 1945.

On the other hand the will-to-live is also spiritually transmuted into the will-to-power or into the desire for "power and glory." Man, being more than a natural creature, is not interested merely in physical survival but in prestige and social approval. Having the intelligence to anticipate the perils in which he stands in nature and history, he invariably seeks to gain security against these perils by enhancing his power, individually and collectively. Possessing a darkly unconscious sense of his insignificance in the total scheme of things, he seeks to compensate for his insignificance by pretensions of pride. The conflicts between men are thus never simple conflicts between competing survival impulses. They are conflicts in which each man or group seeks to guard its power and prestige against the peril of competing expressions of power and pride. Since the very possession of power and prestige always involves some encroachment upon the prestige and power of others, this conflict is by its very nature a more stubborn and difficult one than the mere competition between various survival impulses in nature. It remains to be added that this conflict expresses itself even more cruelly in collective than in individual terms. Human behaviour being less individualistic than secular liberalism assumed, the struggle between classes, races and other groups in human society is not as easily resolved by the expedient of dissolving the groups as liberal democratic idealists assumed.

Since the survival impulse in nature is transmuted into two different and contradictory spiritualized forms, which we may briefly designate as the will-to-live-truly and the will-to-power, man is at variance with himself. The power of the second impulse places him more fundamentally in conflict with his fellowman than democratic liberalism realizes. The fact he cannot realize himself, except in organic relation with his fellows, makes the community more important than bourgeois individualism understands. The fact that the two impulses, though standing in contradiction to each other, are also mixed and compounded with each other on every level of human life, makes the simple distinctions between good and evil, between selfishness and altruism, with which liberal idealism has tried to estimate moral and political facts, invalid. The fact that the will-to-power inevitably justifies itself in terms of the morally more acceptable will to realize man's true nature means that the egoistic corruption of univeral ideals is a much more persistent fact in human conduct than any moralistic creed is inclined to admit.

If we survey any period of history, and not merely the present tragic era of world catastrophe, it becomes quite apparent that human ambitions, lusts and desires are more inevitably inordinate, that both

human creativity and human evil reach greater heights, and that conflicts in the community between varying conceptions of the good and
between competing expressions of vitality are of more tragic proportions than was anticipated in the basic philosophy which underlies
democratic civilization.

There is a specially ironic element in the effort of the seventeenth
century to confine man to the limits of a harmless "nature" or to bring
all his actions under the discipline of a cool prudence. For while
democratic social philosophy was elaborating the picture of a harmless
individual, moved by no more than a survival impulse, living in a
social peace guaranteed by a pre-established harmony of nature, the
advancing natural sciences were enabling man to harness the powers of
nature, and to give his desires and ambitions a more limitless scope than
they previously had. The static inequalities of an agrarian society were
transmuted into the dynamic inequalities of an industrial age. The
temptation to inordinate expressions of the possessive impulse, created
by the new wealth of a technical civilization, stood in curious and ironic
contradiction to the picture of essentially moderate and ordinate
desires which underlay the social philosophy of the physiocrats and of
Adam Smith. Furthermore a technical society developed new and more
intensive forms of social cohesion and a greater centralization of economic process in defiance of the individualistic conception of social
relations which informed the liberal philosophy.[2]

The demonic fury of fascist politics in which a collective will
expresses boundless ambitions and imperial desires and in which the
instruments of a technical civilization are used to arm this will with a
destructive power, previously unknown in history, represents a melancholy historical refutation of the eighteenth- and nineteenth-century
conceptions of a harmless and essentially individual human life.
Human desires are expressed more collectively, are less under the discipline of prudent calculation, and are more the masters of, and less
limited by, natural forces than the democratic creed had understood.

While the fury of fascist politics represents a particularly vivid
refutation of the democratic view of human nature, the developments
within the confines of democratic civilization itself offer almost as

[2] Thus vast collective forms of "free enterprise," embodied in mono-
polistic and large-scale financial and industrial institutions, still rationalize
their desire for freedom from political control in terms of a special philosophy
which Adam Smith elaborated for individuals. Smith was highly critical of the
budding large-scale enterprise of his day and thought it ought to be restricted
to insurance companies and banks.

telling a refutation. The liberal creed is never an explicit instrument of the children of darkness. But it is surprising to what degree the forces of darkness are able to make covert use of the creed. One must therefore, in analyzing the liberal hope of a simple social and political harmony, be equally aware of the universalistic presuppositions which underlie the hope and of the egoistic corruptions (both individual and collective) which inevitably express themselves in our culture in terms of, and in despite of, the creed. One must understand that it is a creed of children of light; but also that it betrays their blindness to the forces of darkness. . . .

Democratic theory, whether in its liberal or in its more radical form, is just as stupid in analyzing the relation between the national and the international community as in seeking a too simple harmony between the individual and the national community. Here, too, modern liberal culture exhibits few traces of moral cynicism. The morally autonomous modern national state does indeed arise; and it acknowledges no law beyond its interests. The actual behaviour of the nations is cynical. But the creed of liberal civilization is sentimental. This is true not only of the theorists whose creed was used by the architects of economic imperialism and of the more covert forms of national egotism in the international community, but also of those whose theories were appropriated by the proponents of an explicit national egotism. A straight line runs from Mazzini to Mussolini in the history of Italian nationalism. Yet there was not a touch of moral cynicism in the thought of Mazzini. He was, on the contrary, a pure universalist.[3]

Even the philosophy of German romanticism, which has been accused with some justification of making specific contributions to the creed of German Nazism, reveals the stupidity of the children of light much more than the malice of the children of darkness. There is of course a strong note of moral nihilism in the final fruit of this romantic movement as we have it in Nietzsche; though even Nietzsche was no

---

[3] "Your first duty." wrote Mazzini, "first as regards importance, is toward humanity. You are men before you are citizens and fathers. If you do not embrace the whole human family in your affections, if you do not bear witness to the unity of that family, if—you are not ready, if able, to aid the unhappy,—you violate your law of life and you comprehend not that religion which will be the guide and blessing of the future."

Mazzini held kings responsible for national egotism: "The first priests of the fatal worship [of self-interest] were the kings, princes and evil governments. They invented the horrible formula: every one for himself. They knew that they would thus create egoism and that between the egoist and the slave there is but one step." *The Duties of Man*, ch. xii.

nationalist. But the earlier romantics usually express the same combination of individualism and universalism which characterizes the theory of the more naturalistic and rationalistic democrats of the western countries. Fichte resolved the conflict between the individual and the community through the instrumentality of the "just law" almost as easily as the utilitarians resolved it by the calculations of the prudent egotist and as easily as Rousseau resolved it by his conception of a "general will," which would fulfill the best purposes of each individual will. This was no creed of a community, making itself the idolatrous end of human existence. The theory was actually truer than the more individualistic and naturalistic forms of the democratic creed; for romanticism understood that the individual requires the community for his fulfillment. Thus even Hegel, who is sometimes regarded as the father of state absolutism in modern culture, thought of the national state as providing "for the reasonable will, insofar as it is in the individual only implicitly the universal will coming to a consciousness and an understanding of itself and being found."[4]

This was not the creed of a collective egotism which negated the right of the individual. Rather it was a theory which, unlike the more purely democratic creed, understood the necessity of social fulfillment for the individual, and which, in common with the more liberal theories, regarded this as a much too simple process. . . .

The democratic idealists of practically all schools of thought have managed to remain remarkably oblivious to the obvious facts. Democratic theory therefore has not squared with the facts of history. This grave defect in democratic theory was comparatively innocuous in the heyday of the bourgeois period, when the youth and the power of democratic civilization surmounted all errors of judgment and confusions of mind. But in this latter day, when it has become important to save what is valuable in democratic life from the destruction of what is false in bourgeois civilization, it has also become necessary to distinguish what is false in democratic theory from what is true in democratic life.

The preservation of a democratic civilization requires the wisdom of the serpent and the harmlessness of the dove. The children of light must be armed with the wisdom of the children of darkness but remain free from their malice. They must know the power of self-interest in human society without giving it moral justification. They must have this wisdom in order that they may beguile, deflect, harness and restrain self-interest, individual and collective, for the sake of the community.

---

[4] *Philosophy of Mind,* Sect. II, par. 539.

HERBERT MARCUSE (1898–)

Ethics and Revolution

I propose to discuss the relation between ethics and revolution by taking as guidance the following question: Can a revolution be justified as right, as good, perhaps even as necessary, and justified not merely in political terms (as expedient for certain interests) but in ethical terms, that is to say, justified with respect to the human condition as such, to the potential of man in a given historical situation? This means that ethical terms such as "right" or "good" will be applied to political and social movements, with the hypothesis that the moral evaluation of such movements is (in a sense to be defined) more than subjective, more than a matter of preference. Under this hypothesis, "good" and "right" would mean serving to establish, to promote, or to extend human freedom and happiness in a commonwealth, regardless of the form of government. This preliminary definition combines individual and personal, private and public welfare. It tries to recapture a basic concept of classical political philosophy which has been all too often repressed, namely, that the end of government is not only the greatest possible freedom, but also the greatest possible happiness of man, that is to say, a life without fear and misery, and a life in peace.

Here we encounter the first vexing question, namely, who determines, who can and by what right determine the general interest of a commonwealth, and thereby determine the range and limits of individual freedom and happiness, and the sacrifices imposed upon individual freedom and happiness in the name and on behalf of the commonwealth? For as long as the general and individual welfare do not immediately coincide, the latter will be *made* to conform with the former. And if we ask this question we are at once confronted with an equally serious and embarrassing problem: granted even that freedom is not only an individual and private affair, that it is rather determined by the society, by the state in which we live, what about happiness? Is the happiness of an individual his own private affair, or is it too, in a very definite sense, subject to the limitations and even the definitions imposed upon it by a commonwealth? The extreme position that human happiness is and must remain individual and the individual's own affair cannot be defended if we give it only a few minutes' thought. There are certainly modes and types of individual happiness which cannot be tolerated by any kind of commonwealth. It is perfectly possible—as a matter of fact we know it to be the fact—that the people who were the master torturers in the Hitler concentration camps were often quite happy doing their job. This is one of the many cases of individual happiness where we do not hesitate to say that it is not merely the individual himself who can be and who can remain the judge of his own happiness. We assume a tribunal which is (actually or morally) entitled to "define" individual happiness.

Now after these preliminary clarifications, let me define what I mean by "revolution." By "revolution" I understand the overthrow of a legally established government and constitution by a social class or movement with the aim of altering the social as well as the political structure. This definition excludes all military coups, palace revolutions, and "preventive" counterrevolutions (such as Fascism and Nazism) because they do not alter the basic social structure. If we define revolution in this way we can move one step forward by saying that such a radical and qualitative change implies violence. Peaceful revolutions, if there are such things, if there can be such things, do not present any problem. We can therefore reformulate the initial question by asking: Is the revolutionary use of violence justifiable as a means for establishing or promoting human freedom and happiness? The question implies a very important assumption, namely, that there are rational criteria for determining the possibilities of human freedom and happiness available to a society in a specific historical situation. If there are no such rational criteria, it would be impossible to evaluate a political movement in terms of its chances to attain a greater extent or a higher degree of freedom and happiness in society.

But postulating the availability of rational standards and criteria for judging the given possibilities of human freedom and happiness means assuming that the ethical, moral standards are *historical* standards. If they are not, they remain meaningless abstractions. Applied to our question, this means that to claim an ethical and moral right, a revolutionary movement must be able to give rational grounds for its chances to grasp real possibilities of human freedom and happiness, and it must be able to demonstrate the adequacy of its means for obtaining this end. Only if the problem is placed in such a historical context, is it susceptible to rational discussion. Otherwise, only two positions remain open, namely, to reject *a priori* or to endorse *a priori* all revolution and revolutionary violence. Both positions, the affirmative as well as the negative one, offend against historical facts. It is, for example, meaningless to say that modern society *could* have come about without the English, American, and French Revolutions. It is also meaningless to say that all revolutionary violence had the same social function and consequences. The violence of the Civil Wars in seventeenth century England, the violence of the first French Revolution certainly had effects and consequences very different from those of the Bolshevik Revolution, and very different from the counterrevolutionary violence perpetrated by the Nazi and Fascist regimes. Moreover, the positions of *a priori* rejecting or *a priori* approving social and political violence would amount to sanctioning any change brought about in history, regardless of whether it would be in a progressive or regressive, liberating or enslaving direction. . . .

The ethics of revolution thus testifies to the clash and conflict of two historical rights: on the one side, the right of that which *is*, the established commonwealth on which the life and perhaps even the happiness of the individuals depend; and on the other side, the right of that which can be and perhaps even *ought* to be because it may reduce toil, misery, and injustice, provided always that this chance can be demonstrated as a real possibility. Such a demonstration must provide rational criteria; we can now add: these must be *historical* criteria. As such, they amount to an "historical calculus," namely, calculation of the chances of a future society as against the chances of the existing society with respect to human progress, that is to say, technical and material progress used in such a way that it increases individual freedom and happiness. Now if such an historical calculus is to have any rational basis, it must, on the one side, take into account the sacrifices exacted from the living generations on behalf of the established society, the established law and order, the number of victims made in defense of this society in war and peace, in the struggle for existence, individual and national. The calculus would further have to take into account the intellectual and material resources available to the society and the manner in which they are actually used with respect to their full capacity of satisfying vital human needs and pacifying the struggle for existence. On the other side, the historical calculus would have to project the chances of the contesting revolutionary movement of improving the prevailing conditions, namely, whether the revolutionary plan or program demonstrates the technical, material, and mental possibility of reducing the sacrifices and the number of victims. Even prior to the question as to the possibility of such a calculus (which, I believe, does exist), its inhuman quantifying character is evident. But its inhumanity is that of history itself, token of its empirical, rational foundation. No hypocrisy should from the beginning distort the examination. Nor is this brutal calculus an empty intellectual abstraction; in fact, at its decisive turns, history became such a calculated experiment.

The ethics of revolution, if there is such a thing, will therefore be in accordance not with absolute, but with historical standards. They do not cancel the validity of those general norms which formulate requirements for the progress of mankind toward humanity. No matter how rationally one may justify revolutionary means in terms of the demonstrable chance of obtaining freedom and happiness for future generations, and thereby justify violating existing rights and liberties and life itself, there are forms of violence and suppression which no revolutionary situation can justify because they negate the very end for which the revolution is a means. Such are arbitrary violence, cruelty, and indiscriminate terror. However, within the historical continuum, revolutions establish a moral and ethical code of their own and in this way become the origin, the fountainhead and source of new general norms and values. In fact some of today's most generally-professed values originated in revolutions, for example, the value of tolerance in the English Civil Wars, the inalienable rights of man in the American and French Revolutions. These ideas become an historical force, first as partial ideas, instruments of a revolutionary movement for specific political ends. Their realization originally involved violence; they then assumed not only partial political but general ethical validity and rejected violence. In this way, revolutions place themselves under ethical standards.

Violence *per se* has never been made a revolutionary value by the leaders of the historical revolutions. His contemporaries rejected Georges Sorel's attempt to cut the link between violence and reason, which was at the same time the attempt to free the class struggle from all ethical considerations. In comparing the violence of the class struggle in its revolutionary phase with the violence of military operations in war, he made the former subject to strategic calculations only: the end was the total defeat of the enemy; violence a means to attain this end—the relation between means and end was a technical one. Sorel's defense of violence this side of good and evil remained isolated from the revolutionary reality of his time; if he had any influence, it was on the side of the counterrevolution. Otherwise, violence was defended, not *per se,* but as part of rational suppression, suppression of counterrevolutionary activity, of established rights and privileges, and, for the society at large, of material and intellectual needs, that is, enforcement of austerity, rationing, censorship.

Now this suppression which includes violence is practiced in the interest of the objectives of the revolution, and these objectives are presented not only as political but also as moral values, ethical imperatives, namely greater freedom for the greater number of people. And in this sense the objectives and the ends of the revolution itself claim general validity and become subject to moral standards and evaluation.

Here we are confronted with the problem of all ethics, namely, the question as to the ultimate sanction of moral values. Or, in plain language, who or what determines the validity of ethical norms? The question becomes acute only with the secularization of the West; it was no problem in the Middle Ages as long as a transcendent sanction of ethics was accepted. The infidels could justly be exterminated, heretics could justly be burned—in spite of all protest. This was justice in terms of the prevailing values, which in turn were those of transcendent ethics. But today, where is the sanction of ethical values—sanction not in terms of the enforcement but in terms of the acceptance of ethical values, the proof of their validity? Sanction today, it seems, rests mainly in a precarious and flexible syndrome of custom, fear, utility, and religion; flexible because, within the syndrome, there is a large range of change. I refer, for example, to the high degree of liberalization in sexual morality which we have witnessed during the last thirty years, or, to the easy suspension of practically all ethical values in so-called emergency situations. The sanction and validity of ethical norms is thus restricted to the normal state of affairs in social and political relations.

Now in terms of the normal established state of affairs, a revolution is by definition immoral; it offends against the right of the existing commonwealth; it permits and even demands deception, cunning, suppression, destruction of life and property, and so on. But a judgment by definition is an inadequate judgment. Ethical standards by virtue of their imperative claim transcend any given state of affairs, and they transcend it, not to any metaphysical entities but to the historical continuum in which every given state of affairs has emerged, by which every given state of affairs is defined, and in which every given state of affairs will be altered and surpassed by other states. And in the historical continuum which defines its place and function, the ethics of revolution appeal to an historical calculus. Can the intended new society, the society intended by the revolution, offer better chances for progress in freedom than the existing society? In the historical continuum, these chances can only be measured by going beyond the given state of affairs, going beyond it not simply into an abstract vacuum of speculation, but going beyond it by calculating the resources, intellectual as well as material, scientific as well as technical, available to a given society, and projecting the most rational ways of utilizing these resources. Now if such projection is possible, then it can yield objective criteria for judging revolutions as to their historical function in terms of progress or regression, in terms of the development of *humanitas*.

A preliminary answer is suggested by a glance at the historical process itself. Historically, the objective tendency of the great revolutions of the modern period was the enlargement of the social range of freedom and the enlargement of the satisfaction of needs. No matter how much the social interpretations of the English and French Revolutions may differ, they seem to agree in that a redistribution of the social wealth took place, so that previously less privileged or under-privileged classes were the beneficiaries of this change, economically and/or politically. In spite of subsequent periods of reaction and restoration, the result and objective function of these revolutions was the establishment of more liberal governments, a gradual democratization of society, and technical progress. I said "objective function" because this evaluation of the revolution is obviously a judgment *ex post facto*. The intention and ideology of the leaders of the revolution, and the drives of the masses may have had quite different aims and motives. By virtue of their objective function, these revolutions attained progress in the sense defined, namely, a demonstrable enlargement of the range of human freedom; they thus established, in spite of the terrible sacrifices exacted by them, an ethical right over and above all political justification.

But if such ethical right and its criteria are always and necessarily after the fact, it serves for nought and leaves us with the irrational choice of either a *priori* accepting or *a priori* rejecting all revolution. Now I submit that, while the historical function of a revolution becomes identifiable only after the fact, its prospective direction, progressive or regressive is, with the certainty of a reasonable *chance*, demonstrable *before* the fact—to the same degree to which the historical conditions of progress are demonstrable. For example, it could be demonstrated—and it was demonstrated before the fact—that the French Revolution of 1789 would give, in terms of the historical calculus, a better chance for the development of human freedom than the Ancien Régime. Contrariwise, it could be demonstrated, and was demonstrated long before the fact, that Fascist and National-Socialist regimes would do the exact opposite, namely, necessarily restrict the range of human freedom. Moreover, and I think this is a very important point, such demonstration of the historical *chances* before the fact becomes increasingly rational with the development of our scientific, technical, and material resources and capabilities, with our progress in the scientific mastery of man and nature. The possibilities and contents of freedom today are coming more and more under the control of man: they are becoming increasingly calculable. And with this advance in effective control and calculability, the inhuman distinction between violence and violence, sacrifice and sacrifice becomes increasingly rational. For throughout history, the happiness and freedom, and even the life of individuals, have been sacrificed. If we consider human life *per se* sacred under all conditions, the distinction is meaningless, and we have to admit that history is *per se* amoral and immoral, because it has never respected the sanctity of human life as such. But in fact we do distinguish between sacrifices which are legitimate and sacrifices which are not legitimate. This distinction is an historical one, and with this qualification, ethical standards are also applicable to violence.

PUNISHMENT

Governmental agencies, at least in our society, have been entrusted with a monopoly on police power, presumably a necessity in light of their obligation to maintain public order. But monopolies always create the conditions for abuse, and increasingly, social critics refuse to look upon law enforcement and punishment procedures as apolitical—divorced from the interests and biases of those who hold power. Particularly in periods when faith in the governmental structure is threatened, or when persons are broadly disillusioned about the health of their social environment, the debate about legal punishment is likely to flourish. There, in the law's ability to punish—even to deprive citizens of their lives—the issues of power and abuse, cruelty and excess, arbitrariness and responsibility are sharply focused.

Surprisingly, it was not until the eighteenth century that Western thinkers began to protest the abuse of police power in the form of cruel and excessive punishment. Cesare Bonesano, Marquis of Beccaria, for example, was the first to denounce capital punishment, on grounds that the state had not been granted power to take human life. The state, he argued, rests on a social contract, involving the responsibility to protect life, property, and the ability to seek happiness. Life is an inalienable natural right, not to be casually withdrawn under the pretext of maintaining social order. The execution of criminals is an abuse—a violation of the very agreement on which political institutions are founded.

318

In an argument that clearly prefigured current discussion about judicial brutality, Beccaria also questioned the excessive character of capital punishment. He protested the barbaric example set by the state in executing criminals and argued that public morality is certain to suffer. Capital punishment cannot be defended, even pragmatically, in that its deterrent effect cannot be established.

In the nineteenth century, the discussion about legal punishment was extended. Jeremy Bentham carefully distinguished various situations in which punitive action by the state can be sanctioned and attempted to develop guidelines by which punishments become proportionate to crimes. The interesting thing about Bentham's approach is the degree to which the question is subsumed within his larger endeavor to make jurisprudence a science. Punishment is acknowledged as a thoroughly political phenomenon—one of the instruments by which governments maintain a humane environment. But Bentham wanted to base legislation on a firmer ground than the flammable, shifting line of power politics. Judicial reform ought to grow from a knowledge of the stable purposes of government itself.

The nineteenth century idealist, F. H. Bradley, was broadly sympathetic with Bentham's attempt. But he was under the spell of Darwin and looked upon politics in a more aggressive, positive manner. In his surprising "Some Remarks on Punishment," Bradley argues that the older doctrines of punishment—educational, deterrent and retributive—should not be discarded. They should, however, be made subordinate to the "principle of social surgery," which he described as the right and responsibility of the social organism to suppress undesirable growths. To contemporary minds, Bradley's comment may appear almost grotesque, insensitive to the high value we place upon individual worth. But he was forging important philosophical foundations for the Western welfare state, and he was putting the problem of legal punishment squarely in the open-ended political process.

John F. Ford's defense of capital punishment rests on a similar philosophical position. He argued that society as a whole has the right to chart its course, that the welfare of the whole must precede that of individuals, and that society must be able to protect itself from criminal internal threats. The state is an organ through which society achieves the common good; and thus the state, in its procedures of legal punishment, acts as an implementer of divine purposes.

The other two selections that follow relate to the broad discussion of punishment in quite specific ways. John Dewey is concerned about the reform of criminal procedures, in ways consistent with experimentalism and with a compassionate sense of justice. Schlick, a leader within the Vienna Circle's articulation of logical positivism, explores the character of responsibility in relation to punishment. Both Dewey and Schlick deal with punishment out of an appreciation of new social scientific data. But unlike Dewey, Schlick does not believe that progress in the sciences can contribute directly to the solution of moral problems. He approaches classical ethical issues with the purpose of giving a scientific explanation of moral conduct, and as a positivist, he intended his *Problems of Ethics*, from which our selection is taken, to be a social scientific, not a classical philosophical work. It was to be an occasion in which thought about ethical problems might be stimulated.

MARCHESE DE BECCARIA (1738–1794)

Capital Punishment

The useless prodigality of punishments, by which men have never been made any better, has driven me to examine whether the punishment of death be really useful and just in a well organized government. What kind of right can that be which men claim for the slaughter of their fellow beings? Certainly not that right which is the source of sovereignty and of laws. For these are nothing but the sum total of the smallest portions of individual liberty, and represent the general will, that is, the aggregate of individual wills. But who ever wished to leave to other men the option of killing him? How in the least possible sacrifice of each man's liberty can there be a sacrifice of the greatest of all goods, namely, of life? And if there could be that sacrifice, how would such a principle accord with the other, that a man is not the master of his own life? Yet he must have been so, could he have given to himself or to society as a body this right of killing him.

The death penalty therefore is not a right; I have proved that it cannot be so; but it is a war of a nation against one of its members, because his annihilation is deemed necessary and expedient. But if I

The selection is from Marchese de Beccaria, *On Crimes and Punishments*, trans. J. A. Farrer (London: Chatto and Windus, 1880).

can show that his death is neither necessary nor expedient, I shall have won the cause of humanity.

The death of a citizen can only be deemed necessary for two reasons. The first is when, though deprived of his personal freedom, he has still such connections and power as threaten the national security; when his existence is capable of producing a dangerous revolution in the established form of government. The death of a citizen becomes then necessary when the nation is recovering or losing its liberty, or in a time of anarchy, when confusion takes the place of laws: but in times when the laws hold undisturbed sway, when the form of government corresponds with the wishes of a united nation, and is defended internally and externally by force, and by opinion which is perhaps even stronger than force, where the supreme power rests only with the real sovereign, and riches serve to purchase pleasures but not places, I see no necessity for destroying a citizen, except when his death might be the real and only restraint for diverting others from committing crimes; this latter case constituting the second reason for which one may believe capital punishment to be both just and necessary.

Since mankind generally, suspicious always of the language of reason, but ready to bow to that of authority, remain unpersuaded by the experience of all ages, in which the supreme punishment has never diverted resolute men from committing offences against society; since also they are equally unmoved by the example of the Romans and by twenty years of the reign of the Empress Elizabeth of Russia, during which she presented this illustrious example to the fathers of their people, an example which is at least equivalent to many conquests bought by the blood of her country's sons, it is sufficient merely to consult human nature itself, to perceive the truth of the assertion I have made.

The greatest effect that any punishment has upon the human mind is not to be measured by its intensity but by its duration, for our sensibility is more easily and permanently affected by very slight but repeated impressions than by a strong but brief shock. Habit holds universal sway over every sentient being, and as we speak and walk and satisfy our needs by its aid, so moral ideas only stamp themselves on our mind by long and repeated impressions. It is not the terrible yet brief sight of a criminal's death, but the long and painful example of a man deprived of his liberty, who, having become as it were a beast of burthen, repays with his toil the society he has offended, which is the strongest restraint from crimes. Far more potent than the fear of death, which men have ever before their eyes in the remote distance, is the thought, so efficacious from its constant recurrence; "I myself shall be reduced to as long and miserable a condition if I commit similar misdeeds."

Capital punishment makes an impression in prospect which, with all its force, does not fully meet that ready spirit of forgetfulness, so natural to man even in his most important concerns, and so liable to be accelerated by his passions. As a general rule, men are startled by the sight of violent sufferings, but not for long, and therefore such impressions are wont so to transform them as to make of ordinary men either Persians or Spartans, but in a free and settled government impressions should rather be frequent than strong.

Capital punishment becomes a spectacle for the majority of mankind, and a subject for compassion and abhorrence for others; the minds of the spectators are more filled with these feelings than with the wholesome terror the law pretends to inspire. But in moderate and continuing penalties the latter is the predominant feeling, because it is the only one. The limit, which the legislator should affix to the severity of penalties, appears to lie in the first signs of a feeling of compassion becoming uppermost in the minds of the spectators, when they look upon the punishment rather as their own than as that of the criminal.

In order that a punishment may be just, it must contain only such degrees of intensity as suffice to deter men from crimes. But as there is no one who on reflection would choose the total and perpetual loss of his liberty, however great the advantages offered him by a crime, the intensity of the punishment of servitude for life, substituted for capital punishment, has that in it which is sufficient to daunt the most determined courage. I will add that it is even more deterrent than death. Very many men face death calmly and firmly, some from fanaticism, some from vanity, which almost always attends a man to the tomb; others from a last desperate attempt either no longer to live or to escape from their misery; but neither fanaticism nor vanity have any place among fetters and chains, under the stick, under the yoke, in a cage of iron; the wretch thus punished is so far from terminating his miseries that with his punishment he only begins them.

The mind of man offers more resistance to violence and to extreme but brief pains than it does to time and to incessant weariness; for whilst it can, so to speak, gather itself together for a moment to repel the former, its vigorous elasticity is insufficient to resist the long and repeated action of the latter. In the case of capital punishment, each example presented of it is all that a single crime affords; in penal servitude for life, a single crime serves to present numerous and lasting warnings. And if it be important that the power of the laws should often be witnessed, there ought to be no long intervals between the examples of the death penalty; but this would presuppose the frequency of crimes, so that, to render the punishment effective, it must not make on all men the impression that it ought to make, in other words, it must be useful and not useful at the same time. And should it be objected that perpetual servitude is as painful as death and therefore equally cruel, I will reply that, taking into consideration all the unhappy moments of servitude, it will perhaps be even more painful than death; but whilst these moments are spread over the whole of a lifetime, death exercises all its force in a single moment. There is also this advantage in penal servitude, that it has more terrors for him who sees it than for him who suffers it, for the former thinks of the whole sum-total of unhappy moments, whilst the latter, by the unhappiness of the present moment, has his thoughts diverted from that which is to come. All evils are magnified in imagination, and every sufferer finds resources and consolations unknown to and unbelieved in by spectators, who substitute their own sensibility for the hardened soul of a criminal.

The following is the kind of reasoning adopted by the thief or the assassin, whose only motives for not breaking the laws are the gallows or the wheel. (I know that the analysis of one's own thoughts is an art only learnt by education, but a thief does not the less act according to certain principles because he is unable to express them.) "Of what sort," he argues, "are these laws that I am bound to observe, that leave so great an interval between myself and the rich man? He denies me the penny I ask of him, and excuses himself by ordering from me a work of which he himself knows nothing. Who has made these laws? Were they not made by rich and powerful men, who have never deigned to visit the wretched hovels of the poor, who have never divided a musty loaf of bread amid the innocent cries of famished children and the tears of a wife? Let us break these bonds, which are fatal to the greater number, and only useful to a few indolent tyrants; let us attack injustice in its source. I will return to my state of natural independence; I will live for some time happy and free on the fruits of my courage and address; and if the day should ever come when I have to suffer and repent for it, the time of suffering will be short, and I shall have one day of misery for many years of liberty and pleasure. As the king of a small band, I will correct the errors of fortune, and see these tyrants pale and tremble before one, whom in their insolent arrogance they rated lower than their horses or their dogs," Then religion hovers before the mind of the criminal, who turns everything to a bad use, and offering him a facile repentance and an almost certain eternity of bliss does much to diminish in his eyes the horror of that last tragedy of all.

But the man who sees in prospect a great number of years, or perhaps the whole of his life, to be passed in servitude and suffering before the eyes of fellow citizens with whom he is living in freedom and friendship, the slave of those laws which had once protected him, makes a useful comparison of all these circumstances with the uncertain result of his crimes and with the shortness of the time for which he would enjoy their fruits. The ever present example of those whom he actually sees the victims of their own imprudence, impresses him much more strongly than the sight of a punishment which hardens rather than corrects him.

Capital punishment is injurious by the example of barbarity it presents. If human passions, or the necessities of war, have taught men to shed one another's blood, the laws, which are intended to moderate human conduct, ought not to extend the savage example, which in the case of a legal execution is all the more baneful in that it is carried out with studied formalities. To me it seems an absurdity, that laws, which are the expression of the public will, which abhor and which punish murder, should themselves commit one; and that, to deter citizens from private assassination, they should themselves order a public murder. What are the true and the most useful laws? Are they not those covenants and conditions which all would wish observed and proposed, when the incessant voice of private interest is hushed or is united with the interest of the people? What are every man's feelings about capital punishment? Let us read them in the gestures of indignation and scorn with which everyone looks upon the executioner, who is, after all, an innocent administrator of the public will, a good citizen contributory to the public welfare, an instrument as necessary for the internal security of a State as brave soldiers are for its external. What, then, is the source of this contradiction; and why is this feeling, in spite of reason, ineradicable in mankind? Because men in their most secret hearts, that part of them which more than any other still preserves the original form of their first nature, have ever believed that their lives lie at no one's disposal, save in that of necessity alone which, with its iron sceptre, rules the universe.

What should men think when they see wise magistrates and grave priests of justice with calm indifference causing a criminal to be dragged by their slow procedure to death; or when they see a judge, whilst a miserable wretch in the convulsions of his last agonies is awaiting the fatal blow, pass away coldly and unfeelingly, perhaps even with a secret satisfaction in his authority, to enjoy the comforts and pleasures of life? "Ah," they will say, "these laws are but the pretexts of force, and the studied cruel formalities of justice are but a conventional language, used for the purpose of immolating us with greater safety, like victims destined in sacrifice to the insatiable idol of tyranny. That assassination which they preach to us as so terrible a misdeed we see nevertheless employed by them without either scruple or passion. Let us profit by the example. A violent death seemed to us a terrible thing in the descriptions of it that were made to us, but we see it is a matter of a moment. How much less terrible will it be for a man who, not expecting it, is spared all that there is of painful in it."

Such are the fatal arguments employed, if not clearly, at least vaguely, by men disposed to crimes among whom, as we have seen, the abuse of religion is more potent than religion itself.

If I am confronted with the example of almost all ages and almost all nations who have inflicted the punishment of death upon some crimes, I will reply, that the example avails nothing before truth, against which there is no prescription of time; and that the history of mankind conveys to us the idea of an immense sea of errors, among which a few truths, confusedly and at long intervals, float on the surface. Human sacrifices were once common to almost all nations, yet who for that reason will dare defend them? That some few states, and for a short time only, should have abstained from inflicting death, rather favours my argument than otherwise, because such a fact is in keeping with the lot of all great truths, whose duration is but as of a lightning flash in comparison with the long and darksome night that envelopes mankind. That happy time has not yet arrived when truth, as error has hitherto done, shall belong to the majority of men; and from this universal law of the reign of error those truths alone have hitherto been exempt, which supreme wisdom has seen fit to distinguish from others, by making them the subject of a special revelation.

The voice of a philosopher is too feeble against the noise and cries of so many followers of blind custom, but the few wise men scattered over the face of the earth will respond to me from their inmost hearts; and, amid the many obstacles that keep it from a monarch, should truth perchance arrive in spite of him at his throne, let him know that it comes there attended by the secret wishes of all men; let him know that before his praises the bloody fame of conquerors will be silenced, and that posterity, which is just, will assign him the foremost place among the pacific triumphs of a Titus, an Antoninus, or a Trajan.

Happy were humanity, if laws were now dictated to it for the first time, when we see on the thrones of Europe beneficent monarchs, men who encourage the virtues of peace, the sciences and the arts, who are fathers to their people, who are crowned citizens, and the increase of whose authority forms the happiness of their subjects, because it removes that intermediate despotism, more cruel because less secure, by which the people's wishes, always sincere, and always attended to when they can reach the throne, have been usually intercepted and suppressed. If they, I say suffer the ancient laws to exist, it is owing to the infinite difficulties of removing from errors the revered rust of many ages; which is a reason for enlightened citizens to desire with all the greater ardour the continual increase of their authority.

JEREMY BENTHAM (1748–1832)

The Rationale of Punishment

DEFINITIONS AND DISTINCTIONS

To afford a clear apprehension of the subject of the following work, which subject is Punishment, it is necessary that what punishment *is,* and what punishment *is not*, should be clearly understood. For this purpose it will be proper to distinguish it from those objects with which it is in danger of being confounded, and also to point out the different shapes which it may assume.

Punishment, whatever shape it may assume, is an evil. The matter of *evil*, therefore, is the sort of matter here in question: the matter of evil in almost all the shapes of which it is susceptible. In considering this matter, two objects, constant accompaniments one to the other, will require to be distinguished, viz. 1. The act by which the evil is considered as being produced; and, 2. What is considered as being the result of that same act, the evil itself which is thus produced.

The English language affords but one single-worded appellative in common use for designating both these objects, viz. *Punishment*.

Punishment may be defined—an evil resulting to an individual from the direct intention of another, on account of some act that

The selection is from Jeremy Bentham, "Principles of Penal Law," in *The Works of Jeremy Bentham*, ed. John Bowring (Edinburgh: William Tait, 1843).

appears to have been done, or omitted. The propriety of this definition will appear, and its use be manifested, by taking it to pieces, and examining its several constituent parts.

Punishment, then, is an *evil*—that is, a physical evil; either a pain, or a loss of pleasure, or else of that situation or condition of the party affected, which is the immediate cause of such pain or loss of pleasure. It is an evil resulting from the *direct* intention of another. It is not punishment, if it be obliquely intentional on the part of the person from whose agency it results, but an evil of some other nature, but which, however, is not in all cases distinguished by a specific name.

It is an evil resulting to a person from the direct intention of another, *on account of* some act that has been done or omitted. An evil resulting to an individual, although it be from the direct intention of another, if it be not on account of some act that has been done or omitted, is not a punishment. If, out of *wantonness*, for the sake of *sport*, or out of *ill-will*, resulting from an *antipathy* you entertain against a man's person, without having any particular act of his to ground it upon, you do him a mischief, the evil produced in this case is what nobody would understand to come under the name of punishment.

But so it be on account of some act that has been done, it matters not by whom the act was done. The most common case is for the act to have been done by the same person by whom the evil is suffered. But the evil may light upon a different person, and still bear the name of punishment. In such case it may be styled punishment *in alienam personam*, in contradistinction to the more common case in which it may be styled punishment *in propriam personam*. Whether the act be ultimately or only mediately intentional, it may, consistently enough with common usage, bear the name of punishment; though, according as it was in the one or other way that the intention happened to regard it, the act will assume a different name, as we shall have occasion to mention presently.

It must be on account of some act that at least *appears* to have been done; but whether such an act as appears to have been done, or any act actually was done, is not material.

By the denomination thus given to the act, by the word punishment, taken by itself, no limitation is put to the description of the person of the agent; but on the occasion of the present work, this person is all along considered as a person invested for this purpose with the authority of the state; a legislator appointing the species of evil to be inflicted in a species of case; or a judge appointing the individual lot of evil to be inflicted in this or that individual case.

Vengeance, antipathy, amendment, disablement, determent, self-defense, self-preservation, safe custody, restraint, compulsion, torture, compensation in the sense in which it means a particular mode of satisfaction for injury or damage—burthen in any such phrase as that of imposition of a burthen, and taxation: by all these several words, ideas are presented which will require in each instance to be compared, and in most instances to be distinguished from the ideas presented by the word *punishment.*

Take whatever portion of the matter of evil is upon the carpet: whether the term punishment shall or shall not with propriety be applied depends upon the position in which the actual result stands with reference to the time in which the *will* or intention of the agent acts.

Intention or unintentional: if intentional, directly or indirectly, or, to use another word, collaterally intentional; if directly, ultimately, or but mediately intentional, such are the modifications which the matter of evil may be considered as receiving, when considered in the character of an object to which the will or intention turns itself.

In some cases, the man in power, or some person or persons, having, as he supposes, received, at the hands of some person or other, evil in some shape or other, the object which he has in view, in the affliction of the evil in question, is an enjoyment of a certain kind, which he derives, or expects to derive, from the contemplation of the evil thus sustained. In this case, the act in question is termed an act of *vengeance.*

So far as this, and this alone, is his object, this evil thus produced is not only directly but ultimately intentional.

Whether in the character of a sole object, a result of this nature be a fit object for the man in power to propose to himself, is indeed a very important question, but one which has no place here: punishment, by being misapplied, is not the less punishment.

Laying out of the above case the supposed antecedent evil, you have no longer an act of vengeance, but an act performed for the mere gratification of *antipathy.* But by the supposition having for its author or agent the legislator or the judge, it is still not the less an act of punishment.

Of the cases in which the act productive of the evil, intentionally produced by the hand of power, is termed an act of punishment, the most common class is that which is composed of those in which, on the part of the agent, the evil thus produced is, though intentional, and even directly intentional, yet not ultimately, but only mediately intentional.

In this case, the ultimately intentional object—the object in relation to which the act of punishment is intended to minister in the character of a means to an end—may be either an act of the negative or the positive cast.

When the act to which the punishment is annexed is of the positive cast, the ultimately intentional object aimed at by the act of punishment is of the opposite cast; and so, when the offence is negative, the result, the production of which is aimed at by the punishment, is positive.

If the offence be of the positive cast, then come the following string of appellatives, expressive of the results, the production of which is in different ways aimed at, viz. 1. Amendment or reformation; 2. Disablement; 3. Determent; 4. Self-defence; 5. Self-preservation; 6. Safe custody; and 7. Restraint.

If the offence be of the negative cast, then comes another string of appellatives, expressive, as above, of the results aimed at, viz. 1. Compulsion or restraint; 2. Torture; 3. Compensation, in the sense in which it is equivalent to *satisfaction*, rendered in consideration of injury resulting from an offence, or in consideration of damage produced without intentional injury; 4. Taxation.

Whether the result aimed at be of the negative or positive cast, the terms, coercion, obligation, burthen, or the phrase *imposition* of a burthen, are competent to the designation of it.

Amendment, or reformation, and *disablement*, are words expressive of the result aimed at, in so far as the conduct of the supposed delinquent is concerned. In the case of *amendment* or *reformation*, the obnoxious act is regarded as being of such a nature, that by a single instance of its being committed, such a degree of disorder in the moral constitution is indicated, as requires a general change to remove it, and bring the patient to a state of ordinary purity.

Few, if any, offences of the negative class being to be found which exhibit any such degree of malignity,—the use of the terms amendment and reformation is nearly confined to the case when the obnoxious act, the prevention of which is the ultimate end of the punishment, is of the positive kind.

Disablement is a term for which, with reference to an act of the negative kind, a place is hardly to be found. Doing nothing is a sort of offence to which every man is so competent, that all endeavours on the part of government to disable a man from committing it may be set at defiance.

Determent is a result equally applicable to the case either of a positive or negative offence. It is moreover equally applicable to the situation of the already-punished delinquent, and that of other persons at large; nor does it involve, on the part of the punished delinquent, the supposition of any such general disorder as is implied by the words *amendment* or *reformation*.

When the ultimately intentional result is amendment or reformation, it is by the impression made by the action of the evil on the will of the offender that, in so far as it is produced, the result is considered as being produced. In this case, the *act of punishment* is also termed an act of *correction*.

When the ultimately intentional result is disablement, it is by depriving the offender of the power of committing obnoxious acts of the like description, that, in so far as it is produced, the result is considered as being produced. In this case, the course taken to produce the result may either be such the nature of which is to produce it only for a time, as is done by temporary imprisonment, confinement, or deportation; or for ever, as would in some cases be done by mutilation.

In so far as by the act of punishment exercised on the delinquent, other persons at large are considered as deterred from the commission of acts of the like obnoxious description, and the act of punishment is in consequence considered as endued with the quality of *determent*; it is by the impression made on the will of those persons, an impression made in this case not by the act itself, but by the idea of it, accompanied with the eventual expectation of a similar *evil*, as about to be eventually produced in their own instances, that the ultimately intentional result is considered as produced; and in this case it is also said to be produced by the *example*, or by the force of *example*.

Between self-defence and punishment, the relation is of this sort, viz. that to the same act which ministers to the one of those purposes, it may happen to minister to the other. This coincidence may have place in either of two ways: an act which has self-defence for its direct object and result, may have punishment for its collateral result; or an act which has punishment for its direct object and result, may have self-defence for its collateral result.

In repelling a personal assault, it may happen to an individual, intentionally or unintentionally, to inflict on the assailant a suffering by any amount greater than that of any which by the assault, was inflicted on himself: if unintentionally, self-defence was not only the sole ultimately intentional, but the sole intentional result: but the suffering of the assailant, though not the collaterally intentional, was not in effect less truly the collateral result.

On the other hand, in inflicting punishment on a delinquent, it may happen to the *man in authority* to be exercising on his own behalf an act of *self-defence;* in regard to all offences, such as *rebellion* and *treason,* which have for their object or their effect the subversion of the government, or the weakening of its powers. But it is only in reference to such offences that an act of punishment can, with reference to the constituted authorities, be with propriety called an act of self-defence.

But if in lieu of the constituted authorities, the members of the community at large be considered as the persons by whom the punishment is inflicted; then is all punishment an act of *self-defence*, in relation to the particular species of evil with which the offence thus punished is pregnant: an act tending to defend the community against offences of the sort in question, with their attendant evils, viz. by means of reformation, disablement, and determent, one or more of them as above.

In the signification of the word *self-defence*, it is implied that the evil against which the party is endeavouring to guard himself has, for its cause, an act done by some sentient being, with the intention of producing that same evil.

The word self-preservation is alike applicable, whatsoever be the source or quarter from which the evil is considered as about to come. In so far, therefore, as the act of punishment is with propriety capable of being termed an act of self-defence, it is, with the same propriety, capable of being termed an act of *self-preservation.*

Between safe custody and punishment, the relation is of this sort: —To one and the same operation, or factitious state of things, it may happen to be productive of both of these effects. But in the instance of the same individual, it is only to a limited degree that there can be a sufficient reason for making provision for both at the same time.

To a considerable extent, imprisonment with propriety may be and every where is applied, under the name and to the purpose of punishment. In this case, safe custody is in part the same thing with the intended punishment itself; in part, a concomitant necessary to the existence and continuance of whatsoever inflictions it may be deemed proper to add to those which are inseparable from the safe custody itself.

But in another case, imprisonment, or an infliction of the same name, at least, as that which is employed as above, for the purpose of punishment, is to a great extent administered ultimately for the purpose of eventual forthcomingness, and mediately for the purpose of safe custody, though no such thing as punishment is, or, at least, ought to be intended, because no ground for punishment has as yet been, and perhaps never may be, established.

Between restraint and punishment, the relation is of this sort. In some shape or other, restraint is the *directly* intentional result of every prohibitive law. The evil, whatever it be, that constitutes an inseparable accompaniment of the state thus denominated, is a collaterally intentional result of that same law. The evil of the restraint may be very moderate; but still, by every general prohibitive law, evil in some shape or other, in some quantity or other, must come.

At the same time, restraint is, in a great variety of shapes, capable of being employed in the character of a punishment. As a punishment, restraint is not incapable of being employed for the purpose of securing submission to restraint. But in this case, the coincidence is but verbal, and arises from the generality of the word restraint. In the character of a punishment, we cannot employ the restraint collaterally resulting from the negative act, the production of which is the object of the prohibition in the character of the eventual punishment, to secure obedience to that same prohibitive law. To prevent a man from stealing, a law threatening to prevent him from stealing, would be but an indifferent resource. To secure, by means of eventual punishment, restraint in this shape, you must employ restraint in some other shape; for example, the restraint attached to imprisonment.

Between compulsion and punishment, the relation is of this sort. In the case of compulsion, as in the case of restraint, the act in question is the act which is regarded as the efficient cause of the evil, the prevention of which is the ultimate object of the act of punishment. What *restraint* is, in the case when the act in question is of the positive cast, *compulsion* is, in the case when the act is of the negative cast.

Between torture and punishment, the relation is of this sort. The term torture is employed, and perhaps with nearly equal frequency, in two different senses. In its most extended sense, it is employed to designate pain, especially pain of body, when considered as being intense in its degree, and this without reference to the cause by which it is produced.

In its more restricted sense, being that in which it is most apt to be employed, when considered as the result of law, it is employed to signify pain of body in its degree intense as above, employed in due course of law, or, at any rate, by the hand of power, in the character of an instrument of compulsion.

But the account given of it, when employed in this sense, wants much, as yet, of being complete. The compulsion, or constraint, may be produced which is denounced.

By this circumstance, torture stands distinguished not only from compulsion itself, but from any lot of punishment considered as applied to the purpose of compulsion in the ordinary mode.

The notion of torture is not included in a punishment attached to an act of disobedience, of which no remission is allowed; but suppose the same lot of pain attached to the same offence, with power to remit any part of it, in case of, and immediately upon compliance with the requisition of the law, and here the punishment comes under the notion and denomination of torture.

Between compensation, or satisfaction and punishment, the relation is of this sort: in all cases, if compensation be the end in view, so far as concerns pecuniary compensation, by whatsoever is done for the purpose of compensation, the effect of pecuniary punishment is produced likewise. More suffering, however, will in general be produced by what is taken for the purpose of compensation, than if the same amount were taken for the purpose of punishment: it will be accompanied by the regret produced by the idea of the advantage not only reaped by an adversary, but reaped at one's own expense.

On the other hand, by the contemplation of the suffering inflicted by punishment on the delinquents, good in the shape of compensation, or say vindictive satisfaction, is administered to the party injured.

Between taxation and punishment of the pecuniary kind, for it is only in this form that they can be compared, the relation is of this sort; they both consist in the application of compulsion to the extracting out of the pocket in question a certain sum; the difference between them consists in the end in view. In the case of taxation, the object is the obtainment of a certain sum; in the case of punishment, the object is the prevention of the obnoxious act, to the commission of which the obligation of paying the money is attached in the character of a punishment. In the case of taxation, the wish of the legislator is, that the money may be paid; and, consequently, if it be to the performance of a certain act that the obligation of paying the money is annexed, his wish is that the act may be performed.

As in the two cases the result intended is opposite, the actual results are accordingly incompatible, in so far as either result is obtained the other is missed. Whether the effect of any given law shall be taxation, or effectual prohibition, depends, in the instance of each individual, upon the value, which, in the case in question, he is called upon to pay, compared with the value in his estimation of the advantage which stands annexed to the exercise of the act; if the advantage appear the greater, he pays the money and exercises the act; if the value of the money to be eventually paid appear the greater, he obeys the prohibitory law, and abstains from the performance of the act.

When the face assumed by any law is that of a prohibition, if the penalty be nothing but pecuniary and the amount is fixed, while the profits of the offence are variable, the probability is, that in many instances the penalty, even if levied, which could not be without detection, prosecution, and conviction, would but operate as a taxed licence.

This circumstance is so obvious, that one would have thought it could not have been overlooked; had it, however, been observed with any tolerable steadiness in England, the law of that country would wear a face widely different from that which it wears at present.

In relation to all these several results or concomitants of punishment, one observation useful to be borne in mind, that it may operate as a preservative against much error, is—that it is but in very few, if any of these instances, that from the name by which the object is here designated, any true judgment can be formed on any such question as whether and how far the object is a fit object of pursuit or aim in the character of an end.

Take any one of them for example,—if taken by itself that object be of the nature of good, yet, in the first place, that good may be in any degree minute; in the next place, to the quantity of evil with which it may happen to it to be followed, there are no limits: and thus it is that false must be that proposition, which, without leaving room for exceptions, should pronounce the attainment of that object to be universally an end fit to be aimed at, whether through the intervention of punishment, or any other means; and conversely.

Of the distinctions here pointed out between punishment and the several objects that are of kin to it, five distinguishable practical uses may be made.

1. They may serve as a memento to the legislator, to see on every occasion, that for the several objects which may have place, and present a demand for legislative provision, due and adequate provision is accordingly made.

2. To preserve him from the delusion which would have place, wheresoever it happens that by one and the same lot of evil, due and adequate provision may be made for two or more of these purposes, if by the difference of their respective denominations, he were led to give birth to two or more lots of evil for the purpose of effecting the good, for the effectuation of which one of them would suffice.

3. That in each instance, in comparing the end he has in view with the means which he proposes to employ for the attainment of it, the view he takes of such proposed means may be sufficiently clear, correct, and complete, to enable him to form a correct judgment of the

mode and degree in which they promise to be conducive to the attainment of the end.

4. That he may be upon his guard against that sort of rhetorical artifice which operates by substituting for the proper name of the object or result in question, according to the purpose in view, the name of some other object or result, the name of which is either more or less popular than the proper one.

5. That while in pursuit of any one of these objects, in the character of an *end*, he employs such means as to his conception appear conducive to that end, he may be correctly and completely aware of any tendency which such arrangements may have to be conducive or obstructive, with reference to any other of these same ends. . . .

MEASURE OF PUNISHMENT

" . . . . . . *Adsit*
Regula, peccatis quae poenas irroget aequas,
Ne scutica dignum, horribili sectere flagello."

HOR. *L.* I. *Sat.* iii.

Establish a proportion between crimes and punishments, has been said by Montesquieu, Beccaria, and many others. The maxim is, without doubt, a good one; but whilst it is thus confined to general terms, it must be confessed it is more oracular than instructive. Nothing has been accomplished, till wherein this proportion consists has been explained, and the rules have been laid down by which it may be determined that a certain measure of punishment ought to be applied to a certain crime.

Punishments may be too small or too great; and there are reasons for not making them too small, as well as for not making them too great. The terms *minimum* and *maximum* may serve to mark the two extremes of this question, which require equal attention.

With a view of marking out the limits of punishment on the side of the first of these extremes, we may lay it down as a rule—

RULE I. That the value of the punishment must not be less, in any case, than what is sufficient to outweigh that of the profit of the offence.

By the profit of the crime, must be understood not only pecuniary profit, but every advantage, real or apparent, which has operated as a motive to the commission of the crime.

The profit of the crime is the force which urges a man to delinquency: the pain of the punishment is the force employed to restrain him from it. If the first of these forces be the greater, the crime will be committed; if the second, the crime will not be committed. If, then, a man, having reaped the profit of a crime, and undergone the punishment, finds the former more than equivalent to the latter, he will go on offending for ever; there is nothing to restrain him. If those, also, who behold him, reckon that the balance of gain is in favour of the delinquent, the punishment will be useless for the purposes of example.

The Anglo-Saxon laws, which fixed a price upon the lives of men —200 shillings for the murder of a peasant, six times as much for that of a nobleman, and thirty-six times as much for that of the king—evidently transgressed against this rule. In a great number of cases, the punishment would appear nothing, compared with the profit of the crime.

The same error is committed whenever a punishment is established which reaches only to a certain fixed point, which the advantage of the crime may surpass.

Authors of celebrity have been found desirous of establishing a rule precisely the reverse: they have said, that the greatness of temptation is a reason for lessening the punishment; because it lessens the fault; because the more powerful the seduction, the less reason is there for concluding that the offender is depraved. Those, therefore, who are overcome, in this case, naturally inspire us with commiseration.

This may all be very true, and yet afford no reason for departing from the rule. That it may prove effectual, the punishment must be more dreaded than the profit of the crime desired. Besides, an inefficacious punishment is doubly mischievous;—mischievous to the public, since it permits the crime to be committed,—mischievous to the delinquent, since the punishment inflicted upon him is just so much misery in waste. What should we say to the surgeon, who, that he might save his patient a small degree of pain, should only half cure him? What should we think of his humanity, if he should add to his disease the torment of a useless operation?

It is therefore desirable that punishment should correspond to every degree of temptation; at the same time, the power of mitigation might be reserved in those cases where the nature of the temptation itself indicates the absence of confirmed depravity, or the possession of benevolence—as might be the case should a father commit a theft that he might supply his starving family with bread.

RULE II. *The greater the mischief of the offence, the greater is the expense it may be worth while to be at, in the way of punishment.*

This rule is so obvious in itself, that to say any thing in proof of it would be needless; but how few are the instances in which it has been observed? It is not long since that women were condemned to be burnt alive for uttering bad money. The punishment of death is still lavished on a multitude of offences of the least mischievous description. The punishment of burning is still in use in many countries for offences which might safely be left to the restraint of the moral sanction. If it can be worth while to be at the expense of so terrible a punishment as that of burning alive, it ought to be reserved for murder or incendiarism.

It will be said, perhaps, that the intention of legislators has always been to follow this rule, but that their opinions, as well as those of the people, have fluctuated respecting the relative magnitude and nature of crimes. At one period, witchcraft was regarded as the most mischievous offence. Sorcerers, who sold their souls to the devil, were objects of abhorrence. A heretic, the enemy of the Almighty, drew down divine wrath upon a whole kingdom. To steal property consecrated to divine uses was an offence of a more malignant nature than ordinary theft, the crime being directed against the Divinity. A false estimate being made of these crimes, an undue measure of punishment was applied to them.

RULE III. *When two offences come in competition, the punishment for the greater offence must be sufficient to induce a man to prefer the less.*

Two offences may be said to be in competition, when it is in the power of an individual to commit both. When thieves break into a house, they may execute their purpose in different manners: by simply stealing, by theft accompanied with bodily injury, or murder, or incendiarism. If the punishment is the same for simple theft, as for theft and murder, you give the thieves a motive for committing murder, because this crime adds to the facility of committing the former, and the chance of impunity when it is committed.

The great inconvenience resulting from the infliction of great punishments for small offences, is, that the power of increasing them in proportion to the magnitude of the offence is thereby lost.

RULE IV. *The punishment should be adjusted in such manner to each particular offence, that for every part of the mischief there may be a motive to restrain the offender from giving birth to it.*

Thus, for example, in adjusting the punishment for stealing a sum of money, let the magnitude of the punishment be determined by the amount of the sum stolen. If for stealing ten shillings an offender is punished no more than for stealing five, the stealing of the remaining five of those ten shillings is an offence for which there is no punishment at all.

The last object is, whatever mischief is guarded against, to guard against it at as cheap a rate as possible; therefore—

RULE V. *The punishment ought in no case to be more than what is necessary to bring it into conformity with the rules here given.*

RULE VI. *That the quantity of punishment actually inflicted on each individual offender may correspond to the quantity intended for similar offenders in general, the several circumstances influencing sensibility ought always to be taken into the account.*

The same *nominal* punishment is not, for different individuals, the same *real* punishment. Let the punishment in question be a fine: the sum that would not be felt by a rich man, would be ruin to a poor one. The same ignominious punishment that would fix an indelible stigma upon a man of a certain rank, would not affect a man of a lower rank. The same imprisonment that would be ruin to a man of business, death to an old man, and destruction of reputation to a woman, would be as nothing, or next to nothing, to persons placed in other circumstances.

The law may, by anticipation, provide that such or such a degree of mitigation shall be made in the amount of the punishment, in consideration of such or such circumstances influencing the sensibility of the patient; such as age, sex, rank, &c. But in these cases, considerable latitude must be left to the judge.

Of the above rules of proportion, the four first may serve to mark out the limits on the minimum side—the limits *below* which a punishment ought not to be diminished; the fifth will mark out the limits on the maximum side—the limits above which it ought not to be increased.

The minimum of punishment is more clearly marked than its maximum. What is *too little* is more clearly observed than what is *too much*. What is not sufficient is easily seen, but it is not possible so exactly to distinguish an excess: an approximation only can be attained. The irregularities in the force of temptations compel the legislator to increase his punishments, till they are not merely sufficient to restrain the ordinary desires of men, but also the violence of their desires when unusually excited.

The greatest danger lies in an error on the minimum side, because in this case the punishment is inefficacious; but this error is least likely to occur, a slight degree of attention sufficing for its escape; and when it does exist, it is at the same time clear and manifest, and easy to be remedied. An error on the maximum side, on the contrary, is that to which legislators and men in general are naturally inclined: antipathy, or a want of compassion for individuals who are represented as dangerous and vile, pushes them onward to an undue severity. It is on this side, therefore, that we should take the most precautions, as on this side there has been shown the greatest disposition to err.

By way of supplement and explanation to the first rule, and to make sure of giving to the punishment the superiority over the offence, the three following rules may be laid down:—

RULE VII. *That the value of the punishment may outweigh the profit of the offence, it must be increased in point of magnitude, in proportion as it falls short in point of certainty.*

RULE VIII. *Punishment must be further increased in point of magnitude, in proportion as it falls short of proximity.*

The profit of a crime is commonly more certain than its punishment; or, what amounts to the same thing, appears so to the offender. It is generally more immediate: the temptation to offend is present; the punishment is at a distance. Hence there are two circumstances which weaken the effect of punishment, its *uncertainty* and its *distance*. . . .

It is therefore true, that the more the certainty of punishment can be augmented, the more it may be diminished in amount. This is one advantage resulting from simplicity of legislation, and excellence of legal procedure.

For the same reason, it is necessary that the punishment should be as near, in point of time, to the crime as possible; because its impression upon the minds of men is weakened by distance; and because this distance adds to the uncertainty of its infliction, by affording fresh chances of escape.

RULE IX. *When the act is conclusively indicative of a habit, such an increase must be given to the punishment as may enable it to outweigh the profit, not only of the individual offence, but of such other like offences as are likely to have been committed with impunity by the same offender.*

Severe as this conjectural calculation may appear, it is absolutely necessary in some cases. Of this kind are fraudulent crimes; using false weights or measures, and issuing base coin. If the coiner was only punished according to the value of the single crime of which he is convicted, his fraudulent practice would, upon the whole, be a lucrative one. Punishment would therefore be inefficacious, if it did not bear a proportion to the total gain which may be supposed to have been derived not from one particular act, but from a train of actions of the same kind.

There may be a few other circumstances or considerations which may influence, in some small degree, the demand for punishment; but as the propriety of these is either not so demonstrable, or not so constant, or the application of them not so determinate, as that of the foregoing, it may be doubted whether they are worth putting on a level with the others.

RULE X. *When a punishment, which in point of quality is particularly well calculated to answer its intention, cannot exist in less than a certain quantity, it may sometimes be of use, for the sake of employing it, to stretch a little beyond that quantity which, on other accounts, would be strictly necessary.*

RULE XI. *In particular, this may be the case where the punishment proposed is of such a nature as to be particularly well calculated to answer the purpose of a moral lesson.*

RULE XII. *In adjusting the quantum of punishment, the circumstances by which all punishment may be rendered unprofitable ought to be attended to.*

And lastly, as too great a nicety in establishing proportions between punishment and crime would tend to defeat its own object, by rendering the whole matter too complex, we may add—

RULE XIII. *Among provisions designated to perfect the proportion between punishments and offences, if any occur which by their own particular good effects would not make up for the harm they would do by adding to the intricacy of the code, they should be omitted.*

The observation of rules of proportion between crimes and punishments has been objected to as useless, because they seem to suppose, that a spirit of calculation has place among the passions of men who, it is said, never calculate. But dogmatic as this proposition is, it is altogether false. In matters of importance, every one calculates. Each individual calculates with more or less correctness, according to the degrees of his information, and the power of the motives which actuate him; but all calculate. It would be hard to say that a madman does not calculate. Happily, the passion of cupidity, which on account of its power, its constancy, and its extent, is most formidable to society, is the passion which is most given to calculation. This, therefore, will be more successfully combated, the more carefully the law turns the balance of profit against it.

F. H. BRADLEY (1846–1924)

Some Remarks on Punishment

Darwinism, we may presume, should modify the view which we take of punishment. This does not mean that any of our old doctrines need quite be given up. The educational, the deterrent, and the retributive view may each retain, we may rather presume, a certain value. But all of these, it seems, must be in part superseded. They must be made subordinate to another and a higher law,—what we may call the principle of social surgery. The right and the duty of the organism to suppress its undesirable growths is the idea of punishment directly suggested by Darwinism. It is an old doctrine which has but gained fresh meaning and force. And its principle is the old principle and the one ground for any sound theory of punishment. The moral supremacy of the community, its unrestricted right to deal with its members, is the sole basis on which rational punishment can rest. . . .

There is a way of thinking and feeling about punishment, not uncommon in our days, which exhibits a high degree of inconsistency. It more or less explicitly accepts the doctrine that crime (all of it or some of it) is mere disease. Or, rather, crime is taken as a natural deviation from the type. And rightly from this ground a protest is made against such unwilled defects being imputed and judged of morally. Now, with this protest no one can fail more or less to sympathize. But here is the beginning of blind and thoughtless confusion. For, protesting against the principle of the retributive view, or at least partially against its application, and thus, at least in effect, withdrawing part of life from that principle's sway, these moral innovators stand at the same time on its absolute supremacy. Justice on its positive side is restricted, but on its negative side is to retain unlimited sovereignty. Criminals, some or all, are diseased, and are therefore innocent, and the innocent, of course, are by justice proclaimed to be sacred. They are to enjoy therefore that treatment which was assigned to mere disease, when mere disease was not taken to include and cover crime. And surely such an attitude and such a claim are most inconsistent. This insane murderer, we may hear it said, is not to be destroyed. Justice is the assignment of benefit and injury according to desert; but this man is not a moral agent, and hence it

The selection is from F. H. Bradley, "Some Remarks on Punishment," *International Journal of Ethics*, April, 1894.

is unjust to injure him. But, if he is not a moral agent, I reply, surely what follows is that justice is indifferent to his case. What is just or unjust has surely nothing to do with our disposal of his destiny. And hence, so long only as we do not pretend retributively to punish him, we may cut him off, if that seems best for the general good. For justice, we have found, is but a subordinate and inferior principle. It can hear no appeal from the tribunal of the common welfare. And to take a view of crime which seems to abolish all accountability, to make in this way everywhere impossible any application of strict justice, and then in the name of justice to claim protection for ravishers and murderers, seems really preposterous. The claim is rational only as an appeal to us to modify our principles. It is a confused request to us in the name of justice to dethrone justice. But when justice (as it must be) is dethroned, and when Darwinism (as it will be) is listened to, there will be a favourable hearing for the claims of ethical surgery. And we may now dismiss both forms of the retributive view.

But against the unlimited right of the moral organism to dispose of its members is there anything to be set? There is nothing, so far as I see, but superstition and prejudice. The idea that justice is paramount, that, with the individual, gain or loss must correspond to desert, and that, without this, the Universe has somehow broken down—this popular idea is, after all, the merest prejudice. It seems to rest either on the assumption that there is no principle above justice, or on the common error as to the absolute validity of principles. But the necessary collision both of rights and duties, their mere conditional force, and the subordination of all else to the one principle of general welfare, are truths not to be refuted. And, dwelling no more on this crude popular superstition about justice, I will pass on to consider an opposite error. There is a belief that (not animal, but) human life is sacred. The former prejudice as to justice is, I suppose, anti-Christian; but the sacredness of human life seems largely a Christian idea. And I exhibited the root of this error in a former discussion.[1] The individual in the next world has an infinite value; the things of this world, our human ends and interests, are all alike counted worthless, and the rights and duties founded on these interests, of course, bodily disappear. The good of the whole, worthless in itself, can therefore confer no right to interfere with its members; and each individual, on the other side, is, to so speak, the preserve of Providence. Violence, immoral in itself, or, at least, immoral for us men, is forbidden us, and is left in the hands of the Deity.

[1] Unpublished. *Eds.*

Now, to criticise this view, otherwise than by stating it, seems here not necessary. Once admit that life in this world is an end in itself, and the pure Christian doctrine is at once uprooted. For, measured by that end and standard, individuals have unequal worth, and the value of each individual is but relative, and in no case infinite. And the community, we have seen, is itself its own Providence, and therefore against its rights the individual is not sacred. With this we may pass from the Christian error, and may proceed to consider a fresh form of delusion. The individual may be taken, as such, to have positive and negative rights, rights not derived from another world, but still inhering in him independent of his place in the community. But both the individual and his rights, in this sense, certainly do not belong to our human world, and hence, unless they exist in some other world, they are existent nowhere. They are survivals, in short, from obsolete metaphysics, and about their vital principle I do not intend to speak further. But the rights of these supposed individuals, once placed in a community, must necessarily collide, and all attempts to avoid this collision are idle. And to find a rational ground on which mutual interference is here legitimate and there unlawful, is once more impossible. This question is one which called for discussion a century ago, but at the present time it can be considered a question no longer. The rights of the individual are, in short, to-day not worth serious criticism.

What is the result which, so far, we have gained? The welfare of the community is the end and is the ultimate standard. And over its members the right of the moral organism is absolute. Its duty and its right is to dispose of these members as seems to it best. Its right and duty is, in brief, to be a Providence to itself. And what went counter to this doctrine we found to be mere superstition. . . .

On another planet, if you like, it may all be quite otherwise. But on our planet, so far as we know, some hardship is inevitable. And if we are to play at Providence, as we must, then we must by commission or by neglect ourselves inflict hardship. Surely, then, the least cruel, the most merciful course of conduct—the best means in our power to diminish suffering—is to regard nothing but the conditions of general advantage. And as to these conditions Darwinism offers a positive doctrine. It teaches, in a word, the necessity of constant selection. It insists that the way to improve—the way even not to degenerate—is on the whole unchanging. That way consists in the destruction of worse varieties, or at least in the hinderance of such varieties from reproduction. Merely bring the fittest in each generation to the front—do nothing to secure that the next generation shall come from these fittest

—and, in short, you are trifling with your mission as Providence. This is what Darwinism teaches, and it adds that society at present sins grossly by commission as well as by neglect. Not content with inaction, society works directly in the very interest of evil. It secures artificially the maintenance and the propagation of the unfit, while the fit are even injured in order to contribute to this general injury. And against such ruinous perversity Darwinism protests. It insists on the necessity of social amputation. The wholesale confinement, or, again, the mutilation of worse specimens, is not a satisfactory substitute. For it seems wrong to load the community with the useless burden of these lives, and, in the second place, there is a consideration too often ignored. To maintain in existence a creature, while depriving that creature of the conditions of happiness, is surely to inflict on it the direst suffering. Now, to pass such a sentence worse than death would, of course, be right if it were necessary and an ultimate resort. But in any other case it would be the extreme of indefensible cruelty. To remove from the social organism, as it were, by ligature a member sentient and miserably conscious through life of its own protracted dying, seems a most barbarous device. And by comparison clearly there is more kindness and mercy in the knife. . . .

The real question is, on which side lies the balance of harm? Measured by the good of the community, is moral surgery the less or the greater of two evils? We have to choose, in brief, between the complex results of alternative courses, and I do not propose to attempt a detailed estimate. I wish not to advocate any result to which my mind has been led, so much as to press for a serious consideration of the problem. I am satisfied if I have shown that the claim of moral surgery, however inconvenient it may be, cannot at least be ignored. . . .[2]

But, for myself as a bystander, there are some feelings which I am not careful to hide. I am oppressed by the ineffectual cruelty of our imprisonments. I am disgusted at the inviolable sanctity of the noxious lunatic. The right of the individual to spawn without restriction his

[2] It is no good answer to urge that, after all, we have progressed so far in spite of neglect. For the conditions certainly have not remained the same. They are changing every day, and in great part unfavorably. The positive checks to population, in the shape of hardship and disease, acted as a selection of stronger varieties; and these checks every day are lessened. It is far easier now for weak and diseased specimens to survive and to breed. The struggle again, if we retain free trade in reproduction together with protection of the results, is becoming largely a mere struggle between rival fertilities. And from this competition the morally superior more and more refrain. I do not think that in the past such conditions have ever prevailed.

diseased offspring on the community, the duty of the state to rear
wholesale and without limit an unselected progeny—such duties and
rights are to my mind a sheer outrage on Providence. A society that
can endure such things will merit the degeneracy which it courts.
More and more on certain points we seem warned to return in part to
older and to less impracticable principles of conduct. And these are
views of Plato which, to me at least, every day seem less of an anach-
ronism and more of a prophecy.

JOHN J. FORD (1865–1923)

A Defense of Capital Punishment

Is capital punishment lawful? If this question is answered by
sentiment or passion the answer will vary with varying times and
interests.

But what does reason say in the matter? Reason invariably answers "yes." Its argument? The necessity of capital punishment for
the preservation of the public welfare.

If capital punishment is ever necessary for the preservation of the
public welfare, and it is at times necessary for that end, then according
to reason capital punishment is lawful. For then there arises a collision
of rights, and the lesser right must naturally give way to the greater. A
collision arises between the natural right of the individual to the preservation of his own life and the natural right of civil society to its own
preservation. Of the two the latter is clearly the greater right: for the
good of the whole is above the good of the part in the same order of
goods.

"Every part," says St. Thomas, "is referred to the whole as the
imperfect to the perfect, and therefore every part naturally exists for the
whole. And hence we see that if it be expedient for the welfare of
the whole human body that some member should be amputated, as
being rotten and corrupting the other members, the amputation is
praiseworthy and wholesome. But every individual stands to the
whole community as the part to the whole. Therefore, if any man be

The selection is from *Catholic Mind,* March 18, 1915.

dangerous to the community and be corrupting it by any crime, the killing of him for the common good is praiseworthy and wholesome" (Aquinas, *Ethicus*, vol. ii, p. 40).

But mark well. "The slaying of an evildoer is lawful, inasmuch as it is directed to the welfare of the whole community, and therefore appertains to him alone who has charge of the preservation of the community; as the amputation of an unsound limb belongs to the surgeon when the care of the welfare of the whole body has been entrusted to him. Now, the care of the common good is entrusted to rulers having public authority; and therefore to them is it lawful to slay evildoers, not to private individuals" (Aquinas, *Ethicus*, vol. ii, p. 42).

The argument of reason, as you will notice, does not base the right of capital punishment on the mere proportion or equation that must exist between the crime and the punishment. The gravity of the crime must of course be considered, but together with it the necessity of the public welfare. Hence even if there were question of a very grave crime worthy of death, still if such punishment were not necessary for the preservation of the public welfare it should not be inflicted by public authority on the criminal. He should then be corrected by other punishments.

An illustration will confirm the argument of reason. All agree that an innocent man who has taken refuge in a city to escape the death with which he has been threatened by a very powerful foe would be obliged to leave that city, even at the risk of certain death, should that city be besieged on his account and gravely imperiled. All agree, moreover, that were he to refuse to leave, and were he disposed rather to see the city taken and sacked than give himself up to his persecutor, he would render himself guilty against society, and it would be lawful for that city thus endangered to give him over to the enemy to escape extermination. How much more lawful, then, is it for public authority to do a criminal to death if his death is necessary for public security, as often happens, particularly in the case of murder and conspiracy, where the fate of society and the rebellious faction depends for the most part on some leader whose death would wipe out the very name of rebellion.

From what has been said, then, it is plain that if capital punishment is ever necessary for the preservation of the common weal it is lawful. Nor does this way of reasoning proceed on the principle that the end justifies the means. For the slaying of a man is not intrinsically evil in itself, but only inasmuch as it is unjust. Were it evil of itself it would not under any circumstances be allowed. Now, whatever some may hold with regard to the right of killing in a just war, all will certainly admit that it is allowable "to repel by force with the moderation of a blameless defense," and accordingly if necessary even to slay a man in self-defense. But were homicide evil in itself, it could never be allowed.

The principal error of most of those who look upon capital punishment as unlawful is founded on the false theory of the social contract. According to this false theory of Rousseau, the individuals of a country create the State by agreeing to give certain powers to the government. Civil power or authority in this theory is not from God through nature, but from the will of the people. Hence, as no individual has a right over his own life or another's, and except in the case of unjust aggression is never allowed to kill another, so the state, whose limit of power in this theory is the power of the individuals that compose it, may not kill a malefactor save in the very act of aggression. And accordingly capital punishment from this viewpoint is nothing more than legalized murder.

As the false theory of the social contract underlies not only this error about the justice of capital punishment, but all or nearly all the other ethical and political errors of our country, it may be well here to refute that theory briefly. Its absurdity is evident from this reason alone among many that might be given. Even had the founders of civil society made such a contract, of which there is not the slightest memorial, it would not suffice to explain the existence of the obligations by which we are bound in civil society. For either we are bound as citizens by virtue of the contract made by our forefathers, or not. If such an obligation exists, we do not render obedience to ourselves, as Rousseau would have it, but to our forefathers; hence we would be bound by a will not our own—a thing contrary to the very essence of the theory of the social contract. If however, no such obligation exists, then there is no civil authority at all; for that is no authority which everyone is free at any moment to set aside. There can be no true right to command where there is no corresponding duty to obey. Nor can it be said that this consent is obligatory and that it is to be presumed it is given. For then man is not freely made subject to civil authority, as it is clear that a forced consent is not free.

The theory of Rousseau, that man is naturally a savage, perpetually at war with his fellow-man, and that society is an afterthought, something artificial superadded to his nature, is as opposed to historical facts as it is degrading to the human race.

Civil authority, considered in general, does not depend on the consent of men, and is not, as many foolishly imagine, from the people, but from nature. For willy-nilly the people must be ruled by somebody unless they wish the human race to perish. The people may in certain cases choose their form of government and their ruler, but they do not give him what they cannot give: civil power or authority. This is concreted in the people, but not created by the people. Let me illustrate: Two persons live far apart from each other and do not even know each other. There exists between them no actual relation and therefore no actual duty. They meet, and as soon as they meet they are obliged as men to love each other, to help each other, to live according to the laws of humanity. Shall we say that they have created these laws? True, it was of their own accord that they abandoned their solitude, but once they meet they find the laws of humanity formed by the hand of nature. Now civil power or authority is a law of nature; it does not, therefore, depend on the will of the people, though from their associating together flows the actualization of such authority. Nature, or rather the author of nature, God, bids men live in civil society. This is clear from the power of speech, the great former of civil society, and from the many innate desires and needs of the mind, which men cannot attain except in civil society. Civil society, therefore, is natural. But there can be no civil society without someone to govern the wills of all and direct them rightly to the common end. Civil power or authority, therefore, is also natural.

To put the same truth in other words, "Man's natural instinct moves him to live in civil society, for he cannot, if dwelling apart, provide himself with the necessary requirements of life, nor procure the means of developing his mental and moral faculties. Hence it is divinely ordained that he should lead his life—be it family, social or civic—with his fellow-men, amongst whom alone his several wants can be adequately supplied. But as no society can hold together unless someone be over all, directing all to strive earnestly for the common good, every civilized community must have a ruling authority, and this authority, no less than society itself, has its source in nature, and has consequently God for its author. "There is no power but from God" (Leo XIII on the Christian Constitution of States). The right to rule is not necessarily, however, bound up with any special form of government; nor, except in the case of the theocratic form, is the ruler immediately chosen by God.

Civil authority, therefore, comes from nature, and the end of such authority is the preservation of order in the State. Consequently, if for the preservation of order capital punishment is necessary, the right to inflict capital punishment must be comprised in civil authority. For nature never gives the end without the means. Capital punishment then is not legalized murder.

The people are not the whole state. They are but an element, the material element, going to make up the state. That which gives the state its form and being is authority, and that is something distinct from and over and above the multitude. It is a thing of nature, and not of the general will. Authority is certainly in the people, for where there are no people there is no authority; authority is through the people, for the people are the principle of its unity; but authority is not from the people, for the people can neither make nor unmake it. It is something independent of them. All they can do at best is to designate the subject of authority. And so, when after a fair trial a man who has committed a certain grave crime or crimes, and whose death is necessary for the common weal, is sentenced by the judge to die, and is actually put to death by the executioner, no murder is committed by the state. The state is then merely acting in self-defense and using a right given it by the author of nature for a necessary end. And so it is not the case of man killing his fellow-man without authority from God, but it is God the Master of life and death by means of man executing justice. For he (the ruler) is God's minister and beareth not the sword in vain.

II

But is capital punishment ever necessary? There are those who freely grant my major premise, that if capital punishment is ever necessary for the public welfare it is just, but who deny that such necessity ever exists. When asked for their proofs they give the usual amount of sentimentality and sophistry. Leaving out the sentimentality, which is too maudlin to be noticed, let us examine the chief sophisms which they take to be unanswerable arguments.

And first they assert that it is not true that the death penalty inspires more horror in criminals than any other kind of punishment. This gratuitous assertion, however, is refuted by the facts of the case and by reason. By the facts of the case, for with very few if any exceptions there is no one condemned to die who does not look upon it as a great favor to have his sentence commuted into one of imprisonment, even though perpetual. And this goes to show that death is held in greater abhorrence than any other evil, not excluding the lasting loss of liberty. It is refuted by reason, for as life is the foundation of every other good, the repugnance to its loss is by far the greatest that man experiences. And such a repugnance is a necessary offshoot of our nature. To overcome this repugnance a man must make the greatest efforts; and hence, except in the case of foolishness or fatalism, contempt for death constitutes the highest degree of fortitude. In the deprivation of life man sees the absolute cessation of every kind of good, without a ray of hope remaining to comfort him, at least here below. Hence he looks upon death as the greatest of evils, and his natural aversion for it is as great as his natural desire for felicity. As long as he lives he can hope for pardon, he can hope for escape, he can hope for a revolution, he can hope for a mitigation of his sentence. And such hope was never better founded than at present. As to exceptions, if any such there be, we must bear in mind that in the making of laws and sanctions the rule must be considered, not the exception. Moreover, it is one thing to throw oneself rashly into the certain peril of death, and quite another to be executed ignominiously as a rotten member of society. Even those who do not fear the former, fear the latter.

This salutary fear is needed more in a free government like our own than in a monarchy; and therefore so is capital punishment more needed. In a monarchy a man who is known to be on the point of committing a crime is forthwith arrested and brought to his senses by the solitude of the prison walls. "If I do this murder," he reasons with himself, "I am arrested, judged, sentenced, executed—there is no escape. Therefore I will not do this murder." In a free government like our own such a man may not be sent to prison beforehand. He may be watched, but the watch kept over him, especially if protracted, ends in being deluded and therefore useless; and the crime can be committed. Whence it follows that in a free government it is more difficult to prevent crimes than in an absolute government; and this renders the necessity of a greater fear of committing grave crimes in a free government than in an absolute one—a fear that capital punishment alone can inspire into the minds of those given over to wickedness.

The apparent argument from statistics, which is considered unanswerable by our adversaries, proves nothing at all in the matter. For even if the statistics were genuine, and complete, a thing that is not so, and a real nexus existed between the two facts, i.e., the abolition of capital punishment and the diminution of crime; if, in other words, it would be shown clearly and certainly that the number of murders and other grave crimes had diminished because capital punishment was abolished, this would not make for the contention of our opponents. It would merely go to prove, according to strict logic, that capital punishment, by which such crimes were formerly punished, was a lesser punishment than imprisonment, and that instead of diverting men from crime, it rather by some mysterious allurement, the secret of which is known only to the abolitionists, incited men to crime. Witness the demonstrative power of your statistics in the matter! The decrease of crime, then, after the abolition of capital punishment, if ever really proved to be a fact, must be sought from other causes, especially if the interval of time between the terms of comparison is long. The decrease might arise from the diminution of misery or poverty, which is wont to move men to commit certain crimes, from the bettering of the conditions of the working classes, from the greater skill and vigilance of the military or police force which renders the probability of hiding the crime smaller, from the greater care bestowed on the moral education of children, from the larger number of well-made and well-lighted streets and highways, and many other causes. Everyone knows that the morality of a country does not depend solely or even mainly on the fear of punishment. Crime is diminished principally by precautionary measures. The penalties of the codex are only a last resort necessary for those who in a well-regulated community, but composed of men, will always be found in need of a check less noble but still efficacious. It has been well said that statistics tell the truth when read aright, but read upside down they say any extravagance whatever. Now the man that brings statistics, even though genuine and complete, to prove that where capital punishment has been abolished, crime has, on account of that abolition, diminished, is surely reading statistics upside down. He should first show logically—a thing that can not be done, as we have seen—that the diminution was owing to the abolition. Otherwise he will be guilty of the fallacy of attributing a fact (?) to a false cause. *Post hoc, ergo propter hoc.* He who makes use of statistics to demonstrate that capital punishment is not only unnecessary but the cause of greater evil, is either utterly ignorant of the elements of logic or is wanting in good faith. I have answered the objection polemically. But did I care to do so ,I could give counter statistics.

III

The lawfulness and justice of capital punishment considered in itself has in its favor not only the vote of reason, as we have seen, but also the vote of all the peoples and of all the legislators of the world—the votes of the whole human race. For in all nations, at all times, amongst civilized people and barbarous, in aristocracies and democracies, for certain crimes capital punishment has always been in use. The use varied in various nations. A particular crime was punished by capital punishment in one country and not in another, but everywhere the right of capital punishment has always been admitted. Would you have us believe that the whole human race could agree to establish murder by law? Neither will it do to bring forward certain errors of the nations. For these errors were not everywhere and always the same, and at any rate they were corrected by Christianity. But capital punishment has been universal and most constant even after the announcement of the Gospel; and twenty centuries of Christian civilization are not to be despised so easily—all the chorus of your namby-pamby sentimentalists to the contrary notwithstanding.

And if besides reason and human authority we consult Revelation we shall find the same truth confirmed—the justice of capital punishment. Thus Exodus xxi, 12: "He that striketh a man with a will to kill him, shall be put to death," and Leviticus xxiv, 17: "He that striketh and killeth a man, dying let him die." And so Moses, Joshua, Samuel, David, Elias and other holy men used this power and put to death malefactors. And St. Paul in his epistle to the Romans, c.xiii, v.4 "If thou do that which is evil, fear, for he beareth not the sword in vain. For he is God's minister." Here the Apostle tells us that the right of the sword, or capital punishment, has been given by God to rulers against criminals. The lawful ruler holds from God the right of life and death, according to the exigency of the eternal reasons of justice; and therefore he does not bear the sword in vain. He bears it as the symbol of the right he has to put to death the wicked and to use this right against them when reason and justice require it for the security of the public welfare. True, Christ the God-man said in the New Testament: "Thou shalt not kill." But as God He had said the same thing in the Old Testament, and had also said what I have quoted from Exodus and Leviticus and what I might quote from Genesis. Unless, then, one wishes to say that Christ is not God or that He is self-contradictory, it must be admitted that the words of the Fifth Commandment have not the meaning ascribed to them by some of our sensational abolitionists. Their obvious meaning taken in the light of all revelation and reason, is "Thou shalt not kill" by private authority except when it is necessary in case of self-defense. But this does not forbid the killing of a man by public authority in a just war, or when, as in the case of a great criminal, it is necessary for the common weal. For Christ is God, and God does not contradict Himself. Besides, it is a canon of criticism, and particularly biblical criticism, that the obscurer passage should be interpreted in the light of the clearer.

To sum up the argument of reason, justice inflicts punishment for three ends—for the correction of the culprit, for the restoration of order and for the defence of society. Capital punishment is not absolutely necessary for the first end, or even the second, but it is for the third. For there are men so hardened in crime, so unyielding to every social remedy, whose company is so pernicious that where the State does not employ extreme remedies and does not make of them an example for those who might be tempted to imitate them, they become the terror and ruin of society. But by taking their life society first renders their fall again impossible, and then by the horror of the punishment it makes them undergo, and the infamy with which it covers them it takes away the desire from others of following in their footsteps. Death then may be an efficacious and therefore a necessary remedy in certain cases for the security of society, and in such cases the collision of rights is evidently in favor of society. Capital punishment is lawful in itself because it is not intrinsically evil, and it can be an efficacious and necessary remedy for the ends of punishment but especially for public safety. Capital punishment should be used when it is a necessary means for the security of the commonwealth. The argument of reason is confirmed by the belief and practice of the whole human race through all the ages. It is confirmed by the infallible word of God Himself. Let the ancient wisdom, then, remain in possession of the veneration of the people, and let us absolve society from the pretended legal murder imputed to it by the sentimentalists.

IV

So much for the question of the justice of capital punishment. But some well-meaning persons, who do not belong to the class I have been refuting, may ask what is to be thought about the opportunities of abolishing capital punishment. "Is not more obtained," they will say, "by clemency than by rigor, by pardon than by execution?" Great certainly is mercy.

> *It is an attribute to God Himself:*
> *And earthly power doth then show likest God's*
> *When mercy seasons justice.*

And so when a ruler pardons as God would pardon he deserves praise, not blame.

But should anyone think that pardon and amnesty ought to be the only or the main means of a wise government, he would be quite wrong. For, though at times there should be an assuasion of justice, a mitigation of rigor, compassion for human weakness, were pardon for crime to become very frequent and almost the ordinary thing, all the sinews of justice would be shattered, the evil-doer would plunge into all kinds of crimes, and society would be exposed to the gravest dangers. Justice would be disarmed in the face of malefactors. To their eyes the frequency of pardon forms a happy perspective that takes from crime its punishment and horror, and leads to consequences which even they know who have only newspaper knowledge of current events. Great certainly is mercy, but in the government of nations it can never take the place of justice, it can only season it. When mercy displaces justice it becomes the highest injustice. For then the wicked can overpower the good with impunity, and the rebellious can shake society to its foundations.

Capital punishment has three advantages: it acts as a repressive force against the savage nature of criminals; it acts as a protective force in favor of honest citizens; it acts as a reintegrating force of moral order deeply disturbed by certain crimes. It may not always correct the criminal. But we must remember that the correction of the culprit is not the primary, but the secondary end of punishment inflicted by the civil power. The primary end of such punishment is the safety of society and the maintaining of justice among the citizens. And when the two ends cannot be attained the secondary must give way to the primary. It may happen by mistake that an innocent man is put to death. But this is on account of the fallibility of human judgment, which is a general condition in human affairs. This only shows that in inflicting this punishment the State should proceed with the greatest caution and certitude possible. If the State knowingly acts unjustly in the matter and abuses its power against the poor and the innocent, and in favor of the rich and the powerful, the abuse of the thing should be abolished, not the use. For, except virtue, there is nothing in this world that cannot be abused. Abolish capital punishment, just exercised when necessity requires it, and you will open the door of our State to crime and criminals, and as a natural consequence to lynching, vigilanteism and *dementia Americana.*

It is true that in proportion as a people acquires religion, culture, honor and delicacy, it takes to means less violent, and hence the mitigation of punishment may become necessary and just. And this is why in civilized Europe the severity of punishment went on naturally diminishing by itself long before philanthropy had started its loud boasting, and the codes had been altered. Nature and religion worked together in the heart of men and brought its fruits to maturity.

But, unfortunately, nowadays religion and the things that go with it, true culture and honor and delicacy, have little or no sway over the minds of many, as daily experience teaches us. The time has not yet come, therefore, when we can afford to do away with capital punishment. What barbarous philanthropy were it, then, to listen to the neurasthenics and the socialists, and in order to save the life of a scoundrel keep innocent men and women and their sons and daughters in perpetual agony!

JOHN DEWEY (1859–1952)

Justice and Criminality

Our own time has seen a generous quickening of the idea of social justice due to the growth of love, or philanthropy, as a working social motive. In the older scheme of morals, justice was supposed to meet all the necessary requirements of virtue; charity was doing good in ways not obligatory or strictly exacted. Hence it was a source of peculiar merit in the doer, a means of storing up a surplus of virtue to offset vice. But a more generous sense of inherent social relationships binding the aims of all into one comprehensive good, which is the result of increase of human intercourse, democratic institutions, and biological science, has made men recognize that the greater part of the sufferings and miseries which afford on the part of a few the opportunity for charity (and hence superior merit), are really social inequities, due to causes which may be remedied. That justice requires radical improvement of these conditions displaces the notion that their effects may be here and there palliated by the voluntary merit of morally superior individuals. The change illustrates, on a wide scale, the transformation of the conception of justice so that it joins hands with love and sympathy. That human nature should have justice done it under all circumstances is an infinitely complicated and difficult requirement, and only a vision of the capacities and accomplishments of human beings rooted in affection and sympathy can perceive and execute justly.

The selection is from John Dewey and James H. Tufts, *Ethics* (New York: Henry Holt and Company, 1908).

TRANSFORMATION OF PUNITIVE JUSTICE

The conception of punitive or corrective justice is undergoing the same transformation. Aristotle stated the rule of equity in the case of wrongdoing as an arithmetical requital: the individual was to suffer according to his deed. Later, through conjunction with the idea of a divine judge inflicting retribution upon the sinner, this notion passed into the belief that punishment is a form of justice restoring the balance of disturbed law by inflicting suffering upon the one who has done wrong. The end and aim of punishment was retribution, bringing back to the agent the evil consequences of his own deed. That punishment *is* suffering, that it inevitably involves pain to the guilty one, there can be no question; this, whether the punishment is externally inflicted or is in the pangs of conscience, and whether administered by parent, teacher, or civil authority. But that suffering is for the sake of suffering, or that suffering can in any way restore or affect the violated majesty of law, is a different matter.

What erring human nature deserves or merits, it is just it should have. But in the end, a moral agent deserves to *be* a moral agent; and hence deserves that punishments inflicted should be *corrective*, not merely retributive. Every wrongdoer should have his due. But what is his due? Can we measure it by his past alone; or is it due every one to regard him as a man with a future as well? as having possibilities for good as well as achievements in bad? Those who are responsible for the infliction of punishment have, as well as those punished, to meet the requirements of justice; and failure to employ the means and instrumentalities of punishment in a way to lead, so far as possible, the wrongdoer to reconsideration of conduct and re-formation of disposition, cannot shelter itself under the plea that it vindicates law. Such failure comes rather from thoughtless custom; from a lazy unwillingness to find better means; from an admixture of pride with lack of sympathy for others; from a desire to maintain things as they are rather than go to the causes which generate criminals. . . .

REFORM OF CRIMINAL PROCEDURE

The negative side of morality is never so important as the positive, because the pathological cannot be as important as the physiological of which it is a disturbance and perversion. But no fair survey of our methods, either of locating criminality or of punishing it, can fail to note that they contain far too many survivals of barbarism. Compared with primitive times we have indeed won a precious conquest. Even as late as 1813, a proposal to change the penalty for stealing five shillings from death to transportation to a remote colony, was defeated in England. But we are likely in flattering ourselves upon the progress made to overlook that which it remains to make. Our trials are technical rather than human: they assume that just about so much persistent criminality must persist in any case. They endeavor, in rather routine and perfunctory ways, to label this and that person as criminal in such and such degrees, or, by technical devices and resources, to acquit. In many American states, distrust of government, inherited from days of tyrannical monarchy or oligarchy, protects the accused in all sorts of ways. For fear the government will unjustly infringe upon the liberty of the individual, the latter is not only—as is just—regarded as innocent till proved guilty; but is provided with every possible technical advantage in rules of evidence, postponements and appeals, advantages backed up, in many cities, by association with political bosses which gives him a corrupt "pull."

On the other hand, there is as yet no general recognition of the possibility of an unbiased scientific investigation into all the antecedents (hereditary and environmental) of evildoers; an investigation which would connect the wrong done with the *character of the individual* committing it, and not merely with one of a number of technical degrees of crime, laid down in the statute books in the abstract, without reference to particular characters and circumstances. Thus while the evildoer has in one direction altogether too much of a chance to evade justice, he has in another direction a chance at only technical, rather than at moral, justice—justice as an individual human being. It is not possible to discuss here various methods which have been proposed for remedying these defects. But it is clearly the business of the more thoughtful members of society to consider the evils seriously and to interest themselves actively in their reform. We need, above all, a change in two respects: (a) recognition of the possibilities of new methods of judgment which the sciences of physiology, psychology, and sociology have brought about; and (b) surrender of that feudal conception according to which men are divided, as it were essentially, into two classes: one the criminal and the other the meritorious. We need to consider the ways in which the pressure and the opportunities of environment and education, of poverty and comfortable living, of extraneous suggestion and stimulation, make the differences between one man and another; and to recognize how fundamentally one human nature is at bottom. Juvenile courts, probation officers, detention officers, mark the beginnings of what is possible, but only the beginnings. For the most part crime is still treated sordidly and by routine, except when, being sensational, it is the occasion for a great battle of wits between keen prosecuting attorney and clever "criminal lawyer," with the world through the newspapers watching the display.

REFORM OF PUNISHMENT

Emerson's bitter words are still too applicable. "Our distrust is very expensive. The money we spend for courts and prisons is very ill laid out. We make, by distrust, the thief and burglar and incendiary, and by our court and jail we keep him so." Reformatories, whose purpose is change of disposition, not mere penalization, have been founded; but there are still many more prisons than reformatories. And, if it be argued that most criminals are so hardened in evil-doing that reformatories are of no use, the answer is twofold. We do not know, because we have never systematically and intelligently tried to find out; and, even if it were so, nothing is more illogical than to turn the unreformed criminal, at the end of a certain number of months or years, loose to prey again upon society. Either reform or else permanent segregation is the logical alternative. Indeterminate sentences, release on probation, discrimination of classes of offenders, separation of the first and more or less accidental and immature offender from the old and experienced hand, special matrons for women offenders, introduction of education and industrial training into penitentiaries, the finding of employment for those released—all mark improvements. They are, however, as yet inchoate. Intelligent members of society need to recognize their own responsibility for the promotion of such reforms and for the discovery of new ones.

MORITZ SCHLICK (1882–1936)

Punishment and Responsibility

Ethics has, so to speak, no moral interest in the purely theoretical question of "determinism or indeterminism?," but only a theoretical interest, namely: in so far as it seeks the laws of conduct, and can find them only to the extent that causality holds. But the question of whether man is morally free (that is, has that freedom which, as we shall show, is the presupposition of moral responsibility) is altogether different from the problem of determinism. Hume was especially clear on this point. He indicated the inadmissible confusion of the concepts of "indeterminism" and "freedom"; but he retained, inappropriately, the word "freedom" for both, calling the one freedom of "the will," the other, genuine kind, "freedom of conduct." He showed that morality is interested only in the latter, and that such freedom, in general, is unquestionably to be attributed to mankind. And this is quite correct. Freedom means the opposite of compulsion; a man is *free* if he does not act under *compulsion*, and he is compelled or unfree when he is hindered from without in the realization of his natural desires. Hence he is unfree when he is locked up, or chained, or when someone forces him at the point of a gun to do what otherwise he would not do. This is quite clear, and everyone will admit that the everyday or legal notion of the lack of freedom is thus correctly interpreted, and that a man will be considered quite free and responsible if no such external compulsion is exerted upon him. There are certain cases which lie between these clearly described ones, as, say, when someone acts under the influence of alcohol or a narcotic. In such cases we consider the man to be more or less unfree, and hold him less accountable, because we rightly view the influence of the drug as "external," even though it is found within the body; it prevents him from making decisions in the manner peculiar to his nature. If he takes the narcotic of his own will, we make him completely responsible for *this* act and transfer a part of the responsibility to the consequences, making, as it were, an average or mean condemnation of the whole. In the case also of a person who is mentally ill we do not consider him free with respect to those acts in which the disease expresses itself, because we view the illness as a

The selection is from Moritz Schlick, *Problems of Ethics* (New York: Dover Publications, Inc., 1962) pp. 149–158. Reprinted through permission of the publisher.

disturbing factor which hinders the normal functioning of his natural tendencies. We make not him but his disease responsible.

THE NATURE OF RESPONSIBILITY

But what does this really signify? What do we mean by this concept of responsibility which goes along with that of "freedom," and which plays such an important role in morality? It is easy to attain complete clarity in this matter; we need only carefully determine the manner in which the concept is used. What is the case in practice when we impute "responsibility" to a person? What is our aim in doing this? The judge has to discover who is responsible for a given act in order that he may *punish* him. We are inclined to be less concerned with the inquiry as to who deserves *reward* for an act, and we have no special officials for this; but of course the principle would be the same. But let us stick to punishment in order to make the idea clear. What is punishment, actually? The view still often expressed, that it is a natural *retaliation* for past wrong, ought no longer to be defended in cultivated society; for the opinion that an increase in sorrow can be "made good again" by further sorrow is altogether barbarous. Certainly the origin of punishment may lie in an impulse of retaliation or vengeance; but what is such an impulse except the instinctive desire to destroy the *cause* of the deed to be avenged, by the destruction of or injury to the malefactor? Punishment is concerned only with the institution of causes, of *motives* of conduct, and this alone is its meaning. Punishment is an educative measure, and as such is a means to the formation of motives, which are in part to prevent the wrongdoer from repeating the act (reformation) and in part to prevent others from committing a similar act (intimidation). Analogously, in the case of reward we are concerned with an incentive.

Hence the question regarding responsibility is the question: Who, in a given case, is to be punished? Who is to be considered the true wrongdoer? This problem is not identical with that regarding the original instigator of the act; for the great-grandparents of the man, from whom he inherited his character, might in the end be the cause, or the statesmen who are responsible for his social milieu, and so forth. But the "doer" is the one *upon whom the motive must have acted* in order, with certainty, to have prevented the act (or called it forth, as the case may be). Consideration of remote causes is of no help here, for in the first place their actual contribution cannot be determined, and in the second place they are generally out of reach. Rather, we must find the person in whom the decisive junction of causes lies. The question of who is responsible is the question concerning the *correct point of application of the motive*. And the important thing is that in this its meaning is completely exhausted; behind it there lurks no mysterious connection between transgression and requital, which is merely *indicated* by the described state of affairs. It is a matter only of knowing who is to be punished or rewarded, in order that punishment and reward function as such—be able to achieve their goal.

Thus, all the facts connected with the concepts of responsibility and imputation are at once made intelligible. We do not charge an insane person with responsibility, for the very reason that he offers no unified point for the application of a motive. It would be pointless to try to affect him by means of promises or threats, when his confused soul fails to respond to such influence because its normal mechanism is out of order. We do not try to give him motives, but try to heal him (metaphorically, we make his sickness responsible, and try to remove its causes). When a man is forced by threats to commit certain acts we do not blame him, but the one who held the pistol at his breast. The reason is clear: the act would have been prevented had we been able to restrain the person who threatened him; and this person is the one whom we must influence in order to prevent similar acts in the future.

THE CONSCIOUSNESS OF RESPONSIBILITY

But much more important than the question of when a man is said to be responsible is that of when he *himself* feels responsible. Our whole treatment would be untenable if it gave no explanation of this. It is, then, a welcome confirmation of the view here developed that the subjective feeling of responsibility coincides with the objective judgment. It is a fact of experience that, in general, the person blamed or condemned is conscious of the fact that he was "rightly" taken to account —of course, under the supposition that no error has been made, that the assumed state of affairs actually occurred. What is this consciousness of having been the true doer of the act, the actual instigator? Evidently not merely that it was he who took the steps required for its performance; but there must be added the awareness that he did it "independently," "of his own initiative," or however it be expressed. This feeling is simply the consciousness of *freedom*, which is merely the knowledge of having acted of one's *own* desires. And "one's own desires" are those which have their origin in the regularity of one's character in the given situation, and are not imposed by an external power, as explained above. The absence of the external power expresses itself in the well-known feeling (usually considered characteristic of the consciousness of freedom) *that one could also have acted otherwise.* How this indubitable experience ever came to be an argument in favor of indeterminism is incomprehensible to me. It is of course obvious that I should have acted differently had I *willed* something else; but the feeling never says that I could also have willed something else, even though this is true, if, that is, other motives had been present. And it says even less that under *exactly the same* inner and outer conditions I could also have willed something else. How could such a feeling inform me of anything regarding the purely theoretical question of whether the principle of causality holds or not? Of course, after what has been said on the subject, I do not undertake to demonstrate the principle, but I do deny that from any such fact of consciousness the least follows regarding the principle's validity. This feeling is not the consciousness of the absence of a cause, but of something altogether different, namely, of *freedom*, which consists in the fact that I can act as I desire.

Thus the feeling of responsibility assumes that I acted freely, that my own desires impelled me; and if because of this feeling I willingly suffer blame for my behavior or reproach myself, and thereby admit that I might have acted otherwise, this means that other behavior was compatible with the laws of volition—of course, granted other motives. And I myself desire the existence of such motives and bear the pain (regret and sorrow) caused me by my behavior so that its repetition will be prevented. To blame oneself means just to apply motives of improvement to oneself, which is usually the task of the educator. But if, for example, one does something under the influence of torture, feelings of guilt and regret are absent, for one knows that according to the laws of volition no other behavior was possible—no matter what ideas, because of their feeling tones, might have functioned as motives. The important thing, always, is that the feeling of responsibility means the realization that one's self, one's own psychic processes constitute the point at which motives must be applied in order to govern the acts of one's body.

CAUSALITY AS THE PRESUPPOSITION OF RESPONSIBILITY

We can speak of motives only in a causal context; thus it becomes clear how very much the concept of responsibility rests upon that of causation, that is, upon the regularity of volitional decisions. In fact if we should conceive of a decision as utterly without any cause (this would in all strictness be the indeterministic presupposition) then the act would be entirely a matter of *chance*, for chance is identical with the absence of a cause; there is no other opposite of causality. Could we under such conditions make the agent responsible? Certainly not. Imagine a man, always calm, peaceful and blameless, who suddenly falls upon and begins to beat a stranger. He is held and questioned regarding the motive of his action, to which he answers, in his opinion truthfully, as we assume: "There was no motive for my behavior. Try as I may I can discover no reason. My volition was without any cause— I desired to do so, and there is simply nothing else to be said about it." We should shake our heads and call him insane, because we have to believe that there was a cause, and lacking any other we must assume some mental disturbance as the only cause remaining; but certainly no one would hold him to be responsible. If decisions were causeless there would be no sense in trying to influence men; and we see at once that this is the reason why we could not bring such a man to account, but would always have only a shrug of the shoulders in answer to his behavior. One can easily determine that in practice we make an agent the more responsible the more motives we can find for his conduct. If a man guilty of an atrocity was an enemy of his victim, if previously he had shown violent tendencies, if some special circumstance angered him, then we impose severe punishment upon him; while the fewer the reasons to be found for an offense the less do we condemn the agent, but make "unlucky chance," a momentary aberration, or something of the sort, responsible. We do not find the causes of misconduct in his character, and therefore we do not try to influence it for the better: this and only this is the significance of the fact that we do not put the responsibility upon him. And he too feels this to be so, and says, "I cannot understand how such a thing could have happened to me."

In general we know very well how to discover the causes of conduct in the characters of our fellow men; and how to use this knowledge in the prediction of their future behavior, often with as much certainty as that with which we know that a lion and a rabbit will behave quite differently in the same situation. From all this it is evident that in practice no one thinks of questioning the principle of causality, that, thus, the attitude of the practical man offers no excuse to the metaphysician for confusing freedom from compulsion with the absence of a cause. If one makes clear to himself that a causeless happening is identical with a chance happening, and that, consequently, an indetermined will would destroy all responsibility, then every desire will cease which might be father to an indeterministic thought. No one can prove determinism, but it is certain that we assume its validity in all of our practical life, and that in particular we can apply the concept of responsibility to human conduct only in so far as the causal principle holds of volition a processes.

SECTION EIGHT

WAR

Everyone accepts the desirability of peace, at least as an ultimate goal. Even fascist propagandists argued that their rejection of pacificism was a precondition for a thousand years of peace; and Karl Marx founded his gospel of conflict on the vision of a classless, harmonious society. In our own era, we are experiencing an almost frantic demand that ways be found to end the bitter sequence of twentieth century wars. Weary with the apparent moral compromises of an affluent society, statesmen, intellectuals, and especially university students fix upon warfare as the symbol of a confusing and frustrating unwillingness to construct a world that nurtures human dignity. In fact, few moral issues appear so clear-cut as that of war and peace, so amenable to unambiguous judgments about good and bad.

Where then are the differences of conviction about warfare, particularly those that can be called philosophical? On what grounds do serious thinkers qualify the facile slogan, "War is hell"? Why do apparently intelligent persons disagree about the morality or immorality of particular wars? Can we hope for a resolution of such disagreement through an impartial survey of facts?

Philosophy begins its consideration of war, not by looking at a specific conflict or treaty or at a particular attempt to negotiate peace, but by trying to understand the human situation out of which such phenomena emerge. War produces the philosophical urge to explain what it is in man's nature that makes peace so elusive. So the starting

365

point for the philosophical analysis of war is man himself, and a writer's opinion about armed conflict will inevitably express a broad theory about human nature—about persons in their interrelations, their institutions, even about persons "in themselves" as emotional-rational-willful creatures.

Often philosophical disagreement in the analysis of war appears to be little more than disagreement over questions of fact. Was Plato correct, for example, in his belief that the basic cause of war is in the corruption of souls, expressed in the growth of luxury, in respect for the strong as over against the just, and in the disregard of truth as the basis for legislation? Or is Thorstein Veblen correct that war is consequent upon changes in economic and technological structures? Does Marx improve on Veblen's analysis by seeing war in the context of class conflict?

In the readings that follow, the student should look for these expressed or unexpressed disagreements about the "facts of human nature." What kind of "facts" are they? Can disagreements about them be resolved through empirical studies as found in the social sciences? Or are some of them more like axioms, that is, assumptions on the basis of which analysis can proceed, but which are not themselves verifiable in a way that commands universal agreement? If the latter should be the case, then one can ask for the reasons thinkers cite for their choice of certain axioms rather than others and can as well assess the force of such reasons.

Broad theories about human nature are closely related to estimates of the attainability of peace, and it is often in their prescription of peace-creating mechanisms that philosophers tip their philosophic hand. Theories of human nature usually involve attempts to implement moral judgments, and the following readings do not resist this temptation. The confrontation of William James and Merleau-Ponty provides a case in point. Here the student should note how conflicting diagnoses of the social nature of man give rise to differing prescriptions.

Of course, theories of human nature and their related peace-creating prescriptions do not evolve in vacuums, unaffected by the peculiarities of a particular time and place in the history of man. Discussions about war and peace are always dated. Greek and Roman writers, for example, could not entirely divorce the problem of war from issues related to a slave economy, and contemporary war theorists cannot help but betray signs of a shattered idealism. If it is to be evaluated with sensitivity, a philosophical approach to war has to be seen in its proper historical context. But, it may be asked, is relativity to be made an absolute? Are there no general statements we can make about the human propensity to war and its amelioration that have more than a transitory significance? Is it possible to distinguish transient elements from universal views of man? Indeed, is it desirable for us to draw from the history of Western thought about war in an approach to our own situation?

In the following readings, Augustine raises the perennial discussion concerning the morality of warfare—whether wars can be fought in a just manner and whether one can distinguish between just and unjust wars. Augustine is an important architect of the "just war" tradition, which has had a profound influence on Western thought and which is assuming a major place in contemporary argument about American military engagements. T. H. Green sees warfare as an occasion for confusion with regard to the rights of individuals, and Bertrand Russell's appeal to intellectuals is a sophisticated exploration of the moral self-deception found in societies that are at war. William James deals with the nexus of general theories about man and theories about the causes and amelioration of international conflict; his essay constitutes one of the major contributions to the philosophical consideration of war, interesting particularly in its attempt to pioneer in what is now known as moral psychology. H. Richard Niebuhr's utilization of metaphor to understand the moral significance of World War II prefigured his later attempts to explore the meaning of symbolic forms in ethical theory. His essay is related to the just war tradition, but it finds the imagery of crucifixion to be more fruitful in illumining the fact of collective guilt than the casuistry of just war theorists. An equally helpful exploration of collective guilt is developed in Merleau-Ponty's "The War Has Taken Place." Both Niebuhr and Merleau-Ponty are phenomenologists, and a comparison of their essays can serve to show the diverse possibilities of that methodological commitment as well as the complexity of warfare as a dimension of the human experience.

Concerning the Just War

What is the evil in war? Is it the death of some who will soon die in any case, that others may live in peaceful subjection? This is mere cowardly dislike, not any religious feeling. The real evils in war are love of violence, revengeful cruelty, fierce and implacable enmity, wild resistance, and the lust of power, and such like; and it is generally to punish these things, when force is required to inflict the punishment, that, in obedience to God or some lawful authority, good men undertake wars, when they find themselves in such a position as regards the conduct of human affairs, that right conduct requires them to act, or to make others act in this way. Otherwise John, when the soldiers who came to be baptized asked, What shall we do? would have replied, Throw away your arms; give up the service; never strike, or wound, or disable any one. But knowing that such actions in battle were not murderous, but authorized by law, and that the soldiers did not thus avenge themselves, but defend the public safety, he replied, "Do violence to no man, accuse no man falsely, and be content with your wages." But as the Manichæans are in the habit of speaking evil of John, let them hear the Lord Jesus Christ Himself ordering this money to be given to Cæsar, which John tells the soldiers to be content with. "Give," He says, "to Cæsar the things that are Cæsar's." For tribute-money is given on purpose to pay the soldiers for war. Again, in the case of the centurion who said, "I am a man under authority, and have soldiers under me: and I say to one, Go, and he goeth; and to another, Come, and he cometh; and to my servant, Do this, and he doeth it," Christ gave due praise to his faith; He did not tell him to leave the service. But there is no need here to enter on the long discussion of just and unjust wars.

A great deal depends on the causes for which men undertake wars, and on the authority they have for doing so; for the natural order which seeks the peace of mankind, ordains that the monarch should have the power of undertaking war if he thinks it advisable, and that the soldiers should perform their military duties in behalf of the peace and safety of the community. When war is undertaken in obedience to God,

The selection is from Augustine, "Reply to Faustus the Manichæan," *in Writings in Connection with the Manichæan Controversy,* trans. Richard Stothert and Albert Newman (Buffalo: The Christian Literature Society, 1887).

who would rebuke, or humble, or crush the pride of man, it must be allowed to be a righteous war; for even the wars which arise from human passion cannot harm the eternal well-being of God, nor even hurt His saints; for in the trial of their patience, and the chastening of their spirit, and in bearing fatherly correction, they are rather benefited than injured. No one can have any power against them but what is given him from above. For there is no power but of God, who either orders or permits. Since, therefore, a righteous man, serving it may be under an ungodly king, may do the duty belonging to his position in the State in fighting by the order of his sovereign,—for in some cases it is plainly the will of God that he should fight, and in others, where this is not so plain, it may be an unrighteous command on the part of the king, while the soldier is innocent, because his position makes obedience a duty,—how much more must the man be blameless who carries on war on the authority of God, of whom every one who serves Him knows that He can never require what is wrong?

If it is supposed that God could not enjoin warfare, because in after times it was said by the Lord Jesus Christ, "I say unto you, That ye resist not evil: but if any one strike thee on the right cheek, turn to him the left also," the answer is, that what is here required is not a bodily action, but an inward disposition. The sacred seat of virtue is the heart, and such were the hearts of our fathers, the righteous men of old. But order required such a regulation of events, and such a distinction of times, as to show first of all that even earthly blessings (for so temporal kingdoms and victory over enemies are considered to be, and these are the things which the community of the ungodly all over the world are continually begging from idols and devils) are entirely under the control and at the disposal of the one true God. Thus, under the Old Testament, the secret of the kingdom of heaven, which was to be disclosed in due time, was veiled, and so far obscured, in the disguise of earthly promises. But when the fullness of time came for the revelation of the New Testament, which was hidden under the types of the Old, clear testimony was to be borne to the truth, that there is another life for which this life ought to be disregarded, and another kingdom for which the opposition of all earthly kingdoms should be patiently borne. Thus the name martyrs, which means witnesses, was given to those who, by the will of God, bore this testimony, by their confessions, their sufferings, and their death. The number of such witnesses is so great, that if it pleased Christ —who called Saul by a voice from heaven, and having changed him from a wolf to a sheep, sent him into the midst of wolves—to unite them all in one army, and to give them success in battle, as He gave to the

Hebrews, what nation could withstand them? what kingdom would remain unsubdued? But as the doctrine of the New Testament is, that we must serve God not for temporal happiness in this life, but for eternal felicity hereafter, this truth was most strikingly confirmed by the patient endurance of what is commonly called adversity for the sake of that felicity. So in fullness of time the Son of God, made of a woman, made under the law, that He might redeem them that were under the law, made of the seed of David according to the flesh, sends His disciples as sheep into the midst of wolves, and bids them not fear those that can kill the body, but cannot kill the soul, and promises that even the body will be entirely restored, so that not a hair shall be lost. Peter's sword He orders back into its sheath, restoring as it was before the ear of His enemy that had been cut off. He says that He could obtain legions of angels to destroy His enemies, but that He must drink the cup which His Father's will had given Him. He sets the example of drinking this cup, then hands it to His followers, manifesting thus, both in word and deed, the grace of patience. Therefore God raised Him from the dead, and has given Him a name which is above every name; that in the name of Jesus every knee should bow, of things in heaven and of things in earth, and of things under the earth; and that every tongue should confess that Jesus is Lord, to the glory of God the Father. The patriarchs and prophets, then, have a kingdom in this world, to show that these kingdoms, too, are given and taken away by God: the apostles and martyrs had no kingdom here, to show the superior desirableness of the kingdom of heaven. The prophets, however, could even in those times die for the truth, as the Lord Himself says, "From the blood of Abel to the blood of Zacharia"; and in these days, since the commencement of the fulfillment of what is prophesied in the psalm of Christ, under the figure of Solomon, which means the peacemaker, as Christ is our peace, "All kings of the earth shall bow to Him, all nations shall serve Him," we have seen Christian emperors, who have put all their confidence in Christ, gaining splendid victories over ungodly enemies, whose hope was in the rites of idolatry and devil-worship. There are public and undeniable proofs of the fact, that on one side the prognostications of devils were found to be fallacious, and on the other, the predictions of saints were a means of support; and we have now writings in which those facts are recorded.

If our foolish opponents are surprised at the difference between the precepts given by God to the ministers of the Old Testament, at a time when the grace of the New was still undisclosed, and those given to the preachers of the New Testament, now that the obscurity of the Old is removed, they will find Christ Himself saying one thing at one time, and another at another. "When I sent you," He says, "without scrip, or purse, or shoes, did ye lack anything? And they said, Nothing. Then saith He to them, But now, he that hath a scrip, let him take it, and also a purse; and he that hath not a sword, let him sell his garment, and buy one." If the Manichæans found passages in the Old and New Testaments differing in this way, they would proclaim it as a proof that the Testaments are opposed to each other. But here the difference is in the utterances of one and the same person. At one time He says, "I sent you without scrip, or purse, or shoes, and ye lacked nothing;" at another, "Now let him that hath a scrip take it, and also a purse; and he that hath a tunic, let him sell it and buy a sword." Does not this show how, without any inconsistency, precepts and counsels and permissions may be changed, as different times require different arrangements? If it is said that there was a symbolical meaning in the command to take a scrip and purse, and to buy a sword, why may there not be a symbolical meaning in the fact, that one and the same God commanded the prophets in old times to make war, and forbade the apostles? And we find in the passage that we have quoted from the Gospel, that the words spoken by the Lord were carried into effect by His disciples. For, besides going at first without scrip or purse, and yet lacking nothing, as from the Lord's question and their answer it is plain they did, now that He speaks of buying a sword, they say, "Lo, here are two swords;" and He replied, "It is enough." Hence we find Peter with a weapon when he cut off the assailant's ear, on which occasion his spontaneous boldness was checked, because, although he had been told to take a sword, he had not been told to use it. Doubtless, it was mysterious that the Lord should require them to carry weapons, and forbid the use of them. But it was His part to give the suitable precepts, and it was their part to obey without reserve.

It is therefore mere groundless calumny to charge Moses with making war, for there would have been less harm in making war of his own accord, than in not doing it when God commanded him. And to dare to find fault with God Himself for giving such a command, or not to believe it possible that a just and good God did so, shows, to say the least, an inability to consider that in the view of divine providence, which pervades all things from the highest to the lowest, time can neither add anything nor take away; but all things go, or come, or remain according to the order of nature or desert in each separate case, while in men a right will is in union with the divine law, and ungoverned passion is restrained by the order of divine law; so that a good man wills only what is commanded, and a bad man can do only what he is permitted, at the same time that he is punished for what he wills to do unjustly. Thus, in all the things which appear shocking and terrible to human feebleness, the real evil is the injustice; the rest is only the result of natural properties or of moral demerit. This injustice is seen in every case where a man loves for their own sake things which are desirable only as means to an end, and seeks for the sake of something else things which ought to be loved for themselves. For thus, as far as he can, he disturbs in himself the natural order which the eternal law requires us to observe. Again, a man is just when he seeks to use things only for the end for which God appointed them, and to enjoy God as the end of all, while he enjoys himself and his friend in God and for God. For to love in a friend the love of God is to love the friend for God. Now both justice and injustice, to be acts at all, must be voluntary; otherwise, there can be no just rewards or punishments; which no man in his senses will assert. The ignorance and infirmity which prevent a man from knowing his duty, or from doing all he wishes to do, belong to God's secret penal arrangement, and to His unfathomable judgments, for with Him there is no iniquity. Thus we are informed by the sure word of God of Adam's sin; and Scripture truly declares that in him all die, and that by him sin entered into the world, and death by sin. And our experience gives abundant evidence, that in punishment for this sin our body is corrupted, and weighs down the soul, and the clay tabernacle clogs the mind in its manifold activity; and we know that we can be freed from this punishment only by gracious interposition. So the apostle cries out in distress, "O wretched man that I am! who shall deliver me from the body of this death? The grace of God through Jesus Christ our Lord." So much we know; but the reasons for the distribution of divine judgment and mercy, why one is in this condition, and another in that, though just, are unknown. Still, we are sure that all these things are due either to the mercy or the judgment of God, while the measures and numbers and weights by which the Creator of all natural productions arranges all things are concealed from our view. For God is not the author, but He is the controller of sin; so that sinful actions, which are sinful because they are against nature, are judged and controlled, and assigned to their proper place and condition, in order that they may not bring discord and disgrace on universal nature. This being the case, and as the judgments of God and the movements of man's will contain the hidden reason why the same prosperous circumstances which some make a right use of are the ruin of others, and the same afflictions under which some give way are profitable to others, and since the whole mortal life of man upon earth is a trial, who can tell whether it may be good or bad in any particular case—in time of peace, to reign or to serve, or to be at ease or to die—or in time of war, to command or to fight, or to conquer or to be killed? At the same time, it remains true, that whatever is good is so by the divine blessing, and whatever is bad is so by the divine judgment.

T. H. GREEN (1836–1882)

The Right of the State Over the Individual in War

It may be admitted that to describe war as 'multitudinous murder' is a figure of speech. The essence of murder does not lie in the fact that one man takes away the life of another, but that he does this to 'gain his private ends' and with 'malice' against the person killed. I am not here speaking of the legal definition of murder, but of murder as a term of moral reprobation, in which sense it must be used by those who speak of war as 'multitudinous murder.' They cannot mean murder in the legal sense, because in that sense only 'unlawful killing,' which killing in war is not, is murder. . . . Of murder in the moral sense the characteristics are those stated, and these are not present in the case of a soldier who kills one on the other side in battle. He has no ill-will to that particular person or to any particular person. He incurs an equal risk with the person whom he kills, and incurs that risk not for the sake of killing him. His object in undergoing it is not private to himself, but a service (or what he supposes to be a service) to his country, a good which is his own no doubt (that is implied in his desiring it), but which he presents to himself as common to him with others. Indeed, those who might speak of war as 'multitudinous murder' would not look upon the soldier as a murderer. . . .

It does not follow from this, however, that war is ever other than a great wrong, as a violation on a multitudinous scale of the individual's right to life. Whether it is so or not must be discussed on other grounds. If there is such a thing as a right to life on the part of the individual

The selection is from T. H. Green, *Lectures on the Principles of Political Obligation,* in Vol. II of the *Works of Thomas Hill Green* (London : Longmans, Green, and Co., 1900).

374 STUDIES IN SOCIAL ETHICS

man as such, is there any reason to doubt that this right is violated in the case of every man killed in war? It is not to the purpose to allege that in order to a violation of right there must be not only a suffering of some kind on the part of the subject of a right, but an intentional act causing it on the part of a human agent. There is of course no violation of right when a man is killed by a wild beast or a stroke of lightning, because there is no right as between a man and a beast or between a man and a natural force. But the deaths in a battle are caused distinctly by human agency and intentional agency. The individual soldier may not have any very distinct intention when he fires his rifle except to obey orders, but the commanders of the army and the statesmen who send it into the field intend the death of as many men as may be necessary for their purpose. . . .

Is there then any condition on the part of the persons killed that saves the act from having this character? It may be urged that when the war is conducted according to usages that obtain between civilised nations, (not when it is a village-burning war like that between the English and Afghans), the persons killed are voluntary combatants, and οὐδεὶς ἀδικεῖται ἑκών. Soldiers, it may be said, are in the position of men who voluntarily undertake a dangerous employment. If some of them are killed, this is not more a violation of the human right to life than is the death of men who have engaged to work in a dangerous coal-pit. To this it must be answered that if soldiers did in fact voluntarily incur the special risk of death incidental to their calling, it would not follow that the right to life was not violated in their being killed. It is not a right which it rests with a man to retain or give up at his pleasure. It is not the less a wrong that a man should be a slave because he has sold himself into slavery. The individual's right to live is but the other side of the right which society has in his living. The individual can no more voluntarily rid himself of it than he can of the social capacity, the human nature, on which it is founded. Thus, however ready men may be for high wages to work in a dangerous pit, a wrong is held to be done if they are killed in it. If provisions which might have made it safe have been neglected, someone is held responsible. If nothing could make it safe, the working of the pit would not be allowed. The reason for not more generally applying the power of the state to prevent voluntary noxious employments, is not that there is no wrong in the death of the individual through the incidents of an employment which he has voluntarily undertaken, but that the wrong is more effectually prevented by training and trusting individuals to protect themselves than by the state protecting them. Thus the waste of life in war would not be the less a wrong,—not the less a violation of the right, which subsists between all members of society, and which none can alienate, that each should have his life respected by society,—if it were the fact that those whose lives are wasted voluntarily incurred the risk of losing them. But it can scarcely be held to be the fact. Not only is it impossible, even when war is conducted on the most civilised methods, to prevent great incidental loss of life (to say nothing of other injury) among non-combatants; the waste of the life of the combatants is one which the power of the state compels. This is equally true whether the army is raised by voluntary enlistment or by conscription. It is obviously so in the case of conscription; but under a system of voluntary enlistment, though the individual soldier cannot say that he in particular has been compelled by the government to risk his life, it is still the case that the state compels the risk of a certain number of lives. It decrees that an army of such a size shall be raised, though if it can get the men by voluntary hiring it does not exercise compulsion on the men of a particular age, and it sends the army into the field. Its compulsive agency causes the death of the soldiers killed, not any voluntary action on the part of the soldiers themselves. The action of the soldiers no doubt contributes to the result, for if they all refused to fight there would be no killing, but it is an action put in motion and directed by the power of the state, which is compulsive in the sense that it operates on the individual in the last resort through fear of death.

We have then in war a destruction of human life inflicted on the sufferers intentionally by voluntary human agency. It is true, as we saw, that it is not easy to say in any case by whose agency in particular. We may say indeed that it is by the agency of the state, but what exactly does that mean? The state here must=the sovereign power in the state; but it is always difficult to say by whom that power is wielded, and if we could in any case specify its present holders, the further question will arise whether their course of action has not been shaped for them by previous holders of power. But however widely distributed the agency may be which causes the destruction of life in war, it is still intentional human agency. The destruction is not the work of accident or of nature. If then it is to be other than a wrong, because a violation of the right to mutual protection of life involved in the membership of human society, it can only be because there is exercised in war some right that is paramount to this. It may be argued that this is the case; that there is no right to the preservation of life at the cost of losing the necessary conditions of 'living well'; that war is in some cases the only means of maintaining these conditions, and that where this is so, the wrong of causing the destruction of physical life disappears in the paramount right of preserving the conditions under which alone moral life is possible.

This argument, however, seems to be only available for shifting the quarter in which we might be at first disposed to lay the blame of the wrong involved in war, not for changing the character of that wrong. It goes to show that the wrong involved in the death of certain soldiers does not necessarily lie with the government which sends those soldiers into the field, because this may be the only means by which the government can prevent more serious wrong; it does not show that there is no wrong in their death. If the integrity of any state can only be maintained at the cost of war, and if that state is more than what many so-called states have been,—more than an aggregation of individuals or communities under one ruling power,—if it so far fulfils the idea of a state, that its maintenance is necessary to the free development of the people belonging to it; then by the authorities or people of that state no wrong is done by the destruction of life which war involves, except so far as they are responsible for the state of things which renders the maintenance of the integrity of the state impossible by other means. But how does it come about that the integrity of such a state is endangered? Not by accident or by the forces of nature, but by intentional human agency in some form or other, however complicated; and with that agency lies the wrong-doing. To determine it (as we might be able to do if a horde of barbarians broke in on a civilised state, compelling it to resort to war for its defence) is a matter of small importance: what *is* important to bear in mind (being one of those obvious truths out of which we may allow ourselves to be sophisticated), is that the destruction of life in war is always wrong-doing, whoever be the wrong-doer, and that in the wars most strictly defensive of political freedom the wrong-doing is only removed from the defenders of political freedom to be transfered elsewhere. If it is difficult in any case to say precisely where, that is only a reason for more general self-reproach, for a more humbling sense (as the preachers would say) of complicity in that radical (but conquerable, because moral) evil of mankind which renders such a means of maintaining political freedom necessary. The language, indeed, which we hear from the pulpit about war being a punishment for the sins of mankind, is perfectly true, but it needs to be accompanied by the reminder that this punishment of sin is simply a consequence of the sin and itself a further sin, brought about by the action of the sinner, not an external infliction brought about by agencies to which man is not a party.

In fact, however, if most wars had been wars for the maintenance or acquisition of political freedom, the difficulty of fixing the blame of them, or at any rate of freeing one of the parties in each case from blame, would be much less than it really is. Of the European wars of the last four hundred years, how many could be fairly said to have been wars in which either or any of the parties were fighting for this end? Perhaps the wars in which the Dutch Republics defended themselves against Spain and against Louis XIV, and that in which Germany shook off the dominion of Napoleon. Perhaps the more recent struggles of Italy and Hungary against the Austrian Government. Perhaps in the first outset of the war of 1792 the French may be fairly held to have been defending institutions necessary for the development of social freedom and equality. In this war, however, the issue very soon ceased to be one between the defenders of such institutions on the one side, and their assailants on the other, and in most modern wars the issue has not been of this kind at all. The wars have arisen primarily out of the rival ambition of kings and dynasties for territorial aggrandisement, with national antipathies and ecclesiastical ambitions, and the passions arising out of religious partisanship, as complicating influences. As nations have come more and more to distinguish and solidify themselves, and a national consciousness has come definitely to be formed in each, the rival ambitions of nations have tended more and more first to support, then perhaps to supersede, the ambitions of dynasties as causes of war. The delusion has been practically dominant that the gain of one nation must mean the loss of another. Hence national jealousies in regard to colonial extension, hostile tariffs and the effort of each nation to exclude others from its markets. The explosion of this idea in the region of political economy has had little effect in weakening its hold on men's minds. The people of one nation still hear with jealousy of another nation's advance in commerce, as if it meant some decay of their own. And if the commercial jealousy of nations is very slow in disappearing, their vanity, their desire apart from trade each to become or to seem stronger than the other, has very much increased. A hundred and fifty years ago national vanity could scarcely be said to be an influence in politics. The people under one ruler were not homogeneous enough, had not enough of a corporate consciousness, to develope a national vanity. Now (under the name of patriotism) it has become a more serious disturber of peace than dynastic ambition. Where the latter is dangerous, it is because it has national vanity to work upon.

Our conclusion then is that the destruction of life in war (to say nothing of other evils incidental to it with which we are not here con-cerned) is always wrong-doing, with whomsoever the guilt of the wrong-doing may lie; that only those parties to a war are exempt from a share in the guilt who can truly plead that to them war is the only means of maintaining the social conditions of the moral development of man, and that there have been very few cases in which this plea could be truly made. In saying this it is not forgotten, either that many virtues are called into exercise by war, or that wars have been a means by which the movement of mankind, which there is reason for considering a progress to higher good, has been carried on. These facts do not make the wrong-doing involved in war any less so. If nothing is to be accoun-ted wrong-doing through which final good is wrought, we must give up either the idea of there being such a thing as wrong-doing, or the idea of there being such a thing as final good. If final good results from the world of our experience, it results from processes in which wrong-doing is an inseparable element. Wrong-doing is voluntary action, either (in the deeper moral sense) proceeding from a will uninfluenced by the desire to be good on the part of the agent (which may be taken to include action tending to produce such action), or (in the sense contemplated by the 'jus naturæ') it is action that interferes with the conditions necessary to the free-play and development of a good-will on the part of others. It may be that, according to the divine scheme of the world, such wrong-doing is an element in a process by which men gradually approximate more nearly to good (in the sense of a good will). We cannot think of God as a moral being without supposing this to be the case. But this makes no difference to wrong-doing in those relations in which it *is* wrong-doing, and with which alone we are concerned, viz. in relation to the will of human agents and to the results which those agents can fore-see and intend to produce. If an action, so far as any results go which the agent can have in view or over which he has control, interferes with conditions necessary to the free-play and development of a good-will on the part of others, it is not the less wrong-doing because, through some agency which is not his, the effects which he intended, and which rendered it wrong-doing, come to contribute to an ulterior good. Nor, if it issues from bad will (in the sense explained), is it less wrong (in the moral sense) because this will is itself, in the view of some higher being, contributory to a moral good which is not, in whole or part, within the view of the agent. If then war is wrong-doing in both the above senses (as it is always, at any rate on the part of those with whom the ultimate responsibility for it lies), it does not cease to be so on account of any good resulting from it in a scheme of providence....

Reverting then to the questions which arose out of the assertion of a right to free life on the part of the individual man as such, it appears that the first must be answered in the negative. No state of war can make the destruction of man's life by man other than a wrong, though the wrong is not always chargeable upon all the parties to a war. The second question is virtually answered by what has been said about the first. In regard to the state according to its idea the question could not arise, for according to its idea the state is an institution in which all rights are harmoniously maintained, in which all the capacities that give rise to rights have free-play given to them. No action in its own interest of a state that fulfilled this idea could conflict with any true interest or right of general society, of the men not subject to its law taken as a whole. There is no such thing as an inevitable conflict between states. There is nothing in the nature of the state that, given a multiplicity of states, should make the gain of the one the loss of the other. The more perfectly each one of them attains its proper object of giving free scope to the capacities of all persons living on a certain range of territory, the easier it is for others to do so; and in proportion as they all do so the danger of conflict disappears.

On the other hand, the imperfect realisation of civil equality in the full sense of the term in certain states, is in greater or less degree a source of danger to all. The presence in states either of a prerogatived class or of a body of people who, whether by open denial of civil rights or by restrictive laws, are thwarted in the free development of their capacities, or of an ecclesiastical organisation which disputes the authority of the state on matters of right and thus prevents the perfect civil fusion of its members with other citizens, always breeds an imagination of there being some competition of interests between states. The privileged class involuntarily believes and spreads the belief that the interest of the state lies in some extension without, not in an improvement of organisation within. A suffering class attracts sympathy from without and invites interference with the state which contains it; and that state responds, not by healing the sore, but by defending against aggression what it conceives to be its special interests, but which are only special on account of its bad organisation. Or perhaps the suffering population overflows into another state, as the Irish into America, and there becomes a source not only of internal difficulty but of hostile feeling between it and the state where the suffering population still survives. People, again, who, in matters which the state treats as belonging to itself, take their direction from an ecclesiastical power external to the state under which they live, are necessarily in certain relations alien to that state, and may at any time prove a source of apparently conflicting interests between it and some other state, which under the influence of the hostile ecclesiastical power espouses their cause. Remove from European states, as they are and have been during the last hundred years, the occasions of conflict, the sources of apparently competing interests, which arise in one or other of the ways mentioned,—either from the mistaken view of state-interests which a privileged class inevitably takes, or from the presence in them of oppressed populations, or from what we improperly call the antagonism of religious confessions,—and there would not be or have been anything to disturb the peace between them. And this is to say that the source of war between states lies in their incomplete fulfilment of their function; in the fact that there is some defect in the maintenance or reconciliation of rights among their subjects. . . .

It will be said, perhaps, that these formal arguments in proof of the wrong-doing involved in war, and of the unjustifiability of the policy which nations constantly adopt in defence of their apparent interests, carry very little conviction; that a state is not an abstract complex of institutions for the maintenance of rights, but a nation, a people, possessing such institutions; that the nation has its passions which inevitably lead it to judge all questions of international right from its own point of view, and to consider its apparent national interests as justifying anything; that if it were otherwise, if the cosmopolitan point of view could be adopted by nations, patriotism would be at an end; that whether this be desirable or no, such an extinction of national passions is impossible; that while they continue, wars are as inevitable between nations as they would be between individuals, if individuals were living in what philosophers have imagined to be the state of nature, without recognition of a common superior; that nations in short are in the position of men judging their own causes, which it is admitted that no one can do impartially; and that this state of things cannot be altered without the establishment of a common constraining power, which would mean the extinction of the life of independent states,—a result as undesirable as it is unattainable. Projects of perpetual peace, to be logical, must be projects of all-embracing empire.

There is some cogency in language of this kind. It is true that when we speak of a state as a living agency, we mean, not an institution or complex of institutions, but a nation organised in a certain way; and that members of the nation in their corporate or associated action are animated by certain passions, arising out of their association, which, though not egoistic relatively to the individual subjects of them (for they are motives to self-sacrifice), may, in their influence on the dealings of one nation with another, have an effect analogous to that which egoistic passions, properly so called, have upon the dealings of individuals with each other. On the other hand, it must be remembered that the national passion, which in any good sense is simply the public spirit of the good citizen, may take, and every day is taking, directions which lead to no collision between one nation and another; (or, to say the same thing negatively, that it is utterly false to speak as if the desire for one's own nation to show more military strength than others were the only or the right form of patriotism); and that though a nation, with national feeling of its own, must everywhere underlie a state, properly so called, yet still, just so far as the perfect organisation of rights within each nation, which entitles it to be called a state, is attained, the occasions of conflict between nations disappear; and again, that by the same process, just so far as it is satisfactorily carried out, an organ of expression and action is established for each nation in dealing with other nations, which is not really liable to be influenced by the same egoistic passions in dealing with the government of another nation as embroil individuals with each other. The love of mankind, no doubt, needs to be particularised in order to have any power over life and action. Just as there can be no true friendship except towards this or that individual, so there can be no true public spirit which is not localised in some way. The man whose desire to serve his kind is not centred primarily in some home, radiating from it to a commune, a municipality, and a nation, presumably has no effectual desire to serve his kind at all. But there is no reason why this localised or nationalised philanthropy should take the form of a jealousy of other nations or a desire to fight them, personally or by proxy. Those in whom it is strongest are every day expressing it in good works which benefit their fellow-citizens without interfering with the men of other nations. Those who from time to time talk of the need of a great war to bring unselfish impulses into play, give us reason to suspect that they are too selfish themselves to recognise the unselfish activity that is going on all round them. Till all the methods have been exhausted by which nature can be brought into the service of man, till society is so organised that everyone's capacities have free scope for their development, there is no need to resort to war for a field in which patriotism may display itself.

WILLIAM JAMES (1842–1910)

The Moral Equivalent of War

The war against war is going to be no holiday excursion or camping party. The military feelings are too deeply grounded to abdicate their place among our ideals until better substitutes are offered than the glory and shame that come to nations as well as to individuals from the ups and downs of politics and the vicissitudes of trade. There is something highly paradoxical in the modern man's relation to war. Ask all our millions, north and south, whether they would vote now (were such a thing possible) to have our war for the Union expunged from history, and the record of a peaceful transition to the present time substituted for that of its marches and battles, and probably hardly a handful of eccentrics would say yes. Those ancestors, those efforts, those memories and legends, are the most ideal part of what we now own together, a sacred spiritual possession worth more than all the blood poured out. Yet ask those same people whether they would be willing in cold blood to start another civil war now to gain another similar possession, and not one man or woman would vote for the proposition. In modern eyes, precious though wars may be, they must not be waged solely for the sake of the ideal harvest. Only when forced upon one, only when an enemy's injustice leaves us no alternative, is a war now thought permissible. . . .

In my remarks, pacificist though I am, I will refuse to speak of the bestial side of the war-*régime* (already done justice to by many writers) and consider only the higher aspects of militaristic sentiment. Patriotism no one thinks discreditable; nor does any one deny that war is the romance of history. But inordinate ambitions are the soul of every patriotism, and the possibility of violent death the soul of all romance. The militarily patriotic and romantic-minded everywhere, and especially the professional military class, refuse to admit for a moment that war may be a transitory phenomenon in social evolution. The notion of a sheep's paradise like that revolts, they say, our higher imagination. Where then would be the steeps of life? If war had ever stopped, we should have to re-invent it, on this view, to redeem life from flat degeneration.

Written for and first published by the Association for International Conciliation (Leaflet No. 27) and also published in *McClure's Magazine,* August, 1910, and *The Popular Science Monthly,* October, 1910.

Reflective apologists for war at the present day all take it religiously. It is a sort of sacrament. Its profits are to the vanquished as well as to the victor; and quite apart from any question of profit, it is an absolute good, we are told, for it is human nature at its highest dynamic. Its "horrors" are a cheap price to pay for rescue from the only alternative supposed, of a world of clerks and teachers, of co-educational and zo-ophily, of "consumer's leagues" and "associated charities," of industrialism unlimited, and femininism unabashed. No scorn, no hardness, no valor any more! Fie upon such a cattleyard of a planet.

So far as the central essence of this feeling goes, no healthy minded person, it seems to me, can help to some degree partaking of it. Militarism is the great preserver of our ideals of hardihood, and human life with no use for hardihood would be contemptible. Without risks or prizes for the darer, history would be insipid indeed; and there is a type of military character which every one feels that the race should never cease to breed, for every one is sensitive to its superiority. The duty is incumbent on mankind, of keeping military characters in stock—of keeping them, if not for use, then as ends in themselves and as pure pieces of perfection,—so that Roosevelt's weaklings and mollycoddles may not end by making everything else disappear from the face of nature.

This natural sort of feeling forms, I think, the innermost soul of army-writings. Without any exception known to me, militarist authors take a highly mystical view of their subject, and regard war as a biological or sociological necessity, uncontrolled by ordinary psychological checks and motives. When the time of development is ripe the war must come, reason or no reason, for the justifications pleaded are invariably fictitious. War is, in short, a permanent human *obligation*. General Homer Lea, in his recent book "The Valor of Ignorance," plants himself squarely on this ground. Readiness for war is for him the essence of nationality, and ability in it the supreme measure of the health of nations.

Nations, General Lea says, are never stationary—they must necessarily expand or shrink, according to their vitality or decrepitude. Japan now is culminating; and by the fatal law in question it is impossible that her statesmen should not long since have entered, with extraordinary foresight, upon a vast policy of conquest—the game in which the first moves were her wars with China and Russia and her treaty with England, and of which the final objective is the capture of the Philippines, the Hawaiian Islands, Alaska, and the whole of our Coast west of the Sierra Passes. This will give Japan what her ineluctable vocation as a state absolutely forces her to claim, the possession of the entire Pacific Ocean; and to oppose these deep designs we Americans have, according to our author, nothing but our conceit, our ignorance, our commercialism, our corruption, and our feminism. General Lea makes a minute technical comparison of the military strength which we at present could oppose to the strength of Japan, and concludes that the islands, Alaska, Oregon, and Southern California, would fall almost without resistance, that San Francisco must surrender in a fortnight to a Japanese investment, that in three or four months the war would be over, and our republic, unable to regain what it had heedlessly neglected to protect sufficiently, would then "disintegrate," until perhaps some Caesar should arise to weld us again into a nation.

A dismal forecast indeed! Yet not unplausible, if the mentality of Japan's statesmen be of the Caesarian type of which history shows so many examples, and which is all that General Lea seems able to imagine. But there is no reason to think that women can no longer be the mothers of Napoleonic or Alexandrian characters; and if these come in Japan and find their opportunity, just such surprises as "The Valor of Ignorance" paints may lurk in ambush for us. Ignorant as we still are of the innermost recesses of Japanese mentality, we may be foolhardy to disregard such possibilities.

Other militarists are more complex and more moral in their considerations. The "Philosophie des Krieges," by S. R. Steinmetz is a good example. War, according to this author, is an ordeal instituted by God, who weighs the nations in its balance. It is the essential form of the State, and the only function in which peoples can employ all their powers at once and convergently. No victory is possible save as the resultant of a totality of virtues, no defeat for which some vice or weakness is not responsible. Fidelity, cohesiveness, tenacity, heroism, conscience, education, inventiveness, economy, wealth, physical health and vigor—there isn't a moral or intellectual point of superiority that doesn't tell, when God holds his assizes and hurls the peoples upon one another. *Die Weltgeschichte ist das Weltgericht*; and Dr. Steinmetz does not believe that in the long run chance and luck play any part in apportioning the issues.

The virtues that prevail, it must be noted, are virtues anyhow, superiorities that count in peaceful as well as in military competition; but the strain on them, being infinitely intenser in the latter case, makes war infinitely more searching as a trial. No ordeal is comparable to its winnowings. Its dread hammer is the welder of men into cohesive states, and nowhere but in such states can human nature adequately develop its capacity. The only alternative is "degeneration."

Dr. Steinmetz is a conscientious thinker, and his book, short as it is, takes much into account. Its upshot can, it seems to me, be summed up in Simon Patten's word, that mankind was nursed in pain and fear, and that the transition to a "pleasure-economy" may be fatal to a being wielding no powers of defence against its disintegrative influences. If we speak of the *fear of emancipation from the fear-régime,* we put the whole situation into a single phrase; fear regarding ourselves now taking the place of the ancient fear of the enemy.

Turn the fear over as I will in my mind, it all seems to lead back to two unwillingnesses of the imagination, one aesthetic, and the other moral; unwillingness, first to envisage a future in which army-life, with its many elements of charm, shall be forever impossible, and in which the destinies of peoples shall nevermore be decided quickly, thrillingly, and tragically, by force, but only gradually and insipidly by "evolution"; and, secondly, unwillingness to see the supreme military aptitudes of men doomed to keep always in a state of latency and never show themselves in action. These insistent unwillingnesses, no less than other aesthetic and ethical insistencies, have, it seems to me, to be listened to and respected. One cannot meet them effectively by mere counter-insistency on war's expensiveness and horror. The horror makes the thrill; and when the question is of getting the extremest and supremest out of human nature, talk of expense sounds ignominious. The weakness of so much merely negative criticism is evident—pacificism makes no converts from the military party. The military party denies neither the bestiality nor the horror, nor the expense; it only says that these things tell but half the story. It only says that war is *worth* them; that, taking human nature as a whole, its wars are its best protection against its weaker and more cowardly self, and that mankind cannot *afford* to adopt a peace-economy.

Pacificists ought to enter more deeply into the aesthetical and ethical point of view of their opponents. Do that first in any controversy, says J. J. Chapman, *then move the point,* and your opponent will follow. So long as anti-militarists propose no substitute for war's disciplinary function, no *moral equivalent* of war, analogous, as one might say, to the mechanical equivalent of heat, so long they fail to realize the full inwardness of the situation. And as a rule they do fail. The duties, penalties, and sanctions pictured in the utopias they paint are all too weak and tame to touch the military-minded. Tolstoi's pacificism is the only exception to this rule, for it is profoundly mystic as regards all this world's values, and makes the fear of the Lord furnish the moral spur provided elsewhere by the fear of the enemy. But our socialistic peace-advocates all believe absolutely in this world's values; and instead of the fear of the Lord and the fear of the enemy, the only fear they reckon with is the fear of poverty if one be lazy. This weakness pervades all the socialistic literature with which I am acquainted. Even in Lowes Dickinson's exquisite dialogue,[1] high wages and short hours are the only forces invoked for overcoming man's distaste for repulsive kinds of labor. Meanwhile men at large still live as they always have lived, under a pain-and-fear economy—for those of us who live in an ease-economy are but an island in the stormy ocean—and the whole atmosphere of present-day utopian literature tastes mawkish and dishwatery to people who still keep a sense for life's more bitter flavors. It suggests, in truth, ubiquitous inferiority.

Inferiority is always with us, and merciless scorn of it is the keynote of the military temper. "Dogs, would you live forever?" shouted Frederick the Great. "Yes," say our utopians, "let us live forever, and raise our level gradually." The best thing about our "inferiors" today is that they are as tough as nails, and physically and morally almost as squeamish, while militarism would keep their callousness, but transfigure it into a meritorious characteristic, needed by "the service," and redeemed by that from the suspicion of inferiority. All the qualities of a man acquire dignity when he knows that the service of the collectivity that owns him needs them. If proud of the collectivity, his own pride rises in proportion. No collectivity is like an army for nourishing such pride; but it has to be confessed that the only sentiment which the image of pacific cosmopolitan industrialism is capable of arousing in countless worthy breasts is shame at the idea of belonging to *such* a collectivity. It is obvious that the United States of America as they exist today impress a mind like General Lea's as so much human blubber. Where is the sharpness and precipitousness, the contempt for life, whether one's own, or another's? Where is the savage "yes" and "no," the unconditional duty? Where is anything that one feels honored by belonging to?

Having thus much in preparation, I will now confess my own utopia. I devoutly believe in the reign of peace and in the gradual advent of some sort of a socialistic equilibrium. The fatalistic view of the war-function is to me nonsense, for I know that war-making is due to definite motives and subject to prudential checks and reasonable criticisms, just like any other form of enterprise. And when whole

[1] "Justice and Liberty," N.Y., 1909.

nations are the armies, and the science of destruction vies in intellectual refinement with the sciences of production, I see that war becomes absurd and impossible from its own monstrosity. Extravagant ambitions will have to be replaced by reasonable claims, and nations must make common cause against them. I see no reason why all this should not apply to yellow as well as to white countries, and I look forward to a future when acts of war shall be formally outlawed as between civilized peoples.

All these beliefs of mine put me squarely into the anti-militarist party. But I do not believe that peace either ought to be or will be permanent on this globe, unless the states pacifically organized preserve some of the old elements of army-discipline. A permanently successful peace-economy cannot be a simple pleasure-economy. In the more or less socialistic future towards which mankind seems drifting we must still subject ourselves collectively to those severities which answer to our real position upon this only partly hospitable globe. We must make new energies and hardihoods continue the manliness to which the military mind so faithfully clings. Martial virtues must be the enduring cement; intrepidity, contempt of softness, surrender of private interest, obedience to command, must still remain the rock upon which states are built— unless, indeed, we wish for dangerous reactions against commonwealths fit only for contempt, and liable to invite attack whenever a centre of crystallization for military-minded enterprise gets formed anywhere in their neighborhood.

The war-party is assuredly right in affirming and reaffirming that the martial virtues, although originally gained by the race through war, are absolute and permanent human goods. Patriotic pride and ambition in their military form are, after all, only specifications of a more general competitive passion. They are its first form, but that is no reason for supposing them to be its last form. Men now are proud of belonging to a conquering nation, and without a murmur they lay down their persons and their wealth, if by so doing they may fend off subjection. But who can be sure that *other aspects of one's country* may not, with time and education and suggestion enough, come to be regarded with similarly effective feelings of pride and shame? Why should men not some day feel that it is worth a blood-tax to belong to a collectivity superior in *any* ideal respect? Why should they not blush with indignant shame if the community that owns them is vile in any way whatsoever? Individuals, daily more numerous, now feel this civic passion. It is only a question of blowing on the spark till the whole population gets incandescent, and on the ruins of the old morals of military honor, a stable system of morals of civic honor builds itself up. What the whole community comes to believe in grasps the individual as in a vise. The war-function has grasped us so far; but constructive interests may some day seem no less imperative, and impose on the individual a hardly lighter burden.

Let me illustrate my idea more concretely. There is nothing to make one indignant in the mere fact that life is hard, that men should toil and suffer pain. The planetary conditions once for all are such, and we can stand it. But that so many men, by mere accidents of birth and opportunity, should have a life of *nothing else* but toil and pain and hardness and inferiority imposed upon them, should have *no* vacation, while others natively no more deserving never get any taste of this campaigning life at all—*this* is capable of arousing indignation reflective minds. It may end by seeming shameful to all of us that some of us have nothing but campaigning, and others nothing but unmanly ease. If now—and this is my idea—there were, instead of military conscription a conscription of the whole youthful population to form for a certain number of years a part of the army enlisted against *Nature*, the injustice would tend to be evened out, and numerous other goods to the commonwealth would follow. The military ideals of hardihood and discipline would be wrought into the growing fibre of the people; no one would remain blind as the luxurious classes now are blind, to man's relations to the globe he lives on, and to the permanently sour and hard foundations of his higher life. To coal and iron mines, to freight trains, to fishing fleets in December, to dishwashing, clothes-washing, window-washing, to road-building, and tunnel-making to, foundries and stoke-holes, and to the frames of skyscrapers, would our gilded youths be drafted off, according to their choice, to get the childishness knocked out of them, and to come back into society with healthier sympathies and soberer ideas. They would have paid their blood-tax, done their own part in the immemorial human warfare against nature; they would tread the earth more proudly, the women would value them more highly, they would be better fathers and teachers of the following generation.

Such a conscription, with the state of public opinion that would have required it, and the many moral fruits it would bear, would preserve in the midst of a pacific civilization the manly virtues which the military party is so afraid of seeing disappear in peace. We should get toughness without callousness, authority with as little criminal cruelty as possible, and painful work done cheerily because the duty is temporary, and threatens not, as now, to degrade the whole remainder of one's life

I spoke of the "moral equivalent" of war. So far, war has been the only force that can discipline a whole community, and until an equivalent discipline is organized, I believe that war must have its way. But I have no serious doubt that the ordinary prides and shames of social man, once developed to a certain intensity, are capable of organizing such a moral equivalent as I have sketched, or some other just as effective for preserving manliness of type. It is but a question of time, of skilful propagandism, and of opinion-making men seizing historic opportunities.

The martial type of character can be bred without war. Strenuous honor and disinterestedness abound elsewhere. Priests and medical men are in a fashion educated to it, and we should all feel some degree of it imperative if we were conscious of our work as an obligatory service to the state. We should be *owned*, as soldiers are by the army, and our pride would rise accordingly. We could be poor, then, without humiliation, as army officers now are. The only thing needed henceforward is to inflame the civic temper as past history has inflamed the military temper. H. G. Wells, as usual, sees the centre of the situation. "In many ways," he says, "military organization is the most peaceful of activities. When the contemporary man steps from the street, of clamorous insincere advertisement, push, adulteration, underselling and intermittent employment into the barrack-yard, he steps on to a higher social plane, into an atmosphere of service and cooperation and of infinitely more honorable emulations. Here at least men are not flung out of employment to degenerate because there is no immediate work for them to do. They are fed and drilled and trained for better services. Here at least a man is supposed to win promotion by self-forgetfulness and not by self-seeking. And beside the feeble and irregular endowment of research by commercialism, its little short-sighted snatches at profit by innovation and scientific economy, see how remarkable is the steady and rapid development of method and appliances in naval and military affairs! Nothing is more striking than to compare the progress of civil conveniences which has been left almost entirely to the trader, to the progress in military apparatus during the last few decades. The house-appliances of today, for example, are little better than they were fifty years ago. A house of today is still almost as ill-ventilated, badly heated by wasteful fires, clumsily arranged and furnished as the house of 1858. Houses a couple of hundred years old are still satisfactory places of residence, so little have our standards risen. But the rifle or battleship of fifty years ago was beyond all comparison inferior to those we possess; in power, in speed, in convenience alike. No one has a use now for such superannuated things."[2]

Wells adds[3] that he thinks that the conceptions of order and discipline, the tradition of service and devotion, of physical fitness, unstinted exertion, and universal responsibility, which universal military duty is now teaching European nations, will remain a permanent acquisition, when the last ammunition has been used in the fireworks that celebrate the final peace. I believe as he does. It would be simply preposterous if the only force that could work ideals of honor and standards of efficiency into English or American natures should be the fear of being killed by the Germans or Japanese. Great indeed is Fear; but it is not, as our military enthusiasts believe and try to make us believe, the only stimulus known for awakening the higher ranges of men's spiritual energy. The amount of alteration in public opinion which my utopia postulates is vastly less than the difference between the mentality of those black warriors who pursued Stanley's party on the Congo with their cannibal war-cry of "Meat! Meat!" and that of the "general staff" of any civilized nation. History has seen the latter interval bridged over: the former one can be bridged over much more easily.

BERTRAND RUSSELL (1872–1970)

An Appeal to the Intellectuals of Europe

Leibniz, writing to a French correspondent at a time when France and Hanover were at war, speaks of "this war, in which philosophy takes no interest." [Philosophische Werke, Gerhardt's edition, I., p. 420.] We have travelled far since those days. In modern times, philosophers, professors, and intellectuals generally undertake willingly to provide their respective governments with those ingenious distortions and those subtle untruths by which it is made to appear that all good is

[2] "First and Last Things," 1908, p. 215.
[3] "First and Last Things," 1908, p. 226.

The selection is from Bertrand Russell, *Justice in War Time* (LaSalle, Illinois: Open Court Publishing Company, 1917). Used by permission of the publisher.

on one side and all wickedness on the other. Side by side, in the pages of the *Scientia*, are to be read articles by learned men, all betraying shamelessly their national bias, all as incapable of justice as any cheap newspaper, all as full of special pleading and garbled history. And all accept, as a matter of course, the inevitability of each other's bias; disagreeing with each other's conclusions, yet they agree perfectly with each other's spirit. All agree that the whole of a writer's duty is to make out a case for his own country. . . .

I cannot but think that the men of learning, by allowing partiality to colour their thoughts and words, have missed the opportunity of performing a service to mankind for which their training should have specially fitted them. The truth, whatever it may be, is the same in England, France, and Germany, in Russia and in Austria. It will not adapt itself to national needs: it is in its essence neutral. It stands outside the clash of passions and hatreds, revealing, to those who seek it, the tragic irony of strife with its attendent world of illusions. Men of learning, who should be accustomed to the pursuit of truth in their daily work, might have attempted, at this time, to make themselves the mouthpiece of truth, to see what was false on their own side, what was valid on the side of their enemies. They might have used their reputation and their freedom from political entanglements to mitigate the abhorrence with which the nations have come to regard each other, to help towards mutual understanding, to make the peace, when it comes, not a mere cessation due to weariness, but a fraternal reconciliation, springing from realisation that the strife has been a folly of blindness. They have chosen to do nothing of all this. Allegiance to country has swept away allegiance to truth. Thought has become the slave of instinct, not its master. The guardians of the temple of Truth have betrayed it to idolaters, and have been the first to promote the idolatrous worship.

One of the most surprising things in this war is the universal appeal to atavistic moral notions which, in times of peace, civilised men would have repudiated with contempt. Germans speak of England's brutal national egotism, and represent Germany as fighting to maintain a great ideal of civilisation against an envious world. Englishmen speak of Germany's ruthless militarism and lust of dominion, and represent themselves as fighting to uphold the sacredness of treaties and the rights of small nations. In a sober mood, many of the men who use such language would recognise that it is melodramatic and mythical. All nations, at all times, are egotistic. It may happen, accidentally, that in pursuing its own interest a nation is also spreading civilisation or upholding the sacredness of treaties; but no impartial person can believe that for such ends a nation will sacrifice a million lives and a thousand millions of pounds. Such sacrifices are only made for nationally selfish ends, and until it is recognised that all the nations engaged in the war are equally and wholly selfish, no true thought about the issues involved is possible.

Moral judgments, as applied to others than oneself, are a somewhat subtilised police force: they make use of men's desire for approbation to bring self-interest into harmony with the interest of one's neighbours. But when a man is already trying to kill you, you will not feel much additional discomfort in the thought that he has a low opinion of your moral character. For this reason, disapproval of our enemies in wartime is useless, so far as any possible effect upon them is concerned. It has, however, a certain unconscious purpose, which is, to prevent humane feelings towards the enemy, and to nip in the bud any nascent sympathy for his sufferings. Under the stress of danger, beliefs and emotions all become subservient to the one end of self-preservation. Since it is repugnant to civilised men to kill and maim others just like themselves, it becomes necessary to conquer repugnance by denying the likeness and imputing wickedness to those whom we wish to injure. And so it comes about that the harshest moral judgments of the enemy are formed by the nations which have the strongest impulses of kindliness to overcome.

In order to support this belief in the peculiar wickedness of the enemy, a whole mythology of falsehood grows up, partly through the deliberate action of newspapers and governments, but chiefly through the inherent myth-making tendency of strong collective emotions. Every powerful passion brings with it an impulse to an attendant system of false beliefs. A man in love will attribute innumerable non-existent perfections to the object of his devotion; a jealous man will attribute equally non-existent crimes to the object of his jealousy. But in ordinary life, this tendency is continually held in check by intercourse with people who do not share our private passions, and who therefore are critical of our irrational beliefs. In national questions, this corrective is absent. Most men meet few foreigners, especially in time of war, and beliefs inspired by passion can be communicated to others without fear of an unsympathetic response. The supposed facts intensify the passion which they embody, and are magnified still further by those to whom they are told. Individual passions, except in lunatics, produce only the germs of myths, perpetually neutralised by the indifference of others; but collective passions escape this corrective, and generate in time what appears like overwhelming evidence for wholly false beliefs.

Men of learning, who are acquainted with the part played by collective error in the history of religion, ought to have been on their guard against assaults upon their credulity. They ought to have realised, from the obvious falsehood of the correlative opposite beliefs in enemy countries, that the myth-making impulse was unusually active, and could only be repelled by an unusual intellectual vigour. But I do not find that they were appreciably less credulous than the multitude. In the early days of last September, when the Germans were carrying all before them in France, the need for some source of hope produced in England an all but universal belief that a large Russian army had travelled from Archangel, through England, to Belgium. The evidence was very much better than the evidence for most facts of history: most men knew many eye-witnesses of their transit, and at last a newspaper published a telegram from its correspondent saying that he had discovered them in Belgium. Only then was the story officially denied, but for a long time many continued to believe it. And the intellectuals were not by any means less ready to believe it than the rest of the country.

The really harmful beliefs are those which produce hatred of the enemy. The devastation and maltreatment of Belgium might naturally have aroused some qualms among humane Germans. But the instinct of self-protection produced a harvest of accusations against the Belgians: that they put out the eyes of wounded Germans, or cut off their hands; that they behaved brutally to German women in Belgium; and, generally that they had shown such depravity as rendered them unworthy of consideration. At the very same time, innumerable German atrocities were reported in England. It cannot, unfortunately, be denied that many very shocking atrocities occurred, but not nearly so many as the English at first believed. Many men stated confidently that they knew people in England who had staying with them Belgian children whose hands had been cut off by German soldiers. Some such cases there were in Belgium, but I know of no evidence that any reached England. No effect whatever was produced by pointing out that if there were so many cases, at least one with a name and address would have been mentioned in the newspaper. Such arguments have no power against a belief which stimulates ferocity, and is on that account felt to be useful. No doubt atrocities have occurred on both sides. But it is certain that they have been far less numerous, and (for the most part) less unnatural, than they are almost universally believed to have been. . . .

The fundamental irrational belief, on which all the others rest, is the belief that the victory of one's own side is of enormous and indubitable importance, and even of such importance as to outweigh all the

evils involved in prolonging the war. It is possible, in view of the uncertainty of all human affairs, that the victory of one side or the other
might bring great good to humanity. But even if this be the case, the
beliefs of the combatants are none the less irrational, since there is no
evidence such as would convince an impartial outsider. The Allies are
convinced that their victory is for the good of mankind, and the Germans and Austrians are no less convinced in the opposite sense. When
a large mass of men hold one opinion, and another large mass hold
another, and when in each case the opinion is in accordance with self-
interest, it is hardly to be supposed that it is based on rational grounds
either on the one side or on the other. Meanwhile the evils produced by
the war increase from day to day, and they, at least, must be admitted by
both sides equally.

The difference of opinion as to the desirable issue of the war is not
wholly due to self-interest, though that is no doubt the chief cause. The
difference is due in part to divergent ideals embodying divergent desires.
Putting the matter crudely, and considering only the Western war, we
may say that the Germans love order, learning, and music, all of which
are good things, while the French and English love democracy and
liberty, which are also good things. In order to force their respective
ideals upon nations which do not value them, the Germans are willing
to replace order in Europe by the universal chaos of war, and to send the
young men who pursue learning or music to be killed on the battlefield,
while the French and English have found it necessary to suppress democracy and liberty for the present, without any guarantee that they will
be restored when the war is over. If the war lasts long, all that was good
in the ideals of Germany, France, and England will have perished, as the
ideals of Spartans and Athenians perished in the Peloponnesian War.
All three races, with all that they have added to our civilisation, will
have become exhausted, and victory, when it comes, will be as barren
and as hopeless as defeat.

Under the distorting influence of war, the doubtful and microscopic differences between different European nations have been exaggerated when it has become treason to question their overwhelming
importance. Every educated man knew and acknowledged before the
war began, and every educated man now knows without acknowledging,
that the likenesses among European nations are immeasurably greater
than their differences. Congresses, conferences, and international
bodies of many kinds testified to the diffused consciousness of a common purpose, a common task in the life of civilisation. Suddenly, between one day and the next, all this is forgotten: German scholars

repudiate English honours, English scholars say that Germany has done nothing of importance in learning. In a moment, all the great co-operative work for which academic bodies exist is set aside for the pleasure of indulging a bitter and trivial hatred.

This war is trivial, for all its vastness. No great principle is at stake, no great human purpose is involved on either side. The supposed ideal ends for which it is being fought are merely part of the myth. Every nation is fighting in self-defence, every nation is fighting to destroy the tyranny of armaments, every nation is fighting to show that unprovoked aggression cannot be practised with impunity. Every nation pays homage to peace by maintaining that its enemies began the war. The fact that these assertions carry equal conviction on both sides shows that they are not based on reason, but are merely inspired by prejudice. But besides these common objects there are some in which the two sides differ. Probably the two Kaisers would say, and perhaps believe, that they are fighting to prove it a crime to assassinate heirs to thrones. It can hardly be supposed that the Tsar would deny that this is a crime, but he would say, as the English do, that it is a crime for a great nation to oppress a small one. This proposition, however, is only true in certain latitudes; it does not apply to Finland or Persia. The English and French say they are fighting in defence of democracy, but they do not wish their words to be heard in Petrograd or Calcutta. And, oddly enough, those who most bitterly hate democracy at home are the most ferocious in defending it against Germany.

This war is not being fought for any rational end; it is being fought because, at first, the nations wished to fight, and now they are angry and determined to win victory. Everything else is idle talk, artificial rationalising of instinctive actions and passions. When two dogs fight in the street, no one supposes that anything but instinct prompts them, or that they are inspired by high and noble ends. But if they were capable of what is called thought, if they had been taught that Dog is a rational animal, we may be sure that a superstructure of belief would grow up in them during the combat. They fight really because something angers them in each other's smell. But if their fighting were accompanied by intellectual activity, the one would say he was fighting to promote the right kind of smell (*Kultur*), and the other to uphold the inherent canine right of running on the pavement (democracy). Yet this would not prevent the bystanders from seeing that their action was foolish, and that they ought to be parted as soon as possible. And what is true of dogs in the street is equally true of nations in the present war.

The original impulse towards war, though by now it has spent its force, was very strong in the first days. Fighting and killing are among the natural activities of males, both of human beings and of the higher animals. The spectacle of males killing each other in sexual combat is pleasant, presumably, to animal females, and certainly to many of those of the species *homo sapiens.* Owing to the activities of the police, opportunities for these pleasures are much curtailed in civilised countries. For this reason, when war is coming there is a liberation of a whole set of instinctive activities normally repressed. This brings with it an exhilaration comparable to that of falling in love. Instead of being oppressed by the prospect of the horrors of war—friends and relations killed or maimed, countries ravaged, civilisation bleeding in the mire— most men, in the first days, were excited and happy, feeling an unusual freedom, and inventing, with unconscious hypocrisy, all sorts of humane reasons to excuse their joy. In this mood there is no great hatred of the enemy: he has his uses, since without him there could be no fighting. The injury to him is a merely incidental and almost regrettable result of the battle. Primitive poetry is full of this mood, and the early days of August showed that it is still possible to civilised men.

But when, as in this war, neither side wins decisive successes, and the utmost effort is required to avert disaster, the honeymoon intoxication of the first moments is soon succeeded by a sterner mood. Checks cause fury, and injuries suffered produce hatred. More and more men's thought become concentrated on humbling the pride of their enemies. If the war remains undecided for a long time, if the new levies on both sides are exterminated without either victory or defeat, there will be a growing ferocity, leading to horrors such as even this war has not yet brought into the imaginations of men. One by one soldiers will pass suddenly from ferocity to apathy: the spring of will will break, leaving millions of derelicts fit only for the hospital or the asylum. This is what the German military authorities mean when they say that the war will be decided by nervous endurance. They hope that a smaller percentage of the Germans than of the Allies will be broken by the strain. Militarists on both sides look forward cheerfully to the extinction, for all purposes of national life, of most of the men now between twenty and forty. And yet they continue to pretend that the victory of their side is more important than an early peace. And in this infamy their professorial parasites support them and egg them on.

The worst disasters would have been averted if either side had won a rapid victory, and are even now not inevitable if the war comes to an end during this year. But if peace is not made soon if no military decision is reached, there will have to be an increasing passionate concentration of will in all countries upon the one common purpose of mutual destruction. As the effort of will required grows greater and more difficult through weariness, the vital force of the nations will be more and more weakened. When at last peace comes, it is to be feared that no stimulus will be adequate to rouse men to action. After the fierce tension of combat, nothing will seem important; a weak and relaxed dissipation will succeed the terrible unnatural concentration. There is no parallel in history to the conflict in which the world is now engaged. Never before have so large a proportion of the population been engaged in fighting, and never before has the fighting been so murderous. All that science and organisation have done to increase the efficiency of labour has been utilised to set free more men for the destructive work of the battlefield. Man's greater command over Nature has only magnified the disaster, because it has not been accomplished by greater command over his own passions. And if he does not acquire command over his own passions, whatever destruction is not achieved now is only postponed to a later day.

The degradation of science from its high function in ameliorating the lot of man is one of the most painful aspects of this war. Savage man, like the brutes, lives in bondage to matter: the task of securing a bare subsistence absorbs his energies, leaving no leisure for art and thought and the goods of the mind. From this bondage science has been progressively liberating the populations of civilized countries. One man's labour now will produce a great deal more than one man's food. Out of the time set free in this way have grown literature and music, poetry and philosophy, and the intoxicating triumphs of science itself. On the basis of the greater productivity of labour, education, democracy, and all the political advances of the modern State have been built. Suddenly, now, because a madness of destruction has swept over Europe, the men of science have abandoned their beneficent activities: physicists invent swifter aircraft, chemists devise more deadly explosives, and almost all who can, devote themselves to the labour of death. The place of science in human development, one is compelled to think, has never become present to their minds, since they are willing to prostitute it to the undoing of its own work.

Knowledge with elevation of mind is the chief instrument of human progress; knowledge without elevation of mind easily becomes devilish, and increases the wounds which man inflicts on man. Men of learning should be the guardians of one of the sacred fires that illumine the darkness into which the human spirit is born: upon them depends the ideal of just thought, of disinterested pursuit of truth, which, if it had existed more widely, would have sufficed alone to prevent the present horror. To serve this ideal, to keep alive a purpose remote from strife, is more worthy of the intellectual leaders of Europe than to help Governments in stimulating hatred or slaughtering more of the young men upon whom the future of the world depends. It is time to forget our supposed separate duty toward Germany, Austria, Russia, France, or England, and remember that higher duty to mankind in which we can still be at one.

MAURICE MERLEAU-PONTY (1908–1961)

The War Has Taken Place

. . . We have been led to take upon ourselves and consider as our own not only our intentions—what our actions mean for us—but also the external consequences of these actions, what they mean in a historical context. Twenty years ago a historian denounced the Allies' share of responsibility for World War I. During the Occupation we were stupefied that this same historian should publish—with the permission of the censors—a pamphlet denouncing England's role in starting World War II. He did not understand that to implicate England with the Germans occupying Paris was to accept responsibility for propaganda no pacifist had the right to further, since it was the instrument of a martial regime. In the spring of 1944 all professors were asked to sign a petition entreating Pétain to intervene and stop the war. It would be overly simple to assume that the men who composed and signed this petition were agents of the Germans trying to end the war before the German defeat. Treason is rarely committed with such clarity, at least among professors, and they are the type of men who are never swayed by self-interest alone, but also by ideas. Let us then try to imagine one of the authors of this petition. For him, the passions of war *do not exist:* they gain their apparent strength from the consent of men who are *equally free at*

The selection is from Maurice Merleau-Ponty, *Sense and Non-Sense,* trans. Hubert L. Dreyfus and Patricia Allen Dreyfus (Chicago: Northwestern University Press, 1964), pp. 145–150. French edition by Les Éditions Nagel, Paris. Used by permission of the publishers.

every moment. Therefore there is no world at war, with democracies on one side and Fascist states on the other, or with the established empires lined up against the late-comer nations eager to found empires for themselves (the former accidentally allied to a "proletarian" state). There are no empires, no nations, no classes. On every side there are only men who are always ready for freedom and happiness, always able to attain them under any regime, provided they take hold of themselves and recover the only freedom that exists: their free judgment. There is only one evil, war itself, and one duty, refusing to believe in victories of right and civilization and putting an end to war. So this solitary Cartesian thinks—but he does not see his shadow behind him projected onto history as onto a wall, that meaning, that appearance which his actions assume on the outside, that Objective Spirit which is himself.

The Cartesian would doubtless reply that if we hold ourselves responsible for the most distant consequences of our thoughts and actions, the only thing left for us to do is refuse all compromise as does the hero. And, he would add, how many heroes are there among the men who today take pride in their having resisted? Some were civil servants and continued to draw their salary, swearing in writing— since they had to—that they were neither Jews nor Masons. Others of them agreed to seek authorization of what they wrote or staged from a censorship which let nothing pass which did not serve its purpose. Each in his own way marked out the frontier of the permissible. "Don't publish anything," said one. "Don't publish anything in the newspapers or magazines," said another. "Just publish your books." And a third said, "I will let this theater have my play if the director is a good man, but if he is a servant of the government, I will withdraw it." The truth is that each of them settled with outward necessity, all except a few who gave their lives. One could either stop living, refusing that corrupted air, that poisoned bread, or one could continue, which meant contriving a little hide-out of private freedom in the midst of the common misery; and this is what most of them did, putting their consciences to rest by means of some carefully weighed sacrifices. Our compromise does not acquit the traitors who called this regime down upon us, aided it more than what was absolutely necessary, and were the self-appointed keepers of the new law. It does, however, prohibit us from judging them in the name of a morality which no one followed to the letter and from basing a new philosophy on the experience of those four years, since we lived according to the old one. Only the heroes really were outwardly what they inwardly wished to be; only they became one with history at the moment when it claimed their lives.

Those who survived, even at the greatest risk, did not consummate this cruel marriage, and no one can speak of this silence or recommend it to others. Heroism a thing not of words but of deeds, and any preaching would be presumptuous here, since the man who is still able to speak does not know what he is speaking of.

This line of reasoning is hard, but it leads in the direction we want to go. It is true that we are not innocent and that the situation in which we found ourselves admitted of no irreproachable conduct. By staying here we all became accomplices to some extent, and we must say of the Resistance what the combatants said about the war: no one comes back except the man who at some moment or another reduced the risks he was running, who, in that sense, elected to save his life. Nor can those who left France to pursue the war elsewhere with arms or propaganda lay any more claim to purity, for they escaped a direct compromise only by yielding the ground for a while, and in this sense they too had a part in the ravages of the Occupation. Several of our comrades asked themselves the question and made the best choice, but nothing can turn their decision into a true solution. One compromised oneself whether one stayed or left; no one's hands are clean (which is perhaps why the Germans found the corpses of Martel and several others at Paris). We have unlearned "pure morality" and learned a kind of vulgar immoralism, which is healthy. The moral man does not want to dirty his hands. It is because he usually has enough time, talent, or money to stand back from enterprises of which he disapproves and to prepare a good conscience for himself. The common people do not have that freedom: the garage mechanic had to repair German cars if he wanted to live. One of our comrades used to go to the Rive Gauche Bookstore for the German philosophy books he needed. When the day came, he took part in the uprising, and was shot by the Germans. We are in the world, mingled with it, compromised with it. This is no reason to surrender all that is exterior and to confine ourselves to our thoughts, which are always free, even in the mind of a slave. This division of interior and exterior is abstract. We give the world both too little and too much credit. Too much because we bring weight to it when the time comes, and the State as was evident with the Vichy State, is nothing without our consent. Too little because it arouses our *interest*, because we exist in it, and the wish to be free on the fringe of the world will end in our not being free at all. A judgment without words is incomplete; a word to which there can be no reply is nonsense; my freedom is interwoven with that of others by way of the world. Of course, those of us who were neither Jews nor declared Communists could manage to meditate during those four years:

we were not denied Plato or Descartes or rehearsals at the Conservatory on Saturday mornings. We could begin our adolescence all over again, return to our gods and our great writers as if they were vices. This did not bring us any nearer to ourselves or to the spirit of the times. Yet for all that, we did not get out of history. Our finest thoughts, seen from London, New York, or Moscow, had a place in the world, and they had a name—the reveries of captives—and even their value as thoughts was altered as a result. One cannot get beyond history and time; all one can do is manufacture a private eternity in their midst, as artificial as the eternity of the madman who believes he is God. There is no vital spirit in gloomy isolated dreams; spirit only appears in the full-light of dialogue. We were no more free, as we meditated on our great men, and no more pure consciousness, than the Jew or the deportee who became pure suffering, unable to see and unable to choose. No effective freedom exists without some power. Freedom exists in contact with the world, not outside it.

·   ·   ·   ·

In this we rediscovered one of the truths of Marxism. But even Marxism had to be taken up anew, for it threatened to confirm our prewar prejudices. Under the pretext that history is the history of class struggle and that ideological conflicts are only its superstructure, a certain kind of Marxism detaches us from all situations in which the fate of the classes is not immediately at stake. Marxists of this type classed the Second World War as imperialistic, at least until the intervention of the U.S.S.R., and were not interested in it. True history would recommence for them on the day when the social struggle could again manifest itself. Since fascism was, after all, nothing but a poor relative of capitalism, the Marxist didn't have to take sides in this family quarrel, and whichever faction won made little difference to him. Certain of us thought that capitalism could not allow itself to be liberal in a crisis, that it would become rigid in all things, and that the same necessities which gave birth to fascism would stifle freedom in the pretended democracies. The worldwide war was just an appearance; what remained real beneath that appearance was the common fate of the proletariats of all nations and the profound solidarity of all forms of capitalism through the internal contradictions of the regime. Thus there could be no question of the national proletarians in any way assuming responsibility for the events in which they found themselves involved: no proletarian in uniform can feel *anything but* proletarian.

Thus certain among us frowned on their own delight at the news of some German defeat and pretended not to share the general satisfaction. When we presented the situation of an occupied country to them as the prototype of an inhuman situation, they did their best to dissolve this phenomenon in the more general one of capitalistic exploitation and oppression. Entrusted from the start with the secret of history, they understood patriotic rebellion better than it understood itself and absolved it in the name of the class struggle. And yet when liberation came they called it by name, just like everyone else.

They didn't have to give up Marxism in order to do so. The experience of those four years had, in fact, brought a better under-standing of the concrete relationship of the class struggle to Marxist ideology. The class struggle is not *more real* than ideological conflicts; they cannot be reduced to it, as appearances to reality. Marx himself pointed out that, once they become established, ideologists have a weight of their own and set history in motion in the same way that the flywheel drives the motor. There must be more, consequently, to a Marxist analysis of Hitlerism than summarily classifying it as "a capitalistic episode." Such an analysis undoubtedly lays bare the com-bination of economic events without which it would not have existed, but this situation is unique, and to define it fully, to bring it back into contact with actual history, we must take local particularities into account and consider naziism's human function as well as its economic one. The Marxist must not simply keep applying the capital-work formula in some mechanical way but must think each new event through afresh to determine in each case the serpentine route of the proletarian future. He is not obliged to consider oppression in an occupied country as a surface phenomenon, beneath which the truth of history is to be sought. There are not two histories, one true and the other empirical; there is only one, in which everything that happens plays a part, if one only knows how to interpret it. For a Marxist in a French environment, the German Occupation was not a historical accident but an event of the first magnitude. The German and Anglo-Saxon victories are not equivalent from the point of view of the class struggle. No matter how reactionary the Anglo-Saxon governments are and wish to be, they are curbed in their own countries by their liberal ideology, and the social struggle's imminent re-emergence into the spotlight gains in interest for men who do not have a hundred years to live and who would have had to spend perhaps fifty years under Fascist oppression. Marxism does not suppress history's subjective factors in favor of objective ones; it binds the two together. The ideology of nationalism cannot be classed once and for all as bourgeois: its function in shaping the historical conjunction must be newly appreciated at every moment, and this function may at times be progressive and at other times reactionary. Nationalistic feeling (which is not to say chauvinism) is revolutionary in the France of today and was so in 1940. This does not merely mean that national feeling is in fact opposed to the immediate interest of French capitalism and that, by a pious trick, the Marxists can make it serve their own struggle. It means that the historical conjuncture frees the national reality from the reactionary mortgages which encumbered it and authorizes the proletarian consciousness to integrate it. One might try to argue that in Marxist political thinking the nation can only be a means, never an end, that Marxist patriotism can only be tactical, and that for the Marxist a purgation of morals, for example, serves the ends of revolution, whereas the primary concern of the patriot is, on the contrary, the integration of the movement of the masses into the nation. But even this kind of language is not Marxist. It is the particular attribute of Marxism not to distinguish the means from the end, and, in principle, no system of political thought is less hypocritical and less Machiavellian. It is not a question of abusing the patriot's good faith and leading them were they do not wish to go. Not the Marxist but history transforms nationalist feeling into the will to revolution. It is a question of making the patriots see (and events as well as Marxists undertake to do this) that in a weakened country like France which the movement of history has reduced to a second-rate power, a certain political and economic independence is possible only through a dangerous oscillation or within the framework of a Socialist Confederation of States which has no chance of becoming a reality except through revolution. To be a Marxist is not to renounce all differences, to give up one's identity as a Frenchman, a native of Tours or Paris, or to forego individuality in order to blend into the world proletariat. It is indeed to become part of the universal, but without ceasing to be what we are. Even in a Marxist perspective the world proletariat is not a revolutionary factor so long as it only exists objectively, in economic analysis. It will become such a factor when it realizes that it is a world proletariat, and this will only happen through the concerted pressure or a meeting at the crossroads of actual proletarians, such as they exist in the different countries, and not through an ascetic internationalism wherein each of them loses his most compelling reasons for being a Marxist.

H. RICHARD NIEBUHR (1895–1962)

War as Crucifixion

Man, being incurably rational, cannot act without some theory of the events in which he is participating. This truth is clearly apparent in the case of war. A blaze of unreasoning emotion may induce men to exchange a few blows but any long conflict, especially between groups, requires propaganda, which at its worst is an effort to supply a theory that will fit the emotions and at its best is an attempt to direct and restrain emotion by understanding of the situation. To be sure, theories of war in general and of any particular conflict in which we are engaged are not the only factors which influence action, but they are nevertheless important elements in any responsible behavior.

Two main theories of the nature of war are being applied to our present struggle and are influencing in various ways the responses of individuals and communities to the situation. They may be named the amoral and the moral theories. The former interprets war as a conflict of powers in which victory with its fruits belongs to the stronger and in which moral words or phrases are nothing but instruments of power by means of which emotions are aroused and men are unified. This view is held both by certain balance-of-power advocates of unlimited participation in war, so long as national self-interest is involved, and by certain pacifists who wash their hands of war because it makes no moral difference which side wins in a conflict of pure power.

MORAL AND AMORAL THEORIES INADEQUATE

The moral view of war, on the other hand, interprets it as an event in a universe in which the laws of retribution hold sway. According to this theory war begins with a transgression of international, or natural, or human, or divine law and continues in the effort of the law's upholders to bring the offenders to justice. Those who hold this view make a distinction between unjust war—the act of transgression—and just war—the act of retribution and of defense of order. Again, both

The selection is from H. Richard Niebuhr, "War as Crucifixion," Copyright 1943 Christian Century Foundation. Reprinted by permission from the April 28, 1943 issue of *The Christian Century*.

participants and non-participants in any particular war may use this theory; their differences are largely due to their estimate of this war as just or as unjust.

Both theories are inadequate and misleading, for both fail to account for all the relevant phenomena and must be abandoned at some point in practice, not because emotion is too powerful to submit to their control, but because they appear unreasonable. Since man is a self-interested being and always desires to extend his power, the amoral theory is partly true. But since man is always interested in values beyond the self and desires not only power but also the enjoyment of the good, the amoral theory is wholly inadequate. It forgets that wars are fought by men and that human power cannot be abstracted from human rationality and morality.

Among men, might not only makes right, but the conviction of being right makes might, and it is impossible to reduce such a conviction to an emotional reaction. However much the power realists may regret the fact, it remains true that in war men do not fight simply for their own interests but make great sacrifices for distant values, for their own country, or Poland, or "democracy," or "the new order," or "the Four Freedoms." It may be said that while individuals do this in war, nations always act amorally. But this again is to deal with unreal, wholly abstract beings, since nations and their governments are human, so that the mixture of motives which is discernible in individuals is always present in groups also.

RETRIBUTION FAILS

The moral view of war seems to take into account those elements which the power theory ignores, yet it also remains inadequate and is in some respects more misleading than its rival. Its failure does not necessarily lie at the point in which the power theory is interested, for it may be very much aware of men's love of power and of the necessity for taking this into account in the making of moral judgments. Its inadequacy appears rather in the impossibility of applying the whole scheme of moral judgment and retributive justice to social relations. It has often been observed that a people cannot be indicted, that the question of war-guilt which appears so easily determinable in time of conflict becomes more difficult with longer perspective, that retribution itself is impractical since the community which is to be punished cannot be excluded from the society of nations as an individual can be banished from his community by imprisonment.

The greatest difficulty of all which the moral theory faces is the fact that in war the burden of suffering does not fall on the guilty, even when guilt is relatively determinable, but on the innocent. Retribution for the sins of a Nazi party and a Hitler falls on Russian and German soldiers, on the children of Cologne and Coventry, on the Finns and the French. In order that the moral theory may be used it becomes necessary to convict all the common men, the whole opposing nation of guilt. Even if that were possible the theory does not hold since the suffering for guilt is shared by those who are on the side of "justice." Hence those who hold to the moral theory find themselves unable to follow it in practice. If they declare a present war to be just they must participate in inflicting suffering and death on the "just" with the "unjust"; if they regard a present war as unjust they must stand idly by while the "just" are being made to suffer with the "unjust."

IS WAR CRUCIFIXION?

Since neither theory will do for men who want to act reasonably, on the basis of an intelligible interpretation of the facts of experience, the question arises whether there is not some other pattern than that of the survival of the fittest or that of retributive justice by means of which war may be understood and response to it guided. The question must arise for Christians whether that understanding of the nature of cosmic justice which the crucifixion of Jesus Christ discovered to men must not and may not be applied to war, as it must and may be applied to many personal events that are unintelligible save through the cross. Is war, then, crucifixion?

War is at least very much like the crucifixion. In both events there is a strange intermixture of justice and injustice on the side alike of those who regard themselves as the upholders of the right and on the side of the vanquished. Three men were crucified on Calvary, all, it appears, on more or less the same charge of insurrection. Two of them were malefactors who actually desired to overturn the established order, whether for patriotic or personal motives; yet they were not alike since one recognized the at least relative justice of his punishment while the other remained unrepentant. The third cross carried one who was innocent of the charge made against him; yet ambiguously so, since he was establishing a kingdom of a strange sort which held unknown dangers for the Roman order and the Jewish law.

Nor were the crucifiers less mixed in their justice and injustice: soldiers who did their duty in obedience to their oath, priests who acted according to their lights—though their light was darkness—a judge who failed in his duty, citizens who were devoted to the maintenance of the sacred values of Jewish culture, a mob overborne by emotion. They knew not what they did. War is like that—apparently indiscriminate in the choice of victims and of victors, whether these be thought of as individuals or as communities.

CROSS REVEALS GOD'S MORAL EARNESTNESS

A second point of resemblance between war and the crucifixion is no less striking. The cross which will not yield to analysis in terms of retributive justice, will not yield either to analysis in terms of brute power. If the alternative before men were simply either that God is just in the sense that he rewards the good and punishes the guilty, or that the world is indifferent to good and evil, then the cross would be the final demonstration of God's injustice or, rather, of his non-existence. If that were the alternative then men would need to conclude that "Whirl is king and hath dethroned Zeus."

But the cross does not encourage moral indifference; it requires men to take their moral decisions with greater rather than less seriousness; it demonstrates the sublime character of real goodness; it is a revelation, though "in a glass darkly," of the intense moral earnestness of a God who will not abandon mankind to self-destruction; it confronts us with the tragic consequences of moral failure. It does all this because it is sacrifice—the self-sacrifice of Jesus Christ for those whom he loves and God's sacrifice of his best-loved Son for the sake of the just and the unjust. War is like the cross in this respect. In its presence men must abandon their moral cynicism along with other peacetime luxuries.

We are moved in the presence of war to think more rather than less seriously of the importance of our decisions and of the evil and good possibilities of our existence. For war also is not only a great slaughter but a great sacrifice. It is the moving sacrifice of our youth for the sake of that which they love; the sacrifice by parents of their best-loved sons. In the midst of its cruelties, falsehoods and betrayals there appear sublime examples of human courage and devotion and selflessness that uplift us as we see the greatness of man revealed alongside his depravity. An almost infinite capacity for goodness is reflected in the dark glass of sinfulness. Vicarious suffering shows up dramatically the tragic issue of our wrongdoings and wrong-being in the midst of our human solidarity. War does not make for moral indifference.

THE CROSS IS RELEVANT

The analogy of war and crucifixion suggests that we are dealing with more than analogy. It indicates that the cross is relevant to the understanding of our world and to our social action in ways which neither the sacerdotal nor the moral influence theory of its meanings has made evident. Hence it directs Christians to wrestle with the problem of the cross in new ways so that new light from it may fall upon the scenes of their present social life as well as upon their personal problems and tragedies. It may well be that the meaning of the cross must become apparent to our time in new situations somewhat as the meaning of the spherical nature of the earth has become apparent in a new way to us in recent years.

The knowledge of the fact that we live on a globe has been a relatively abstract knowledge for hundreds of years. It was found significant for certain purposes, but on the whole men continued to live their daily lives on the practical assumption of the earth's flatness. All the maps translated our spherical relations into relations on a plane, and so we persisted in the thought that Europe lay to the east of us, never to the north, Asia to the west, never to the north or east. What we have known for hundreds of years we now need to learn because the old pattern of the flat earth no longer suffices even for the life of one who never leaves his continent. The existence of this nation, at least, begins to depend on his now taking seriously a known but unappropriated knowledge. Perhaps it is like this with the cross of Christ and war and every social suffering.

What we shall find when we concern ourselves more seriously with the cross and with its meaning for our war cannot be prophesied There is one point, however, which seems of great importance and to which all efforts to understand war through the cross must give heed. It is the point which Paul made. The crucifixion illuminated many things for him, but in particular it was the revelation of the righteousness of God which was distinct from the righteousness of the law and which when it became apparent, showed man's righteousness to be as unrighteous as his unrighteousness.

WHAT KIND OF UNIVERSE?

Perhaps we may understand Paul's point like this: The cross of Jesus Christ is the final, convincing demonstration of the fact that the order of the universe is not one of retribution in which goodness is rewarded and evil punished, but rather an order of graciousness wherein, as Jesus had observed, the sun is made to shine on evil and on good and the rain to descend on the just and the unjust. To live in this divine order of graciousness on the basis of the assumption that reward must be merited and evil avenged is to come into conflict with the real order in things. The pattern of retributive justice simply will not work; it is like the effort to translate the global earth into the terms of a plane. To make distinctions between the just and unjust, and to employ for that purpose the standard of good works performed by them, will not work.

If men are to live at all, as souls or as communities, they must begin with the acceptance not of some standard of judgment—not even the standard of graciousness—but of an act of graciousness to which they respond graciously. The cross is not the demonstration of the fact that man has a wrong standard of judgment which he must correct or for which he must substitute a right standard of judgment by means of which to assess goodness and sinfulness, but it shows that the whole effort to assess and judge the goodness and the evil of self and others, and to reward or punish accordingly, is mistaken.

WAR AND GOD'S GRACIOUSNESS

God's righteousness is his graciousness and his grace is not an addition to his justice; hence man's rightness does not lie in a new order of judging justice, but in the acceptance of grace and in thankful response to it. The cross does not so much reveal that God judges by other standards than men do, but that he does not judge; it does not demonstrate that men judge by the wrong standards but that their wrongness lies in trying to judge each other, instead of beginning where they can begin—with the acceptance of graciousness and response to it.

If the cross is not only a historical event but a revelation of the order of reality, then war is not only like the cross but must be a demonstration of that same order of God. How it demonstrates the disorderliness of human righteousness and unrighteousness is apparent enough. How it demonstrates the fundamental ungraciousness of both the apparently righteous and the apparently unrighteous is perhaps also clear. But that it should be the hidden demonstration of divine graciousness is hard for us to understand. The cross in ancient history is acceptable to us; the cross in "religious" history, in the history of man's relation to a purely spiritual God, is also acceptable; but the cross in our present history is a stumbling block and a folly which illustrates human sinfulness, but not divine graciousness.

Yet how the divine grace appears in the crucifixion of war may become somewhat clear when the cross of Christ is used to interpret it. Then our attention is directed to the death of the guiltless, the gracious, and the suffering of the innocent becomes a call to repentance, to a total revolution of our minds and hearts. And such a call to repentance— not to sorrow but to spiritual revolution—is an act of grace, a great recall from the road to death which we all travel together, the just and the unjust, the victors and the vanquished. Interpreted through the cross of Jesus Christ the suffering of the innocent is seen not as the suffering of temporal men but of the eternal victim "slain from the foundations of the world." If the Son of God is being crucified in this war along with the malefactors—and he is being crucified on many an obscure hill—then the graciousness of God, the self-giving love, is more manifest here than in all the years of peace.

It will be asked, If these suggestions, these vague gestures in the direction of the interpretation of war as crucifixion, are followed, what will be the result for action? No single answer can be given since the cross does not impose a new law on man. But one thing will be common to all actions which are based on such an understanding of war: there will be in them no effort to establish a righteousness of our own, no excusing of self because one has fallen less short of the glory of God than others; there will be no vengeance in them. They will also share one positive characteristic: they will be performed in hope, in reliance on the continued grace of God in the midst of our ungraciousness.

Part III

Editorial Essays

ROBERT N. BECK

Commitment and Practical Philosophy

It is perhaps no exaggeration to observe that the whole of moral philosophy, as it is generally taught today, rests on the contrast between statements of facts and evaluations. This contrast runs roughly as follows: the truth or falsity of a factual statement is shown by means of evidence, and what counts as evidence is laid down by the rules for the meaning of that statement. Evaluations are quite different, however, for they are not linguistically or logically connected with the factual statements on which they are based or to which they are related. The factual statement, "There is oil in Arabia," is true as long as oil is found in Arabia (perhaps after that too), and anyone who rejected the statement or questioned the evidence as evidence could be shown to have made a logical mistake. But a man's statement that something is good because of some fact about it is not, it is commonly held, so connected with fact. Indeed, one may refuse to take that fact as any evidence for a valuation at all, for nothing connects 'good' with one piece of evidence rather than another. To be sure, to say that something is good is not to fall into meaninglessness; but what saves good here is its (usually non-cognitive) 'action-provoking' or imperative, commending function. The connection of good is to 'pro-attitudes', not to evidence or objects at all.

Such a position—and there are many interesting variants the details of which have been omitted here—is partly a consequence of the way in which the modern world has come to view the intellectual life. Questions about fact, about objects and the world, many are likely now to say, are exclusively and exhaustively in the domain of the sciences. Although the bulk of the work of reason lies here, a second task, however, remains open to intellect, namely analysis or elucidation. Viewed as a second-order activity, analysis—the work of philosophy—aims not at increasing our knowledge of the world or the human condition, but at clarification of the concepts we use (or misuse) in seeking such knowledge.

Now these two activities, it should be noted, however definitive of intellectual activity they are taken by some philosophers, do not in fact exhaust the range of human needs. From neither of them, science or analysis, comes any consequence that is directive of our choices and commitments. Science, ever attempting to determine more adequately what is the case, says nothing about our obligations and values; and analysis may clarify the role of 'good' or 'right' (usually done within the science-analysis context), but it will help us not at all about any commitment to a good. Yet it is precisely this last issue—seen in questions of choosing or being committed on the very topics of this book—that takes human if not logical precedence over the others. In other words, and more generally, man's conception of himself does not consist only of what he knows: it includes also and perhaps more importantly what he aspires to be.

Much of traditional philosophy was directed toward understanding these aspirations. The pursuit of this understanding was within the province of an activity usually called practical[1] philosophy, which aimed at (was even defined as) systematic thinking about human choices and commitments. Philosophers tried to produce reasons for acting in some ways rather than others and to suggest choices consistent with means to what we want or ought to want. This they did by seeking to enunciate and justify a set of practical principles regarding choice and value.

Many contemporary philosophers, especially those accepting the science-analysis classification, have been extremely skeptical of past writings in practical philosophy. They believe them to contain confused mixtures of primitive science, personal prejudices and recommendations, and defective analyses. Then, too, beliefs about how we should behave were often derived in traditional theories from metaphysics or theology. Life, philosophers said, should be organized according to God's intentions for man or according to the nature of the world or of man's rational nature. But with the decay of religion and metaphysical thinking in many parts of the modern world came a deprecation of the practical philosophies connected with them. Even more, there came a deprecation—to which the science-analysis division contributed—of the very task of developing a systematic practical philosophy

Yet it is this intellectual task which is demanded in contemporary society—the more so, perhaps, because of the general decline of religious and metaphysical thought. A set of customs and prejudices, however coherent and therefore valuable they may be, is insufficient to

---

[1] The word 'practical' in this terminology has reference to conduct, and is used in contrast to 'theoretical'.

Much of normative ethics (when the discipline is admitted) as developed today would fall under the term practical philosophy. The latter term rather than the former is used here, however, in order to refer to the whole range of human choice and conduct.

men's aspirations: they need as well a coherent set of values and principles that will provide reasons for acting. Indeed, such is an intellectual need apart from science and analysis: these do not fulfill the need, nor do they remove it. To say this, of course, is not to deny philosophy in the narrower sense of analysis, nor necessarily to try to retain the word philosophy for something other than analysis: usage may soon restrict its meaning to analysis alone. But it is to suggest that the effort to produce a coherent system of practical principles, to establish what needs to be done to enable men to live in conformity with them, and to show how they can be directive of men's choices, remains a significant intellectual activity.

Neither a scientist nor a philosopher in the contemporary analytic sense, the practical philosopher thus aims to meet a distinctive human need. His concern, to put it perhaps over-briefly, is to develop a systematic basis for choice. This involves primarily a set of justified[2] principles ordering values and obligation, and therefore implying duties.[3] In short, practical philosophy seeks reasons for acting which are consistent and realistic.

Suppose that someone were to urge that certain actions during a lightning storm, for example standing under a large tree, were dangerous and therefore bad. Clearly his judgment is intended as an action-guiding force: he is seeking to have persons not stand under trees. Much of current analysis would suggest that there are two elements in this judgment—the facts or evidence about lightning and the commendation, "I dislike lightning, so ought you." But surely the whole notion of commendations and pro-attitudes is artificial in this context, however we recognize an element of urging and recommending. The critical question is: can a reason be given why one should avoid the danger or evil? To be commended to avoid "danger" or "evil" (the words) is hardly to the point, nor are the speaker's emotions—his likes and dislikes—very relevant to the danger-status of the situation.

In general, a reason for acting is given when one is shown the way to what one values, in itself and coherently with other experiences which are valued. One might also say, when one is shown the way to what one wants, for this would link reasons for acting to human experience or "human nature" in a loose, uninterpreted sense. Standing

---

[2] 'Justified' as against demonstrated or verified. Further reference to this term is given below; see also the second editorial essay, "The Logic of Moral Argument."

[3] Cf. the discussion of the data of ethics in the "Introduction" above, pp. xi–xvii.

under a tree in a lightning storm is at least potentially incoherent with other wants—health rather than injury, life rather than death—and these latter become a reason (or part of a reason) for avoiding the danger. The possible coherence or incoherence of wants is an element of the deliberative basis of choice. To be sure, not all choices need be reasoned about in this way. For some desires the question, "Why do you want that?" will make sense, for others it will not. To avoid injury and boredom and to experience their opposites are reasons for acting in themselves—though in saying this one needs carefully to distinguish a reason for acting from actually doing something.

Thus practical philosophy, in the first instance, is concerned to elaborate an estimate of human wants—"a table of values"—that will be deliberatively directive of choice. The second element is to elaborate principles that will relate choices and values to facts. This element needs careful attention, for it runs head-on against two dogmas of contemporary philosophy. The first is that no ought or choice can be 'derived' from facts; the second is that value terms are externally related to facts in such a way that they are usable with any fact (evidence never determines an evaluation). Both of these dogmas are less obvious now than their proponents once thought. They suggest something important about evaluations, but do so in a simplistic way that conceals and distorts many complex relationships. To be suggestive only: no moral judgment can be derived from the facts about lightning alone, but man-with-wants-in-storm does provide a basis for deliberations about what ought to be done. One might in fact say that the practical philosopher does not so much evaluate the world of facts and descriptions as describe the world of evaluation—though one would have to accept such a world as a kind of presupposition of practical reasoning.[4]

This important philosophic topic cannot be further pursued here. Still it must be emphasized that facts and objects (in the broadest sense) are a component in practical reasoning. Man's sexual nature and wants are an element in deliberations about choices relative to sexual integrity; the social conditions of mass society have significance in developing reasons for acting in the face of the experience of alienation. A tenet of philosophical idealism may be helpful here. Facts, idealists have said, become objects only in reference to human desires and wants. But even the most objectless human life, they insist, points toward a

---

[4] Cf. the discussion of context in the essay below, "The Logic of Moral Argument."

system in which particular desires (and hence objects and deeds) meet and are qualified by a conception of something desirable on the whole. In so forming even an elementary and partial system, desires are permeated by reason or order. As is suggested further in the next essay, deliberate moral thought is never "mere" emotion because of the presence in it of context and order. It is therefore one of the functions of practical reason to articulate that system of desires, wants, and values and therewith to relate it to the domain of fact.

Mention of reason and system leads to the third factor at work in practical philosophy, namely, the criterion of coherence. The need for consistency is common to all intellectual endeavor, demonstration, verification, and deliberation alike. In the domain of the practical, this need is present in order to maintain the integrity—even the existence—of the objects of deliberation. To choose to stand under a tree, and to choose not so to stand, involves two choices and as well, in a way, no choice. It is like the command, Open and shut the door, or the description, The wall is green and pink all over. Two commands or descriptions seem to be given; yet because they contradict each other, there is a sense in which neither a command or description has been given. In like manner, inconsistent values can annul the value experience itself. To want certain kinds of sexual experience and also to want certain values in marriage may (or, of course, may not—that is the problem) contradict each other so that instead of two values being experienced, none is.

The classical meaning of coherence is such consistency. Recent uses of the criterion, however, have suggested that it involves cognitive ideals of inclusiveness and system as well. Such additional meanings are necessary to an adequate practical philosophy, or one might be led to the extreme inference that a life of one choice and one value would be the most coherent of possibilities. But this surely would be a *reductio ad absurdum* of the criterion.

Practical reasoning, then, aims at developing a systematic body of principles regulative of values and obligation and, therefore, regulative or directive of choice. Its aim is to provide a basis for rational decision, and it pursues this aim not, as has been said above, by demonstration (which is the procedure of logic and analysis) nor by verification (which is appropriate to science) but by deliberation. Much of the disparagement of practical philosophy in contemporary analytic philosophy is a direct result of its identification of intellectual activity and knowledge with the first two of these modes, to the exclusion of the third. But the human need for directive deliberation remains, and it is ultimately to be satisfied only by a philosophy than can combine coherence and realism.

The traditional question, How can reason be practical? has been answered here roughly by suggesting that reason *is* practical, that in deliberation it can to some extent make the passions its slave, and that the need for practical reason remains even in an age of advanced science and logic. But while arguing that practical philosophy is neither a fancy nor a parade of prejudice and ideology, it may be necessary to conclude by observing that the traditional hope of a single philosophy for all men may be vain. A universally accepted position would be one of which we could say that if any man understood its principles and also understood human nature, then he would accept that position. But systems of coherence, since they are finite (and we need not raise the metaphysical question of a single ultimate coherent system), may be many and varied; the scope of possibilities and the ranges of inclusiveness vary greatly in the human condition. These facts, together with an absence of a single accepted position, may have led some philosophers too easily into a purely emotive interpretation of practical philosophy.

But the argument here has not been for a single inclusive philosophy. It has rather been only that the conditions of modern society demand the production of practical philosophy, and that that production should be and can be guided by the goals of coherence and realism. Nor has a practical philosophy been stated here: the goal has simply been to reawaken interest in the wider range of man's intellectual concerns.

JOHN B. ORR

The Logic of Moral Argument

Ethics has traditionally been concerned with logic, that is, with the principles or rules of inference that allow us to determine the validity of arguments. Logical analysis becomes important in ethics when one want to find reasons—hopefully good, well ordered reasons—for justifying his moral choices and for guiding his deliberations. One also turns to logic when arguments which invite agreement are suspect and sloppily or deceptively constructed. In developing an awareness of the rules of inference, many believe, one is helped to find ways to be certain that moral choices are correct or incorrect—granted, to be sure, a number of broad assumptions about the nature of morality itself.

This essay[1] does not intend, however, to prescribe a system of logical inference within which moral reasoning can be measured. Its intent is more modest, namely to observe what is actually happening when philosophers and theologians come to conclusions about concrete moral choices or social policies. Most of the writers included in this volume have been fairly explicit in defining their foundational value theories. But now the focus is on another dimension of their writing— the rhetoric that belongs to their conclusions about particular cases. The intent is to discover what happens in the transition from the abstract to the concrete, from value theories and practical philosophies to specific commitments. Do various writers employ different "logics"? Or is it possible to discover a pattern of reasoning, independent of the content of moral belief, that all rational men will have to acknowledge as authoritative?

In all fairness, it should be said that very few philosophers and theologians develop their practical conclusions in a pristine manner, as logical inferences from theoretical generalizations. Most write about war, alienation, or violence because, in the course of affairs, there are baffling human problems to be faced and decisions to be made, for example, whether *this* war is just, whether industrial society generates an inhumane culture, and which forms of coercion can justly be used as instruments of civil reform. The relation of practical conclusions to the principles of a practical philosophy would seem initially to be dialectical; that is, theory is born as writers reflect on situations where choices must be made, but, in turn, these very choices are guided by assumptions about the nature of value and obligation. The impression our case studies convey, then, is one of serious deliberation, where both general and specific decisions are being made.

But the logical problem remains. Whatever the process might be in which philosophers come to their conclusions, they still must answer two classical questions: "according to which principles should the moral agent make his decisions?" and, "what is the moral thing to do in a given situation?" The problem of this essay is to explore how these

---

[1] A more extended treatment of this argument, with fuller attention to theological issues, can be found in John B. Orr, "Another Pronouncement on Pronouncements," *Encounter*, Spring, 1969, pp. 89–104.

questions are related. We want to know whether the acceptance of certain principles makes necessary a number of practical conclusions, should one be willing to reason logically. If all men reasoned correctly and if they agreed on their principles, would they all come to the same conclusions about the morality of specified acts or political policies?

The safest initial generalization to make is that moral argumentation is astonishingly diverse and that it is extremely unclear what constitutes rules of inference for it. In the first place, not all principles function in exactly the same way. They have been developed at different levels of abstraction, ranging from natural law's dictum that "good is to be done and promoted, and evil is to be avoided," through Kant's imperative that no man should make a moral exception of himself, to F. H. Bradley's "principle of social surgery." Although this diversity is in part the product of attempts to reason from the more abstract to the more concrete, it also reflects the fact that in moral argument principles do not all serve the same function. Some are used to justify particular policies, others to explain why a given object is valued, and still others to justify our choice of a particular system of moral rules. The practical philosophies which purportedly embody wisdom within a given community cannot be understood simply as spectra from the white of pious generality to the black of specific policy directive. Instead, they are more found to be a heterogeneous congregation whose principles ˈulfill different functions and assume the forms appropriate to their various capacities.

When philosophers and theologians presume to offer practical advice about individual and social behavior, their arguments become even more diverse. Their appeals often simultaneously combine empirical judgments (many of which may be "loaded"), principles, customs, precedents, theological-metaphysical assertions, parables, proverbs, authorities, stories, and descriptions of moral styles. Some may argue, as does Moritz Schlick, in the form of an extended social scientific description in which explicit moral conclusions are avoided like malaria, but in which conclusions seem to be implicit nevertheless. Others, like Richard Niebuhr in his "War as Crucifixion," seem to be painting images, the value of which exists in their ability to illumine analogically the moral topography of a complex situation.

That such diversity is not wholly the product of sloppiness or the shabbiness of authors enamored with the process of giving practical advice is the thesis of James Gustafson's now classical essay, "Context versus Principles: A Misplaced Debate in Christian Ethics."[2] Speaking to his theological colleagues, Gustafson tries to show that the tension between so-called contextualists (who refuse to submit to the rigors of formal logic) and so-called casuists (who do) rests on a misunderstanding of the procedures these authors actually utilize in their work. He identifies four base points, across which moralists move in their analyses, even though they may protest that one of the base points is normative for moral reflection. Some authors, he says, begin with a disciplined situation-analysis, appropriating both the methods and conclusions of the social sciences. Others begin with an analysis of religious style, or the quality of life that belongs to an individual when he participates in a community of faith. Others begin with theological assertions, while still others believe that moral reflection ought to proceed at the level of principles. The point that Gustafson makes with eloquence, though, is that religious moral discourse does not maintain the discipline of staying within the bounds of any one of these spheres of discourse (or on any one base). Authors inevitably move from one to consideration of the other three bases, sometimes with self-conscious delineation of the breaking points and sometimes in a fashion that cries out for a greater carefulness. Gustafson, however, does not try to discern the logic which actually governs theological moral reflection in its movement across the base points, mainly because his essay is narrowly conceived to deal with the exhaustion of a faddish casuist-contextualist debate. He is content to assert the plurality and diversity of moral argument, while leaving the larger analytic task to another author or another time.

Thus, it seems inevitable, to adopt Gustafson's deterministic vocabulary, that moral argument is too multifaceted an activity to be measured against systems of formal logic alone. In the case studies included within this volume, Gustafson's comments seem equally applicable. To take only one example: Bertrand Russell's "Appeal to the Intellectuals of Europe" begins with a statement about moral styles within the community of Western intellectuals, but then it quickly proceeds to a descriptive analysis of the patterns of self-deception apparent in a society during wartime. As he does this, he reveals an idealistic theory of social causation which leads him to say

---

[2] James M. Gustafson, "Context versus Principles: A Misplaced Debate in Christian Ethics," reprinted from *Harvard Theological Review* (April, 1965) in Martin Marty and Dean G. Peerman (eds.), *New Theology No. 3* (New York: The Macmillan Company, 1966), pp. 69–102.

that, at least in part, war grows from the imperialistic process in which nations feel impelled to extend their values. Finally, he announces a principle: "Knowledge with elevation of mind is the chief instrument of human progress; knowledge without elevation of mind easily becomes devilish, and increases the wounds which man inflicts on man." Russell's essay is quite representative; and his procedures amply demonstrate that models of formal logic, while helpful, do not sufficiently account for the flexible use of data in the process of moral argument.

Chaim Perelman has helpfully suggested that the appropriate model for moral argument is not the theory of demonstration used in formal logic but is rather the long-neglected logic of rhetoric, treated at length in the *Topics* of Aristotle and described there as "dialectical." It is a theory of argumentation complementary to, but not identical with, the theory of demonstration, which is more appropriate to the sciences. Perelman writes that the logic of ethics is one that describes the techniques useful in criticizing and justifying opinions, choices, claims, and demands. Thus, the logic of argument is a process of becoming convincing. In order to justify particular policies or acts that are controversial, Perelman concludes, the moralist reaches into his community's consensus and uses elements that will serve to associate the controversial with the accepted. "These acts, these persons, these values, and these beliefs, furnish precedents, models, convictions, and norms which in turn permit the elaboration of criteria by which to criticize and to justify attitudes, dispositions, and propositions."[3]

If Perelman is correct, the time may be ripe to return to C. L. Stevenson's *Ethics and Language*[4] for some lessons in the logic of moral reasoning. This book, published in 1944, is a product of the logical positivist movement, and as such, it is not willing to say that moral argument is subject to rules of inference. In fact, moral argument is emotive—an expression of passions. It is no rational process at all, and propositions about moral obligation are therefore neither true nor false. But Stevenson does not deny that there is a kind of order to moral argument. In fact, he carefully develops a number of models,

---

[3] See C. H. Perelman, *Justice* (New York: Random House, 1967), pp. 53–70.

[4] Charles L. Stevenson, *Ethics and Language* (New Haven: Yale University Press, 1944).

and he helps his readers to see that the art of being emotively convincing requires discipline and argumentative craftsmanship.

The analysis of logical positivism fails exhaustively to describe the logic of moral argument, but Perelman's proposal concerning rhetorical logic is not merely emotivism. Rhetoric in moral argument works in terms of rational order, in the form of a system or shape of beliefs, aspirations, and values which lend legitimacy to particular policies and which form the perspective or frame of reference within which practical decisions are considered. Such a general perspective may be only partly visible, being present in the myths, parables, maxims, and presuppositions of a given thinker or community, and being often articulated mainly in response to internal and external crises. For example, in the 1950's, when Americans became uneasy about the extension of Soviet influence, they found themselves expressing all kinds of truisms which in other circumstances would appear to be flabbily sentimental. In that context, however, the truisms reflected a sense of cultural identity and a perspective within which Americans expected their officialdom to operate. To a significant extent, such moral and political judgment serves both to legitimate controversial acts or policies and to articulate and strengthen the consensus or perspective which the argument must assume. Although popular moral argument seldom takes the form of a systematic development, the implicit principles appear to exhibit a consistency sufficient to maintain the moral identity of a people and to provide a tolerably coherent interpretative frame of reference. And the more a community perspective is referred to in moral argument, the more useful it can become.

The British philosopher, Ian Ramsey, has recently described the process of justifying moral conclusions with reference to the perspective of another community, namely the Christian community, broadly conceived. In his essay, "Towards a Rehabilitation of Natural Law," he notes in Christian moral discourse the presence of certain key ideas or primitives such as the resurrection, salvation by faith, and unconditional love. He observes that different Christians have, to be sure, chosen different key ideas, but this diversity does not really matter since each "must be positioned by reference to the whole pattern of Christian discourse."[5] "Unconditional love," for example,

[5] Ian Ramsey, "Towards a Rehabilitation of Natural Law," *Christian Ethics and Contemporary Philosophy* (New York: The Macmillan Company, 1966), pp. 391–392.

is empty unless it presupposes the parables of the Good Samaritan and the father and two sons; sayings such as "forgiveness seventy times seven" assume the atonement and grace. In other words, the key ideas are already associated with "certain principles of behaviour implicit in the discourse," and "will be grounded in the kind of disclosure which e.g. the Gospel narratives and Christian doctrines were expressly designed to evoke and perpetuate, a disclosure to which the Christian responds with characteristic commitment."[6] Thus, Ramsey finds a perspective or order which provides principles together with a world-view in terms of which particular issues are interpreted and argued. The way of working out practical Christian conclusions in a given moral or political situation, he claims, is "to set various possible behaviour patterns alongside this Christian perspective of behaviour patterns and principles and see which is the best match."[7] In *On Being Sure in Religion*, Ramsey is even more explicit. He urges a method in which Christians first deal with "concrete situations," getting the issues as clearly explicated as possible from a number of perspectives and disciplines, and then returning to the more general principles. Such an interplay of specific and general never ends:

> . . . the very social judgment brought to bear on the empirical situation will develop and modify it, and as likely as not raise other questions and issues. These will then need, in turn, to be brought again into relation with the biblical and doctrinal narrative, until some other insight is generated, and other principles enunciated. So the process repeats itself.[8]

Ramsey places his position in contrast to that of the logical positivist. He agrees that moral argument is emotive and intended to evoke commitment and the ability to see things from the perspective of a given community. But he argues that this perspective is ordered and that this order lends structure to argument. It is, in short, a more or less explicit practical philosophy, and it provides a way of describing and interpreting one's experience, be that experience individually or socially oriented.

What is the place for specific, practical policy directives and

[6] *Ibid*, p. 392.
[7] *Ibid*.
[8] Ian Ramsey, *On Being Sure in Religion* (London: Athlone Press, 1963), p. 36.

moral conclusions in the rhetorical model? The marks of an adequate interpretive frame appear to be its ability to provide for reasonable intellectual coherence, its ability to be comprehensive, and its ability to deal intensely with particular experiences or issues. Perspectives do contain grounds to determine whether specific social policies "match" or are consistent with particular sensitivities. But they do not function as an axiomatic foundation for policy conclusions; they seek rather to provide good reasons—compelling reasons—by evoking grounds that grant legitimacy. Thus, the role of an appeal to general principles in particular moral arguments is threefold: (1) it provides an order calculated to legitimate an act or policy; (2) it provides an order calculated to evoke commitment to a perspective, i.e., the willingness to see matters in a particular way; and (3) it is the order calculated to indicate the further lines of development of that perspective. Such a logic is really not concerned about movement across otherwise disparate spheres of discourse, such as the scientific, mythical, artistic-literary, theological, and metaphysical.

But thus to specify the role of order in ethical argument is not to claim that the process of reasoning can insure one against the baptism of parochialism. Such a conclusion would assume the possibility of a stance above historical limitations—a position to which we poor mortals are denied access. No system includes within itself rigorous protection against assertions such as "a, b, c, d, and e (a motley assemblage) are all examples of x, and x is obligatory." For what is to prevent one from supplementing that already long list through the *ad hoc* addition of f, g, h, i, j, and k? Such specifications, which are always possible, rest upon an arbitrary act of saying which cases are representative of a class. Thus, it appears that in ethical reasoning (as perhaps in all reasoning?) there is no complete insurance against parochialism and bias. Still, if these cannot be avoided, we had best not become involved in a sham ritual of self-flagellation for the sins necessary to finitude. Various systems of moral principle and argumentation can be pluralistically recognized, yet accepted as critically significant to the human condition.

Finally, we may note that in the rhetorical model, it is important that reasoning be dialectical, moving between behavioral particulars and a variety of warrants consistent with a general frame of reference. Only thus can a particular be viewed in its uniqueness as the locus of conflicting pressures, interests, and principles. Apart from the particular, warrants of a practical philosophy tend to be diffuse and artificially enshrined in a harmony of pious generality. But by reference to the particular they are vitalized by their involvement in a tension of values and by their ability to supplement each other as a coherent rationale for decision.

JOHN B. ORR

A Postscript Concerning Case Study Ethics

In the past few years, the use of case studies in the analysis of ethical theory has enjoyed a kind of renaissance. Teachers of ethics are discovering that it is possible, perhaps desirable, to approach theoretical generalization inductively, and thus to let particular moral issues suggest the broad configuration of problems and potential theoretical moves. At least one association of ethics teachers regularly schedules seminars in the development of case study techniques— seminars which betray the evangelical verve one usually associates with persons who recently have experienced a conversion.

This increased interest in case study ethics perhaps grows in part from a reaction against philosophy's recent preoccupation with linguistic analysis. In a period of civil turmoil when fundamental choices are being formulated about the direction of social change, it has been difficult to maintain that ethics' contribution should be limited to historical studies and to linguistic clarification. Philosophy, like most other disciplines within the college and university, now finds itself in the position of rethinking its self-definition, particularly in light of pressures "to be more relevant" or to be involved as an advocate in society's decision-making processes. Although once rejected, the image of the philosopher as a moral contender is receiving new energy. Jeremy Bentham, John Stuart Mill, and T. H. Green, nineteenth century philosophers who developed their ethical theories within the milieu of politics and who measured their ethical theories in terms of political reform, again seem to be assuming importance as models for philosophical activity.

This postscript is an attempt to understand what happens when philosophers move into particular cases—when they deal as pre-scribers or advocates or at least as persons who believe that moral issues are most fruitfully viewed from a particular perspective. Does particularity take one out of philosophy altogether? That is, does philosophy, by definition, have to do only with abstractions, and must one lay down his academic mantle when particular commitments are espoused?

We do not think so. In fact, one of the presuppositions of this volume has been that, on the one hand, the case study approach is germane to ethical studies, and, on the other, that the justification of a moral position may be made more effective when developed in a philosophical context. Case study philosophy is just that. It is philosophy, not something else. And its development should not be viewed simply as a clever means of enlivening the classroom, but as a level of ethical discourse that has integrity in its own right.

Henry David Aiken's helpful essay "Levels of Moral Discourse" suggests why case studies cannot be neglected by the serious student of moral reasoning. He argues that philosophers are too ready to limit ethical investigation in the belief that the discipline of ethics is concerned solely with articulating principles or with describing the relationships within which moral behavior is determined. But moral reflection proceeds at several levels of generality, each contributing to a full understanding of the moral life and each having its own logic and criteria for evaluation. Discourse takes place on at least four levels, Aiken says: (1) the expressive level, where no problem of justification can possibly arise; (2) the level of moral rules, which asks about patterns of conduct and about the rules of behavior that are appropriate under various circumstances; (3) the level of ethical principles, on which we attempt to justify the principles we hold and, therefore, in which we make explicit our definition of what it is to be moral; and (4) the post-ethical level, on which we deal with the question, "Why be moral?" At the post-ethical level, we are no longer in ethics proper: we are rather building an image of human nature which clarifies our assumption that man ultimately must be regarded as a moral animal.[1]

In terms of Aiken's vocabulary, the case study approach focuses on the level of moral rules. And something conceptually different happens here from what occurs when persons deal at other levels. The attempt to answer the questions, "What should the moral agent do?" or, "What is the moral shape of a particular situation?" draws from a number of sources, often including social scientific research as well as principles, parables, precedents, and other normative

[1] Henry David Aiken, "Levels of Moral Discourse," *Reason and Conduct* (New York: Alfred A. Knopf, 1962), pp. 65–87.

symbols. And characteristically, the attempt involves persons in a consideration of the stark conflicts that form the stuff of moral decision. To make a serious decision about any course of action is to choose for a fragile balance of principles that includes always the sacrifice of some which—all things being equal—we would want to maximize. In social ethics, the root meaning of justice as a "binding" or a "holding-together" of values (that cannot simultaneously be maximized) seems painfully appropriate in ethical reflection at the level of moral rules. Justice here has to do with discerning in each case what is a viable, humane balance of values.

It follows that a theory of moral behavior is not complete until it deals with case studies. Case studies are by no means all there is to ethics. Ethics is finally neither a loose collection of prescriptions nor a moral encyclopedia where correct examples of casuistry are offered for the student's mastery. Nor can case studies legitimately be isolated from the systematic exposition of more abstract problems of value theory. But when particular issues are ignored, ethics becomes bloodless, and philosophy deprives itself of self-consciousness at that important moment when theories of commitment contribute to the formulation of moral styles and acts.

It also follows that the moralist does not sell his philosophical soul when he enters the arena on behalf of a moral-political position. Rather, he is doing what classical philosophers have always done when they have moved from the analytical to the constructive mood in their professional activity. At the level of ethical principles, the move involves constructing theories of commitment, frames of reference within which moral styles are structured. But at the level of moral rules, the constructive mood may easily involve the philosopher in arguing the justice of a particular act of civil disobedience, the need for a piece of legislation, or in explicating the claims of truthfulness within a certain context. To believe that the development of theories of commitment is more germane to the work of a philosopher is evidence of an indefensible bias. There is little reason why the philosopher should expend his energy in constructive activity at the level of ethical principles and at the post-ethical level but should fear a loss of academic integrity in assuming the role of moral advocate. Indeed, philosophers should be grateful that what others must do in their extracurricular time, they can do in the interest of developing a richly conceived and rounded ethical literature. Ethics happily does not share with other disciplines the methodological barriers to becoming involved as an interpreter and advocate of social change.

Likewise, there seems little reason to perpetuate the habitual pattern of arguing from the abstract to the concrete in ethics—of starting, as did Hobbes, with a general philosophy of human nature, then moving to a theory of values, and only then to concrete moral prescriptions. We suspect that it may be healthy for ethical theorists occasionally to start with concrete issues of moral decision and to let the experiential phenomena suggest directions for reflection. Phenomenologists aptly remind us that premature abstraction can blind persons to the complexity of moral experience and can contribute to failures in dealing imaginatively with changing moral possibilities. No procedural chronology deserves final loyalty, and ethics especially is a discipline that derives energy from the peculiar contribution that various starting points can make.

This postscript, then, constitutes something of an appeal for moralists to accept with enthusiasm the tasks of case study philosophy. The context for such an appeal is clearly a period wherein moral-political advocacy has great utility. But the context is also an academic one, where advocacy and the analysis of advocacy are fully in place, and where such activities are necessary to a comprehensive implementation of the discipline's purposes. The moral philosopher is neither politician nor minister, yet his interests sometimes draw close to theirs—particularly in case studies, when he constructs his advocacy as a healing, reforming presence. Yet, fortunately, the gift of prophecy does not require a denial of analytical honesty, and the several dimensions of ethics are not engaged in mutually destructive combat. Case studies provide a rounding-out and an enrichment to a discipline that has traditionally given its greatest enthusiasm to more abstract tasks. Their development would represent a victory of theoretical completion.

BIBLIOGRAPHICAL ESSAY

The number of books, textbooks, and monographs in ethics is exceedingly large. The student will become aware both of the number and variety of publications simply by browsing in the ethics section of his school library. Books of selections, surveys, histories of ethics, works on ethical theory, and studies of special topics such as suicide and alienation can be found. Some familiarity with a library collection is very useful as one seeks to explore special topics or problems in detail. A representative sample of survey works includes: Crane Brinton, *A History of Western Morals* (New York: Harcourt, Brace & Co., Inc., 1959); C. D. Broad, *Five Types of Ethical Theory* (New York: Harcourt, Brace & Co., Inc., 1934); Philippa Foot (ed.), *Theories of Ethics* (London: Oxford University Press, 1967); Thomas E. Hill, *Contemporary Ethical Theories* (New York: The Macmillan Company, 1957); W. T. Jones, *et al* (eds.), *Approaches to Ethics* (New York: McGraw-Hill Book Company, Inc., 1962); Joseph Margolis (ed.), *Contemporary Ethical Theory* (New York: Random House, Inc., 1966); Henry Sidgwick, *Outline of the History of Ethics* (London: Macmillan & Company, 1886, and later editions); and M. Warnock, *Ethics Since 1900* (London: Oxford University Press, 1960). A good introductory paperback is William K. Frankena, *Ethics* (Englewood Cliffs: Prentice-Hall, Inc., 1963); and an introductory series of paperbacks has been published by St. Martin's Press, New York, which includes Anthony Flew, *Evolutionary Ethics* (1967), W. D. Hudson, *Ethical Intuitionism* (1967), and M. Warnock, *Existentialist Ethics* (1967). A great number of books on ethical theory have been produced in our century; ethics has been a very active philosophical field. A suggestive sample of these includes: Kurt Baier, *The Moral Point of View* (Ithaca: Cornell University Press, 1958); Brand Blanshard, *Reason and Goodness* (New York: The Macmillan Company, 1961); F. H. Bradley, *Ethical Studies* (London: H. S. King & Co., 1904, and later editions); R. M. Hare, *Freedom and Reason* (Oxford: Clarendon Press, 1963); G. E. Moore, *Principia Ethica* (Cambridge: University Press, 1903); P. H. Nowell-Smith, *Ethics* (Baltimore: Penguin Books, 1954); H. A. Prichard, *Moral Obligation: Essays and Lectures* (Oxford: Clarendon Press, 1949); Henry Sidgwick, *The Methods of Ethics* (New York: Dover Publications, Inc., 1966, and earlier editions); G. M. Singer, *Generalization in Ethics* (New York: Alfred A. Knopf, Inc., 1961); and Charles L. Stevenson, *Ethics and Language* (New Haven: Yale University Press, 1944).

The topics covered in this anthology have been written on extensively, both in books and in articles. *The Philosopher's Index* and *The Readers' Guide to Periodical Literature* are helpful in locating significant articles, and the *Bibliographie de Philosophie* is useful for books. The problem of truth-telling has not been explored in book-length form as much as some of the other topics, although most texts will include reference to it. Truth-telling in medical ethics is an interesting variant on the problem; see, for example, the chapter in Joseph Fletcher, *Morals and Medicine* (Princeton: Princeton University Press, 1954). The problem of suicide has been widely discussed by writers in many fields. Some of the sociological and psychological studies of it are now available in paperback, and they will provide important background material for the student of ethics. Professional journals in these fields contain many articles reporting studies of suicide. Many textbooks will contain sections discussing the issue, and an interesting survey is found in S. E. Sprott, *The English Debate on Suicide from Donne to Hume* {LaSalle: Open Court Publishing Co., Inc., 1961).

Sexual morality has also been discussed by writers from many different fields, and the literature on this problem has become very extensive. Among the important books on the topic are the following: Ronald Atkinson, *Sexual Morality* (New York: Harcourt, Brace & World, Inc., 1965); M. C. D'Arcy, *The Mind and Heart of Love* (New

York: Meridian Books, 1956); Erich Fromm, *The Art of Loving* (New York: Bantam Books, 1963); H. A. Grunwald (ed.), *Sex in America* (New York: Bantam Books, 1964); Hans Hofman, *Sex Incorporated: A Positive View of the Sexual Revolution* (Boston: Beacon Press, 1967); C. S. Lewis, *The Four Loves* (New York: Harcourt, Brace & World, Inc., 1960); and John Wilson, *Logic and Sexual Morality* (Baltimore: Penguin Books, 1956).

The problem of alienation has been surveyed in two fine anthologies, Gerald Sykes (ed.), *Alienation: The Cultural Climate of our Time*, two vols. (New York: Braziller, 1964), and Eric and Mary Josephson (eds.), *Man Alone: Alienation in Modern Society* (New York: Dell Publishing Company, Inc., 1962). Professional journals in psychology, sociology, and philosophy contain many studies on this widely discussed current problem. A good survey article on the background and development of alienation has been written by Bernard Murchland, "The Advent of Alienation," in *Buffalo Studies*, 4 (1968), 21-67.

The field of social ethics has been treated less frequently in introductory textbook form. Still, helpful introductions can be found. Illustrative of them are: Richard B. Brandt (ed.), *Social Justice* (Englewood Cliffs: Prentice-Hall, Inc., 1962); Gibson Winter (ed.), *Social Ethics: Issues in Ethics and Society* (New York: Harper & Row Publishers, Inc., 1968); and Wayne Leys, *Ethics and Social Policy* (New York: Prentice-Hall, Inc., 1941). Some representative works helpful on the topics covered in this anthology are the following. Frank Grace, *The Concept of Property in Modern Christian Thought* (Urbana: University of Illinois Press, 1953), written as a doctoral dissertation, is still one of the better sources available. In recent years, a number of more specialized works have appeared that deal with specific problems of reform in the distribution of income, that is, which join the problems of property and welfare. Among the best is Paul Harbrecht, *Toward the Paraproprietal Society* (New York: The Twentieth Century Fund, 1960), which explores the confusing character of pension funds as a form of property. One of the few contemporary restatements of an orthodox theory of property rights is developed by Richard M. Weaver, *Ideas Have Consequences* (Chicago: University of Chicago Press, 1948), although a number of similar ideas are developed, usually less adequately, in a wide variety of popular journals.

Henry Bieren, *Violence and Social Change; a Review of the Current Literature* (Chicago: University of Chicago Press, 1968), can introduce students to a body of literature that is widely dispersed in professional and semi-popular publications From the theological perspective, Thomas Merton, *Faith and Violence* (Ann Arbor: University of Michigan Press, 1968) is one of the few ecent works that comments on violence within the contemporary situation. The eighth *Yearbook* of the American Society for Political and Legal Philosophy is on the topic of revolution and is very helpful. The entire series of yearbooks is valuable for students of social ethics.

Punishment has been treated extensively as a legal and moral problem, particularly in the context of the nineteenth and twentieth century prison reform movement. A. C. Ewing, *The Morality of Punishment* (London: K. Paul, Trench, Trubner and Co., Ltd., 1929) is still regarded as a classical statement of the philosophical issues involved, as is H. L. A. Hart's recent *Punishment and Responsibility* (New York: Oxford University Press, 1968). Hugo Bedau's *The Death Penalty in America* (New York: Anchor Books, 1964), while on a more specialized topic, is nevertheless important for the whole problem of punishment.

Within the ethical consideration of warfare, Ralph Potter, *War and Moral Discourse* (Richmond: John Knox Press, 1969) is a helpful resource. Potter includes an invaluable bibliographical essay, which gives extended attention to the just war tradition within theological ethics but which is comprehensive also. Irving Horowitz, *The Idea of War and Peace in Contemporary Philosophy* (New York: Paine-Whitman, 1957) is an excellent expositor of various philosophical positions, with much sensitivity to the concerns of the American peace movement. From a different perspective, Richard Falk, *Law, Morality, and War in the Contemporary World* (Princeton: Princeton University Press, 1963) investigates warfare as a problem of international law.

SYSTEMATIC OUTLINE OF SELECTIONS

The following is a classification of the authors selected for these case studies in ethics. Instructors who wish to relate them to major ethical traditions may find the outline helpful. Numbers in parenthesis refer to selections in the text.

Classifications of this kind are usually somewhat loose and are always debatable. Our hope is, however, that the outline is sufficiently useful to relate our materials to those in standard ethics texts.

I. Formalism
  Stoicism: Seneca (8)
  Deontological theories: Immanuel Kant (3)
I. Teleological Ethics
  Hedonism: Thomas Hobbes (34)
  Utilitarianism: Jeremy Bentham (40), David Hume (11), John Stuart Mill (4)
  Naturalism: Marchise de Beccaria (39), John Dewey (43), Charles Frankel (31), William James (13, 47), Walter Lippmann (17), Niccolo Machiavelli (2), Karl Marx (22), Bertrand Russell (48)
  Voluntarism: Joseph Fletcher (18), Friedrich Nietzsche (5), Pierre-Joseph Proudhon (28), Arthur Schopenhauer (12)

III. Perfectionist Ethics

Self-realization: Aristotle (33), Peter A. Bertocci (19), F. H. Bradley (41), T. H. Green (46), G. W. F. Hegel (21), Plato (1)

Natural law and contract: St. Thomas Aquinas (10), St. Augustine (9, 45), John J. Ford (42), John Locke (27), Paul VI (15)

IV. Phenomenological Ethics

Maurice Merleau-Ponty (49)

Theistic existentialism: Dietrich Bonhoeffer (7), Karl Jaspers (25), Sören Kierkegaard (16), H. Richard Niebuhr (50), Reinhold Niebuhr (37), Leo Tolstoy (36)

Atheistic existentialism: Albert Camus (14), Oswald Spengler (30)

Phenomenological-scientific: Hannah Arendt (26), Erich Fromm (32), Nicolai Hartmann (6), Herbert Marcuse (38), Thomas Nagel (20), Moritz Schlick (44), Georg Simmel (23), Georges Sorel (35), Frederick A. Weiss (24)

INDEX

Italicized numbers refer to authors' selections used in the text.

Abortion, 102
Abraham, 65
Absurd, the, 53, 88-95
Addams, Jane, xii-vi
Aiken, H. D., 427
Alexander VI, 17
Alienation, 151-214, 432
Anarchism, 237-39
Anarchy, 218
Antinomianism, 129
Anxiety, 81, 192-93, 205-06
Aquinas, St. Thomas, 52, *67-69,*
    345-46, 435
Aristocracy, 283-85
Aristotle, 67n, 68, 69, 212n, 276,
    278-86, 356, 423, 435
Arendt, Hannah, 152, *207-14,*
    435
Atkinson, C. F., 252n
Atkinson, Ronald, 431
Auden, W. H., 186
Augustine, St., 52, *59-66,* 67, 69,
    128, 129, 145, 210n, 276, 367,
    368-73, 435
Authority, 301, 347-49

Baier, Kurt, 431
Baillie, J. B., 153n
Barnes, Hazel E., 142n
Bax, E. B., 77n
Beauty, 107, 166
Beccaria, Marchese de, 318-19,
    335, 434
Bedau, Hugo, 433
Being, 14-15
Belief, 86, 92
Bell, Daniel, 131
    entham, Jeremy, 319, *326-40,*
    426, 434
Bergman, Ingmar, 195
Bertocci, P. A., 98, *133-37,* 435
Bieren, Henry, 432
Birth, 98. *See also* Life
Birth control, 98, 102-05, 117-27
Blanc, Louis, 248
Blanshard, Brand, 431
Bonhoeffer, Dietrich, 4, *43-50,*
    129, 435
Bowring, John, 326n
Bradley, F. H., 319, *341-45,* 420,
    431, 435

Brandt, R. B., 432
Brinton, Crane, 430
Broad, C. D., 430
Buber, Martin, 197, 198
Byron, Lord, 108

Caesar, Julius, 62
Calvin, John, 209
Calvinism, 295-96
Camus, Albert, 53, *88-95*, 187,
    196, 435
Capital punishment, 318-19,
    320-26, 345-55
Capitalism, 162, 209, 212,
    299-300, 401
Carlyle, Thomas, 246n
Casuistry, 41
Cato the Elder, 57, 61-62
Causality, 37, 362-64
Chapman, J. J., 385
Character, 44
Choice, xiii, 415-16
Christianity, 80-81, 97, 107, 111,
    113, 128-30, 202-03, 211, 295,
    304-05, 342-43, 352
Cicero, xi, 54n, 70
City, 171-84
Coherence, 417
Coit, Stanton, 39n
Common good, 346
Communism, 242. *See also* Karl
    Marx; Marxism
Community, 40. *See also* Society
Comte, Charles, 233
Conjugal act, 101-03. *See also*
    Sex; Marriage
Conscience, 42
Consciousness, 52, 89, 92, 142-43,
    153-59, 166
Constant, Benjamin, 19-23
Contraception, 138. *See also* Birth
    control

Crime, 336, 350-51

D'Arcy, M. C., 431
Darwin, Charles, 319
Darwinism, 341-44
David, 352
Davies, J. L., 5n
Death, 99
DeGeorge, R. T., 311n
Deontological, xvi, 434
Democracy, 278-80, 283, 284,
    299, 309, 310
Democritus, 252, 256
Descartes, René, 207n, 211, 256,
    401
Desire, 146
Determinism, xiii, 359
Dewey, John, 266, 319-20,
    355-58, 434
Dickinson, Lowes, 386
Disinterestedness, 127
Divorce, 121, 124-25, 132
Dreyfus, H. L., 398n
Dreyfus, P. A., 398n
Dumas, Alexandre, 109n
Duty, 19, 97, 115-16

Easton, L. D., 160n
Easton, W. B., Jr., 133n
Eavey, C. B., 128n
Elias, 352
Eliot, T. S., 133
Ellis, Havelock, 117-19, 122, 123
Emerson, R. W., 358
Epistemology, 3
Equality, 21, 22-23, 230, 231,
    235-37, 288, 379
Eternity, 107-10, 113-15
Ethics, xi, xivn, xv, 93, 428
Evaluation, 416
Evil, xiv, 90, 303, 326-28
Ewing, A. C., 433

Existence, 6, 15, 30-31
Existentialism, 435
Experience, 22, 26, 94

Faith, 87
Falk, Richard, 433
Family, 97, 214. *See also*
    Marriage
Farrer, J. A., 320n
Fear, 288-89
Ferdinand, 18n
Fichte, J. G., 310
Fletcher, Joseph, *128-33,* 431,
    434
Flew, Anthony, 431
Foot, Philippa, 430
Force, 17
Ford, J. J., 319, *345-55,* 435
Formalism, 434
Fortune, *54-55,* 56
Fourier, François, 235
Frankel, Charles, 219, *259-69,*
    434
Frankena, W. K., 430
Frankl, Victor, 190
Frederick the Great, 386
Free will, xiii, 99
Freedom, 4, 22-23, 26, 56, 90-93,
    179-80, 194, 270, 274-75,
    316-17, 359, 362-63, 377, 401
Freud, Sigmund, 185, 191
Fromm, Erich, 135n, 219,
    269-75, 432, 435

Galbraith, J. K., 262n
Galilei, Galileo, 207, 256
Gerth, H. H., 171n
Gleason, Robert, 128
God, 43-45, 48, 52, 54n, 60, 62,
    64, 68, 70, 71-74, 79n, 82, 90,
    99-105, 112, 202, 220, 222-24,

348, 349, 352, 368-72, 378,
    407, 409-10
Good, 311, 413
Goethe, J. W. von, 255
Government, 25
Grace, Frank, 432
Green, T. H., 266, 367, *373-81,*
    426, 435
Grenier, Jean, 95n
Grice, H. P., 145
Grunwald, H. A., 432
Guaranteed income, 269-75
Guddat, K. H., 160n
Gumere, R. M., 53n
Gustafson, James, 420-21

Happiness, xiv, 311-12
Harbrecht, Paul, 432
Hare, R. M., 431
Hart, H. L. A., 433
Hartmann, Heinz, 294, 295
Hartmann, Nicolai, 3, 4, *39-42,*
    435
Hayek, F. V., 262-63
Healy, John, 59n
Hedonism, 122, 434. *See also*
    Pleasure
Hegel, G. W. F., 151, 152,
    153-59, 185, 212n, 310, 435
Heinemann, F. H., 152
Hill, T. E., 430
History, 313-14, 317
Hitler, Adolf, 406
Hobbes, Thomas, 207n, 276, 277,
    286-91, 429, 434
Hofman, Hans, 432
Homer, 252
Homosexuality, 148-49, 190-91
Honesty, 34, 49n
Horace, 110n
Horney, Karen, 184, 190, 191
Horowitz, Irving, 433

Hudson, W. D., 431
Hulme, T. E., 292n
Human nature, 75, 83, 137,
 164-65, 306-07, 366. *See also*
 Man
Hume, David, 52, *69-77*, 80, 359,
 434
Huxley, Thomas, 131

Idea, 33-34
Idealism, 37, 38, 416-17
Ideology, 130-32
Individualism, 183
Infallibility, 24
Inge, Dean, 127
Instrumental value, 4
Intellect, 31, 172-73
Intrinsic value, 4
Isabella, 18n

James, William, 53, *82-88*, 366,
 367, *382-90*, 434
Jaspers, Karl, 152 '*99-206*, 207n,
 435
Joad, C. E. M., 119
Job, 62
John XXIII, 102
Jones, W. T., 430
Josephson, Eric, 151, 432
Josephson, Mary, 151, 432
Joshua, 352
Judaism, 111
"Just war," 367, 368-73, 404-05
Justice, 20, 22, 68, 239, 341-42,
 352, 354, 355-56, 372, 406, 428
Juvenal, 57n

Kant, Immanuel, xiv, 4, *19-23*,
 47n, 50n, 420, 434
Kennedy, John F., 131
Kierkegaard, Sören, 97, *105-16*,
 189, 190, 193, 194, 195, 435

King, Martin Luther, 131
Knowledge, 7, 27-28, 29, 193
Koyré, Alexandre, 207n
Kroeger, A. E., 19n

Labor, 160-71, 212-13, 219,
 220-25, 228, 232-35, 245
Language, 33
Law, 20, 23. *See also* Rights
Lawrence, D. H., 147
Lea, Homer, 383-84
LeClercq, J., 131n
Legalism, 98, 129-31
Leibniz, G. W. von, 390
Leo XIII, 348
Lessing, G. E., 30
Levy, Oscar, 30n
Lewis, C. S., 432
Leys, Wayne, 432
Liberalism, 306-09
Liberty, 230, 242, 265-68. *See
 also* Freedom
Lie, 39-40, 41-42, 47-48
Life, 52, 54, 82, 86-87, 89, 93,
 98, 100-02, 104, 165, 204-06,
 317, 342-43, 349, 373-74
Lindsay, A. D., 276
Lippmann, Walter, 97-98, *117-27*,
 434
Locke, John, 218, *220-28*, 435
Logic, 418-19
Love, 97-100, 107-16, 118-19,
 122, 123-27, 128-33, 135-37
Lowrie, Walter, 105n
Lucretius, 203
Lust, 107
Luther, Martin, 207, 209
Lysimachus, 54n

Machiavelli, Niccolò, 4, *16-18*,
 434
Mailer, Norman, 147

Malthus, T. R., 243
Man, 96, 98, 123-24, 126, 172, 405. *See also* Human nature
Marcuse, Herbert, 277, *311-17*, 435
Margolis, Joseph, 430
Marriage, 97, 98, 99-103, 105-16, 125-27, 135-37
Marty, Martin, 421n
Marx, Karl, 152, *160-71*, 185, 212-13, 257, 258, 296, 298-300, 365, 366, 434
Marxism, 401-03
Masochism, 147, 190
Maugham, Somerset, 191
Mazzini, Giuseppe, 296, 309
Merleau-Ponty, Maurice, 366, *398-403*, 435
Merton, Thomas, 43
Metaethics, xv, 152
Metaphor, 34-36, 38
Metaphysics, 414
Migne, J. P., 129n
Militarism, 383
Mill, John Stuart, 218, 240-51, *424-29*, 434
Mills, C. W., 171n
Molesworth, William, 286n
Mommsen, Theodor, 253
Monarchy, 350
Money, 173-74, 176, 227-28, 252-59
Montesquieu, Baron de, 335
Moore, G. E., 431
Moore, Kenneth, 128n
Moral argument, 418-26
Moral experience, xi-vii
Moral law, xiv, 105
Moral order, 100
Morality, 20, 108, 149. *See also* Ethics
Morals, xi, xivn

Morgan, J. S., 259n
Moses, 352, 371
Murchland, Bernard, 432
Murder, 68, 373
Musaeus, 112
Mussolini, Benito, 309
Myth, 297

Nagel, Thomas, 98, *137-50*, 435
Natural law, 101, 435
Nature, 165, 167, 171, 348-49
Newman, Albert, 368n
Newton, Isaac, 256
Niebuhr, H. Richard, 367, *404-10*, 420, 435
Niebuhr, Reinhold, 276, *306-10*, 435
Nietzsche, Friedrich, 4, *30-38*, 50n, 171, 175, 183, 309, 434
Normative, 96
Normative ethics, xv, 152, 414
Nothingness, 94
Nowell-Smith, P. H., 431

Obligation, xiv
O'Brien, Justin, 88n
Oligarchy, 280-83
Optimism, 86, 292, 294
Owen, Robert, 248, 249

Pacioli, Fra Luca, 255
Pain, 81
Parenthood, 100. *See also* Family; Marriage
Patten, Simon, 385
Paul, Cedar, 199n
Paul, Eden, 199n
Paul VI, 97, *98-105*, 435
Peace, 365, 366, 385
Peerman, D. G., 421n
Perception, 35, 37, 143-46
Perelman, Chaim, 422-23

Perversion, sexual, 133, 137-50
Pessimism, 86, 292-95
Peter, St., 370, 371
Philolaus, 54n
Philosophy, 7-8, 28, 69-70,
  413-14, 426, 428
Pius XII, 104
Plato, 4, *5-16*, 28, 55n, 61, 136,
  141, 345, 366, 401, 435
Pleasure, *9-15*, 119, 122, 133,
  175, 327
Pliny, 77n, 78-79
Political economy, 160-61, 163,
  169, 170
Politics, 23
Positivism, 320, 422-23
Possibility, 87
Potter, Ralph, 433
Practical philosophy, 413-18, 419
Pragmatism, 53
Prichard, H. A., 431
Procreation, 97, 101-05, 117, 130
Production, 163
Property, 160-71, 179, 211,
  217-39, 241-42, 284-85, 432
Prostitution, 119
Proudhon, Pierre-Joseph, 169,
  218, 219, *228-39*, 434
Psychoanalysis, 193-94, 199
Punishment, 20, 55, 78, 318-64,
  433
Pythagoras, 256

Ramsey, Ian, 423-24
Rand, Ayn, 128
Rationalism, 200
Reality, 44, 48
Reason, 59, 418, 425
Regulus, 62-63
Religion, 77-78, 82-83, 164, 211,
  325

Renan, J. E., 297
Responsibility, 42, 360-64
Retribution, 341-42, 356, 405-06
Revolution, 88-89, 277, 278-86,
  297-98, 300, 311-17
Rhythm method, 103-04
Riesman, David, 188
Right, 20, 23. *See also* Justice
Rights, 19, 20, 22, 217, 228, 230,
  289-90
Rigorism, 41
Roosevelt, Theodore, 383
Roth, J., 292n
Rousseau, Jean Jacques, 310, 347
Ruskin, John, 175
Russell, Bertrand, 120-21, 125,
  367, *390-98*, 421, 422, 434

Sade, Marquis de, 146
Sadism, 146-47
St. Paul, 128, 145, 267, 352, 408
Saint-Simon, Comte de, 235, 237
Salter, William, 87
Samson, 64, 67, 69
Samuel, 352
Santayana, George, 126
Sartre, Jean-Paul, 142-43, 145,
  191
Schiller, Johann, 202
Schopenhauer, Arthur, 52, *77-81*,
  434
Schilder, Paul, 185
Schlick, Moritz, 320, *359-64*, 420,
  435
Science, 37, 83-84, 239, 397,
  413
Self, 200, 211
Self-alienation, 184-99
Self-defense, 330-31
Self-realization, xvin, 306, 435
Seneca, 52, *53-59*, 73n, 79, 434

Sensuality, 108-09, 287
Sex, sexual integrity, 96-150
Sexual perversion, 98, 137-50
Sexuality, 431-32
Sidgwick, Henry, 430, 431
Simmel, Georg, 152, *171-84*, 435
Sin, 294
Singer, G. M., 431
Situation ethics, 98, 128-33
Skepticism, 153, 158
Slavery, 254-55, 366
Smith, Adam, 257, 258, 308
Smith, N. H., 43n
Social contract, 347
Social ethics, xvi, Part II
Socialism, 171, 238, 242, 250-51, 298
Society, 76, 286-91, 348
Socrates, 5-16, 54n, 55, 56n
Sorel, Georges, 278, *292-300*, 314, 435
Soul, 8, 15
Speech, 48-49
Spengler, Oswald, 218-19, *252-59*, 435
Spinoza, Baruch, 275
Sprott, S. E., 431
State, 300-05, 348-49, 354, 375-76, 379
Steinmetz, S. R., 384-85
Sterilization, 102
Stevenson, C. L., 422, 431
Stifter, Adalbert, 50n
Stoicism, 52, 54n, 79, 153-154, 158, 434
Straus, Erwin, 187
Strothert, Richard, 368n
Strozi of Florence, 76
Suicide, 51-95, 431
Swenson, L. M., 105n
Sykes, Gerald, 432

Tacitus, 55n, 74n
Taine, Hippolyte, 294
Tartaglia, Niccolò, 207n
Tasker, R. V. G., 59n
Tawney, R. H., 265-66
Teleological, xvi, 434
Telesphorus, 54n
Terrence, 54n
Thomson, N. H., 16n
Thucydides, 202
Time, 200-01
Tolstoy, Leo, 277, *300-05*, 385, 435
Trustworthiness, 39-42
Truth, 3-50, 431
Tucker, B. R., 228n
Tufts, J. H., 355n
Tully. *See* Cicero
Tyranny, 279

Uprightness, 39-42
Urban, W. M., xiin
Utilitarianism, 434
Utopia, 297-98

Value, xiii-xiv, xv, 4, 96-97, 100, 315, 416
Vaughan, D. J., 5n
Veblen, Thorstein, 366
Violence, 232, 276-317, 342, 368, 432-33
Virgil, 53, 59n
Voluntary, xiii

Wages, 169, 236-37
War, 290-91, 365-410, 433
Warnock, M., 430
Wealth, 240-41
Weaver, R. M., 432
Webber, Max, 209-11
Weiss, F. A., 152, *184-99*, 435

Weldon, J. E. C., 278n
Welfare, 219, 240-51, 259-69, 311, 343, 432
Wells, H. G., 389-90
Whitman, Walt, 82
Williams, Tennessee, 189
Wilson, Edmund, 131
Wilson, John, 432

Winter, Gibson, 432
Wisdom, 7-11, 27, 56
Wolff, K. H., 171n
Wordsworth, William, 86
Work, 257. *See also* Labor
Wright, Chauncey, 83

Youth, 260-61